D1523934

# SCIENCE JOURNALISM

*Science Journalism: An Introduction* gives wide-ranging guidance on producing journalistic content about different areas of scientific research. It provides a step-by-step guide to mastering the practical skills necessary for covering scientific stories and explaining the business behind the industry.

Martin W. Angler, an experienced science and technology journalist, covers the main stages involved in getting an article written and published; from choosing an idea, structuring your pitch, researching and interviewing, to writing effectively for magazines, newspapers and online publications. There are chapters dedicated to investigative reporting, handling scientific data and explaining scientific practice and research findings to a nonspecialist audience. Coverage in the chapters is supported by reading lists, review questions and practical exercises. The book also includes extensive interviews with established science journalists, scholars and scientists that provide tips on building a career in science journalism, address what makes a good reporter and discuss the current issues they face professionally. The book concludes by laying out the numerous available routes into science journalism, such as relevant writing programs, fellowships, awards and successful online science magazines.

For students of journalism and professional journalists at all levels, this book offers an invaluable overview of contemporary science journalism with an emphasis on professional journalistic practice and success in the digital age.

**Martin W. Angler** is a freelance science journalist with a background in technology and environmental journalism. His work has appeared on the BBC, in *Scientific American* and in major German and Swiss newspapers such as *Neue Zürcher Zeitung, ZEIT Online, SPIEGEL Online, Motherboard Germany, P.M. Magazin* and *Bild der Wissenschaft*. He was also a regular contributor to two radio programmes on technology on the Italian public broadcaster RAI, and to leading interdisciplinary science projects at the European Academy of Bolzano.

# SCIENCE JOURNALISM

## An Introduction

*Martin W. Angler*

Routledge
Taylor & Francis Group

LONDON AND NEW YORK

First published 2017
by Routledge
2 Park Square, Milton Park, Abingdon, Oxon OX14 4RN

and by Routledge
711 Third Avenue, New York, NY 10017

*Routledge is an imprint of the Taylor & Francis Group, an informa business*

© 2017 Martin W. Angler

The right of Martin W. Angler to be identified as author of this work has been asserted by him in accordance with sections 77 and 78 of the Copyright, Designs and Patents Act 1988.

*British Library Cataloguing-in-Publication Data*
A catalogue record for this book is available from the British Library

*Library of Congress Cataloging-in-Publication Data*
Names: Angler, Martin W., author.
Title: Science journalism : an introduction / Martin W. Angler.
Description: London ; New York : Routledge, 2017. | Includes index.
Identifiers: LCCN 2016058263 | ISBN 9781138945494 (hardback :
    alk. paper) | ISBN 9781138945500 (pbk. : alk. paper) |
    ISBN 9781315671338 (ebook)
Subjects: LCSH: Science news—Handbooks, manuals, etc.
Classification: LCC Q225 .A54 2017 | DDC 070.4/495—dc23
LC record available at https://lccn.loc.gov/2016058263

ISBN: 978-1-138-94549-4 (hbk)
ISBN: 978-1-138-94550-0 (pbk)
ISBN: 978-1-315-67133-8 (ebk)

Typeset in Sabon
by Apex CoVantage, LLC

To Katia

# CONTENTS

# FIGURES

# ACKNOWLEDGEMENTS

Without the following people this book wouldn't exist. So, without further ado, I would like to thank:

My editors at Routledge. Thank you for believing in this book: Kitty Imbert and Niall Kennedy.

My fantastic interviewees. Thank you for letting me pick your brains: Natalie Angier, Sharon Begley, Deborah Blum, Curtis Brainard, Dean Burnett, Alberto Cairo, Siri Carpenter, Davide Castelvecchi, Erika Check Hayden, Daniel Clery, Deborah Cohen, Quentin Cooper, Richard Craig, Denis Dilba, David Dobbs, Susannah Eliott, Ben Goldacre, Jason Goodyer, Winfried Göpfert, Steve Harrison, Laura Helmuth, Robert Hernandez, Mark Lee Hunter, Hauke Janssen, Paige Jarreau, Adam Johansen, George Johnson, Karen Kaplan, Yarden Katz, Joan Leach, Kate Lunau, Phil McKenna, Alexander McNamara, Greg Miller, Deborah Nelson, Bob O'Hara, Kelly Oakes, Helen Pearson, Angela Posada-Swafford, Tim Radford, Hillary Rosner, John Ross, Ellen Ruppel Shell, Kristin Sainani, Charles Seife, Graham Southorn, Douglas Starr, David Sumner, Fabio Turone, Rob Weatherhead, Simon White, Christie Wilcox, Ed Yong and Carl Zimmer.

Special thanks for your generous permissions to reuse your brilliant material: *BBC Focus* magazine, Civio, Chartbeat, Nick Garnett, Gizmodo, HealthNewsReview.org, Hootsuite, the Knight Science Journalism Program at MIT, Matter Studios, *DER SPIEGEL*, the United Nations Environment Programme, Wiley and the Woods Hole Oceanographic Institution.

My mentors at Edinburgh Napier University. Thank you for inspiring me: Rachel Younger and Simon Pia.

My partner in life. Thank you for always supporting me: Katia Cont.

Final thanks: Bünz.

# 1

# INTRODUCTION

**What you will learn in this chapter:**

- An attempt at a definition
- A short history of science journalism
- Infotainment versus critical science journalism
- Science journalism's main tasks
- How to become a science journalist
- Science and society
- Risk and risk perception
- Science journalism under fire
- What makes a good science journalist? An interview with Tim Radford

## Introduction

Welcome to *Science Journalism: An Introduction*! I invite you to join me as I cover the whole science journalistic process from finding ideas, to pitching them to your colleagues and editors, to writing for print and online media. The book also includes dedicated chapters on storytelling techniques, statistics, investigative journalism in a scientific context, digital science journalism and how you can build a career in this competitive field.

You can read this book in one of two ways. If you are an aspiring science writer without much experience, I recommend you read the book from start to finish. If you are a seasoned science writer, you should look for the gems in this book. The interviews with veteran science writers, science journalism educators, award-winning science bloggers, statisticians and scientists ensure you are not fed one author's opinion; rather, you will get to know the tools of the trade via the first-hand accounts of these experts.

At the end of each chapter you will find a short summary, a set of review questions, exercises to cement your newly acquired know-how and a reading list.

In this chapter, I first try to answer what is science journalism? Is it complete reporting on science? Is it sensationalist, entertaining writing that merely touches science marginally? Isn't science involved in most stories nowadays, at least up to certain degree? In investigating these questions, the section that follows the definition will provide a short overview of how science journalism evolved and how historical science writing differs from today's.

The section on infotainment versus critical science journalism briefly addresses one of the most debated issues of science journalism: its quality. It is certainly true that the availability of online tools has contributed to there being numerous science-related articles and television and radio contributions that have questionable journalistic and educational value; at the same time, it is that very availability of online tools that has rendered the production of news as easy as it possibly gets, making this era the golden age of journalism. Despite the reports that newspapers, magazines and television channels are cutting their science staff (which in some contexts is true), this is a great time to be a science journalist. The readers love well-presented science.

In this chapter, you will also find thoughts on what your tasks as a future science journalist will be and learn about a naïve approach to becoming a science journalist. As you will see, persistence, common sense and a good nose for what people like to read (starting with yourself) will go a long way. (You will find much more about the traits of good science journalists in Chapter 12, Building a Career in Science Journalism.)

This chapter contains a dedicated section on the role of science and science journalists in society in which I try to answer questions such as: Are we pure educators? Are we entertainers? Are we, as science journalists, at fault if we praise a new treatment and people follow our advice and perhaps die because they gave preference to the treatment we championed? There is an infinite pool of such questions, and reading through the book will hopefully not only provide some answers but also raise more of these questions. Along these lines, you will find a section in this chapter dedicated to risk – how we communicate it and how our audience perceives it. This section focuses on our responsibilities and offers thoughts on how we can convey risks without becoming scaremongers.

I will then address current issues in science journalism such as accuracy and sensationalism. In doing so, I draw on a controversy in which science journalism has come under fire. What follows is a discussion with seasoned, award-winning science journalist Tim Radford, whose career spans more than three decades.

## An attempt at a definition

What is science journalism? Ask ten different science journalists and scholars and you will receive ten different answers, but here is an attempt: Science journalism is a journalistic genre that primarily deals with scientific achievements and breakthroughs, the scientific process itself, scientists' quests and difficulties in solving complex problems. If done properly, science journalism questions the methods scientists employ as well as their results and how the media and the public interpret them; it also investigates and unfolds possible conflicts of interest researchers may have. As with every journalistic genre, science journalism demands an in-depth knowledge of the system you operate in, which includes knowledge about science policies, country-specific laws and the scientific disciplines you want to cover. You will need to acquire knowledge that will help you identify flaws in the research and spot from afar when scientists try to misuse you as a surrogate public relations (PR) spokesperson. Without a critical mindset, journalists often produce mediocre and shallow contributions that champion science rather than critically scrutinise it. Such pieces – known as *gee whiz science journalism* – do not put anything into question but rather serve as another public relations communication channel. That said, such shallow science articles do have their merits on the business side: If done well, gee whiz articles draw attention and build an audience. As you will see throughout the book, this works particularly well online.

Every scientific discipline – including the environment, medicine, biology, physics or mathematics – is worth covering. The seeming exception is technology journalism, but the lines between the two genres can be blurry as most technological advancements depend on scientific discoveries and are closely tied to science. According to Badenschier and Wormer (2012), the most successful topics in science journalism worldwide are health and biology, whereas at the *New York Times*, health, medicine and behavioural sciences are the prevailing topics. Moreover, a 2008 survey among leading nationwide German newspapers found that in 2006–2007, 29 per cent of the examined articles covered medicine, 15 per cent covered the environment and 14 per cent covered biology (Badenschier and Wormer 2012). These newspapers also claimed that when they need to decide whether to cover and publish the politics beat or the science beat, they generally give preference to the politics beat.

As of late, science journalism also occupies itself with hitherto largely neglected topics on the sociological modus operandi of science (meta-topics, if you will) such as sexual harassment in science. Previously covered topics, such as science policy, have increasing presence as well. Award-winning science journalist Ed Yong said that such topics should receive more coverage, and he would appreciate seeing more of such content in the near future (Yong 2016).

Journalist and author Ellen Ruppel Shell, co-director of the graduate program in science journalism at Boston University, takes this view:

> The idea that one can just walk into science journalism without having previous experience or knowledge of science has become much more difficult to support in recent decades. I know it's a long-held debate in the field. Some people claim that, if you are a good journalist, you can just write about science. But not only is the science difficult, the sociology, history and politics of science is difficult. It helps enormously to have an awareness of this.
>
> *(Ruppel Shell 2016)*

The *Guardian*'s former science editor, Tim Radford, said that ultimately science journalism is like most other journalistic genres and depends mostly on whether you can find stories that are relevant to your audience:

> When called upon to actually debate these issues with editors of science magazines, I just say we are not science writers, we are journalists, and I make the point we are writing for people about things that matter to them. That's what political writers do, and in fact, that's what sports writers do. We are just journalists who have a specialisation for the time being. Indeed, much of my writing career was not in science. It was in the arts: I was a film critic, and I edited the books pages of the *Guardian* for a while, and certainly I looked after the political comment pages for what seems like an exceptionally long and tedious time. The reason for writing about science is that it's calling with good stories. That's a journalist's test: Is it a good story? I'm not quite sure that we could agree on the definition of a good story, but most of us agree that we know one when we see one.
>
> *(Radford 2016)*

Seasoned science journalist Quentin Cooper, who formerly hosted the radio show *Material World* on BBC Radio 4, largely confirms Radford's opinion that science need not be its own journalistic genre and further claims that as a science journalist, you would address everybody, not just science enthusiasts:

> It is important to get the audience who are not looking for science programmes. I don't want to make science programmes for people who just think they want science programmes. I want to make science programmes and write science pieces for everyone. In the end, it is about getting people to engage with the science rather than getting people to appreciate that they are engaging with science. I think sometimes, we get those priorities wrong: We want people to know that they have

had their daily dose of science, like they have eaten their vegetables. I don't want it to be like that. I just want people to naturally absorb it without explicitly thinking that what they just read was a physics or a biology story.

*(Cooper 2016)*

Consider these deliberations a starting point. By the time you finish this book, you will hopefully have a different view of what science journalism is and what it is not. The diversity and number of opinions expressed is meant to be a help to you in that process. That said, how you define science journalism is closely related to the phases it has traversed. As you will see in the next section, there have been cycles of cheerful and critical science journalism; knowing about the history of science is a must if you want to understand how the practices it employs today have evolved over time.

## A short history of science journalism

To understand today's science journalism, it is important to understand how it has evolved. As Nelkin (1987) affirms, in the 1900s, scientists in Europe and the US started traveling around to promote their research. At that time, newspapers started picking up these scientists' talks and publishing them. Science journalism of that era could generally be subdivided into two categories:

Most science journalism in the nineteenth century consisted either of directly practical information about new farming techniques, the latest home remedies, and the like, or wildly sensational stories. It was the heyday of science hoaxes. In 1835 the press reported that astronomer Sir John Herschel had observed batlike human beings on the moon.

*(Nelkin 1987:17)*

Unsurprisingly, this was not science journalism's breakthrough. Science was often portrayed as a mystical phenomenon. Among the readers, awe and fear of science balanced each other. This mindset changed with World War I, as Germany built bombs with the help of chemistry. All of a sudden, the public discovered that science could have powerful effects on both society and economy, leaving it with a fear that Germany could have an edge on the US in chemistry (Nelkin 1987). With the public's interest the press coverage increased, conveying the notion that "science was a way to get things done" (Nelkin 1987:17).

Science meant progress, but the chasm between early science journalists and the public widened. In 1921, media entrepreneur and publisher Edward Willis Scripps was the first to offer a commercial large-scale science news service, *Science Service*. It reached seven million readers, which was 20 per cent of the US readers (Nelkin 1987). Nelkin (1987) cites *Science Service*'s editor, Edwin Slosson, who demanded that science journalism orient itself to topics that are popular among the public and focus on exceptional events. In addition, he claimed that science should be communicated in short paragraphs that depict scientific advances using superlatives.

The science writers of the 1920s and 1930s adopted *Science Service*'s style and understood themselves as missionaries with the goal of persuading the public about science's benefits. One of these writers, Pulitzer Prize winner Gobind Lal (Nelkin 1987), "was the first journalist to use the term 'science writer' with his byline" (Brennan and Clarage 1999:559). Notably, Lal was also one of the founders of the National Association of Science Writers (NASW), and in 1940, he became the NASW's president (Brennan and Clarage 1999).

The laudatory style of the science writers following World War II can sometimes still be felt in today's science journalism. In the 1960s, journalists started covering a new topic: science policy. The way journalists reported about science was generally optimistic in that post-Sputnik era (Nelkin 1987). In the 1970s, editors like John Lear and David Pearlman, in pursuit of the US ideal of the media's objectivity, demanded that science journalists be as critical as their political counterparts (Nelkind 1987). In the 1980s, however, science journalism in the US returned to its cheerleading roots anew (Nelkin 1987).

Ellen Ruppel Shell confirms this progression of science coverage in the media:

> We had this feeling in the late 1950s that the Russians were getting ahead of us and we needed to get on top of everything, and that included science education. All of a sudden, there was a push to get science journalists on staff at various newspapers. Journalists were pulled off of other beats and put on the science beat. Many of these journalists did not have science backgrounds, for example, Walter Sullivan from the *New York Times*. He had a degree in history and also studied music. But at the *Times*, his enthusiasm for science was boundless. In the 1980s, there was some caution, and the introduction of the idea that science journalists are also journalists and that they should think critically. That was the heyday of science journalism: There were a lot of science magazines, and publishers created special science sections in the newspapers. There was tremendous enthusiasm for new technologies. In the 1990s and 2000s, the idea that science journalists should be more critical, more thoughtful and more analytic came to fore. There was also a swelling interest in science narrative, or storytelling around science issues, rather than just simple explication.
>
> *(Ruppel Shell 2016)*

After that, another significant turning point in science journalism was the advent of the web, which influenced readers' attention spans. At the same time, long-form print contributions began to decline, Ruppel Shell (2016) says. Today, new communication forms like blogs and micro-blogs, Snapchat, live videos and other means add to the scientific debate and help hone the aforementioned storytelling approach. Science journalism has changed throughout history, and so has the role of science journalists, but one central debate will always be the one of quality: Are we entertainers, or educators, or both? The next section sheds some light on the ways science is being reported.

## Infotainment versus critical science journalism

The everlasting debate about whether the quality of science journalism is declining, heated discussions about gee whiz science journalism, championing and cheerleading the reporting of scientific breakthroughs and the lack of criticality are features that perhaps distinguish science journalism from other journalistic genres. Although this is the inherent crux: The cheerleading stories are easy to produce, easy to grasp for the lay reader and at the same time require the lowest effort while attracting a large audience. In contrast, the substantial, deep and investigative stories are those that require the most time and money to produce and sometimes lead nowhere. The reality is, if science publications need to be profitable, they often have to produce both types of stories.

In an op-ed for the *Guardian*, associate professor of medicine and pharmacology at the University of Chicago, Jalees Rehman, draws a clear distinction between infotainment and critical science journalism and defines infotainment-style science journalism in the following way: "The bulk of contemporary science journalism falls under the category of 'infotainment'. This expression describes science writing that informs a non-specialist target audience about new scientific discoveries in an entertaining fashion" (Rehman 2013). Its defining features, he further claims, are using an intuitive approach to explain complex scientific issues using analogies, providing background information, summarising the key findings and addressing the importance of the new discovery. In addition, he claims, such articles foist off the responsibility of fact-checking to the scientific journals, assuming that peer-reviewed studies contain no errors. He then contrasts this approach with critical science writing: Critical science writers scrutinise the research itself and employ investigative methods where applicable. Rehman (2013) also affirms that shallow science writing is going to be the predominant form of science journalism and that the very principles of infotainment articles are nearly incompatible with critical science writing. Finally, Rehman (2013) offers the following list of four criteria that should help you distinguish infotainment-style science articles from critical articles:

1   **Style:** Critical science writing employs soberer words and fewer enthusiastic, judgmental and value-laden words, such as *awesome* or *paradigm shift*, than infotainment-style articles.

2 **Critical analysis of the study:** Either opposing scientists or the science writer can point out flaws and limitations of the study in question. Citing unnamed sources is not the norm yet.

3 **Context:** Critical science writers cover the *how* (for example, how a study compares to related studies), whereas uncritical science articles merely address the reasons a study was conducted in the first place.

4 **Negative studies:** Not all studies are successful in that they can reject the null hypothesis. Such stories are usually not apt for being reported using superlatives or the words mentioned in item 1. Rehman (2013) argues that is why you can categorise articles on negative studies as critical science writing.

In their definition of science journalism, Murcott and Williams (2013) acknowledge both roles of science journalists by stating:

> A science journalist is a specialist whose role is, broadly, to report scientific developments to a wider audience than that reached by the academic journals. A science journalist will also provide analysis and context of research, conduct investigations into the provenance and reliability of research and researchers, and, occasionally, break stories of major significance to a wider audience.
>
> *(Murcott and Williams 2013:152)*

Note that in the latter part of Murcott and Williams' (2013) statement, they emphasise the quality aspect of science journalism that adds value that transcends the mere dissemination of science news. On that note, Schünemann (2013) points out that the public expects science journalists to distinguish between solid facts and sensationalist science, but, this places a burden on the journalist because selecting what to report and how to report it means framing the world in a possibly subjective way. In the next section of this chapter, I will briefly address selection as one of the main tasks of science journalists.

Furthermore, Schünemann (2013) identifies the fast-paced environment of journalism as one of the reasons that fewer critical science journalism pieces are produced: "In journalism, money is most efficiently made by speeding up the writing process, at the expense of accuracy and veracity, to produce more stories, and by hyping those stories to lure in a bigger, sensation-hungry readership" (144). She also points out that such uncritical, sensationalist and merely entertaining articles can be exploited by scientists and "medico-scientific corporations" (144) seeking to promote their work or products. She also addresses the great responsibility that comes with communicating science, as the mainstream media are the main information source for the lay public. Obviously, mere infotainment-style science journalism cannot possibly live up to the expectation to allude the caveats of scientific advances.

If you want to write critically about science, then dissecting and recognising the flaws in scientific papers is one of the main tasks you will have to master. The next section addressed what else you will need to succeed as a science journalist.

## Science journalism's main tasks

What is expected of you as a science journalist? Are you supposed to entertain or educate or both? Or is there a different expectation altogether? The answer is, it depends who you work for, what kinds of articles you write, how much time you have to research your articles and how much of a budget you can get for sourcing original content. The best articles both grip the readers and educate them, so, apart from mastering core journalistic skills such as issue selection and interviewing techniques, you also need to master storytelling techniques. In an increasingly digital world, you will also need to acquire technical skills that help you produce multimedia and online content. This may sound like a lot of skills to learn, but at the end of the day, they all boil down to the same common denominator: making science accessible to people.

Ellen Ruppel Shell (2016) says that as a modern science journalist, it is one of your main tasks to transcend the mere explication of science; instead, you must add value to it. That added value is so important because you will face a lot of competition not only from scientific institutions but also from scientists who start their own blogs that allow them to reach out to the public. So, if you have to add value, how do you do that? I will start with a deliberation of what adding value is not: adapting press releases and republishing them, extracting the quotes and re-using them and packaging this as a journalistic article. There is nothing substantially wrong with that, but merely spreading the word strongly overlaps with public information officers' (PIOs) primary task: advertising science. Instead, what journalism must do is critically question what people would like you to take at face value.

Additionally, Joan Leach, director of the Australian National Centre for the Public Awareness of Science, states that it is a good science journalist's job to provide the lay audience with stories that help explain how science works:

> The same stories get told over and over again, like the search for discoveries or the frontier narrative. Even if science journalists don't write short and snappy broadsheet journalism, if they are writing books or writing a blog, they are giving us a set of stories in which we tell and explain to ourselves the way science works. That is a crucial task. Those people who really care about science journalism are the ones who are giving us a narrative framework for how we understand science now.
>
> *(Leach 2016)*

One of your most important tasks in almost every stage of your work is *selection*. Which topics are newsworthy, and which can you ditch? That is selection at the level of news values. Which sources (including people, documents and databases) do you use for underpinning your story idea, and which lead will you ditch? That is selection at the level of researching your story. Which questions do you need to ask your sources, and which questions do you add impromptu? That is selection at the level of interviewing. Which events do you choose to put together your story, and how do you prioritise them? That is selection at the level of writing and ordering. There is a reason you need to be selective: Time (interviewing, deadlines) and space (characters in a print publication, time on-the-air) are limited.

Your role as science journalist requires you to research, cover and present a wide range of scientific topics to the public. The dissemination of results is an integral part of science, so as a science journalist, you are contributing to and shaping science because research collaborations, grants and funding are often related to a paper's (and its authors' and their institutions') popularity. In addition, you may advise publications and broadcasters on the newsworthiness of science stories, which in turn aids your editors' or programme directors' selection process for which science stories they are going to run. One of your core tasks is to inform the public of new and relevant scientific advances. As a conscientious science journalist, you will also address controversial topics and try to give your audience a balanced view of ongoing scientific debates. If your articles spark debates or dispel myths that your audience previously took for granted, you have certainly succeeded at critically questioning science and conveying it in a fair way to your readers. However, shallow and cheerleading science stories remain the predominant form of science writing because they are easy to produce within a short time and they attract large audiences, which means publishers make a lot of advertising money with them, especially online.

One way you can add value as a science journalist is by being a scientific advisor to your readers and helping them make informed decisions. Especially in health journalism, it is crucial that you provide them with enough context and supporting information that they can, for example, decide whether a new drug may benefit or harm them. In fact, George Johnson, a science journalist at the *New York Times*, said that providing such background information and putting findings in context adds value to scientific research:

> That is actually something we can do as journalists and writers that scientists can't always do. They are so close to the research they are doing that they often take for granted some of the more surprising elements. As a journalist and a knowledgeable outsider, maybe you have a greater ability to step back and see things in a larger context. One of the nicest things that happens is when you write something and a

scientist says "This is really interesting, and I never quite thought of it that way."

*(Johnson 2015)*

Karen Kaplan, science editor at the *Los Angeles Times*, also confirms that helping people make better decisions is one of science journalists' crucial tasks:

> Everything is a teachable moment for science. I just think people are unnecessarily intimidated by science topics and not only should they not be, but we can't afford for them to be like that. So much public policy in our society is based on science, and people better understand it, or they are not going to make good decisions about many things.
>
> *(Kaplan 2015)*

In the UK, what keeps science journalists from fulfilling these roles (and especially the explicative first role of conveying complex scientific issues to a lay audience) is, on the one hand, the online realm that demands a richer skill set from journalists, which in turn leaves less time for actually producing stories; on the other hand, as the number of PR professionals rises, "this might increase the number of science stories, particularly uncritical ones, [and] it means that the primary role of the journalist in holding power to account is worryingly diminished" (Murcott and Williams 2013:155).

Over the course of this book, I try to address the core skills mentioned in this chapter and walk you through the various stages of becoming a science journalist. I highly recommend you re-read this chapter after finishing the book and compare how your views have changed with regard to science journalists' roles and techniques and the difficulties they face.

## How to become a science journalist

This is not a quick tutorial on how to skip the rest of the book and become a science journalist. Rather, it is an attempt to provide you with an intuitive approach to how you can become a science journalist. Let me set up a premise before proceeding: There is no single path that will land you a job as a science editor at the *New York Times*, the *Guardian*, or the *New Yorker*. Each of the several dozen science writers and educators interviewed for this book took a unique path to establish him- or herself in the field. As this book's entire final chapter is dedicated to the formal ways of gaining a foothold in science journalism, this section focuses on an intuitive approach that employs self-learning.

Although a self-taught approach does not require you to invest a lot of money, it does require you to invest a lot of time to read outstanding science writing, be it short- or long-form articles, blog posts or popular science books. There are no good writers who are not avid readers. In this context, *reading* does not mean quickly skimming texts and then ticking them off; rather, it means actively reading and dissecting what you read. It also includes reading a lot of good books on science writing, such as *A Field Guide for Science Writers, The Science Writers' Handbook*, and *Science Blogging*.

George Johnson confirms that reading actively and analytically is not only a good way to get started, but it is also an essential part of every science journalist's life:

> Read people who are good at science writing. Read the *New York Times*' science section, and read books by people who are really good at this. For me, some of the early books were books by John McPhee and books by Isaac Asimov, who is not really an elegant writer, but he explains things in an enthusiastic and simple way. But don't just read it to get the information and for the intellectual entertainment value, but also find out how the writers did what they did: How did they pull it off? Just notice the way they describe, what they are telling you and what they are leaving out. Pay attention to how their words sound on the page, to the rhythms of their sentences and the way they use language to make pictures in your mind. Pay attention to the way they introduce the scientist as a character and tell you just enough about the scientist that you can picture him or her, and pay attention to how they use dialogue and quotations. Just pay attention to all the elements you think that are good, and then figure out why they are good. If you want to be a writer, you are going to spend a huge amount of your life reading.
>
> *(Johnson 2015)*

Also, read the myriad of advice columns on science writing written by seasoned science writers; for example, look at the platform the Open Notebook, which regularly publishes insights into the craft and into the modus operandi of famous science writers. In fact, most are happy to share their knowledge.

A word of advice: Approach one text type at a time (for example, features). Additionally, limit yourself to one scientific discipline at first. Take award-winning science articles. Then start dismantling them: What does the intro tell? Does it involve human interest? At what point does background information come into play? Where is the story's core statement? How does it end? To get the complete picture, you will have to return to the literature and compare your intuitive findings to the theory of what journalistic structures look like. This is an iterative process. Once you have analysed one particular article, pick similar ones and compare them. What common elements can you find? Where do they differ? You will soon find similarities in the ways such articles are structured. The same is true of the writing styles. Clearly, style, voice and tone do differ from writer to writer and from publication to publication, but some basic rules do always hold. I will approach some of these rules throughout the book.

Apart from consuming and analysing, producing is key. You need to practice, practice and practice. This includes not only the production of texts but also practising how to identify valid topics and pitch them. There are two intuitive ways to start out. First, read the publication you plan to pitch to and analyse which topics and angles it usually covers. Second, read the publication's submission guidelines for freelancers. Even while you are a student, consider yourself a freelance writer because you need to establish yourself in the field. Many publications have their guidelines on their websites. There is a third great way to improve your pitching: Study the databases on the web that contain previous successful pitches of science journalists. Most of them are available for free, and I will specifically address them later in the book. Most important, as seasoned science writer Carl Zimmer (2013) points out in an article on careers in science journalism, rejection is normal. In that sense, prepare to fail. Pitches will be rejected. Written articles will be rejected or edited to a point that you can no longer recognise that you wrote it initially. This is part of the learning process.

What about video and radio? The process does not change; no matter the medium, there is always structure behind every contribution, and each medium has its stylistic rules. For example, a radio contribution needs to employ language visually; you must create pictures in listeners' minds. Incidentally, that is true of all forms of successful writing. This is the process: Consume actively, analyse, read the theoretical foundations and then start producing; fail and repeat, and eventually succeed.

Science journalist Greg Miller recommends that you not wait to get started until you have obtained a degree, a certificate or any other legitimation:

> No matter what stage you're at, just start doing it. Don't feel like you have to get a certain degree or a certain internship or job before you start pitching and writing articles. Start writing, start being a journalist, and don't feel like you have to get some accreditation to do it.
>
> *(Miller 2016)*

## Science and society

In a democracy, it is journalism's job to hold power accountable and question what those in power try to make the public believe. Unfortunately, in part, science journalism fails to live up to its watchdog role and merely entertains its audience instead of conveying and discussing the hard science. Whether you are allowed to produce critical articles largely depends on the editorial policy of the publication you work for. The editorial policy, in turn, is modeled after the publication audience's expectations. Nelkin (1987) affirms that the public's expectations have shaped science journalism since its inception: "The early efforts to communicate science to the public defined a role for science journalists, created expectations about their relationship to the scientific community, and shaped the attitudes and norms of an emerging profession" (17). But these roles are not static; they have changed over time, and they continue to change. As for today's primary role of science journalists, Murcott and Williams (2013) have a clear vision that it should be holding the powers accountable that are at work in science. "Much of science across the world is state-funded, and, arguably, an important principle of democracy is that recipients of such funding should be accountable to the funders, the tax payers" (Murcott and Williams 2013:158). Although science can scrutinise itself, additional external journalistic scrutiny can prove advantageous; otherwise, science may become less credible.

Another important role of science journalists is to increase the public's science literacy and help people make better decisions about their lives. Murcott and Williams (2013) note that the rate at which this occurs has been accelerating over the last years.

This educational role was also confirmed by Tim Radford. Specifically, Radford claims that science journalists have an obligation to democracy:

> We are storytellers, but with a special responsibility to democracy – I think that's the fairest way to put it. Our obligation isn't to science, it isn't even to the editor. It is to the notion of democracy itself, that people are entitled to know what is going on and why it is important that they have been told. The fact that most people can't remember what they have read in the newspaper doesn't mean you haven't done a proper job. It just means that you will have to do it again tomorrow and the day after. I find that for the first 20 years, it didn't matter how many times I explained what DNA was, nobody knew – and suddenly, there is a whole generation that knows what DNA is.
>
> *(Radford 2016)*

Quentin Cooper further expands on the responsibility science journalists have to society. When asked whether he thinks science journalism should educate or entertain, he answers:

> I think it's a bit of both. To a certain extent, being a science journalist is about directing people's attention. There are stories unfolding in every corner of the planet, every day. There are far more stories than we could possibly keep up with. The job of journalism is to help people select the stories that are relevant from the trivia, to make them realise that immediate and easy stories may seem relevant, but perhaps a bit of their time they should be thinking about issues that are a bit

harder to understand but have long-term consequences – like science. But you can't do journalism on the basis of "This is good for you." People love mysteries, and science is full of mysteries. If you can get them to engage with it, pretty soon they want to know more. It's a classic headline to say "Scientists have solved the 30-year-old riddle about the nature of sandstone." Immediately, you are interested, even though you have no idea what the mystery is, and you have never thought much about sandstone, either. You don't really care. But now, you are immediately in there, before you even got to any of the science. Hopefully, by the end of it, you have grasped a bit of science en route. You need to get people in before you discuss any of the science. The great thing is, humans are a curious species.

*(Cooper 2016)*

In order to explain science, you must first be able to understand it:

The science journalist needs to be an intelligent critic who understands not only the output of science but also how it was produced in the first place. No political journalist would cover the story of a new piece of legislation without providing context and background, including the procedures of law-making. There is a very strong case for saying that the same should be expected of science journalists.

*(Murcott and Williams 2013:159)*

Reality looks different, as even science journalists perceive their own métier as not critical enough. In reporting on a survey conducted among 592 global science journalists, Bauer et al. (2013) found that 43 per cent of the respondents saw their roles as informants of science, 23 per cent as translators of complex scientific material and only 10 per cent as entertainers of the public or public watchdogs; among the same respondents, 66 per cent deemed science journalism as too uncritical.

While the role of science journalists is subject to discussion, the primary role of public relations, including science PIOs, is clearly defined: promoting science. However, as Göpfert (2008) asserts, how PR officers convey that information has significantly changed: Public relations officers now hire more professional journalists, and the way they package their material (PR kits) makes it readily available and easily accessible to everyone. That said, Göpfert (2008) points out that the tasks of PR and journalism, although there is a symbiotic theory about the relationship between the two, should be divided:

PR has to accept that offers made to journalism have to undergo a necessary process of selection. This means that public relations have to leave the task of subject choice and subject processing to journalism.

> PR should refrain from gaining influence undercover, to infiltrate or even replace journalism. If independent coverage in reality derives from clever PR measures, then the recipient is being cheated.
>
> *(Göpfert 2008:221)*

This influence of science PR begets what Williams and Clifford (2009) call "minor disagreements between specialists and news editors": UK science journalists assume a gate-keeper role in trying to convince their editors not to run sensationalist science stories that are based on press releases (Williams and Clifford 2009). By reducing the publication of poor-quality journalism, they are serving society as better informants of science; although this need not inherently be critical science journalism, such journalists foster a more informed discourse on science.

Your role can also be imposed by your publication's editorial policy and reality. For example, if you work as a staff writer for an online outlet and need to produce a minimum number of science stories per day, you may have little time to actually carry out journalistic work. Instead, this may prompt you to select press releases, regurgitate their contents, select apt images and spruce up the text before publishing it to the web. Such articles do not provide a great service to society. Most of the time, readers can find that same information elsewhere.

This is not to say that short, press release-based articles do not have their merits but to emphasise that as a science journalist you can and should focus on original and sceptical contributions that ensure that your readers do not just champion science but challenge it.

## Risk and risk perception

While writing this section, I received a press release from the United Nations Environment Programme (UNEP) titled "Hundreds of Millions Face Health Risk as Water Pollution Rises Across Three Continents". The press release claimed that pathogenic and organic pollution of rivers in Asia, Africa and Latin America could put 323 million people's lives at risk. This is both a health and an environmental threat. Communicating risks in a different way is one of our duties as science journalists. But how much is too much or not enough? You shouldn't become a scaremonger or a journalist that hides risks due to conflicts of interest.

On a more formal note, what and how you communicate risks depends on a number of factors, including the topic, audience and scope of the risk. According to Lundgren and McMakin (2013), risk communication can be functionally subdivided into three classes:

1 **Care communication:** Communication when there are already established scientific procedures for handling a danger. This class includes health care advice.

2  **Consensus communication:** Groups of people are informed on risk prevention or mitigation. Groups of stakeholders need to be involved in
finding a solution against a danger and come to a consensus.
3  **Crisis communication:** Communication in the face of an imminent danger, both during and after an emergency, like the partial nuclear melt-
down at the Fukushima Daiichi power plant in 2011.

Communicating risk starts with assessing it, potentially creating a risk/
benefit analysis and then deciding which recommendations (for mitigation
and prevention) to communicate, which depends on the audience and on the
class of risk communication (Lundgren and McMakin 2013). While Lundgren and McMakin primarily address companies' risk managers, you can
adopt the same workflow as a journalist: Figure out what is at stake, assess
the risk, decide how to communicate it considering the relevance to your
audience and only then report it.

Wilkinson et al. (2007), in a study of UK press coverage of nanotechnology between 2003 and 2004, found that only 9 per cent assessed the
social implications and associated risks. They also found that the examined
media were inclined to generally report in a positive way about nanotechnology, but they also added that the public's positive attitude could change
as risks associated to nanoparticles become more apparent. Additionally,
they claimed that for both scientists and journalists, "nanoparticle safety
was the most significant risk issue at stake, an issue characterised by considerable uncertainty" (155). Finally, they contended that the media will probably contribute formatively to how the public will debate nanotechnology,
assuming the public has little knowledge of it.

Cherry-picking which risks to portray in an article while withholding
others is like a photographer picking an angle from which to tell the story.
To a certain extent, the selection of events and viewpoints lies in the nature
of journalism, and this and other factors can negatively influence the way
risk-related stories are communicated. For example, Nelkin (1987) says that
in the pursuit of objectivity, norms such as maintaining one's integrity by
not accepting or offering favours, reporting in a fair way and not having
ties to anything or anyone that could compromise this integrity have been
established:

> In the field of science journalism these norms are particularly empha-
> sized in the coverage of risk disputes and other controversies. Report-
> ers try to maintain balance by quoting scientific sources representing
> opposing sides of a controversy, whether it be over toxic wastes, arti-
> ficial sweeteners, or sociobiology.
>
> *(19)*

Nelkin (1987) is quick to add that merely presenting opposing views does
not allow the readers to judge whether these views are balanced. I will cover

this later in the book when addressing balance in the context of climate change deniers.

A number of interests might be in play when it comes to communicating risks. Two of the primary domains that have a special need for pointing out risks are medicine and environment. Medicine and environment are not only scientific disciplines, but they are also big-budget industries. Some stakeholders have a strong interest in hiding the risks of a novel treatment or drug. In his chapter on medical reporting, Whitaker (2013) states that in 1980, the American Psychiatric Association (APA) started allowing pharmaceutical companies to sponsor scientific symposiums. Speakers were paid, and the talks were painstakingly prepared. The result was a certain loss of independence among the psychiatrists. In addition, medical reporters had difficulties finding experts that who would speak openly about medication in psychiatry: "In truth, when they interview psychiatrists from academic medical schools, they are likely to be speaking with physicians paid, in essence, to tell a positive story about the drugs" (Whitaker 2013:152).

Like medicine, environment lends itself particularly well to establishing quality criteria that help discern bad from good science journalism not only to serve the public better but also to protect the profession itself (Rögener and Wormer 2015). Rögener and Wormer (2015) developed a set of quality criteria based on surveys, discussions and pre-tests among expert groups and student groups. In one survey of a student group, the top criterion was the "correct presentation of risks, no scaremongering, no trivialisation" (9). Eventually, the risk-related criterion was included as the first of a list of ten criteria in environmental journalism (see Rögener and Wormer 2015:10, Table 1). They evaluated fifty environmental stories against the developed criteria and found that nine of the stories "were regarded as either scaremongering or playing down environmental risks" (11).

## Science journalism under fire

Is science journalism for you? If you think it is, then you should develop some resilience over the course of your career, as it is quite likely that at some point your work will face criticism. Sometimes this will be justified and sometimes not. In most cases, such criticism boils down to the quality in understanding and reporting science or to journalistic misconduct, including plagiarism and libel. In extreme cases, such practices can put you out of business, such as in the case of Jonah Lehrer, a science journalist who fabricated quotes and plagiarised his own work.

Science journalists produce many contributions that lack depth, research and overall journalistic quality (such as accuracy). The US, Canadian and European media expect the number of such *churnalism* or *McNews* articles to rise (Bauer et al. 2013). Why do such articles prevail? Lack of time and the scientific illiteracy of science journalists are just two of many reasons. At the heart of many quality-related, heated debates lies the relationship between scientists and science journalists. Schünemann (2013) notes that due to the modern news culture and the increasingly corporate-style mentality of both scientists and journalists, their norms and values diverge. On the one hand, scientists complain about journalists dumbing down complex scientific processes; on the other hand, science journalists complain about scientists trying to feed them questionable information to promote their scientific advances. Why? Getting the media's attention can make it easier to secure research funding. But educating journalists in science is not sufficient to settle the differences between them and scientists, Schünemann (2013) notes:

> Problematically, scientists appear to expect these specialist science reporters to then be equipped to have an (at least basic) understanding of any piece of science thrown at them. This is rather naïve, if not presumptuous, considering that scientists themselves are usually highly specialised within one science. Physicists, say, might be hard put to explain certain biological phenomena and vice versa.
>
> *(136)*

There are more criticisms regarding the quality of science journalism, especially regarding how science journalists choose and consult their sources. For example, in citing Ben Goldacre, Schünemann (2013) argues that science journalists often arbitrarily choose their interviewees as opposed to doing so in a planned and informed manner. She also contends that using peer-reviewed journals is no guarantee that the information presented is reliable and correct. Again drawing on Goldacre and others, Schünemann points out that fake balance is a problem in science journalism: Merely selecting one scientist's opinion and then contrasting it to another (perhaps arbitrarily selected) scientist's opinion is not fairness. She furthermore cites Nick Davies' "safety net rule" (141), which states that the depiction of two sides serves only the journalist, so the journalist can protect herself and does not need to assume any responsibility for what she writes. Finally, Schünemann mentions a fourth element: the elimination of uncertainty. In simplifying stories, scientific evidence is removed from articles, studies' limitations are not addressed and the context of the studies is not considered. This practice skews the picture of scientific research in the media (Schünemann 2013).

In this process of sometimes dumbing down complex scientific research, information is lost, misrepresented and perhaps even fabricated. In other cases, science journalists did not understand studies' terminology, methods and implications before reporting on them. Hence, some scientists have assumed the watchdog role and expose the flaws of badly reported science. For instance, biostatistician Bob O'Hara published an article in the *Guardian* in which he and evolutionary biologist GrrlScientist fiercely criticised the sensationalist headlines of some major publications that reported large number of adult cancers were due to bad luck. You can find excerpts of an interview I conducted with O'Hara on that very topic in Chapter 9.

However, misreporting science is not the only scenario that causes tensions between scientists and journalists. When journalists uncover poor practices, misconduct or generally weird behaviour, some scientists lash out at them. For example, in a 2015 *New York Times* article, journalist Eric Lipton wrote that seed company Monsanto had paid academics to lobby for their products with full knowledge that said academics were perceived as scientific authorities (Lipton 2015). One of them was molecular biologist Kevin Folta at the University of Florida. Based on emails obtained by Freedom of Information Act (FOIA) requests, Lipton (2015) writes that Folta received a grant from Monsanto in 2014. Other scientists were also approached to campaign for Monsanto's products. Before Lipton's article, Kloor (2015) wrote that the grant Folta received from Monsanto was $25,000. The article was later updated to state that Folta's employer had donated it (Kloor 2015).

These revelations sparked a heated debate not only about conflicts of interest in science but also about whether the public has a right to obtain scientists' emails. According to the authors of an op-ed in the *Los Angeles Times*, they do: "Scientists should be subject to the same rules as every other civil servant" (Seife and Thacker 2015), although the authors acknowledge that in rare instances, FOIA requests may be misused to bully an opponent. But the story did not end there.

In a Buzzfeed article in October 2015, Brooke Borel uncovered that Folta interviewed himself by playing the fictitious radio host Vern Blazek. In one of the interviews, he stated never having taken any money from Monsanto (Borel 2015b). Borel, a science journalist, faced criticism in a blog post from Folta (2015) and also from other scientists that supported Folta's outreach. In a follow-up article for the *Guardian*, Borel wrote that she had received angry messages and that researchers had accused her of ruining their cause. In that same article, Borel claims that the debate is historically rooted and is nothing new; in addition, she claims that there is a basic misunderstanding of what science journalism is and what it is not, and there is a lack of distinction from other forms of science communication (Borel 2015a).

## What makes a good science journalist? An interview with Tim Radford

So, what traits does a good science journalist need to have? An ability to tell stories is certainly required, as the *Guardian*'s former science editor, Tim Radford (2016), explains:

> You have to know what the story is and you have to be able to say it in a sentence. People have to actually understand that sentence and still

want to know more. There is a certain amount of craft in the work that we do. But most importantly, you need to be telling a story that people want or need to know more about.

When asked about the similarities between scientists' and science journalists' work, Radford said that the naïve approach at researching does match to a certain degree:

> When I'm talking to scientists – because I developed a second career explaining the media to scientists – I tell them that what they do is to ask questions. What they do is respond excitedly to the discovery that they don't know. A scientist is actually stimulated by the phrase "I don't know". But then, so is a journalist. A scientist then sits down and says "What is it I don't know, and how don't I know, and where would I start to find out" and that's also what we do. The scientist finds out by asking just six questions: who, what, how, why, when and where. Those are the ones we ask as well. The process is all the same, right from the identification of the research problem to the moment when the scientist sits down to write a paper. Both the journalist and the scientist compose the paper very carefully and then submit it to peer review, and then it gets published. The difference is not that one takes a very long time and is more likely to be right than the other. We know that science is often incomplete or wrong, so journalistic stories are not all that much more incomplete or wrong. For a journalist, everything I have described [this process] happens in a day, whereas for a scientist, it takes 18 months or a year. The real difference is that you can write a scientific paper, and perhaps nobody reads it. I cannot believe that most science papers are read by anybody, except maybe the author or subeditor. Sometimes you wonder even how the author could bear to read it, whereas if you wrote a story for a newspaper and no one read it, you would be out of the job. We have this additional burden that we have to be read as well as write. That's a serious difference, and it's part of why we are in the business anyway, because who would ever want to tell a story to an audience of zero?

Radford adds that science journalists are supposed to be discriminating, intelligent and responsible, like other journalists:

> I try not to claim the notion that science writers are a separate species. They are really just journalists doing stories.

As the qualities of objectivity and balance are frequently debated, when asked whether it is possible to achieve objectivity in journalism, Radford says complete objectivity is an illusion, and you should rather consider being fair:

> *Objective* is a treacherous word, isn't it? The word I favour is *fair*. You listen carefully to what people say and why they are saying it. It's not hard to hear dangerous and destructive views. But it's sensible to listen to them, because the important question is: Why are people espousing these views and what is their motive? Were somebody to stand up and say "I think we should bring back autocracy," or "I think the country should be only run by the rich," as a citizen I would object to that quite strongly. As a reporter, I would report it, but I would still object to it myself.

Moreover, Radford points out that rejection is part of the job and is actually a useful experience. At the same time, he remembers how a very persistent writer who was bad at pitching stories listened to his advice and eventually managed to become an established journalist:

> You are going to learn better from failure than from anything else. Generally, if you are the sort of person that takes no for an answer, if you are easily discouraged, then journalism is not for you. The very first quality of journalism is tenacity. If you are a reporter working for a daily newspaper, you have to do your best every day. Even when things go wrong, you have to try and make them go right next time. Failure and dismissal and rejection are all quite useful things to experience. My advice to a young writer would be to collect as many rejection slips as you possibly could and start taking pride in them. . . . Secondly, you could actually learn from rejection. I have several stories of people whose submissions were so terrible I sent them back a standard card which I didn't even sign, so they would never know who had dismissed them, because they were just so frightful. But one of them kept on and on and on, and in the end I told him, "You do realise just how bad you are. Let me tell you the sixteen things that you really shouldn't be doing." He listened, and then he sent another one, and it wasn't quite so bad. In the end, he became a colleague and competitor of some distinction. He did it partly by just being determined to write.

Radford adds that being able to boil down your ideas to a minimum is one of the essential traits of journalism:

> If you want to sell an idea to an editor, have it in one sentence. And it better be a good sentence. Because, if you ring up an editor, he is going to give you his full attention for about 8 seconds, and then he'll start doodling or looking something up. For a freelancer, the perfect

conversation consists of simply putting the idea and the editor saying "800 words for four o'clock".

Finding ideas and selling them to editors is addressed in the next two chapters. You will learn that there are many hard criteria that help you decide which ideas are worth pursuing and which ones you can discard.

## Summary

Science journalism is a journalistic genre like all the others: It conforms to the same rules, and it requires critical thinking, scrutinising complex scientific concepts, holding scientists accountable and potentially exposing misconduct. In addition, it requires a deep understanding of the scientific field. This watchdog role of science journalism is contrasted by a light-hearted and often shallow style of reporting that merely worships new scientific advances and puts scientists on pedestals. Nevertheless, this kind of output does have its merit: popularising science among the public.

Many publications treat science as an orphan. Many readers wince at the idea of reading science articles, as their science experiences in high school or even university have left a sour taste. Science is often perceived as dry, too complicated to grasp, overly technical and not entertaining. As science journalists, therefore, you will have to fulfil the essential roles of educating the public and spurring its interest in science. If you succeed in finding the right balance, your contributions will help people make better decisions about their lives.

This duality of science journalism is rooted in its history. There have been periods when science journalists focused on quality journalism, and there have been periods when gee whiz science journalism was all the rage. Currently, short-form articles on new scientific advances prevail; these provide a fertile ground for heated debates between scientists and science journalists about quality.

As a science journalist, you should not only be resilient but also perseverant and, most important, investigative. These attitudes will help you survive criticism and also progress and build a career in this competitive business. Most important, you will also have to be able to wear two hats at once: the science hat and the writing hat, as conflicting as this might seem. Did you notice the duality again? If you can break down complex scientific issues without over-simplifying them and write about them beautifully, chances are this job is for you.

## Review questions

- What are the most successful topic areas in science journalism worldwide?
- Which historical events spurred the public's interest in science?

- What separates science journalists from public information officers?
- Is self-learning a viable way to break into science journalism? If so, how could you achieve this?
- What attitudes of a political reporter are science journalists sometimes lacking?
- To whom are you obliged to as a journalist: your editor, yourself, or your reader?
- What are the three classes of risk communication?
- What does *fake balance* mean in journalism?
- How much should you be able to compress an idea before pitching it?
- Can you name at least three important attitudes every science journalist should have?

## Exercises

- Find two long-form science stories and read them actively, paragraph by paragraph, and note whether each paragraph entertains or educates.
- Take each story and try to summarize it in one sentence.
- For each role of a science journalist, find an article or television or radio programme that clearly shows that its originator fulfils that role. Which elements reveal the role of the journalist (structure, style, topic selection)?
- Find at least two science stories that provide a fake balance. Hint: Climate change stories are a good place to start.

## Reading list

Allan, S. (2002) *Media, Risk and Science*. Buckingham: Open University Press

Schünemann, S. (2013) Science journalism, In Turner, B. and Orange, R. (eds.) *Specialist Journalism*, London: Routledge, 134–146

Whitaker, R. (2013) Medical reporting, In Turner, B. and Orange, R. (eds.) *Specialist Journalism*. London: Routledge, 147–159

## References

Badenschier, F. and Wormer, H. (2012) Issue selection in science journalism: Towards a special theory of news values for science news? In Rödder, S., Franzen, M., and Weingart, P. (eds.) *The Sciences' Media Connection: Public Communication and its Repercussions*. Dordrecht: Springer, 59–85

Bauer, M.W., Howard, S., Romo Ramos, Y.J., Massarani, L. and Amorim, L. (2013) *Global Science Journalism Report: Working Conditions & Practices, Professional Ethos and Future Expectations*. Our learning series, Science and Development Network. London [Online] Available at: http://eprints.lse.ac.uk/48051/ [date accessed 29 August 2016]

Borel, B. (2015a) The problem with science journalism: We've forgotten that reality matters most, *The Guardian* [Online] Available at: www.theguardian.com/

media/2015/dec/30/problem-with-science-journalism-2015-reality-kevin-folta [date accessed 3 September 2016]

Borel, B. (2015b) Seed money, *Buzzfeed* [Online] Available at: www.buzzfeed.com/brookeborel/when-scientists-email-monsanto [date accessed 3 September 2016]

Brennan, E.A. and Clarage, E.C. (1999) *Who's Who of Pulitzer Prize Winners*. Phoenix, AZ: Oryx Press

Cooper, Q. (2016) Personal phone conversation on 6 September 2016

Folta, K. (2015) The Vern Blazek science power hour, *Kevin Folta (Personal Blog)* [Online] Available at: http://kfolta.blogspot.it/2015/10/the-vern-blazek-science-power-hour.html [date accessed 2 September 2016]

Göpfert, W. (2008) The strength of PR and the weakness of science journalism, In Bauer, M.W. and Bucchi, M. (eds.) *Journalism, Science and Society: Science Communication Between News and Public Relations*. New York: Routledge, 215–226

Johnson, G. (2015) Personal phone conversation on 8 October 2015

Kaplan, K. (2015) Personal phone conversation on 9 October 2015

Kloor, K. (2015) GM-crop opponents expand probe into ties between scientists and industry, *Nature* [Online] Available at: www.nature.com/news/gm-crop-opponents-expand-probe-into-ties-between-scientists-and-industry-1.18146 [date accessed 3 September 2016]

Leach, J. (2016) Personal phone conversation on 6 September 2016

Lipton, E. (2015) Food industry enlisted academics in G.M.O. lobbying war, emails show, *The New York Times* [Online] Available at: www.nytimes.com/2015/09/06/us/food-industry-enlisted-academics-in-gmo-lobbying-war-emails-show.html [date accessed 3 September 2016]

Lundgren, R.E. and McMakin, A.H. (2013) *Risk Communication: A Handbook for Communicating Environmental, Safety and Health Risks*. Hoboken: John Wiley & Sons

Miller, G. (2016) Personal phone conversation on 2 September 2016

Murcott, T.H.L. and Williams, A. (2013) The challenges for science journalism in the UK, *Progress in Physical Geography*, vol. 37, no. 2, 152–160

Nelkin, D. (1987) The culture of science journalism, *Society*, vol. 24, no. 6, 17–25

Radford, T. (2016) Personal phone conversation on 12 April 2016

Rehman, J. (2013) The need for critical science journalism, *The Guardian* [Online] Available at: www.theguardian.com/science/blog/2013/may/16/need-for-critical-science-journalism [date accessed 27 August 2016]

Rögener, W. and Wormer, H. (2015) Defining criteria for good environmental journalism and testing their applicability: An environmental news review as a first step to more evidence based environmental science reporting, *Public Understanding of Science* (published online ahead of print 11 August 2015)

Ruppel Shell, E. (2016) Personal phone conversation on 25 August 2016

Schünemann, S. (2013) Science journalism, In Turner, B. and Orange, R. (eds.) *Specialist Journalism*. London: Routledge, 134–146

Seife, C. and Thacker, P. (2015) Why it's OK for taxpayers to 'snoop' on scientists, *Los Angeles Times* [Online] Available at: www.latimes.com/opinion/op-ed/la-oe-0821-seife-thacker-science-transparency-20150821-story.html [date accessed 1 September 2016]

Whitaker, R. (2013) Medical reporting, In Turner, B. and Orange, R. (eds.) *Specialist Journalism*. London: Routledge, 147–159

Wilkinson, C., Allan, S., Anderson, A. and Petersen, A. (2007) From uncertainty to risk?: Scientific and news media portrayals of nanoparticle safety, *Health, Risk & Society*, vol. 9, no. 2, 145–157

Williams, A. and Clifford, S. (2009) *Mapping the Field: Specialist Science News Journalism in the UK National Media*, report for Cardiff University

Yong, E. (2016) Personal phone conversation on 18 August 2016

Zimmer, C. (2013) A note to beginning science writers, *The Loom (National Geographic)* [Online] Available at: http://phenomena.nationalgeographic.com/2013/06/24/a-note-to-beginning-science-writers/ [date accessed 31 August 2016]

# 2
# FINDING SCIENCE STORIES

**What you will learn in this chapter:**

- What makes a good science story?
- Story idea anatomy
- Topics versus ideas
- Understanding news values
- Sourcing science stories
- The scientific method
- Idea protection

## Introduction

Everybody loves a good story. A good idea is at the heart of every good short story, novel and movie. Journalistic stories are no different; they all boil down to a story idea that can be expressed in one or two sentences. Getting there implies working on an initial topic of interest and moulding it into an idea. Finding that topic, conducting initial research and eventually formulating an idea are the foundation of writing a presentable pitch and sending it to a commissioning editor.

Before you do this, you must not only understand the audience of the publication you are pitching to but also how editors define newsworthiness and select pitches. News factors like timeliness, topicality and extremes help you assess the quality of your story idea before pitching it. Most of these news factors are valid in all journalistic disciplines. Additionally, there are a few more factors to consider in science journalism, such as anniversaries or frequently covered topics. In this chapter, you will get to know these news factors and learn how you can apply them in identifying topics worth writing about.

Stories can take very different shapes, but they all have some sort of structure. Structure glues together otherwise arbitrarily ordered events. Story ideas, too, need to be structured. Only when you have a clear picture of what your story is can you pitch it to somebody. That is why this chapter contains a section on the basic anatomy of science stories and story ideas.

Topics, as you will learn, will never get you a commission, regardless of whether you are pitching them internally to your editor or externally as a freelance writer. Rather, topics serve as an inspiration for your further research and for finding stories that are located within that topic's boundaries. Hence, the section dedicated to differentiating topics from ideas will show you a technique that will help you transform topics into elaborate story ideas.

You will also find a dedicated section on the various sources you can use for finding science stories, including journal papers, press releases, conferences and, most importantly, people. But beware that some of these sources come with caveats, so that section will also contain advice on how to use them properly to get the most out of, say, embargoed journal papers.

Journal authors often pursue a larger goal, such as to cure a disease, to find a novel treatment or to reduce air pollution. These superordinate goals are excellent sources for story ideas, as they contain a human interest factor and put the research in a larger context that transcends a single paper's boundaries. If you don't want to miss out on these opportunities, it is crucial to understand how scientists conduct research. That is why you will also find an intuitive explanation of research's standard procedure, the *scientific method*.

The last section of this chapter will briefly touch upon protecting your story ideas. In a nutshell, you cannot protect them, so you must be careful who you share them with. Pre-pitching ideas to your acquaintances is an important part of finding out if your ideas are sound, as are kneading them, re-formulating them, adapting them and finding evidence to support them before you write pitches. By the time you finish this book, you will probably find that the essential way science works is not all that different from how you as a science journalist work, and this chapter lays the foundation to this notion.

## What makes a good science story?

The quality of a science story depends on many aspects, including the type of publication you want to pitch it to, the text type (feature or news story) and the publication's audience. These factors are external to your story. As part of your preparation to craft your pitch, they implicitly flow into your pitch (and eventual story) but are not explicitly written into it. In contrast, internal factors include news factors and the structure of your story idea; you can name these explicitly in your pitch.

You can either start from the publication you want to pitch to, or you can find a story idea and then select a publication. In both cases, you will have to study the publication by reading as many issues as you can. Reading them will tell you a lot about the publication's editorial policy and, most important, its readership. What topics and what types of stories do they prefer? Many magazines and online science outlets categorise and tag their articles, which makes it easy to find the topics they are interested in. Knowing this will help you find a suitable topic (one that is likely to attract the commissioning editor's interest) long before you write the pitch. Additionally, you can follow the publication's Facebook and Twitter accounts and monitor which topics and subject areas generate the most passionate reader reactions.

The former editor of *BBC Focus* magazine, Graham Southorn, says the magazine's most frequently covered subject areas are space and cosmology:

> For *Focus* magazine, it has to be something that is exciting, with a bit of science fiction to it, something that has been developed in the lab and could change the world or that could have some big implications for the future, plus science that is really cutting edge like head transplants. But we also cover everyday science about why you sneeze or what gives you a good night's sleep. Our topics are either connected to everyday life or topics at the opposite extreme that take you into daydreaming about future.
>
> *(Southorn 2015)*

Also, a publication's ads are unmistakable indicators of its readers' preferences. Do they mostly advertise watches, smartphones and cars? If so, chances are the audience is mostly interested in technology. You can safely assume that every publication has done its homework on demographics and publishes only advertisements that its readers relate to. They know their audience, and so should you. Make sure to also intensively study competing publications, as they most certainly share the same audience.

Southorn confirms that reading a lot is key and emphasises that reading is a way to improve your own writing:

> A lot of people don't read these days. They think they are writers, and they do want to write, but they don't put the time in to read. But you can only be a better writer by reading other people. In fact, you can learn a whole lot by reading the best science writers and the best bloggers.
>
> *(Southorn 2015)*

## Story idea anatomy

You can think of a story idea as the essence of a pitch – a miniature version of a written article. Structurally speaking, all stories must have a beginning, a middle and an end. A sound idea encapsulates that whole structure in one or two sentences. The three story parts are further subdivided into paragraphs that must be linked together to make your text flow. This three-act structure is also the foundation of every successful screenplay and novel. Sohn (2013) confirms this structure and adds that every story should contain "characters engaged in some kind of journey or conflict" (Sohn 2013:11). This journey represents a simplification (again, structurally speaking) of the hero's journey in fiction. It must have a protagonist who is confronted with obstacles and is trying to achieve an ultimate goal. The protagonist may fail or succeed in these efforts, but it is important that the protagonist's story comes to a resolution before the end.

In science journalism, your protagonist could be a physician who dedicates his life to finding a cure for lung cancer. While conducting preliminary research, you perhaps discover that his motivation for doing so is that his wife is gravely ill with lung cancer. Will he succeed in finding new medication before she succumbs to it? There you have all the elements of a story: a protagonist, a conflict, a journey and a resolution. For this example, you should tell your audience whether his wife survives. Can you sum this idea up in one or two sentences? Then, test the idea by pitching it to your friends or family. These "pub pitches" often quickly reveal essential flaws in your story.

If you pass the pub pitch test, you will send an editor a pitch that reflects the finished story's structure. Similarly, your idea must be focused and structured. Elements of your idea are the problem and its solution, protagonists as they pursue a goal, and conflicts. You will need to convey some sense of change and be as specific as is necessary. Most of the time, you need to include who did what and why in your story idea, but you can leave out the when, where and how. However, be flexible about that approach; if the story is about a scientist who develops a biogas digester that cleans Mount Everest of piles of human excrement, the location is worth mentioning. Can you remember the essential traits of a journalist from the first chapter? Selection is key.

Naturally, not every news story can have a scientist who goes on a quest to save humanity from diseases as its protagonist. Sometimes you will simply write reports that explain scientific findings that perhaps solve a very specific problem. If this is the case, your story idea will focus on what is new, why it is relevant and what was known before, also known as context and background. For story ideas that result in reports, structure is still important; in that case, the traditional inverted pyramid format – ordering the facts by importance – is the best way to tell the story. Your story idea should reflect that by presenting the most important facts upfront.

Sohn (2013) confirms that a story has to be connected to a superordinate idea – the main idea of a piece. Especially for longer articles, the main idea represents the essential point you are trying to make or an insight you want to provide; for example, a main point could be "lead-tainted water is not as harmful as previously thought." The main idea often manifests as a non-trivial cause-and-effect relationship. The main idea is part of your story idea, so put it in one of the two sentences that express your story idea. In addition, the main idea helps you stay focused as you pile up heaps of research. In fact, it is an excellent selection tool that helps you decide which bits of your research you should keep and which bits you can safely discard.

## Topics versus ideas

Every good story idea is connected to a topic and a theme. It would be probably be quite easy to come up with several topics you would like to write about, for example, carbon trading, antimicrobial resistance or gene editing. If you want to know what topics people worldwide are currently interested in, check out Google Trends (see the Links section at the end of this chapter). You can also read magazine and newspaper science sections and scholarly publications; common topics of interest will easily emerge, and many science publications tend to cover the same topics. You can also find yearly forecasts of upcoming trends in science topics in publications such as *WIRED* or *Science*.

Finding a topic is a good starting point that will help you conduct further research and eventually find a story within that topic, as Sohn (2013) confirms. Perhaps you already have a notion of what the theme will be before you start researching, but it will usually emerge as a result of researching the topic.

One way to turn topics into tangible story ideas is choosing a focused angle and a clear message. Lack of ambiguity is a news factor that makes your story newsworthy. Sumner and Miller (2013) state that one of the five most common mistakes that beginning writers commit is proposing broad topics instead of ideas that have a strongly focused angle. The other four mistakes are a lack of in-depth research, failing to draw on a variety of sources, not using anecdotes and writing boring texts that lack action. Drawing on decades of experience in dealing with students' pitches, Sumner and Miller state that proposing topics instead of elaborate ideas is still the most common error.

Years ago, I proposed to *Scientific American*'s blog editor a post about tweeting sharks that help the government issue warnings to beachgoers. Before I sent him my story idea, I had rummaged databases, newspapers and the internet for additional material and had talked to people until I had piled up a huge amount of information. Full of excitement, I packed the pitch with lots of scientific background but failed to deliver a story and a theme. To my luck, that editor was kind enough to not immediately reject the pitch; instead, he helped me work on it until it was sound because the topic interested him. He told me the proposal was missing an "analytical arc" – it had no main idea. So, I went through all the arguments I had come up with and looked at what superordinate idea these arguments supported: The Western Australian government was acting inconsistently; on the one hand, it had tried various conservation efforts to protect great white sharks, and on the other hand, it had overridden its own laws to cull the sharks and mollify the mob. That was the story's theme. Summarising the story in two sentences became easy:

> Marine scientists equip great white sharks with GPS tags and translate their positions into tweets that warn beachgoers whenever a shark is nearby. But Western Australia's Premier Colin (aptly nicknamed "Cullin") Barnett instead ordered the sharks to be killed, ignoring that great white sharks are an officially protected species.

This contains all the elements of a story: protagonists pursuing a goal (marine scientists whose goal is to protect beachgoers and sharks), an antagonist pursuing his own goal (Barnett, who wants to appease the public), a central conflict and, obviously, the science of tracking sharks in real time. In this case, the underlying topic would simply be shark protection, or shark culling.

Usually, if you fail to deliver a story and instead propose a mere topic or list of arguments, all you earn is a rejection slip – or no reply at all. I can only speculate, but the editor probably could have guessed what peeked through the list of arguments I sent him: a rather opinionated angle to approach the topic.

So, what makes a good angle, and how can you find one? Most of the popular topics have been covered from a variety of perspectives. Most editors will require you to come up with a fresh angle their readers have not yet seen. A fresh angle can also justify writing on a topic that others have written about ad nauseam. Luckily, you can assess the quality of your angle. A good, "focused angle has unity, action and concreteness" (Sumner and Miller 2013:28):

1 **Unity:** Let the story revolve around a single, central idea. This makes your story more homogenous and hence easier for the reader to follow. Unity will also help you find relevant sources and prevent you from losing track while consulting them.
2 **Action:** Describe what the protagonists are doing. In doing so, use active verbs. As an exercise, Sumner and Miller (2013) suggest you check magazine covers for strong action verbs. Look for *who does what*.
3 **Concreteness:** Be specific about the relevant details. Create pictures in the minds of whoever reads or listens to your idea. Eliminate irrelevant details. This is one of the main differences between topics and ideas: Topics are never concrete.

If you want to find an angle, you need to narrow a topic to a particular perspective or a specific instance within that topic. Once you have identified a candidate for your initial idea, you should put it to the test and find out whether the angle is too broad (Sumner and Miller 2013). If other authors have written entire books on your topic, or if your working title contains no verb, you will probably need to further narrow your initial idea. If you can find a local or topical news peg to hang your story on, that will make for a valid angle, too. Also, try to gain access to pundits or unique documents, as those sources often yield fresh insights worth passing on to readers (Sumner and Miller 2013).

One technique for developing an idea out of a mere topic and finding a number of angles worth reporting about is the angle tree (Sumner and Miller 2013), which is shown in Figure 2.1. The angle tree is a brainstorming technique designed to help you narrow a topic to four specific angles (see Figure 2.2). Then, you choose one angle as your main focus and another that could be covered secondarily. Covering all four would be too much for the article to stay focused (Sumner and Miller 2013). In fact, if you cover too many angles in one article, the reader will have a hard time understanding what the article's main idea is. This would violate the principles of unity and clarity, which you will encounter in the next section.

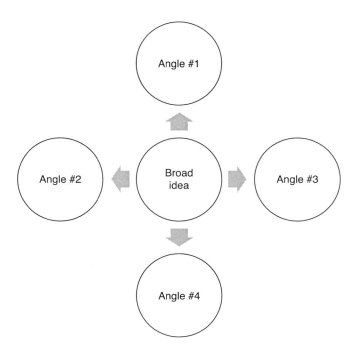

**FIGURE 2.1** The angle tree illustrates how to take a broad idea and break it down into four angles

*Source*: Wiley/Feature and Magazine Writing/Sumner and Miller (2013)

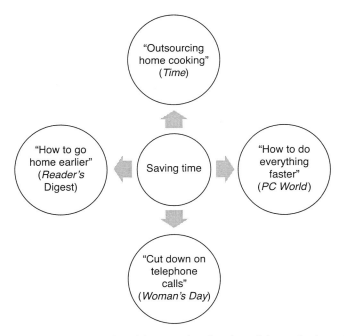

**FIGURE 2.2** This is an example of four angles developed from the broad idea of time management

*Source*: Wiley/Feature and Magazine Writing/Sumner and Miller (2013)

It is also a good exercise to reverse-engineer published articles and try to extract the angles and topics. The article titles are very expressive. For example, the article title of Rose (2015) is:

The Forensics of Identifying Migrants Who Die Exhausted after Crossing from Mexico

In addition, its subtitle reads:

Scientists are identifying the remains of undocumented migrants who died crossing the Mexican border – people whose names would otherwise have been lost forever

Both the title and subtitle hint at the article's story idea and angle. Notice how the title contains active verbs (*die*, as well as *cross* and *identify*, although in gerund form) and nouns (*forensics, migrants, Mexico*). They help narrow down what could have been the original topic: forensics at the Mexican border. The subtitle introduces further details by saying the migrants were undocumented and without the work of these scientists, they would remain anonymous. This answers the who, what, where and why and makes the reader want more. The title and subtitle showcase the principles of unity and action. Readers will find also concreteness in a very specific example later in the article.

Once you have identified one or two angles worth reporting about, try summing up your idea. If you cannot frame your idea in one or two sentences, your angle is probably not tight enough. Those one or two sentences should show unity, action and concreteness, and they should also contain your main idea.

Read as much as you can, and try to extract the angles and story ideas from the articles you read if you want to understand which angles work best. With this in mind, make sure you primarily consume the crème de la crème of science writing. Many award-winning articles are available online for free, such as the yearly *AAAS Kavli Science Journalism Awards* (Lane 2014). Sohn (2013), Sumner and Miller (2013) and *BBC Focus* magazine's former editor Graham Southorn confirm this advice. Philip Yam, editor at *Scientific American*, confirms that reading what your competitors write is essential for developing fresh angles:

> Keeping up with what's going on and learning which kinds of stories are most likely to make it into print, on the Web, or over the air will help you develop news judgment. Having such a background also helps in formulating novel angles and coming up with the day-after analysis that headline news often lacks.
>
> *(Yam 2006:7)*

Sharon Begley, former science and health correspondent at Reuters and former science columnist at *Newsweek*, frequently looks for personal anecdotes to find unique angles:

> I do look for personal anecdotes, for the moment when a scientist had a realisation. For example, I was writing about one of the space missions to repair the *Hubble* space telescope. At that time, one of the mirrors on the telescope was warped when it was manufactured. The telescope was not working, so they had to fix it. The question was: How were they going to fix it? The solution turned out to be to put a new lens on top of the existing lens, which corrected the problem. When asked how he [the scientist] had come up with the idea, he said, "When I was visiting Germany, I was taking a shower in my hotel, and I was looking at this amazing German engineered shower head. There were several circles, one on top of the other, each of which could be rotated, and which would affect the water outlet behind it. Then I realised I could apply that same principle to the *Hubble* space telescope." . . . Whenever you have a scientist in a shower, you go with it.
>
> *(Begley 2015)*

There is one more important quality successful science writing exhibits: the ability to evoke emotions. There are many research papers that confirm we better remember information that evokes emotions. One topic area that evokes emotions is animal abuse. In 1992, science journalist and journalism educator Deborah Blum won the Pulitzer Prize for Beat Reporting for her article series "The Monkey Wars" in the *Sacramento Bee*. In her articles, Blum thoroughly analysed and juxtaposed ethical aspects of primate research. In fact, the series was so successful that she later turned the idea also into a book.

Wahl-Jorgensen (2013) conducted an analysis of emotionality in Pulitzer Prize-winning articles between 1995 and 2011. Her results indicate that successful, award-winning articles do express emotions. However, authors almost never express their own emotions; instead, they describe their protagonists' or sources' emotions. Interestingly, the majority of emotions expressed are negative (Wahl-Jorgensen 2013). This falls perfectly in line with an important news value of the next section: negativity. An award-winning science journalist has a three-point checklist (see Box 2.1) that he

---

**BOX 2.1   DAVID DOBBS: HOW TO ASSESS A SCIENCE STORY IDEA**

Science journalist David Dobbs explains how he evaluates whether a story idea is worth pursuing. He uses this method for long-form feature stories on science:

I have a three-point checklist that helps me decide: Will this thing fly at long length, for example 5,000 to 6,000 words? What I am looking for are three things:

1   A really interesting scientific idea or a finding, with a finding being an instantiated idea. It can be a new idea or an old idea that is suddenly under ferocious attack.
2   You also have to have a person invested in that idea – a scientist. Ask yourself: Do they have an interesting personal story? That's a plus. If they have researched something that is clearly fascinating and amenable to interesting explanation, that is also a plus.
3   Most importantly: Can they talk well? Because the better they can talk, the easier your job is. What you want is a quote machine. You want people who want to talk powerfully and in plain but vivid language about what they are doing.

One of Dobbs's science features, "A Depression Switch?", which has appeared in the *New York Times*, shows that he found such an interesting protagonist. In Chapter 8, Dobbs explains the storytelling techniques he employed for writing this story.

uses to put his ideas to the test before deciding whether to further pursue them. Finally, when you carry out your pub pitch, be sure to observe your listener's emotional reactions. If they react with excitement, awe, disgust or sadness, and if your idea fulfils most or all of the test criteria, you might have found an idea that is worth pitching. But before you do, you should also test it for the classical journalistic news values.

## Understanding news values

Seasoned editors seemingly make intuitive decisions about which stories they commission and which ones they turn down. The same is true of experienced staff writers and freelancers; most have a gut feeling about which story ideas are worth elaborating and eventually pitching. At the heart of these decisions are hard factors that determine whether a story is newsworthy. Knowing these factors explicitly will help you assess the quality of your story ideas and easily discard ideas that seem interesting but are journalistically irrelevant. Over time, you will develop that same intuitive automatism.

Structuring a story idea and showing that you have sufficiently researched the story and its underlying topic is half the battle. The other half is showing an editor what makes your story relevant to readers. Sohn (2013) describes this relevancy as "a news 'hook' – a reason to tell the story *now*".

This is where news values come in: They determine when an event is likely to be turned into a news item based on the psychology of perception (Galtung and Ruge 1965). The news values found by Galtung and Ruge (1965) are still applicable today. You can find the complete list in Box 2.2. These are applicable to all journalistic genres, not just science journalism. Use these news values to test your story ideas. Can you answer one or more questions with *yes*? If so, you probably have a relevant idea.

The first eight news values are culture independent, whereas the last four news values are culture dependent. Especially negative news is likely to be covered in the media because it includes many other news factors such as consonance, unambiguity and unexpectedness.

When asked about additional news values in (popular) science journalism, Graham Southorn replied:

> Anniversaries are a big news value; for example, if ten years ago a special event in science happened. Or it could be something like "this November [2015] it is 100 years [since] Einstein published the general theory of relativity," so I suggested to *Focus* magazine they could write something about gravity and what we know about gravity.
>
> *(Southorn 2015)*

---

## BOX 2.2 NEWS VALUES

- Frequency: Is there a noticeable trend that matches the media's frequency?
- Strength/superlative: Is the event something of a big magnitude?
- Clarity/unambiguity: Does the event have clearly defined implications?
- Meaningfulness/cultural proximity: Is the event related to the audience's culture?
- Consonance: Does the event meet the audience's expectations?
- Unexpectedness: Could the event surprise the audience? Is it "unexpected within the meaningful and consonant" (Galtung and Ruge, 1965:67)?
- Continuity: Has the event been on the news before?
- Composition: Has the publication run a lot of stories of the same kind? If so, an outlier (a story related to a different topic) has better odds of being run.
- Reference to elite nations: Are so-called elite nations, such as the US or Russia, involved in the event?
- Reference to elite people: Are important individuals, such as heads of states, involved in the event?
- Personalisation: Is the event a seeming result of human actions?
- Negativity: Does the event have negative implications?

Source: Based on Galtung and Ruge (1965)

---

Davide Castelvecchi, a senior physical sciences reporter and former online news editor at *Nature*, confirms that anniversaries are worth covering but adds that the *Nature* editors are selective about them:

> We do look at ways to mark certain anniversaries if they are really important. The problem with science anniversaries is that you have to be very selective, because there are so many of them. Some anniversaries are global events, like the anniversary of general relativity last year. A lot of people tend to cover those. I argued for having a special issue of *Nature* last year dedicated to general relativity, but I lost that argument. As far as news is concerned, we do some anniversaries, but we have to be very selective. The fact that something is an anniversary is not news.
>
> *(Castelvecchi 2016)*

Certain topics in science and technology are worth covering even when there is no immediate news peg; for example, "stories like self-driving cars and virtual reality goggles are worth covering now that there is a general trend, with companies producing more and more of these", Castelvecchi (2016) explains. He adds this was also the reason why *Nature* covered virtual reality in 2016: "It was not tied to a specific day or event. It was not a specific anniversary or peg, but it was a general trend that was timely" (Castelvecchi 2016).

Science bloggers are even more independent from classical news values. Paige Jarreau is a science communication specialist at Louisiana State University and former manager of the science blog network Scilogs.com. In her PhD dissertation, she dissected the practices of science bloggers and found that science bloggers do use news values. Also, they may be more likely to adopt news organisations' content decision practices if their blogs are part of such organisations:

> They [science bloggers] may also adopt at least some traditional news values and criteria of newsworthiness in their determination of "blogworthiness" while other values or criteria of blogworthiness may be shared between bloggers to the extent that these emerge as routines unique to the blog format.
>
> *(Jarreau 2015b)*

Most of the science bloggers Jarreau interviewed were either scientists or otherwise rooted in academia. When she asked them about the news values they employ, they were not as strict as trained journalists:

> It was interesting that almost all the science bloggers I talked to are very familiar with news values. Once we started talking about them, they said "News is timely, the bizarre, and other kinds of traditional news values." They were aware of them but not always using them. . . . If the news values fit with their blogging goals, they [would] adopt them. But for many science bloggers, if the traditional news values didn't work for them, they were not worried about it. If they wanted to talk about a paper from last year, they were not worried how timely it was. They don't have an editor, so they can just go with whatever they want to talk about.
>
> *(Jarreau 2015a)*

Interestingly, this intuitive sense of which stories to run seems to resonate with many editors and science journalists. Through their experience, they have internalised these news values. But Jarreau (2015b) also adds that there are science bloggers that have a journalistic background, and they are naturally more likely to adhere to core journalistic values. This can be observed in science blogging networks like *National Geographic*'s Phenomena (Jarreau 2015b).

Some topics in science inherently receive more coverage than others, as Badenschier and Wormer (2012) contend. Medicine, health and biology are all top-sellers in science journalism worldwide. Additional factors affect how and when science news is produced and where it is placed in a newspaper.

First, political news generally trumps science news, even for breakthroughs. If on a specific day nothing happened that editors consider more important than science, science news might also make the front page. Second, the way the news market develops can cause a shift from news values specific to science toward general news values. For example, a science story on tsunamis might get rejected at first but becomes topical when such a catastrophe occurs. As for time-independent factors, two scholars propose a three-factor model for the selection process of science news (Badenschier and Wormer 2012):

1  **Importance:** In terms of politics, economy, society, culture, ethics and/or science.
2  **Surprise:** New and different, exotic.
3  **Usability:** Medical/technical advice for daily life.

Badenschier and Wormer (2012) also developed and tested a draft catalogue of science news values. They eventually reduced the catalogue to the following science news factors with the highest impact on selection (ranked alphabetically):

* Actuality
* Astonishment
* Composition
* Controversy
* Economic relevance
* Graphical material
* Intention
* Personalisation
* Political relevance
* Range (number of affected people)
* Reference to elite persons
* Relevance to recipients/society
* Scientific relevance
* Unexpectedness.

With this newly gained understanding of what a story idea is, how it can be structured and which criteria it needs to meet in order to be journalistically relevant, let's move on to finding inspiration.

## Sourcing science stories

### *People*

People are the most valuable sources for unique ideas. *Scientific American*'s Philip Yam (2006) confirms this: "As is true for any kind of journalism, the best sources are people" (8). Most people have interesting anecdotes to tell you; these help make your article concrete (Sumner and Miller 2013). If you want to get people to talk with you, you will have to establish some kind of relationship with them. Show interest and do preliminary research on the topic they work in. Check out their research interests and read what they have published so far. Find out what they are endorsing or ranting about online. Prepare well and be specific when you ask them for an interview, and also be specific during the interview. Interviewing scientists, patients and officials (the latter perhaps to a lesser extent) often leads to unique tips and leads that are not found on the internet or in newspapers.

Talk to your interviewees in person whenever possible; this way, you get the most information out of them (spoken information, body language, surroundings). Video calls are second best (minus surroundings), followed by phone calls (minus body language and surroundings). Resort to emails only for clarifying or verifying after the interview; email answers are prepared, bland and lack candour. It is also much harder for your interviewee to dodge difficult questions during a face-to-face interview. You can find more on interviewing in Chapter 4.

### Journal papers

Scientific journals will be one of your primary sources as a science journalist. This is where scientists publish their findings, along with their experiment's design, methodology, study limitations and discussions. They are particularly important for your science story's explanatory, hard science passages. Selecting which papers to report about is key. If you are a staff journalist, you will pitch and cover stories from major journals – stories that also other publications will cover. As a freelancer, that does not work, so you need to look for niche topics that a publication's staff has not yet covered. The upside of the latter approach is that it is usually easier to come up with a fresh angle.

Scientific journals produce such a high volume of output that the majority of studies are never read and covered. Online news services can help keep track of relevant stories. They pre-select studies for you and translate the main findings into readable texts. Despite the fact that stories discovered via news services will hardly ever be investigative or scoops, Yam (2006) states that journals can be the right place to uncover original stories that no one else has found yet. He recommends using the online libraries www.arXiv.org (physical sciences) or PubMed (www.ncbi.nlm.nih.gov/pubmed; medicine) for digging up unique research papers. If you are a college student, you can also use your library's subscriptions to many journals to access them for free (Yam 2006).

Apart from the major journals, there are many specialised journals in which you can find quirky and offbeat topics. Sharon Begley, now a science writer at STAT news, recommends looking at these journals:

> Look at the more specialised journals. Everybody is looking at and writing about the papers in *Nature, Science* and *Cell*. The more

specialised journals that sometimes do not send out their results, those tend to have the papers that really break new ground. Once a story is in *Nature* or *Science*, there is almost always a long backstory to it. Just look at the references. Other people have had this idea before. The actual idea tends to have an antecedent, and that antecedent is in the more specialised journals. That is where I have often gotten ideas that nobody else had.

*(Begley 2015)*

Many journals publish studies online ahead of print, and most offer RSS feeds (text notification services that contain paper titles and abstracts). The feeds are immediate and you can access them by using free RSS feed aggregators such as Feedly (see Figure 2.3). You can organise your science journal feeds into categories such as environment, astronomy and medicine. Feedly also has a web interface and is available as an app on almost every mobile platform. There are also other feed readers. These tools aid every journalist's selection process.

What comes after identifying relevant studies? Now you must learn how they are structured and how to read them. The good part about reading scientific papers is that they have similar structures. Raff (2014) breaks that structure down into its elements and explains how to read scientific papers critically. She criticises non-scientists for merely reading the abstracts of scientific papers without paying attention to the other sections. Her approach to critically reading scientific papers consists of the following steps:

1   Read the *introduction.*
2   Find the big research question (this is the paper's central idea).

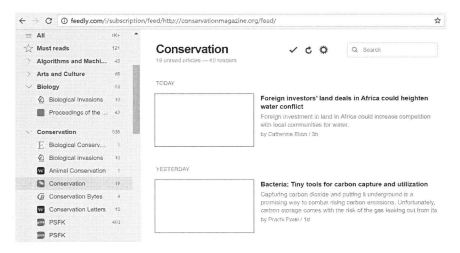

**FIGURE 2.3**   An example of news category organisation in the RSS aggregator Feedly

3  Summarise the background in a few sentences. Who did what to answer the research question?
4  Find the more specific questions; there might be more than one.
5  Identify the scientists' approach. How do they describe their methodology?
6  Analyse the methods section, which contains the experiments. Draw them on paper, and look up any methods you are unfamiliar with.
7  Read the results section. Raff (2014) suggests that you pay particular attention to sample sizes, words like *significant* and *non-significant* and graphs with error bars.
8  Check to see if the results provide answers to the specific questions.
9  Read the conclusion (or discussion) section of the paper. Figure out how the authors interpret their findings and scan this section for concessions of the study's weaknesses.
10  Read the abstract. Does it fall in line with the authors' claims?
11  Find independent experts' opinions about the study.

Raff (2014) also recommends an optional review of the study's literature. She has also written a sample analysis of a paper on a vaccine safety, so you can see her approach in action (Raff 2013). Journals are such good sources because they are primary sources. Secondary sources, such as news services or newspapers, are likely to introduce errors or omit important information because they try to boil down the science to make it readable for non-scientists. The downside of journal papers is that they contain no absolute truths. Some are severely flawed and are later retracted, and some contain irreproducible or fabricated results.

### Press releases

Press releases issued by research institutions and universities are usually easier to understand than scientific papers because they provide an abstract layer on top of those studies. The release authors have already identified the most newsworthy studies and have (hopefully) read, interpreted and processed them into easy-to-digest, short news stories that contain all the necessary information to assemble a journalistic news story.

The drawback is that if you just take the information within the press release without doing further research, asking independent researchers and questioning the results, you are likely to be frowned upon. Slightly rephrasing press releases and failing to add value is not journalism. In fact, this zero-effort approach has been dubbed *churnalism*, and rightfully so. There are online tools like the Media Standards Trust's Churnalism.com that allow you to check whether articles you encounter are merely rewritten press releases or are even plagiarised pieces. All you need to do is enter a URL or text passage into a search box, and the software compares it against a body of published press releases. Churnalism.com is also available as a browser plugin for Chrome and Firefox, so you can check articles' quality as you read them. That browser plugin highlights plagiarised passages once you open a webpage in your browser (Lichterman 2014).

STAT news' Sharon Begley confirms that there are many such texts:

> There are too many stories that only parrot the press releases and that do not even go the next step of asking people who are not involved in the research. If you are just rewriting press releases day in and day out, then you are not really making a contribution.
>
> *(Begley 2015)*

However, press releases can be great stimuli for carrying out deeper research and putting isolated findings in a larger context. In that sense, Sohn (2013) states that press releases can indeed have an additional value: "As you read through study summaries and the coverage that follows them each week you might also start to notice trends and patterns. Then it's just a matter of finding the right spin to distinguish your idea" (14). She adds that press releases also can point out different angles or backstories to you that might be worth writing about.

Online news services like EurekAlert!, AlphaGalileo and ScienceDaily undertake that task for you and organise science news into categories. You can then use a feed reader to subscribe to the latest press releases and receive notifications by category. This acts like a filter by delivering only news on topics that are of interest to you. Alternately, you can browse the news and press releases by category on these services' websites. Some of these services require that you verify your identity as a journalist, while others are freely accessible. Verified access is also required to access most embargoed papers.

## Embargoed papers

When journals send papers to journalists and editors before the actual publication date, they often impose embargoes on them. That means that you cannot publish any of the material before the embargo expires on a specific date and time. But, you do have time to interview researchers and write a story that you can publish as soon as the journal lifts the embargo. The embargo system has advantages and disadvantages. Journals maximise the amount of publicity they get, and journalists can start their research and conduct interviews ahead of time. Although many journals name quality control as the primary motivation for keeping an embargo policy, there is also self-interest involved. After all, embargoes indicate that these research papers are important. On the downside, embargoes hamper the communication between scientists and the public (Marshall 1998).

Whenever you encounter embargoed material, make sure you stick to the formalised agreement until the embargo expires. If you do not, it usually does not have legal consequences; however, it might damage your reputation through public humiliation and a possible future exclusion from further embargoed material by the journal whose policy you violated (Sohn 2013). Figure 2.4 shows a 2014 press release from the United Nations Environment Programme (UNEP), which was embargoed until several hours later. The organisation sent another email when the embargo was lifted. With the embargo cleared, journalists were free to publish their articles based on that press release.

## Conferences

If you want to establish contact with scientists and find ideas by interviewing them on what they are currently working on, scientific meetings and conferences are excellent places to do so. Smaller meetings offer especially good opportunities to meet them in person before or after their talks, an approach seconded by Yam (2006).

If you plan to attend large science conferences, such as the annual meeting of the American Association for the Advancement of Science (AAAS) or the American Physical Society's (APS) annual meeting in the US, be sure to prepare beforehand. Yam (2006) recommends planning your sessions in advance so you do not lose track of what topics have priority. Also, study the conference topics and prepare for them, so you can ask informed questions.

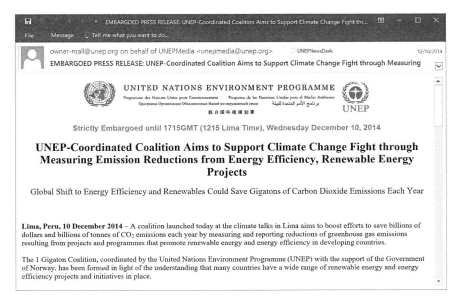

**FIGURE 2.4** An embargoed press release that states when the embargo is lifted

*Source*: United Nations Environment Programme

Study the researchers, their curricula vitae and their previous publications and how these tie in with their planned talks at the conference.

If you come prepared, you can find a lot of unpublished, original research. Sohn (2013) confirms that the story ideas found even at a single conference can last for months. You can find out about upcoming science conferences online. For example, *Nature*'s Nature Events Directory helps you find science events and filter them by date, country and research area. This directory contains many science conferences in the US, UK, Europe and Asia. Moreover, it also offers a free RSS service that you can subscribe to. In the UK, the Wellcome Trust has an excellent database of forthcoming science conferences. The academic publisher Elsevier also offers an online list of global science conferences that you can filter by date, discipline, location and event type. You can find the links to these online databases in the Links section at the end of this chapter.

## Awards and prizes

Prizes can inspire story ideas in two ways. First, science awards and prizes give you an idea of which scientists are currently conducting groundbreaking research while highlighting areas of research that are of special interest to society. Yam (2006) recommends keeping an eye on Nobel Prizes for basic, less recent research and the MacArthur Foundation for more up-to-date research, as well as the Albert Lasker Medical Awards, the Kyoto Prize and the Lemelson-MIT prizes. In addition to highlighting research, the scientists come into focus, too. They have often dedicated their lives to very specific research questions, and many of them have interesting personalities. This provides excellent material for writing profile feature articles, as Yam (2006) confirms. Most awards have websites that exhibit shortlists, candidates and study abstracts, so you can plan and write your articles on them and their research ahead of time. Keep in mind that science prizes are subject to change. Every year, some are discontinued and new ones are introduced. For example, Merali (2013) shows that a number of science prizes have recently mushroomed, many of which are highly remunerated. This includes the Fundamental Physics Prize, the Tang Prize and the Queen Elizabeth Prize for Engineering (Merali 2013), all of which offer greater winnings than the Nobel Prize.

You should also closely monitor science writing awards, such as the AAAS Kavli Science Journalism Awards. Also be sure to have a look at prizes for non-fiction science books, such as the annual Royal Society Prizes for Science Books. Some prizes specifically target science journalism students. For example, the Society for Neuroscience grants two awards per year to science or medical journalism students. Winning such an award can substantially boost your career in science writing. Award-winning science writer Ed Yong recalls what motivated him to participate in the *Daily*

*Telegraph*'s science writing competition in 2007 (which he won): "I needed a notch on my belt" (Yong 2011).

## Blogs

Scientists' blogs are another excellent source for finding science story ideas. There is a lot of research and a variety of opinions that scientists express in their blogs. Such blogs also often show the day-to-day routine in the scientific process. One caveat: Blogs are not peer-reviewed publications, and even if they were, they would not be flawless. That means you have to carefully scrutinise their claims and have them double-checked by independent researchers to confirm their validity.

Science blog networks have professionalised this channel for disseminating science by recruiting blogging scientists, science journalists or both. This way, they can cover a wide variety of scientific disciplines. For instance, the networks ScienceBlogs and SciLogs.com (both are invitation only) cover individual blogs that are written by researchers from all over the world. Many popular science blog networks belong to major publications. For instance, the *WIRED* science blogs, the *Scientific American* blog network, the *Guardian* science blog network or the *Popular Science* blogs are written by staff writers, scientists and freelance writers. Many of them also cover niche research areas, and their often offbeat stories can inspire other story ideas.

## Universities

Universities' bulletin boards and traditional event calendars often present research that cannot be found elsewhere such as event announcements, visiting scientists' guest speeches or inaugural lectures. Perhaps a research group is looking for study participants in research that later turns out to be groundbreaking. Such notices show what the researchers are currently working on, which in turn means they probably have not published any results yet. In fact, as Sumner and Miller (2013) suggest, notice boards can even yield ideas that lead to scoops.

Sharon Begley also supports looking at bulletin boards. Her advice to aspiring students looking for original science ideas is:

> Read the notices in the hallways of research universities. They will read something like this: "There is a department D with this guest speaker. There will be a colloquium on a specific subject." That tends to be where science is bubbling up from the bottom, before it reaches the journals and everything else. That is often where you can find both original ideas and the people who are pursuing them.
>
> *(Begley 2015)*

Online forums and Facebook groups have largely superseded the traditional notice boards, so you can find most announcements online if you do not have physical access to an institution. Research groups primarily announce upcoming events, talks and projects via their faculties' websites. If you want to monitor particular webpages for content changes, you can use a variety of tools. Voo (2013) points out some of the most important online tools, like the browser extension VisualPing. Such tools let you specify website addresses and will send you notifications whenever those websites change their content.

## The scientific method

The structure of scientific papers, as in the breakdown by Raff (2014), is not unlike some science articles in the media. The production processes of science and science journalism are similar in some aspects, too. Both look for unique ideas, formulate hypotheses, observe and measure, analyse the facts and draw conclusions. This claim is at least true of critical, in-depth science journalism.

The approach most scientists take (in slightly different forms depending on the scientific discipline) is called the *scientific method*. As a science journalist, there are two reasons you should get acquainted with it. First, when you interview scientists, you need to know their tools of the trade. How can you ask critical questions if you do not know how they conduct their research? Adam Johansen, director of Warwick University's Academy for PhD Training in Statistics (APTS), says that science writers should know the scientific method:

> If you are going to write about science, it would be useful to have some familiarity with this approach to the world. But whether [the scientific method] is the way all science is done is debatable.
>
> *(Johansen 2016)*

So, what is the scientific method? Developing generalisations out of a few mere observations is certainly not a scientific approach. Instead, scientists come up with testable (and falsifiable) hypotheses, reproducible experiments and measurable results that either confirm or contradict hypotheses and predictions. Royce Murray, Kenan Professor at the University of North California and editor of the journal *Analytical Chemistry*, defines the scientific method as follows: "The scientific method is the systematic, organized gathering of data; the objective formulation and testing of hypotheses (ideas, concepts, theories) with that data; and the stating of conclusions that can be evaluated independently by others" (Murray 1999:153A). Murray's definition sums up the essence of the scientific method very well. On another note, the scientific method is a set of techniques that help scientists conduct their research in a standardised way and eventually gain knowledge of how the world works. The scientific method consists of predefined steps that scientific research passes through in one way or the other. These steps and the order in which they are executed vary depending on the scientific discipline and other factors. That said, you can find the following steps in most representations of the scientific method:

1 Observe a phenomenon in nature or in the universe.
2 Formulate a hypothesis.
3 Make predictions using your hypothesis.
4 Run experiments and collect empirical data.
5 Analyse your data.
6 Draw conclusions.
7 Communicate the results.

Let's look at these steps one by one. The scientific method usually starts with observations of natural phenomena, which lead to questions of how and why these phenomena occur. Following is a very simple example.

You have a few orchids in your living room. First, you notice that one of these orchids blooms all the time, but the others do not. You start thinking about what makes that particular orchid bloom. Asking questions is an important part of the scientific method.

Second, by further observing the orchid's growth, perhaps experimenting with watering, fertilising and cutting branches, you come up with a question: Is it a fertiliser you recently used on that orchid that has caused it to bloom more than the others? Your hypothesis could then be: Fertiliser X causes orchids to bloom. A hypothesis is a generalised, tentative answer to your initial research question. It could prove true or false. To be exact, a hypothesis must be *falsifiable*. That means experiments must exist for which your hypothesis predictions are wrong. In contrast, no hypothesis can be positively tested for all possible combinations. Could you test all orchids in the world for whether fertilising them causes them to bloom? No.

The third step consists of making a prediction using your hypothesis. The prediction is more specific than the hypothesis, which allows you to specifically test it using designed experiments. You might formulate the following prediction: Increasing the amount of fertiliser over time causes orchids to bloom more often than orchids for which the amount of fertiliser used remains constant. Although this is a simplified example, did you notice how much this already sounds like a research paper's title compared to the initial research question and hypothesis?

Fourth, you need to conduct empirical experiments that you design around the prediction you formulated. You need to identify independent and dependent variables that determine the experiment's test runs. For instance, if you willingly change the amount of fertiliser, then that amount of fertiliser is your independent variable, because it is not influenced by anything else other than you. Your dependent variable, on the other hand, could be the number of blooms as a consequence of fertilising your orchids. Since that number potentially depends on the amount of fertiliser used, the blossoms are dependent. Note that you can observe all these intermediary results, hence your experiment is empirical. Since you can easily count and note both the amount of fertiliser used and the amount of blossoms caused by it, you have gathered quantitative data (which, in this case, is desirable). Moreover, experiments frequently employ control groups that help you verify whether your independent variable caused the change in the dependent one or not. In our case, you could place one orchid in another room, maintaining all the other parameters (species, size, amount of watering, light exposure, etc.) except for the fertiliser. If at the end of the experiment the fertilised orchid has grown ten blossoms and the unfertilised one has none, it is possible that the increased amount of fertiliser caused the plant to bloom more than the control.

Fifth, analysing the data will allow you to accept or reject your hypothesis. There are both qualitative and quantitative research methods and statistical tools that you can employ, depending on the nature of your data. In the orchid case, using quantitative statistical methods would be in order. This step often leads scientists to reformulate their hypotheses, or it can lead to observations that either fundamentally change the initial research question or inspire follow-up research projects. Overall, there are many ways to formulate a hypothesis, as Wudka (2006) confirms.

The last two steps consist of drawing conclusions from the experiments and communicating them to the scientific community. It is important to mention that all of your experiments must be reproducible so other scientists will arrive at the same conclusions and results as you did. If they are not, your research paper should not pass peer review, which would result in a rejection from being published in a peer-review journal. Unfortunately, many studies with irreproducible experiments and even fabricated data are published in peer-reviewed journals.

## Idea protection

Once you have an elaborate idea that satisfies the aforementioned criteria, you will want to pitch it to someone who can publish it. Before you do, you should think twice about whom you tell about it.

Once you have written and published an article, it is protected by copyright law. Anyone who copies and publishes your text without obtaining permission is plagiarising. (Note that you also can't re-publish your own texts; you have to seek permission from the copyright holder. You *can* re-publish the same article in different publications if the copyright holder consents to it.)

Using the exact words you have previously used in other articles (without clearly stating it) is called *self-plagiarism*, which is frowned upon. For example, in June 2012, science journalist Jonah Lehrer, who at the time was the *New Yorker*'s newest appointment, was accused of copying and reusing entire passages across a number of publications, including *New York Magazine*, the *New Yorker* and *WIRED* (Brainard 2012). *WIRED* tasked Charles Seife, a journalism professor at New York University, with investigating Lehrer's acts of plagiarism and with either verifying or refuting these accusations. Seife eventually verified that Lehrer had self-plagiarised his work in multiple instances. Lehrer lost his post at the *The New Yorker* and eventually also lost his reputation.

In contrast to published work, mere ideas are impossible to protect (Roberts 2009). How can you prove that you had an idea before someone else turned it into a published article? You cannot. There is no way you can formally protect a story idea. Idea theft is not common if you are a staff writer, but it is if you are a freelancer. The dilemma is that, as a freelancer, you are dependent on sharing your ideas with others because you have to persuade them of your idea before you publish it. If there are journalists among those people you pre-pitch to, it is possible that one of them could take your idea and turn it into an article of their own.

In 2014, this has happened to me. Approximately two years earlier, I started working on a story about Italian citizens who translate their degree titles from Italian to German, deliberately declaring their master's degrees as doctoral degrees via a translation inaccuracy from Italian to German. The issue is known but is a legal grey area. Being a freelancer, at the time I also worked for a small local weekly newspaper in Northern Italy. When I once pitched an IT article idea to my then editor, she agreed to publish it and asked what else I was working on. I told her about my research into the fake doctorates and detailed sources and examples that I had dug up. That was my mistake. Later that year, she published an article in the newspaper she was working for, citing exactly the sources and examples I had told her about. When confronted with her misconduct, she denied I had ever told her about the idea. How could I prove it? After all, I had not recorded the phone call.

The reason I had not published the article earlier was that it still lacked a news peg and a case study of someone who had suffered consequences from upgrading a degree title. Interestingly enough, that editor published her article without an example, case study or news peg. Her story was still reasonably successful because it contained a lot of the aforementioned news values like negativity, cultural proximity, personalisation and reference to elite persons (from a local perspective). Over the course of my career, I have had several more such experiences, especially when proposing ideas for columns and features. This can happen, but that is no reason to give up. You will have to pitch and detail your ideas before you can get them published, so idea theft is sort of an occupational hazard. If you know how to generate ideas, you will never run out of them.

## Summary

It may seem easy to conceive story ideas, but in reality there are hard factors that determine whether your idea stands a chance of being turned into a published article. Seasoned journalists can assess the quality of a story in a matter of minutes because they have internalised the criteria that determine whether a story is worth running. Also, you should know who your target publication's audience is, as this will allow you to choose a suitable topic for that publication.

Topics are not story ideas but merely broad areas that can be part of scientific disciplines. While topics are vague in nature, story ideas are graspable and often convey the notion of a protagonist (not necessarily human) that pursues a goal, meets some resistance and eventually achieves that goal or fails to do so. To understand this pursuit in a scientific context, it is also important to understand the scientific method.

The essence of most story ideas can be expressed in one or two sentences. The aforementioned internalised criteria are specific news factors that determine whether your story is actually worth publishing; topicality, negativity, unexpectedness and the involvement of elite people or corporations are some of the most important of these factors. Use them to test your story ideas.

Inspiration for story ideas lies everywhere; press releases, universities, newly published journal papers (beware of embargoes), conferences, awards and blogs are great sources for finding interesting topics and eventually moulding them into story ideas. The single most important source for finding science stories is people. If you want to write good stories, you must talk to study authors, independent researchers, study participants, corporation spokespeople, lobbyists and anyone else who is involved in science.

## Review questions

- What is the difference between a topic and a story?
- What are the elements of a good story?
- How many angles should a story idea have, and why?
- Which technique helps you find focused angles and turn topics into ideas?
- Why should you read and research the publication you want to write for?
- What role does a publication's audience play regarding story ideas?
- What are the best ways to source story ideas?
- How can you objectively measure a story idea's relevancy?

- How do scientists gather knowledge about nature and the universe?
- How can you protect your story ideas?

## Exercises

- Choose three to five of topics that you think merit further research and idea development.
- For each topic, find five articles covering that same topic and identify their primary and secondary angles. Come up with additional, fresh angles for the underlying topics.
- Try to extrapolate ideas from the identified topics. Use the aforementioned angle tree technique.
- Check the ideas for general and science-centred news factors. Which ones do they use, and how many do they contain?
- Check each idea for the factors of unity, action and concreteness.
- Sum up each idea in one or two sentences.
- Read Rose's (2015) article. For each paragraph, note whether it contains unity, action or concreteness. How many "empty" paragraphs can you find?
- Go to your local university and collect three story ideas from a bulletin board.
- Alternatively, interview a scientist about his research and extract one story idea.
- Take your identified topics and find specialised journals that cover them. Find and organise their RSS feeds using a feed reader.

## Reading list

Blum, D., Knudson, M. and Henig, R.M. (eds.) (2006) *A Field Guide for Science Writers*. 2nd edition. New York: Oxford University Press
Hayden, T. and Nijhuis, M. (eds.) (2013) *The Science Writers' Handbook*. Boston, MA: Da Capo Press
Kosso, P. (2011) *A Summary of Scientific Method*. New York: Springer
Reimold, D. (2013) *Journalism of Ideas*. London: Routledge
Sumner, D.E. and Miller, H.G. (2009) *Feature and Magazine Writing: Action, Angle and Anecdotes*. Chichester: John Wiley & Sons
Wudka, J. (2006) *Space-Time, Relativity, and Cosmology*. Cambridge: Cambridge University Press

## Links

Elsevier global events list: www.globaleventslist.elsevier.com/events/
Google Trends: www.google.com/trends/
*Nature* events directory: www.nature.com/natureevents/science/
Wellcome Trust scientific conferences: www.wellcome.ac.uk/education-resources/courses-and-conferences/advanced-courses-and-scientific-conferences/scientific-conferences/index.htm

## References

Badenschier, F. and Wormer, H. (2012) Issue selection in science journalism: Towards a special theory of news values for science news? In Rödder, S., Franzen, M. and Weingart, P. (eds.) *The Sciences' Media Connection – Public Communication and Its Repercussions*. Dordrecht: Springer, 59–85

Begley, S. (2015) Personal phone conversation on 13 June 2015

Brainard, C. (2012) How creativity works? Not like that, *Columbia Journalism Review* [Online] Available at: www.cjr.org/the_observatory/jonah_lehrer_self_plagiarism_n.php [date accessed 27 June 2015]

Castelvecchi, D. (2016) Personal phone conversation on 20 September 2016

Galtung, J. and Ruge, M.H. (1965) The structure of foreign news the presentation of the Congo, Cuba and Cyprus crises in four Norwegian newspapers, *Journal of Peace Research*, vol. 2, no. 1, 64–90

Jarreau, P. (2015a) Personal Google Hangout conversation on 24 June 2015

Jarreau, P. (2015b) *All the Science That Is Fit to Blog: An Analysis of Science Blogging Practices*, Louisiana State University (PhD dissertation) [Online] Available at: http://etd.lsu.edu/docs/available/etd-04072015-094935/unrestricted/Jarreau_Dissertation.pdf [date accessed 5 May 2015]

Johansen, A. (2016) Personal phone conversation on 23 September 2016

Lane, E. (2014) Winners named in 2014 AAAS Kavli science journalism awards competition, *AAAS* [Online] Available at: www.aaas.org/sja2014 [date accessed 22 May 2015]

Lichterman, J. (2014) Media standards trust updates its 'churnalism' tools, *Nieman Labs* [Online] Available at: www.niemanlab.org/2014/02/media-standards-trust-updates-its-churnalism-tools/ [date accessed 23 June 2015]

Marshall, E. (1998) Good, bad, or 'necessary evil'? *Science*, vol. 282, no. 5390, 860–867

Merali, Z. (2013) Science prizes: The new Nobels, *Nature* [Online] Available at: www.nature.com/news/science-prizes-the-new-nobels-1.13168 [date accessed 19 June 2015]

Murray, R.W. (1999) The scientific method, *Analytical Chemistry*, vol. 71, no. 5, 153A

Raff, J. (2013) How to read a vaccine safety study: An example, *Violent Metaphors* [Online] Available at: http://violentmetaphors.com/2013/09/08/an-example-of-how-to-read-a-vaccine-safety-study/ [date accessed 18 June 2015]

Raff, J. (2014) How to read and understand a scientific paper: A step-by-step guide for non-scientists, *The Huffington Post* [Online] Available at: www.huffingtonpost.com/jennifer-raff/how-to-read-and-understand-a-scientific-paper_b_5501628.html [date accessed 18 June 2015]

Roberts, D. (2009) How to: Protect your ideas as a freelancer, *Journalism.co.uk* [Online] Available at: www.journalism.co.uk/skills/how-to-protect-your-ideas-as-a-freelancer/s7/a533220/ [date accessed 23 June 2015]

Rose, A. (2015) The forensics of identifying migrants who die exhausted after crossing from Mexico, *Scientific American* [Online] Available at: www.scientificamerican.com/article/the-forensics-of-identifying-migrants-who-die-exhausted-after-crossing-from-mexico/ [date accessed 17 June 2015]

Sohn, E. (2013) Finding ideas, In Hayden, T. and Nijhuis, M. (eds.) *The Science Writers' Handbook*. Boston, MA: Da Capo Press, 9–22

Southorn, G. (2015) Personal Skype conversation on 10 June 2015

Sumner, D.E. and Miller, H.G. (2013) *Feature and Magazine Writing: Action, Angle and Anecdotes*. 3rd edition. Chichester: John Wiley & Sons

Voo, B. (2013) 5 free tools to notify you of website content changes, *Hongkiat* [Online] Available at: www.hongkiat.com/blog/detect-website-change-notification/ [date accessed 20 June 2015]

Wahl-Jorgensen, K. (2013) The strategic ritual of emotionality: A case study of Pulitzer Prize-winning articles, *Journalism*, vol. 14, no. 1, 129–145

Wudka, J. (2006) The scientific method, In Wudka, J. (ed.) *Space-time, Relativity, and Cosmology*. Cambridge: Cambridge University Press, 1–22

Yam, P. (2006) Finding story ideas and sources, In Blum, D., Knudson, M. and Henig, R.M. (eds.) *A Field Guide for Science Writers*. 2nd edition. New York: Oxford University Press, 5–10

Yong, E. (2011) You've got seven days left to prove you're a science writer, *The Guardian* [Online] Available at: www.theguardian.com/science/2011/may/13/ wellcome-trust-science-writing-prize [date accessed: 19 June 2015]

# 3

# PITCHING

**What you will learn in this chapter:**

- What makes a good proposal
- How editors read pitches
- Approaching editors
- Workshop: making a pitch
- Case study: analysing a successful pitch
- Internal versus external pitching
- The most common pitching mistakes
- Checklist.

## Introduction

Once you have identified an idea and carried out the initial research, you may be itching to write the article, send it to an editor and wait for it to be published. However, you first need to prepare an exposé that sums up your idea, provides background and shows how you want to structure and approach the article. This is called a *pitch*. If an editor likes your pitch, she may commission a story based on it. She may also ask you to remove parts or add others, suggest you consult more sources and make suggestions about the style and length of your article. No editor wants to receive a finished article because they have no bearing on the article.

You need to know what makes commissioning editors tick and how they assess pitches. That includes understanding the pitching code of conduct. For example, cold-calling an editor and explaining your idea is likely to earn you a rejection. In this chapter, commissioning editors explain what works and what does not in pitching. Understanding their work routine is another key aspect. Every day, editors receive lots of pitches and follow-up emails, and they have only limited time to sift the wheat from the chaff, so you need to draw their attention instantly. By the time you finish this chapter, you will have an idea of how you can make your pitches stand out.

If you want to persuade an editor to commission an article, you must structure your pitch. Most editors expect pitches to contain certain elements. Your story idea is the most important one, but a good idea alone is not enough. You will also need to show to the editor that you are the right person to write this particular article. This chapter contains a section dedicated to how editors read pitches and what structures and elements they expect.

If you want to become a good pitch writer, you will need to read a lot of pitches. Online databases contain many pitches commissioned by high-profile publications; read these carefully and analyse their structure and chain of reasoning. This chapter provides a starting point for where to look for successful pitches online. In addition, it offers an example pitch with commentary from the editor who received the pitch.

As in the previous chapter, research is essential before and during pitch writing. You must research the publication and the publication's audience. In addition, before you write your pitch you should learn as much as you can about your story idea and the editor to whom you will pitch it. Adequate preliminary research will help you find the right details that make the pitch come alive and hook the editor. As a bonus, you will have set the stage for conducting in-depth research; ideally, you will have already reached out to interviewees and talked to some of the scientists, read papers and identified some independent experts who can comment on the research you want to write about. A well-written pitch whets the editor's appetite for the main dish: your story.

The last section of this chapter is a checklist that helps you review your finished pitch, step by step, before submitting it. It is derived from commissioning editors' advice and comments. When you are putting together your first pitches, this list comes in handy. Over time, you will internalise the criteria that make a good story, the elements of a good pitch and the checklist criteria. Finding stories and pitching them will become more automatic, and the more you practice, the more successful your pitches will be.

Do not expect your first pitch to earn you a commission. If your story idea is right and if you pay attention to the pitfalls discussed in this chapter, however, you will significantly increase your chances of getting a commission.

## What makes a good proposal?

Winfried Göpfert (2016), professor emeritus in science journalism at the Free University of Berlin, points out that if you want to persuade an editor, you need to be sure the pitch is written *for* the editor. He says you should first sum up what intrigues you about the topic. This helps you to electrify the editor and incite the audience to read your article. You also write the pitch for yourself, however, as an outlining tool that lays out what kind of story you plan to write, how many interviews you will conduct and your style (Göpfert 2016):

> But make no mistake: A pitch merely lays out how you plan to approach a story. A lot will change after you receive the commission and start digging deeper. Oftentimes, as you are writing the article, other plot threads will emerge, and they will be very different from those you initially imagined. The chain of reasoning you have written by then could perhaps force very different continuations. So it would be illogical to all of a sudden address different aspects than the issues discussed previously.
>
> Any plans laid out in a pitch are to be understood as ideas that illustrate what the final story could look like. It is certainly possible that in the end, it indeed does look as outlined in the pitch. But the author has to have the freedom to be flexible about those initial plans.
>
> *(Göpfert 2016)*

This section presents the elements of a pitch in descending order of importance; this approach is similar to the inverted pyramid structure, which is commonly used for writing news. As Bernstein (2014) notes, the inverted pyramid is most suitable when the reader's time is limited, which is clearly the case when you are pitching your story to editors who give you only a couple of minutes to persuade them to give you that commission.

## Story idea

The number one element of a good science pitch is your story idea, so it goes to the top. If your idea cannot hook an editor instantly, she will not read on. James Randerson (2014), the *Guardian's* former science correspondent, recommends that you "include a clear and concise top line that sums up the story. If you are pitching news, this is probably the top line of your story." This should be followed by context and background that show the relevance of that story idea and further elaborate on it (Randerson 2014). Everything revolves around the story idea in a pitch. No matter how well-structured your pitch is, if the idea is flawed, you can expect a rejection slip.

Let's look at an example of how you can distil your story idea into one or two sentences, starting from a topic. First, assume you initially want to write about Tasmanian devils and how they are on the brink of extinction because of rapidly spreading, transmissible facial tumours. That is your topic, and it already contains a bit of unexpectedness: tumours are normally not transmissible. Still, the looming extinction of the Tasmanian devil is merely a topic. Second, other publications have covered this topic and the how-to-save-Tasmanian-devils angle ad nauseam. This means you need to narrow down your topic and come up with a fresh angle.

So, you conduct some preliminary research and discover a few facts. For example, conservationists brought an insurance population of devils to Maria Island off the shore of Eastern Tasmania. You also find that, according to a study, Tasmanian devils could help fight feral cats because they rival for food. In addition, you find quotes from a Tasmanian local who claims that Tasmanian devils kill ground-breeding rare bird populations in the exact sanctuary the conservationists brought them to escape certain death by cancer. That should provide you with sufficient material to develop offbeat angles. Most published stories explain the disease and show conservationists' efforts to save the devils. Thus, unless you have exclusive access to a unique new conservation technique, you should direct your attention elsewhere. In our example, two possible angles emerge from your preliminary research:

1  Possible effects of re-introducing the Tasmanian devil to mainland Australia.
2  How isolated devils on Maria Island influence its ecosystem.

Let's try to translate the second angle into a pitch capable of hooking an editor. For example, first set the scene to give the editor a feeling of what comes next. Then comes the twist: The well-meaning conservationists are actually damaging the island's fauna.

> *Dear [editor] (put name here),*
>
> *To save the Tasmanian devils from the face-eating tumour disease DFTD, scientists have captured a healthy population and released it on the isolated Maria Island, where it thrives. But their seemingly successful plan has a flaw: The devils feed on rare, ground-breeding birds. Maria Island's birds don't have a chance. Evolution has not prepared them for humans who arbitrarily introduce new predatory species to their habitat.*

Note the one sentence that nails your story: "The devils feed on rare, ground-breeding birds." You could further boil it down until you obtain a candidate title and for a feature. Imagine the following title and subtitle for your story:

**Easy Prey**

Conservationists isolate threatened Tasmanian devils on Maria Island to save them from deadly facial tumours. The downside? The predatory marsupials kill off rare, ground-breeding birds.

Now quickly review the news factors this story idea contains. There is *negativity*, because a well-meant conservation project has some serious side effects. There is *clarity*, because the pitch clearly states its angle. Also, you can find *unexpectedness*, as an attempt to protect one species inadvertently pushes another species to the brink of extinction; *composition*, as lots of publications have covered the conservationists' efforts but missed this angle; and *continuity*, as the topic of Tasmanian devils dying due to DFTD has been all over the media.

This conservation-gone-wrong angle seems suitable for publications that regularly cover the natural sciences, conservation and zoology, such as *Nautilus* or *New Scientist*. Shaping topics into angles can be fun, as this might make your story idea relevant to other publications as well. Imagine the scientists' efforts involved a novel technology they came up with to protect the devils. Approaching the story from a technology-focused angle would make the story relevant for *Technology Review*. On the downside, changing the angle may render your story idea irrelevant to the publication you originally intended it for.

### Motivation and access

Once you have hooked an editor with a compelling story idea, you need to keep her interested. You also need to tell her what makes you the ideal author of the story you proposed. One very good reason is unique access: Do you have access to an exclusive source? Using the previous example, can you get an exclusive interview with the person who initially claimed the devils are razing out bird populations? If so, you are ahead of the curve. After all, editors look for unique and fresh raw material, not previously published quotes from other news articles and features.

You can also gain unique insights by sifting through data and discovering suspicious patterns in governments', companies' or organisations' reports. Spatial proximity can put you in a unique position, too. For example, imagine you pitch a story about the Bento Rodrigues dam disaster in Brazil. If you happen to be in Mariana, the city where it occurred, you have an edge over competing journalists. The same is true if you can get an exclusive interview with someone who lives close or is affected by the catastrophe. Unique access might also mean you get the opportunity to join an Arctic expedition or visit a newly discovered archaeological site. You can gain unique access to story material in many ways, and it almost always involves talking with people beforehand. Your pitch should clearly state what kind of access you have to information that other journalists might not have.

In 2015, *Scientific American*'s Larry Greenemeier (2015) wrote an in-depth feature about the online toolset and database Memex, which tracks down human traffickers in the deep web. One component that made Greenemeier's feature truly stand out from all the other articles is that he obtained exclusive maps that show Memex in action: Bubble maps highlight trafficking hotspots, and directed graphs show internet routes taken by users while detailing the relationships between those users. Whatever kind of unpublished, fresh material (documents, data, images, quotes) you can obtain, be sure to highlight it in your pitch.

## Science

The first paragraph (or lead) of your pitch is meant to hook the editor with an intriguing story idea and show the themes that have emerged so far. The subsequent paragraphs should then highlight your access to the story and further elaborate on the science. This is where you show you understand the science by briefly addressing how scientists have solved a particular problem and how you put the issue in a larger context. You should also point out what makes this approach new and how it differs from previous research in that field. In the example of the Tasmanian devil, you could highlight how conservation normally proceeds and whether isolating a threatened species is a first. You could also highlight how previous attempts to fight the disease have failed. Provide only relevant details and name your sources, but beware of getting bogged down in too many or irrelevant details. Be as specific as necessary but also as brief as possible. This science part lends authority to your pitch and shows that you:

- Have done sufficient preliminary research.
- Know what you are talking about.
- Can structure a story and select relevant bits of research.

*Scientific American*'s digital content manager Curtis Brainard cautions against writing lengthy pitches, as they may reveal lack of experience:

> If somebody has written a 600-word pitch for an 800-word article, you know it's an evidence that they do not have a firm command of what their story is. So I often look at length right off the bat. If it is a really long pitch, I will be less likely to read that whole pitch, either because I do not have the time or because I consider that it is somebody who is not experienced with pitching.
>
> *(Brainard 2015)*

At this point, if you have not yet done so, you can include a separate paragraph that points out the story's implications (see Figure 3.1). This is a technique recommended by science journalism educator Douglas Starr, as you will read in a later section. In our example of Tasmanian devils, the implications are important enough to weave them directly into the story idea.

## Salutation

By all means, get the editor's name and gender right.

## Lead

Get straight to the story idea.
Lay out your theme, if you have already found one.
Link the story to news, pose a question or raise an issue
(if appropriate).

## Background 1

Show your access to the story.
Have you worked on similar stories?
Optionally, the theme can also go here.

## Background 2

Show you know the science behind it.
Show you have done sufficient preliminary research.
Be specific and put in a few details.

## Implications

Put the findings in a larger context.
Explain why this story is important to the readers.

## Credentials

Show whom you have worked for.
Put in only relevant information.
Don't send unsolicited clips.

## Closing

Ask: Could this interest your readers? Then close the pitch.

**FIGURE 3.1** Use this template to structure your pitches

*Source*: Based on an interview with Douglas Starr

### Complementary material and style

Depending on the type of text you want to deliver, near the end of your pitch you can also state which complementary material you plan to add to the story. Winfried Göpfert emphasises the importance of proposing additional material:

> Put details, explanations, or statistical context into boxes. They signal the reader [that] this is ancillary material, important to enthusiasts, but it is not necessary for grasping the big picture. But pictures are most important, like photographs, illustrations, photo series, sketches and drawings. They are appetisers that further seduce the audience to read. Apart from the title, they are the most important entry point into your story.
>
> *(Göpfert 2016)*

Style is important in two different ways. First, the style of your pitch tells the editor a lot about you as a writer. If you write a pitch for a witty column but write it in an academic style and pack it with jargon, you will have a hard time getting a commission. So make sure the pitch's style reflects the proposed article's style. Also, pay attention to errors. One typo will not cost you the commission, but if you consistently make orthographic or grammatical mistakes in your pitch or if your expression is poor, most editors will turn your proposal down. Regarding style, use the active voice in all of your sentences, as the passive voice is likely to bore the editor who reads your pitch. It greatly helps if your writing style (as well as the story) emotionally engages the editor, for example, by creating pictures in your editor's mind. This tells the editor you are able to engage not only her but also the publication's audience.

In this context, the second notion of style is how you intend to tell the story. For example, you explain how applying a specific, creative style might benefit your story. What styles you can apply depends entirely on the story. According to Curtis Brainard, coming up with creative styles can make your pitch stand out from otherwise similar stories:

> We are also interested in creative styles of writing. So you might say, "I am going to play devil's advocate in this piece, or I am going to use some sort of literary device to accomplish this. Or, I am going to write as though I were Albert Einstein," something like that. We are definitely looking for interesting writing styles, too, especially in blogs and op-eds. We want people to be experimental. We want them to be creative and see if it works.
>
> *(Brainard 2015)*

### Author information

The author information (apart from what qualifies you to write the story) is the least important part of the pitch, and it goes to the end. Never start with a lengthy introduction of who you are unless you want the editor to think you are a narcissist. You are trying to sell a story, not yourself. That said, the author part can add an authoritative element to your pitch.

Douglas Starr, co-director of the master's in science journalism programme at Boston University (together with Ellen Ruppel Shell) recommends that there is no need to worry if you have not yet written for major publications. If you have a good story to tell, editors will appreciate it. But in order to do that, you have to invest some time into research upfront. At the very minimum, he conducts a few interviews before preparing a pitch (Starr 2015).

Select every detail about yourself carefully; include only what helps the editor make a decision of whether to commission your article. If you have written articles for important publications and if you have written about topics related to the idea you are pitching, be sure to mention them. Do not mention your education, marital status and writing gigs that do not add anything to underpin your authority. For example, mentioning you are also a fantasy short story writer does not help when you are proposing a short news story on air pollution. Do offer to send the editor clips of relevant, published articles, but never send unsolicited clips.

## How editors read pitches

Different editors have different approaches to reading pitches, and of course their expectations differ very much, depending on their publications' editorial policies and their personal preferences. That is why even within the same publication, editors sometimes have very different expectations of working with science writers. For example, in an interview with *Slate*, editors Dan Kois (culture editor) and Laura Helmuth (then science and health editor) discuss their completely different editing styles and state that they work mostly with freelance writers because the culture and science desks do not employ many staff writers. Helmuth affirms her editing style is less rigorous than Kois's, as she wants to preserve the author's voice (Kois, Helmuth and Lai 2015).

In a personal interview, Helmuth confirmed that this relatively soft editing style influences and reflects the way she wants to receive pitches about science articles for *Slate*. She claims the pitching style should be rather short and informal (Helmuth 2015). Fortunately, many commissioning editors are outspoken about what they expect from a pitch – and with good reason. Like Kois and Helmuth, many editors predominantly work with freelancers. If they make it clear from the beginning how they want their pitches, they receive fewer bad pitches, and journalists can tailor pitches to editors' needs and increase their chances of getting a commission. Some publications publish pitching guidelines that provide details about the format, elements and topics that they expect. You can find links to the submission guidelines of *New*

*Scientist, Scientific American, Slate* and *WIRED* in the Reading List at the end of this chapter.

Jason Goodyer, commissioning editor at *BBC Focus* magazine confirms that such pitching guidelines benefit the publication and the writer, and he also details how he assesses freelance pitches:

> These days, most pitches come in by email. At *Focus*, though, we do something slightly different. Because rather than just somebody sending an email and writing that pitch into the email, we ask them to fill out a form, which you can download from the website. We have done that to make it easier for ourselves and also for the freelancer pitching.
>
> Apart from that, when I get the email, I have a sort of first look over it to see if it is suitable, broadly. Sometimes, we get a pitch and it is just something that we would never cover, obviously that is completely unsuitable to the magazine, so I just get back to them and say "Thank you for sending this, but I am afraid it is unsuitable for *Focus*." If I think it has got a chance, then I will reply to them and say "Thanks for sending this. It looks interesting, and I will get back to you once I've had a proper look at it" – just so they know I have seen it. Then, when I have a spare 10 minutes, I will have a good look through it and see if it fits in with the kind of features that we have planned and also if it fits in with the kind of topics that we would cover in *Focus*. Every month we have a features meeting, and I present all of the pitches that have made it to that point to the team and we discuss them – this is usually me, Graham [Southorn] and Daniel [Bennett] – and we have a discussion about what we think is suitable. We put our own ideas forward as well. Every pitch that comes in has to compete with other freelancers' pitches and with our own ideas, so it is quite a competitive area, really.
>
> *(Goodyer 2015)*

For Helen Pearson, *Nature*'s chief features editor in London, a pitch's lead is crucial and hence the first part of a pitch she assesses. She recalls a particularly well-written pitch by science writer Henry Nicholls for a story that eventually resulted in a published feature in *Nature*:

> The lead-in of his pitch was something along the lines of "Next week I'm going to fly out to Malaysia to see the operation to rescue the uterus of an infertile, three-legged Sumatran rhino." I knew immediately, I'm really interested in that. He wrote that lead in the same way as you would write the first line in a feature. The effect it has is that it just grabs you, so I thought, that is unusual, tell me more.
>
> I didn't commission the story straight off the back of that. We had a back-and-forth of interactions to work out what the story was going

to be. But the fact that he had written that compelling lead to his pitch was just very interesting and fun.

Ultimately, if you are pitching a story, it's the same as if you were writing a lead: You have got to grab people, and something quirky or unusual will grab people. So yes, it always helps if there is a little surprise in the lead.

*(Pearson 2015)*

Curtis Brainard states that he receives about five pitches every day. He limits the time to sift through the pile of pitches and check them for suitability to roughly 10 minutes. When asked what his workflow of reviewing pitches looks like, Brainard said every pitch only gets a couple of minutes to persuade him. If your idea manages to hook him, he will spend a few more minutes to think about how *Scientific American* has approached this topic in the past. He also does an internet search to see how others have covered your topic. If they have not, and if your angle is unique, your pitch might be among the 20 to 25 per cent he accepts on average (Brainard 2015).

For Laura Helmuth, a good pitch starts with a concise subject line. That is what she specifically looks for when opening an email pitch:

The first thing is getting the subject line right. It really helps to put the words *Pitch* or *Story from a Freelancer* in the subject line, just to make sure that I know it is from a real person and not a public relations thing. The other important thing is if a story is time sensitive, it is really important to put that in the subject line, so either use the word *urgent* or *time sensitive*. If something comes in that says urgent or time sensitive, I open that right away, because I know that person needs an answer. If I do not know that it is time sensitive, it might be there as long as a week, although I try to keep it to a day or two to respond.

*(Helmuth 2015)*

Most editors will Google your topic and look for examples to find out which other publications have previously published articles on it. In one case, this revealed an initially promising pitch to be what Helmuth called "the worst pitch" she ever received in her 15-year career:

When I was at *Smithsonian Magazine*, someone sent me a pitch for an animal behaviour story that had to do with animal intelligence. He was talking about some examples of new results on animal intelligence and how animals are smarter and that we might give them credit for it, and he rattled off a few examples in this emailed pitch. One of them was about a cow named Betty that could bend a wire to extract food from a bottle. It was a very well-written pitch, and it had a lot of details, and the author obviously knew a lot about the subject. So I emailed back, started a conversation and asked about how he would approach the story. Then I said, "I am sure this is just a typo, but you must know this is a *crow* named Betty, not a *cow*." But he emailed back and said, "Oh, no, no – my story says: It is a cow." I was like "what?" I was really confused, so I did some Google searching, and I found that he had plagiarised the whole pitch. He had basically copied the entire text of a story that was in the *Guardian*, and the *Guardian* had mistakenly referred to the crow as a cow, so it was their mistake. He basically did everything wrong. So, first of all, plagiarizing is the worst thing you can do as a writer. Even in a pitch, you must not plagiarize. Second of all, when an editor says you made a mistake, instead of saying "Oh, maybe the editor knows what she is talking about," he said "Oh, no, no, I was correct." He was just a terrible human being.

*(Helmuth 2015)*

## Approaching editors

First impressions count, and pitches are no different. With stories pitched via email, the most prominent bits of information are the subject and your name. If an editor decides to open the email, the next thing that will immediately grab her attention is the salutation. If you spell the editor's name wrong, in many cases you are done. Your pitch will go straight to the recycle bin, and rightly so. Why would an editor assume you can research and write a whole article packed with scientific facts if you cannot even spell her name correctly?

Submitting a bad pitch is one thing, but disrespecting an editor is another. The latter misstep easily severs your relationship with an editor, but you can make up for the former by trying again, as Helen Pearson confirms:

You need to be reciprocally respectful: I need to respect writers and their ideas, and they need to respect my opinions and my questions. So, it is just having a level of professionalism. But I also think that writers should not be afraid of approaching editors. We are not actually dragons. I honestly am looking all the time for good, talented writers, and I would like to hear from them. So, it is very important that they get in touch and are confident about pitching their ideas, though it might be those ideas do not go anywhere, but that is okay. I don't mind talking to them and spending time with them, because one day maybe an idea will fit.

*(Pearson 2015)*

You must know the dos and don'ts of approaching editors. The following lists are based on the experiences and advice of this chapter's interviewees:

**Do**

- Behave politely and professionally.
- Call the editor by his or her first name.
- Take criticism constructively.
- Accept proposed amendments to your pitch.
- Show that you have read the publication.
- Show respect for the hard work editors do.
- Appreciate the time editors dedicate to your pitch.
- Thank your editor once your article is published and if you receive an award.
- Send pitches exclusively via email, without attachments.
- Ask for a fast reply only if your story is actually time sensitive.

**Do not**

- Send unsolicited manuscripts.
- Be too informal. ("Cheers, mate!" is not an appropriate salutation.)
- Argue with the editor or offend him or her.
- Ask for explanations of why a pitch was rejected.
- Pitch story ideas via telephone.
- Follow up via telephone.
- Follow up on pitches immediately or too often.
- Be sparing with details out of paranoia that an editor might steal your idea.

The last tip is a bit of a tightrope walk: While you do not want to withhold details that might draw an editor's interest, there are situations when you will want to be a bit more reluctant. It really varies from case to case, and the trade-off is between getting a commission and losing that important story. Randerson (2014) confirms that you should keep unique details to yourself if you have a breaking story on hand. Specifically, he recommends:

> If you really do have a hot idea, try giving enough information in your pitch to whet the editor's appetite without making it easy to follow up the story, for example, by leaving out the name of a key contact. Once you have them hooked you can tell them more.
>
> *(Randerson 2014)*

Do respect that an editor's time is limited, so write succinct pitches. Douglas Starr says your pitch must be so focused and to the point that it is worth an editor's time:

> To me, a query has to be very crisp. An editor gets hundreds and hundreds of queries, and you just got to serve it to them on a beautiful

plate, quickly, clearly. The topic needs to be focused, the audience needs to be defined in your own mind, you have to make sure it is appropriate for the magazine, you have to make it clear that you can do the story and that you can get access.

*(Starr 2015)*

Starr (2015) also asks his students to imagine how an editor responds to the following questions when she reads a newly arrived pitch:

- Is this a good story?
- Why this story?
- Why this author?
- Can this author do the story without giving me too much of a headache?
- Does this author know what she is talking about?
- Is the issue clear?
- Have I heard of it before?
- Do I care?
- Is it timely?

If your pitch allows an editor to answer all these questions positively, you are ready to pitch it. Be sure to also read the later section, Case study: analysing a successful pitch, in which Starr walks you through one of his accepted pitches.

You can also pitch your story at some science journalism conferences. Among the most important conferences are the annual Science Writers conference in the US, which is organised by the National Association of Science Writers (NASW); the biennial UK Conference of Science Journalists, which is organised by the Association of British Science Writers (ABSW); and the biennial World Conference of Science Journalists, which is organised by the World Federation of Science Journalists (WFSJ). Most of these conferences offer public pitching sessions where you can present a story pitch to an international panel of commissioning editors and reporters who will assess that pitch and comment on it. The pitching session at the annual Science Writers conference is called Pitch Slam, and Laura Helmuth regularly organises and assesses the pitches: "Our goal is to help both the editors and the writers to understand each other better, and to show that we [editors] are not intimidating" (2015). The session at the Conference of Science Journalists is called the Dragon's Den, where a panel of editors comment live on three pre-selected pitches. Helen Pearson of *Nature* was one of the dragons in 2014. One of the three pitches eventually earned a commission by the magazine *Research Fortnight*. You can find links to a video of the 2014 edition of the Dragon's Den, as well as links to the mentioned conferences, in the Links section at the end of this chapter.

## Workshop: making a pitch

Now that you know what the basic elements of a pitch are, let us have a look at the necessary steps to craft a pitch. This time, our pitch's starting point is a short news item: On 7 July 2015, Reuters released a short news video that shows Hyperloop, a novel method of long-distance travel (Flynn 2015). Six to eight people are put in capsules that travel through a vacuum in very long, straight glass tubes. The estimated travel time between Los Angeles and San Francisco is 30 minutes (at a speed of 1,200 km/h) – half the time an airplane needs for the same distance. The video contains an interview with the company's CEO. As in any press release or short news item, the most important information is already there: The five Ws and one H (what, who, when, where, why, how) and an interview with the lead researcher (or, in this case, the person in charge of developing a new technology). If you added another interview with an independent expert, you could already write a short news story about Hyperloop.

Instead of writing another short news item that adds little value, you can use this news story as an inspiration for a feature story. First, identify the topic and narrow down the publications you could pitch such a story to. The underlying topic is transportation technology or how we travel in the future. That makes *New Scientist, Scientific American, WIRED, MIT Technology Review* and *BBC Focus* suitable candidates because they all run technology stories and have covered transportation technology in the past. You can clearly exclude *Air & Space, Weatherwise* and *Sky and Telescope*, as they specialise in entirely different topic areas. For this exercise, I wrote a pitch to *BBC Focus* magazine's commissioning editor Jason Goodyer, which is shown in Box 3.1. Please note that this magazine does not usually accept formless pitches but provides a pitch form which you can download on the magazine's website.

Note that the main idea in Box 3.1 is in the second paragraph, in order to draw the editor's attention to it. In this case, the first paragraph presents the problem and simultaneously serves as motivation for writing this feature. I wrote the one-sentence story idea first, and all the other information revolves around and supports that idea. Then I wrote the very first paragraph, which provides the underlying problem and serves to hook the editor. This approach works well with pitches on technology, as new technologies almost always address concrete problems. The third paragraph names the sources I am going to consult and cite. The last paragraph mentions the article's proposed length and additional material that could benefit it. I wrote these two paragraphs last; they are usually the easiest to write. Together with the initial paragraph, their purpose is to show that I have done my homework and conducted sufficient initial research to have an understanding of what the problem is. The hardest part is boiling down your idea to that one sentence that constitutes your thesis – the research question you must answer in writing this feature.

---

### BOX 3.1    A PITCH TO JASON GOODYER, COMMISSIONING EDITOR AT *BBC FOCUS* MAGAZINE

#### How you will travel in the future

Every year, eleven million Britons commute to work, spending a full year of their lives in cars and trains. This is going to get worse, as recent US and UK studies have shown: by 2045, most American roads will be completely ramshackle and constantly congested. Nobody will be able to get anywhere anymore.

New transportation technologies like Hyperloop could replace the road-based, doomed commuting model and revolutionise how we travel between cities. Traffic jams? Gone forever.

The news peg for this story is a recent Reuters news story on the companies that are trying to build the Hyperloop. Apart from Elon Musk's Hyperloop, this feature will cover magnetic levitation trains, a trans-Atlantic underwater train between Manchester and New York City, autonomous pods (like those in Masdar City/Abu Dhabi) and self-driving cars. The feature will also address how ticket fees will change with these new commuting technologies – an important aspect, given that British commuters spend twice as much on train tickets as continental Europeans. Moreover, I will interview Hyperloop Transportation Technologies' CEO Dirk Ahlborn and Professor Roger Goodall of Loughborough University, an expert in transportation technologies.

The feature will run approximately 2,000 words long. I also propose a number of sidebars and boxes that visually explain how traveling in the gigantic Hyperloop vacuum tubes works, how magnetism helps trains levitate and how autonomous transportation pods find their way.

---

Although it runs less than 250 words, a lot of preliminary research went into this pitch. The pitch still may be longer than the length *Scientific American*'s Curtis Brainard suggests, but the proposed length of this feature is 2,000 words, which justifies the length of the pitch.

On 16 July 2015, I sent the pitch outlined in Box 3.1 to Jason Goodyer and waited for his comments. Goodyer replied with a thoughtful email response on 5 August 2015:

> The pitch gets off to a good start by stating why the story is relevant to readers. It also backs up the claims by quoting a couple of studies. It would be more helpful here to name the exact studies and also provide links to them so that the editor is able to determine whether or not they come from a reputable source.

It's good to see that the writer has included the answer to the "why now?" question by stating the news peg. The only thing I would say here is that magazines sometimes have fairly long lead times, so rather than thinking about what's happening now it's always a good idea to think about what is going to be happening. That being said, a feature like this would have a reasonably long shelf life.

The writer mentions two potential interviewees but they don't say whether or not the interviews are secured. Without the interviews the piece would suffer greatly, so an editor would ideally want to know that the writer has already got confirmed access to whomever they are saying will be quoted in the piece.

As an editor, it's always helpful to see that the writer has thought of additional elements to go with the main body copy, so this is a big plus. However, it would be a bit easier to read at a glance if bullet points were used here.

There is also no mention of pictures here. It's generally helpful to at least get across a basic idea of what kind of visual elements the piece could have. Not only photos but also graphics and infographics.

Overall, the pitch is concise and to the point, which is always helpful and some editors receive several pitches per day, if not more, and may not have time to read longer pitches.

Finally, if you've never written for the publication before it's always a good idea to include a brief bio and attach a couple of relevant clippings to help to convince the editor that you are the right person for the job.

*(Goodyer 2015b)*

Goodyer eventually rejected the pitch, stating, "We will have to pass as we ran something very similar relatively recently" (Goodyer 2015a). It seems I had made the classic mistake and not browsed through enough previous *Focus* issues. Take such rejections as an incentive to read more issues of the publication you are pitching to. Dealing constructively with rejection is an important part of the learning process.

## Case study: analysing a successful pitch

As a writer, you must be an avid reader. If you want to excel in writing a particular type of story, you have to analytically read such stories whenever you can. Read, analyse and identify recurring patterns. Get the best texts available and learn from them. Then start writing your own stories. You should do the same with pitches. Unlike science stories, however, pitches can be hard to come by. Many vanish in editors' mailboxes, and most of them never surface publicly. Some brilliant science writers make a few of their former pitches available to online databases from which you can download them.

One of these is the Open Notebook's pitch database, which allows you to search for pitches by author or publication. The database contains 80 science story proposals that were eventually published in high profile newspapers, blogs or magazines. I will dissect one of these pitches and identify what exactly made it successful.

When browsing through the pitch database, you will quickly notice that long pitches outnumber shorter ones. The pitch I am going to dissect is about 550 words. Its author, Douglas Starr, a professor for science journalism at Boston University, got a commission for a 1,400-word article about the James Holmes case for *Slate* (Starr 2012). In it, Starr explains the techniques psychologists use to tell real psychopaths and malingerers apart. You can read his full pitch to then editor Laura Helmuth in Box 3.2, and if you want to read the article, you can find a link to it in the Reading List at the end of the chapter.

---

**BOX 3.2  A PITCH FROM DOUGLAS STARR TO *SLATE* EDITOR LAURA HELMUTH**

Dear Laura [Helmuth, science editor]:

With the receipt of James Holmses's notebook at the University of Colorado detailing his plans for a mass execution and reports of his strange behavior in prison, people have begun speculating whether he is mentally ill or simply laying the groundwork for an insanity defense. Such conjecture often takes place when someone commits a horrific, inexplicable crime. It leads to the question – can a criminal get away with faking insanity?

Experts have been debating that question since the creation of insanity defense in the mid-19th century. Criminals of the era would do anything to avoid the noose or the guillotine, and would fake symptoms from the then-emerging field of psychology. Over the years a rich literature grew, as criminal psychologists wrote case histories and studies on how detect those "malingerers." Most techniques relied on the investigators' experience and powers of observation – looking for inconstancies in symptoms, waiting until the suspect grew tired of the game, or simply catching a telltale look in his eye. As the Austrian criminologist Hans Gross wrote: "The shammer, when he thinks no one is looking, casts a swift and scrutinizing glance on the Investigating Officer to see whether or not he believes him."

Today's forensic psychologists equally worry about malingering. Of the roughly 60,000 Competency to Stand Trial referrals every year, anywhere from 10 per cent to 17 per cent are found to be faking it. Today's experts, like their forbearers, observe the suspects with a practiced clinical eye to see if the symptoms match those of well-studied pathologies and if the symptoms remain consistent over time. They also use a battery of vetted psychological tests. One, called M-FAST, poses a series of 25 questions and gives a numerical score to the suspect's sense of reality. A skilled psychologist using this test can make a preliminary assessment in less than 15 minutes. Other exams involve highly structured interviews that produce additional scores for the subject's memory and claims of psychosis.

Those tests, combined with the psychologists' abilities to categorize symptoms, have produced an enviable track record in screening malingerers. Yet a master-faker will occasionally pass through. For decades the mafia chieftain Vincent Gigante, dubbed "Oddfather" by the New York press, shuffled about Little Italy in his pajamas, slobbering and muttering in order to show he was mentally incompetent. During his trial in 1997 he fooled half a dozen leading psychologists – even Richard Rogers, who wrote the definitive textbook on malingering. It wasn't until 2003 when officials who tapped his phone heard him speaking quite coherently to his wife, that Gigante admitted it had all been an sham. That, as well as other anecdotes and information, could make a fascinating article about the phenomenon of malingering and its detection.

My credentials: I'm co-director of the graduate program in Science Journalism at Boston University and a veteran journalist specializing in science and science policy, especially in regards to the legal system. I've published two award-winning books with Knopf, the most recent of which explores the birth of forensics and criminology. My articles and commentaries have appeared in a variety of media, including *The New Republic, Wired, Science, Smithsonian*, on public television, National Public Radio, *The Los Angeles Times*, and the *Boston Sunday Globe Magazine*. (For more information see: douglasstarr.com/bio.)

Would your readers be interested?

Regards, Doug Starr

Starr expands on how he structured his query and recommends that you tailor it to the publication you are pitching it to:

What you need to do in a query is get the editor's attention right away with the lead. Now in this case, because *Slate* comes out every day, I felt that I needed a lead that was closely linked to the news of the period. Many times I don't. But in this case, I just said, this is a practice that is going on and it's a problem. Because I know *Slate*'s editors have a sense of fun and interest, I thought, this just came up, and this is an interesting issue that is going on. First, I immediately link it to the news, and I give it perspective. Next, I raise the issue: Can a criminal get away with insanity? It's very rare for me to use questions in my writing or in a query. But *Slate* likes that. Here is a case of tailoring the query very specifically to the magazine. At the time, *Slate* used to have these explainer pieces, and everyone ended the first paragraph with a question. This is the *Slate* style. The pitch already sounds like a *Slate* article.

*(Starr 2015)*

Starr then breaks down his pitch by paragraph and explains what goes into each:

The first paragraph puts the question. The second paragraph adds something that few other writers could put in. Because of my book, I was able to add a really interesting historical perspective: They had been discussing this idea for 130 years, and they called them malingerers.

The third paragraph brings it right to the present. They still worry about malingerers. Here are the numbers, here is the kind of test they use, a little bit of scientific stuff to show: This is really authoritative.

The fourth paragraph says they got a great track record. And then I found out about Vincent Gigante, the Oddfather, who faked it [insanity], and I knew they would love a little bit of an anecdote. Most of my queries are a little bit longer, but in essence this is what I do:

The first paragraph is like the lead of a story. It gets the editor's attention in a substantive, interesting way. The next two paragraphs are usually background to show that you really know what you are talking about, and the final paragraph wraps it up. I always end my queries with my credentials. Here is who I am and what I have done. Would your readers be interested in this?

With a query like this, the editor is free to accept or reject this, but she knows what I am talking about. . . . That would be a good structure. The lead, a couple of paragraphs of substance, and in a more serious piece, I would even have a paragraph with implications: Here is why this is so important to your readers. That is the basic structure that I and the people in my program use, and we find it effective.

*(Starr 2015)*

## Internal versus external pitching

So far, this chapter has mostly addressed external pitches, that is, pitches from freelance science journalists to publications' commissioning editors. This ties in with the fact that many science magazines now rely on freelance writers. For instance, at *BBC Focus*, science writers produce most of the magazine's features (Goodyer 2015b). The same is true of other science magazines, such as Germany's highest-circulation popular science magazine, *P.M. Magazin*. This makes it easier for you to get an assignment to write a story, provided your pitch is sound and well-crafted.

Despite the shift from staff to freelance science writing (caused by massive layoffs), there are still many publications that employ staff writers. At its very core, the process of pitching a story internally is the same as pitching it from outside: You have to convince an editor that your story is relevant to the publication's audience. But how you do it differs greatly. For example, if you are pitching a story as a staff writer, your editors know you and vice versa. Because you know which topics and ideas they like and commission, you are less likely to come up with unsuitable proposals. As part of an editorial team, you will soon gain that insight, even as an intern. Additionally, the pitching process can be much less formal if you are on staff. Apart from editorial meetings, you can pitch a story in the elevator or during the lunch break.

There are exceptions, however. Sharon Begley, a former staff journalist for Reuters, says that pitching science stories at Reuters follows a rather strict process:

> At *Newsweek*, it was just a casual conversation with only one editor. Sometimes, in story meetings, I would present ideas to a larger group. At Reuters, however, it is much more formal. Yes, you do put something down on paper or a screen, and it is very regimented: What is the idea? Why does it matter? Why do we care? What are the financial implications? You basically have to fill all those boxes. After writing it down, it goes to your first editor who then sends it to your next editor. There is almost no in-person discussion. So, it is very impersonal and much less fun. That just shows that every publication is different in how it handles new ideas.
>
> *(Begley 2015)*

When asked how internal pitching works at *BBC Focus*, commissioning editor Jason Goodyer replied that he thinks the mode of internal pitching also depends on a news organisation's size:

> I do occasionally write features for *Focus* magazine, but I do not have to write formal pitches. When you are a pitching freelancer and you obviously are not on a set salary, pitching is your bread and butter, whereas, when you are on a set salary, I do not really see it as pitching, although the difference is subtle. Even though we do not formally pitch internally at *Focus*, in my experience, internal pitching can be easier and less formal, because you are in direct contact with somebody every day, so even over lunch you can say "I have got this great idea." I can understand that a massive organisation like Reuters has a more formal pitching process, but we at *Focus* are only eight people. Since we work so closely together, it would be weird to send Graham [Southorn] a formal pitch. However, if I wanted to write for another

BBC magazine like *BBC Wildlife*, then I would go through the formal pitching process – I would not just walk over to their desks and say "Hey guys, I have a great idea."

*(Goodyer 2015)*

Curtis Brainard, blogs editor at *Scientific American,* confirms the point of view that internal pitching is generally less formal and easier than pitching as an outside science journalist:

I have both received and delivered internal pitches, and it is a lot more informal. Often, internal pitching is done verbally, for instance during a news meeting. . . . Often, there is a news meeting on Monday to talk about the week ahead. Someone will come in and say "Okay, so here are the three things that are interesting this week – A, B and C. Should I do one or two of them, or maybe I should do all three of them?" But in that case, which one do I first, which one do I second, and which one third? So, this is a much more verbal and fluid process. When it is an internal matter, generally there are no written pitches a lot of times. Instead, this is just handled in meetings between editors and writers. That is a little different for big features, investigations or big enterprise pieces. In that case, a reporter will draft a short note, sort of a pitch, and present it to their editors. When it is something like that – contrary to what I just said a moment ago – the pitch letter will tend to be a bit longer and a bit more detailed, because what you are actually talking about is more involved. You might describe some travel that you need to do, you might describe some other expenses for equipment that you need to get the story. When the pitching is internal and it is written down, it might actually involve a more detailed, longer written pitch – contrary to working with outside writers. Generally, it is quite a bit easier, because the editor and the reporter know one another. Sometimes, the reporter might not explain his or her idea clearly or as simply as possible. But that is okay, because the editor knows that writer, and the editor understands what that writer is trying to say.

*(Brainard 2015)*

He adds that this eventually also happens between editors and freelancers. The better they know each other, "the easier this process [pitching] becomes" (Brainard 2015). The key to building such relationships is that you need to accept criticism and learn from it. On your way to becoming a professional pitch writer, you will undoubtedly make mistakes, as did I earlier in this chapter. To help you avoid the worst mistakes, some editors and scholars talk freely about the worst mistakes they have encountered in the next section.

## The most common pitching mistakes

When asked to dig up a list of the most common pitching mistakes, most editors interviewed were quick to produce a rather extensive list of deal-breakers they had gathered over the years. The list from Jason Goodyer contains three severe pitching mistakes that will earn you a certain rejection:

> Number one is not researching the magazine. That is definitely the most common and the deadliest mistake – you are just wasting everybody's time. Next, not putting enough information in it would be number two. Completely inappropriate pitches that have not been researched and vague pitches, that is. Finally, number three is a lack of professionalism in approaching editors. Those are the big mistakes.
>
> *(Goodyer 2015)*

Curtis Brainard says the biggest mistakes are sending irrelevant content, not getting to the point quickly and sending in unsolicited manuscripts:

> The biggest mistake they make is obviously pitching just something that is totally inappropriate for our particular publication. That is one of the worst things you could do. Another big mistake would be to structure the piece wrong and to start off with something irrelevant and boring, like "Hello, I'm so and so, I have been working on this." They just start telling me about themselves before they get right to it. All of our editors have very, very limited time to review your pitch. So everything that does not go straight to the point is a mistake. Sending a really long, drawn-out pitch is a mistake. I don't know whether all editors would agree with this, but I think a lot would. Sending in a manuscript, a full, unsolicited manuscript is a mistake. I just won't read it. I don't have the time. So a lot of people say "Hey, I wrote this great post, I have attached a draft, will you take a look?" And then the answer is no, no. You have got to send me a short synopsis first. I don't think all editors are quite as hard-lined about that, but I certainly am. I don't want unsolicited manuscripts. I don't have time to read an 800-word manuscript. I only have got time to read a 100-word pitch, so that is what you get.
>
> *(Brainard 2015)*

When asked about the most common pitching mistakes she has encountered, Laura Helmuth in part confirms Brainard's and Goodyer's lists and adds that asking questions is generally not a good idea:

> One mistake that a lot of people make when pitching is that they tend to ask a lot of questions. They have something they are interested in

and they will say "I want to know why these fish swim in circles" and "why is the health care system so bad at doing XYZ." Those pitches almost never work. I think a lot of editors get such pitches. And our response to those is almost always come back when you [have] the answers to these questions.

But the most common mistake is not being familiar with the publication writers are pitching to. It is not a question of how good a story is, but it is a question of how good a fit a story is for your publication. My most common reason for rejecting a pitch is to say "It would be an interesting story for somebody else, but it is just not the sort of thing we cover here, and it's not the approach we take here." It makes sense that this is by far the most common mistake, because as writers you do not have the time to study every single publication you pitch to. But if you don't, your pitch will not work.

Another classic mistake is pitching a topic rather than a story and just saying "this subject is really interesting" without explaining why your story and the subject would be distinctive. It is very common to receive topic pitches. It was more of a problem when I was at *Smithsonian Magazine* because there I was handling magazine features, and I think people think of magazine features as subjects. They do not understand that magazine features – perhaps more than anything – need to have a strong storyline.

*(Helmuth 2015)*

Douglas Starr adds two things he avoids at all costs: sending links and including too much of the material you have gathered while conducting your preliminary research:

One thing I do not do in queries is send links. I don't know if that should be a principle of religion or if it's just a principle of me. But when I have students send queries to me and they send me a link, they are telling me "Why don't you do some homework?" I don't want to do any homework. I want them to have done the homework. If there is a link, I want them to have them have digested the material and put it in the body of the query. I don't want to have to do anything as an editor. I want to see this and say "This is good. I want to talk to this person."

*(Starr 2015)*

Helen Pearson says that she does not easily feel pestered and is generally willing to work with writers on their ideas, provided they are promising. Pearson recalls some of the mistakes she occasionally encounters:

There are some blunders people make from time to time. An obvious one, you need to make it clear that you are pitching for *Nature*.

> We have had pitches where people said "I think the story would be really great for *The Atlantic*." They didn't even delete the title of the publication they last sent the pitch to, and that is not very good. Also, sometimes it just shows that they have not really read the magazine. They pick something that is a review which should have been sent to a scientific journal, it's just clearly way too dense, there is no story to it, so it is just not going to work.
>
> *(Pearson 2015)*

## Checklist

Use the following checklist before you send your pitch to an editor. Does it meet all of the criteria? If not, it might still be a valid pitch. If it lacks many of the essential building blocks, you should consider rewriting it until it meets these criteria.

**Did you do the following?**

- Spell the editor's name right
- Name the publication you are pitching to
- Start your pitch with a lead
- Include your story idea in that lead
- Detail who the story is about and what that person is pursuing
- Explain how you will gain access to the story
- Provide scientific context and background
- Identify sources, papers and sites you want to visit
- Think about the time needed to research and write the piece
- Address the implications and effects of your story
- Provide information and clips about yourself
- Include that information only at the end
- Structure your pitch in order of importance
- Include transitions between the sections
- Research enough material beforehand
- Read previous issues of the publication you are pitching to
- Verify the publication covers the topic you are pitching
- Check whether the publication offers pitching guidelines
- Make sure your topic fits in with the publication's audience
- Check your proposal for the essential news values
- Make sure you are not submitting the first draft of your proposal
- Check your proposal for logical, linguistic, grammatical and orthographic errors

These are some of the most important basics. Obviously, the requirements of a good pitch may vary for different publications, but the most important point is to lay out a good story in one sentence, which should go in your pitch's lead. As Starr (2015) points out, interviewing is crucial for him before he crafts a pitch, so the next chapter covers interviews before moving on to how you can write for newspapers, magazines and online outlets.

## Summary

Once you have submitted your pitch to an editor, it will be vying for her attention with a myriad of other pitches. That is why you have to get to the point immediately with your summarized story idea. Emphasise what makes the story stand out and why it is relevant to the publication's readers. Most important, point out how your access to the story is unique. This can be an interview with a hard-to-get scientist, previously unreleased documents or photographs. Most publications refuse to publish rehashed stories that add nothing to the discussion. Also, a good pitch contains background information that puts the findings and discoveries in context. If you are pitching a long-form story, it might also be helpful to outline how you are going to structure your text and which elements (interviewees, studies) you are planning to include. Credentials, a list of stories or the publications you have worked for belong at the very end of a good pitch. While previous jobs may make it easier to get the commission, the lack of such credentials should not deter you from pitching a good story to an editor.

Good pitches are structured in three parts. Like news stories, good pitches provide the information in descending order of importance. Rewriting and editing pitches before submitting them is also key, because they should be concise and reasonably short. Many editors are inundated with pitches, and they sometimes take little time to evaluate them. Starting a pitch by blathering on about the importance of cancer research for humanity, or packing your entire biography into the pitch right at the beginning, is worthy of a rejection. To avoid these mistakes, read successful pitches on the Open Notebook's pitch database. Study them carefully and look for the structures and techniques explained in this chapter.

## Review questions

- Which elements must a good proposal contain?
- If you had to reduce your proposal to just one element, which one would that be and why?
- What does the ideal length of a pitch depend on?
- What are most editors looking for in pitches?
- How can you increase the odds of getting your pitch accepted?
- Apart from email pitches, what other ways of pitching your stories are there?

- Find the three most blatant pitching taboos the interviewees encountered.
- How do internal and external pitches differ?
- What are the most common pitching mistakes?

## Exercises

- Pick three pitches from the Open Notebook's pitch database, extract the hook and the main story idea and try to guess how many hours of research are hiding in the pitch.
- Write a 200- to 300-word pitch based on a technology-related press release or short news story. Write the one-sentence idea first, then the motivation and finally the paragraph that reels the editor in.
- Take the pitch you have written and find a publication it could be a fit for. Sift through the publication's archives and find the commissioning editor's contact details.
- Prepare a query email and send it to the editor you previously identified.
- Take an award-winning science story and imagine what the pitch might have looked like. Write it down and discuss it with your classmates.
- Identify and verbally pitch three science story ideas to your classmates.
- Find the shortest and the longest pitches in the Open Notebook's pitching database and compare their structures and approaches.
- Read at least three science publications' or science desks' pitching guidelines.

## Reading list

Chokshi, S. (2014) How to contribute to WIRED's opinion section, *WIRED* [Online] Available at: www.wired.com/2014/03/opinionopedia-contribute-wired-opinion/ [date accessed 13 September 2016]

Hayden, T. (2013) Making the pitch, In Hayden, T. and Nijhuis, M. (eds.) *The Science Writers' Handbook*. Boston, MA: Da Capo Press, 23–38

Huang, T. (2012) 6 questions journalists should be able to answer before pitching a story, *Poynter* [Online] Available at: www.poynter.org/how-tos/writing/185746/6-questions-journalists-should-be-able-to-answer-before-pitching-a-story/ [date accessed 13 July 2015]

LaFrance, A., Beck, J. and Romm, C. (2015) Science, technology and health: A guide to pitching for freelancers, *The Atlantic* [Online] Available at: www.theatlantic.com/health/archive/2015/06/science-technology-health-freelancer-pitching-how-to-pitch-submissions/395762/ [date accessed 27 July 2015]

New Scientist (no date) Guide for freelancers, *New Scientist* [Online] Available at: www.newscientist.com/in209-guide-for-freelancers/ [date accessed 12 October 2016]

Reimold, D. (2013) *Journalism of Ideas*. London: Routledge

Scientific American (no date) Submission instructions, *Scientific American* [Online] Available at: www.scientificamerican.com/page/submission-instructions/ [date accessed 13 September 2016]

Slate (2012) Slate's discussion and submission guidelines, *Slate* [Online] Available at: www.slate.com/articles/briefing/slate_user_agreement_and_privacy_policy/2012/12/slate_s_discussion_and_submission_guidelines.html [date accessed 12 October 2016]

Sumner, D.E. and Miller, H.G. (2013) *Feature and Magazine Writing: Action, Angle and Anecdotes*. Chichester: John Wiley & Sons

## Links

Dragon's Den (at the UKSCJ 2014): www.youtube.com/watch?v=ByHaiCifTgY
The Open Notebook's pitch database: www.theopennotebook.com/pitch-database/
Science Writers 2016: http://sciencewriters2016.org/
Secrets of Good Science Writing: www.theguardian.com/science/series/secrets-science-writing
The UK Conference of Science Journalists: www.ukcsj.org/

## References

Bernstein, J. (2014) What kind of blogger are you? *The Guardian* [Online] Available at: www.theguardian.com/media-network/media-network-blog/2014/oct/09/blogger-blogging-digital-publishing-content [date accessed 11 July 2015]

Brainard, C. (2015) Personal phone conversation on 26 June 2015

Flynn, J. (2015) The future of travel? A glass tube called Hyperloop, *Reuters (via ScienceDaily)* [Online] Available at: www.sciencedaily.com/videos/d5be126450ab9c4b5c94a7455f267d0a.htm [date accessed 15 July 2015]

Goodyer, J. (2015a) Personal email conversation on 5 August 2015

Goodyer, J. (2015b) Personal Skype conversation on 25 June 2015

Göpfert, W. (2016) Personal email conversation on 21 March 2016

Greenemeier, L. (2015) Human traffickers caught on hidden internet, *Scientific American* [Online] Available at: www.scientificamerican.com/article/human-traffickers-caught-on-hidden-internet/ [date accessed 2 July 2015]

Helmuth, L. (2015) Personal phone conversation on 23 July 2015

Kois, D., Helmuth, L. and Lai, J. (2015) The editor's creed, *Slate* [Online] Available at: www.slate.com/articles/slate_plus/slate_plus/2014/05/how_should_editors_edit_two_slate_editors_debate.html [date accessed 25 July 2015]

Pearson, H. (2015) Personal phone conversation on 28 July 2015

Randerson, J. (2014) How to pitch articles to editors, *The Guardian* [Online] Available at: www.theguardian.com/science/2014/may/08/how-to-pitch-freelance-articles-to-editors [date accessed 30 June 2015]

Starr, D. (2015) Personal Skype conversation on 31 July 2015

Starr, D. (2012) Can you fake mental illness? *Slate* [Online] Available at: www.slate.com/articles/health_and_science/science/2012/08/faking_insanity_forensic_psychologists_detect_signs_of_malingering_.html [date accessed 16 July 2015]

# 4

# INTERVIEWING SCIENTISTS

**What you will learn in this chapter:**

- Why interviews are important
- Principles of interviewing
- Essential interviewing equipment
- Preparing for the interview
- Asking questions
- More interviewing techniques
- Transcribing the interview
- Best practices for citing and quoting
- Case study: an interview with a well-known scientist.

## Introduction

Interviews are one of the staples of journalism. They are an essential part of your reporting, and they are essential to your understanding of the subject matter, which is important if you want to explain it to a lay audience. Powerful quotes from your interviews enliven otherwise dull and perhaps lengthy explanatory passages. You can also write entire articles around interviews, such as profiles.

The first section of this chapter discusses why interviews are so important in science journalism; this is followed by a section about the basic rules of interviewing. That section includes advice on how many interviews you should conduct and how much preparation should go into your interviews; that, of course, varies greatly depending on the type of article you are writing.

Interviewing is a craft, and like every good craftsman, you should know the tools of the trade. That is why you will find a dedicated section on interviewing equipment and a comparison between the seemingly old-school note-taking approach and the new digital approach to interviewing.

The section on preparing for the interview covers the preliminary research you should put into your interviews. Gather as much information as you can on your interviewee; this can be challenging, because some scientists have numerous publications. You will also learn where to look for additional background information, which is crucial for understanding the big picture.

The key point of this chapter is formulating questions and how you can ask them. There are many types of questions, and you can employ them in very different scenarios. Some will evoke emotional responses, others will confirm what you already know and still others will bluntly provoke your interviewee. All have their merits, but you will see which ones you should use more often than others.

Once you have conducted an interview, you will have to put the statements to paper, so there is a dedicated section on how to do this most efficiently. That section contains some technical advice for which tools can ease that otherwise boring task.

The more interviews you conduct, the more you will recognise that transcribing and editing your interviews is like digging for gold. The penultimate section deals with best practices in citing and quoting your interviews and extracting those gold nuggets. One of the most important rules is to never change the meaning of a quote or divorce it from its context. In addition, because people make mistakes when talking to you, you will need strategies for dealing with flawed quotes.

Finally, this chapter closes with a case study about how one science journalist interviewed world-famous physicist Kip Thorne for *Science*. It contains a lot of advice you can readily apply to your own interviews. As a preparation, be sure to first read the full interview with Kip Thorne in the appendix at the end of this book.

## Why interviews are important

In science journalism, interviews serve a dual purpose. First, they deepen your own understanding of complex scientific issues. Second, they provide you with first-hand quotes and lively anecdotes that you can weave into your stories. The explanatory science and background passages would otherwise often suffer from dry writing.

Experts' quotes add authority to your pieces, but this can be a double-edged sword. On the one hand, their quotes add credibility to your piece, but on the other hand, too many journalists and readers unquestioningly accept their claims. Physician, researcher and science writer Ben Goldacre confirms this and cautions aspiring science journalists against taking scientists' statements at face value and merely writing them down without questioning them first (Goldacre 2016).

Most stories benefit from interviews. Failing to include good quotes in a story is likely to prompt editors to kill it before it gets published: "In the Anglo-American tradition, interviewing sources and attributing facts and opinions to them is an essential part of reporting. Indeed, in many newspapers, otherwise sound stories that can't be supported by quotes remain unpublished" (Adams and Hicks 2009:2).

You can employ interviews in a variety of ways. First, you can extract quotes or paraphrase the scientists and use them to support your story's ideas or to give your readers first-hand accounts of what research looks like. Second, you can use the interview as the story or publish it as a question-and-answer piece in a newspaper or magazine.

The profile is another type of feature article that heavily draws on interviews. The *New Yorker* frequently publishes profile articles on influential people such as politicians, musicians, actors and scientists. These profile features often refer to current world affairs, such as the profile of marine biologist Sylvia A. Earle in July 1989, which addressed the Exxon Valdez oil spill 3 months earlier (White 1989). The *New Yorker*'s archive also contains a number of evergreen profile articles portraying luminaries such as Albert Einstein. You can find a link to the *New Yorker*'s profiles archive in the Links section at the end of this chapter.

Interviews are also important because, as an outsider, you will often find it difficult to keep track of what positions scientists hold regarding specific issues. The scientists you talk to will often have a good understanding what other seminal papers have been published. They know other luminaries in the field and they know the status quo of the research in their field, so they can often point you to interesting studies, multimedia material and, most importantly, other people you should talk to.

## Principles of interviewing

An interview begins a long time before you actually conduct it. You will need to have a thorough understanding of what your story is and whose statements you need in order to underpin it. Identifying and looking up potential interviewees is hence the first logical step of planning your interviews. You must also know how many interviews you need in your article. However, you cannot plan for everybody. In some interviews, your sources will tell you to talk to other people, and if they don't, you should ask them. Not all statements will make it into the story; they will simply provide background to strengthen your own literacy in the field.

Decide pragmatically how many interviews to include. Weaving ten interviewees' statements into a 200-word news item is almost always unnecessary. A 2,000-word feature, however, could use more than one interview.

The basic principle is to achieve some balance and address all involved and affected parties as well as independent and opposing voices. Be aware this may be false balance; as in statistics, the crux lies in the population you draw your sample from. If your text contains statements from one GMO corn advocate and one GMO corn opponent, it does not mean half of the people in the world are for and half are against GMO corn.

Profiles that revolve around one person rarely rely on just one interview. In fact, it is necessary to interview many more people for a profile to determine who the profiled scientist is and how former colleagues, critics, family and friends perceive her. One *New York Times* writer recommends interviewing five more people from the subject's surroundings:

> Interview at least five other people, representing a variety of perspectives, about the subject of your profile. Ask them for telling anecdotes. . . . Each may provide you with information that will help you ask better questions of your profile subject, or of the next person you interview.
>
> *(New York Times 1999)*

In science, if you are covering studies, the first obvious source is the principal investigator (PI), who is usually listed at the end of the list of contributing authors (von Bubnoff 2013). Unlike lower-profile researchers who contributed to the paper, the PI can help you understand the big picture:

> Graduate students or postdocs, who often do the bulk of the work, can discuss the details of the research but may be afraid to say what they really think – or may simply be too close to the work to comment on its larger implications.
>
> *(von Bubnoff 2013:43)*

Most scientists, just like editors, dislike being cold-called. It is common courtesy to set an appointment beforehand, even if it is just a phone call. Emails work best for scheduling interviews, as this allows your interviewee to check her calendar. On the downside, she may take a long time to respond or even overlook your emails, so you might have to resort to calling when you are pressed for time.

The less known a scientist is, the better your chances of securing an interview. Rock-star scientists like Neil deGrasse Tyson are particularly hard to reach. Some people you will even have to book via their agents, but many work at research institutions, so you can try to contact them via press officers or PIOs. Incidentally, von Bubnoff (2013) recommends taking the PIO route when the researcher is getting a lot of media attention, as "working with a PIO may be the only way to get your source on the phone" (42).

You will conduct interviews for different reasons. Some will confirm or deny claims you made in an article, some will be ends in themselves and some will strengthen your understanding of complex issues. Regardless of why you conduct an interview, the following four principles, as defined by Adams and Hicks (2009), always hold and are your keys to successfully conducting interviews:

1 **Plan:** Know what you need to find out, and know the questions your readers would want answered. Prepare a list of questions.
2 **Research:** Find out as much as possible about your interviewee before the interview takes place, and use both off- and online sources.
3 **Listen:** Do not digress from the interview's set purpose. Employ silence.
4 **Empathise:** Put yourself in your interviewee's shoes.

Note that most of these principles are connected to each other; for example, the more research you conduct about your interviewee, the easier it will be for you to empathise with her. Eventually, this will pay off during the interview, because everybody likes to be understood. Most interviewees, and this is especially true of scientists, will appreciate that you took the time to understand who they are and what they do, which in turn makes it much easier to evoke thoughtful responses and get them to talk at all. If you listen carefully instead of interrupting, you will be able to continuously formulate questions in your head as the interview progresses. When you ask those follow-up questions, not only will it show you paid close attention but it will also prompt a natural conversation.

Until you have built such a relationship, your interviewee might carefully gauge whether she will disclose any information at all. Richard Craig, journalism professor at San José State University, states that showing genuine interest and respect for the people and subject matter you are reporting on is a good way to establish a relationship and even become part of the discourse (Craig 2015). If your sources are secretive, you will find that flattery often works. With public officials, you can even demand that they disclose information (see the section on FOIA requests in Chapter 10).

The types of questions you ask and their order will largely determine the quality of the answers you will get. Open-ended questions will require your interviewee to think and come up with a more elaborate response. Closed-ended questions elicit short answers; these are useful if you want your interviewee to confirm facts.

You should also be an active listener. Let your interviewee know you follow her, and do not interrupt. Silence is king, especially with open-ended questions; after each answer, wait a few seconds before asking the next question. Many interviewees will feel they have to add something important to their previous statements. Also, it allows them to think about their answers. This often leads to interesting, colourful statements. Adams and Hicks (2009), von Bubnoff (2013), Clery (2015), and Mencher (2011) all confirm this.

Another important principle is to establish ground rules before starting the interview. Indicate whether you will record the interview and discuss what is on and off the record. If the interviewee does not state what is off the record before saying it, you can generally use the statements.

Also, be aware that you are the one who controls the interview. As the interviewer you are sort of a director, and as such you have a number of rights; "it's perfectly reasonable to ask sources to repeat themselves; to ask for additional details in follow-up questions to stop sources who give you too much information; or to ask them to speak more slowly if necessary" (Thomas Hayden in von Bubnoff 2013).

Another principle to remember is that good interviews are like good photographs: The closer you get the better. Following are interview types in descending order of preference:

- In-person interviews
- Skype interviews
- Phone interviews
- Email interviews (no real conversation happens).

Siri Carpenter, editor-in-chief (and co-founder with Jeanne Erdmann) of the Open Notebook confirms that emails are not her means of choice for conducting interviews because even the statements' authenticity can become an issue:

> You don't know for sure that the person you are quoting was actually the person sending the email. Some people might have a postdoc do it. Sometimes, I have emailed researchers with a follow-up question when I fact-check, and I have seen them forward their email to a postdoc or a colleague. But the last thing I would want is to be quoting a researcher in a story when actually the words were not his or hers.
>
> *(Carpenter 2015)*

## Essential interviewing equipment

Always prepare for the unexpected. When you ask a scientist for an interview appointment, her answer could be, "Okay, I've got a slot in 5 minutes." If your recorder's batteries are drained or the memory is full, that is it. And even if all your equipment is fully loaded and ready, it may still fail you. That is why I start with the lowest-tech interviewing equipment out there: pen and paper.

### *Pen and paper*

Unless you lose them or they go up in flames, pen and paper will never let you down. But they will also not record anything on their own, and writing down an interview verbatim is impossible. Shorthand is a method of abbreviated note-taking that uses simplified symbols to represent letters, words, phrases and phonemes. There are several standards: In the US, the most commonly used shorthand system is Gregg, while in the UK it is Teeline, which has just superseded the Pitman system. In the UK, the National Council for the Training of Journalists (NCTJ) requires its students to take a course on Teeline shorthand.

Writing in shorthand allows you to increase your writing to 100 or 120 words per minute, and some systems allow even up to 200 words per minute. By comparison, most people are able to write about 30 words per minute in longhand English, which is by far too slow to match the speed of talking. Many journalists still consider shorthand a vital skill because it is technology independent, and it allows for quick note-taking during press conferences and interviews. For example, in an interview with the NCTJ, BBC news correspondent Jane Peel states:

> A lot of people have got the impression shorthand is quite old-fashioned and is not relevant to today's newsrooms, but I happen to think it is as valuable as it ever was. I have obviously been doing it for years and years and years. I think the biggest example is court reporting. Although you now get a lot of people tweeting in court, you cannot actually take a full note of what is being said if you are tweeting 140 characters.
>
> *(Jane Peel in Wilson and Tucker 2013)*

While shorthand has its merits, it also has drawbacks, especially when compared to recording interviews. Physical loss or damage may mean you lose all your work; for example, a reporter's notebook was stolen in a discotheque and was later recovered from a puddle – the thief had thrown it away (Adams and Hicks 2009).

Also, notebook-recorded interviews may allow the interviewee to later deny statements or claim inaccurate recording; this is hard to do if you have a voice recording. As journalist Roy Greenslade (2010) writes in an article for the *Guardian*, Lord Young of Graffham had to step down from his adviser role to David Cameron after a tape-recorded statement of his became public. In an interview with the *Daily Telegraph*, Young claimed that cuts in mortgage rates had left the majority of citizens better off. Greenslade (2010) doubts that putting down that same interview using shorthand would have led to Young's resignation, as such statements could be refuted. But the recorded interview made it impossible for him to deny his affirmations. On top of that, taking notes while interviewing consumes your concentration and takes the focus away from the actual conversation:

> Shorthand, no matter how good the user, is much less efficient than using a tape recorder, which allows a conversation or interview to flow naturally, as quickly as both parties wish.
>
> *(Greenslade 2010)*

## *Audio recorders*

While notes just describe the spoken words, audio recordings allow you to observe whether your interviewee had a trembling voice, chattered or talked calmly or hesitated and whether her answers sounded prepared. Most important, recording the interview allows you to focus on your questions and your interviewee's answers. If you have difficulties understanding your interviewee, you can stop the recording and rewind, slow down the playback speed or even digitally enhance the recording so you can hear the voice better. This is impossible with shorthand.

Digital audio recorders are valuable tools that will cost you around $100. Especially when paired with a professional microphone, they produce high-quality audio that can be broadcast on radio or television. If you want to record landline calls, you can buy adapters that you can interpose between the phone and your audio recorder. These adapters will record both sides of the conversation and rarely cost more than $15.

Two components are crucial when using digital audio recorders: batteries and memory cards. First, be sure your kit is ready to start at all times. Fully charge your batteries ahead of time, and bring spare batteries; especially in cold weather, batteries discharge quicker than usual. Second, prepare your memory cards by backing them up and emptying them beforehand. You do not want to have to select which audio files to delete shortly before or even during the interview. Some recorders have built-in memory (usually 2 to 4 GB), but most fortunately have memory expansion slots so you can upgrade the memory and record much longer interviews. Also, choose a compressed audio format such as MP3, which allows you to squeeze up to 30 hours onto a 2 GB memory card.

Your computer is also a great interview-recording device. Use applications such as Skype or Google Hangout to conduct video interviews. If you need to call your interviewee, these apps offer inexpensive internet phone calls. If you have to make a lot of long-distance calls, this can help you save money. Skype does not support recording video and audio calls, so you need to buy dedicated plugins such as Call Recorder. These save your calls (including video calls) to your hard disk as you talk. Video quickly fills up your disks, so make sure to back them up to external hard disks or save them using cloud storage providers like Dropbox, Google Drive and the like. I conducted virtually all my interviews for this book this way.

Without a doubt, your jack-of-all-trades is already in your pocket or purse: your smartphone. You can use it to record calls and face-to-face interviews. If you conduct an interview outdoors, be sure to use a windscreen, just as you would with a professional-grade microphone. (You can see a similar setup in Figure 4.1, which shows Nick Garnett's (the BBC's mobile reporter) standard mobile reporting kit including his smartphone, windscreen, headphones, microphone, and notepad. He used his kit to report

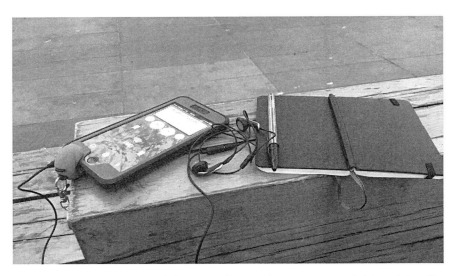

**FIGURE 4.1** The BBC's mobile journalist Nick Garnett used his minimalist broadcasting kit (an iPhone 6s, headphones, a windscreen and a notepad) to cover the aftermath of the Paris attacks

*Source*: Nick Garnett

from the November 2015 Paris attacks.) Recording apps are available, and you can use them to record incoming and outgoing calls as well as in-person interviews.

Take the time to acquaint yourself with your smartphone, make a few test calls, save them and then review the settings. Is the volume right? What is the right distance between the microphone and your interviewee? While smartphones can replace a lot of devices, they suffer from quickly draining batteries, they are chronically low on memory and sometimes the recording apps just don't work. Be sure to carry backup recording solutions.

Bradshaw and Rohumaa (2013) recommend that a mobile journalist's kit should contain a mobile phone, a laptop computer, a sufficient number of chargers, batteries and cables, and "the failsafe option of a notepad and pen."

## Preparing for the interview

What are the ingredients of an effective business meeting? You need to bring some input, which requires research and preparation. You need define the meeting purpose and determine the goals or decisions you want to achieve. Interviews are no different. Especially in science journalism, do your research. First, you must become acquainted with the topic you are writing about. If you cover a journal paper, read the paper you are writing about, and take notes of passages and claims that you do not understand yet. Also, get acquainted with context and background. Read that same author's and other authors' papers on the same topic and see if patterns emerge or whether you find fundamental discrepancies. Become an expert yourself and only then start interviewing, as award-winning investigative journalist Mark Lee Hunter confirms:

> You should not be interviewing someone unless you have read their papers, and you should make the effort to understand what their research is about before you talk to them. Journalists should learn how to read statistical tables, to look up the numbers, to pick up anomalies in papers and also to be able to call scientists not just asking for data, but bringing data of their own.
>
> *(Hunter 2016)*

Second, become acquainted with the authors. Look up their curricula, read their online profiles, read what others have written about them. Identify their areas of expertise and try to understand the big picture. Use social media, blogs, websites, Wikipedia articles, newspaper clips, online radio interviews and online videos to find out more about your interviewee. You would be surprised how many researchers give conference presentations or *TED Talks* that you can find online. Often, during or after conferences, they briefly comment on a topical issue; you will often find this online, too. Such interviews will show you which topics and types of questions they enjoy, which ones they avoid and how they react to tough questions. Richard Craig tells me he also teaches his students to find out as much as possible about their interviewees as part of their preparation, because the better prepared you are, the less time you have to waste asking simple confirmatory questions that you could have read elsewhere:

> What I usually try to do is learn as much as I can about who I am going to interview in advance of the interview itself. When I first started, it was a lot harder than it is today with the internet. One thing I keep telling my students is: Do your homework and prepare for the interview. Find out as much as you can about these persons or the companies they work for. You need to double-check all the facts about the people you interview.
>
> *(Craig 2015)*

Also, keep a list of independent experts in the field that you would like to contact. That list will grow as you immerse yourself in the research and conduct your first interviews. For example, some interviewees will put you in contact with other people and suggest you talk to them as well. This will deepen your understanding of the subject area and at the same time help you put together more specific questions.

In fact, the more people you interview (even if the they are just background interviews) and the more context material you read, watch and listen to beforehand, the more questions will come to your mind. Write them down and keep a catalogue of these questions so you can refer to them during your interviews (especially in case the conversation gets stuck). Add more questions of your own to the list: What do you need to know to give your readers the complete picture? What would they want to know? What do you need to know to fully understand the story before telling it to your audience? Also, have your previous interviewees raised specific, unanswered questions? Add those to your catalogue as well. As handy as prepared questions are, though, do not adhere too closely to them or you will run the risk of conducting a boring, mechanical interview. Instead, focus on having a conversation that flows naturally, as Friedman (2013) confirms: "There's certain information you know you want to get, but you also want to put your sources at ease so they give you that information in an interesting way. No one wants to be interrogated." Speaking of getting what you want: You need to know the purpose of each of your questions. Some questions evoke vivid anecdotes, others confirm facts and still others elicit hitherto unknown facts that you can add to your article. That will be the output you are looking for, while your catalogue and your newly acquired expertise will be your interview's input. Be sure to define beforehand what your interview's purpose is. That purpose will also help you formulate better questions:

> Preparation means defining a clear purpose for the interview. What kind of information do you hope to obtain? Is your purpose learning about your subject's personal life or obtaining information based on his or her professional expertise? Just as every article needs a clearly defined angle, so does each interview. All of the questions you ask should be focused around that purpose.
>
> *(Sumner and Miller 2013:57)*

With a purpose in mind and a list of questions in your hand, what is left to do? Setting up the interview. As with pitching, try asking for interviews via email first. If you cannot find an email address, try agents or press officers. If you still can't contact the person, call an assistant, agent or institute press officer. My experience is that you can address many scientists from English-speaking countries by their given name. This is unimaginable in continental Europe, as not addressing scientists by their full academic titles is frowned upon in many cases. As an interviewer, you should never become intimidated by high-profile scientists; "the scientist knows more than you (about his subject, anyway), but he can't do what you do. Each of you is doing something important. The two of you need each other" (Kunzig 2006:128). Behave like a professional, introduce yourself and clearly state the interview's purpose and what you need the interviewee to comment on, and chances are you will secure that interview. All of this chapter's reviewed literature unanimously recommends that you clearly state the following information when asking for an interview appointment:

- Your name
- The publication that has commissioned your piece (or the one you plan on pitching it to)
- What you need to know from the interviewee
- How long the interview will last.

Finally, being persistent when setting up interview appointments is vital and one of the most important traits of every journalist. Scientists are busy doing research, going to conferences, publishing papers and giving talks. In addition, they have their own private lives. Do not give up too quickly. Mencher (2011) gives his advice on what makes you succeed as an interviewer:

> There's a saying in newsrooms that good interviews follow the two "P's" – persistence and preparation. Persistence is necessary to persuade people to be interviewed, and it is essential in following a line of questioning that the subject may find uncomfortable.
>
> *(295)*

For example, in writing this book, I had to contact about 60 interviewees. Some of them were eager to speak with me, others had to reschedule one or several times and still others were flattered initially but then became unreachable all of a sudden, so I had to replace them. Some I simply could not persuade to do the interview, because they were working on their own projects or because they simply did not want to talk – and that is perfectly fine. If people absolutely refuse to talk with you, talk with others.

## Asking questions

Formulating questions is a vital part of your preparation. Mencher (2011) identifies four different types of questions that interviewers may ask. The latter three types, Mencher adds, are those questions that will invite your interviewee to speak verbosely:

1  Direct questions
2  Open- and closed-ended questions
3  Tough questions
4  Intrusive questions.

Direct questions, Mencher (2011) argues, stem directly from themes you identified before the interview while conducting your research. Open- and closed-ended questions both have their merits. The former induce your interviewee to reflect on the question and then answer verbosely, while the latter will elicit a short and specific answer. Closed-ended questions work well if you want facts confirmed.

Tough questions can possibly offend your interviewee, and they are difficult to ask because they might end your interview abruptly. That is why it is important that you leave your most difficult questions for the end of the interview. Still, your interviewee may try to dodge difficult questions. What you can do to mitigate that risk is ask really simple questions that lack details and loaded words, blame somebody else for your questions or play down how serious your questions really are (Adams and Hicks 2009). Alternatively, you can also explicitly warn your interviewee about your next question:

> You tell your interviewee you are going to ask a difficult/hard/rude/impertinent/offensive question and then you do. Because they are prepared, the sting goes out of the question and they feel more able – and more obliged – to answer. Try it.
>
> *(Adams and Hicks 2009:59)*

The problem with open-ended questions in science journalism is that they can cause scientists to rattle out one jargon word after the other. While such questions can yield colourful quotes and beautiful anecdotes, they are the type with the highest potential of causing you a headache. It can take a long time to transcribe them and then tidy them and identify the quotable portions. Most of the time, you will be able to use only a small fraction of answers to open-ended questions. If your interviewee is not able to produce a directly quotable answer, you will have to paraphrase. In the worst case, you can toss away the entire interview.

You can improve the odds of collecting useful quotes that you can weave into your article right away. Among others, von Bubnoff (2013) cites Jessica Marshall in recommending the following strategies to provoke original statements:

- Directly ask for metaphors.
- Ask them to put their work into a context that the audience can understand.
- Ask for the scientific field's status quo and controversies.
- Ask for the interviewee's emotions.

Drawing on his experience as journalism educator, Richard Craig mentions that, in order to avoid jargon, you should not be afraid to interrupt your interviewee and ask for clarification:

> For some students, admitting they don't understand something is admitting some kind of a failing. I tell them [that] it is not a dumb

but a smart question to ask "What do you mean by that?" You need to develop the reflex that whenever you encounter a piece of jargon and you don't immediately know what it is, to stop them, slow them down and ask "What exactly do you mean by that? I don't know if my readers will understand that."

*(Craig 2015)*

But Craig is also quick to add that not every scientist can perfectly boil down and explain her work. If you encounter someone who cannot, you should consider interviewing another scientist within the same area of expertise.

In a personal phone call, Daniel Clery, *Science*'s senior correspondent in the UK, confirms that asking emotion-provoking questions can lead to great quotes, and at the same time, you can use them as a tool to get quotes from otherwise tight-lipped interviewees:

If you are having real trouble getting any sort of reaction out of them, then you start asking questions that will provoke them to say more interesting things, for example: "Were you surprised by these results?" or "Were you expecting these results?" That sort of question gets them to reflect on their emotions about a piece of research.

*(Clery 2015)*

According to Mencher (2011), the main method of getting a good quote is being a good and empathic listener. Also, you should keep an open ear for the one good quote that will bring your piece alive. One technique for doing so is watching out for quotes that address the theme of your story. Now your preparation work, like identifying purpose and themes, pays off: "The reporter is alert to the statement that will illustrate the theme of the article" (Mencher 2011:300).

Asking short, clear questions helps your interviewee understand what the question's focus is so she can better tailor her response to it. More often than not, one long question in fact hides a multitude of shorter questions. Split it up into separate, shorter questions. Scanlan (2013) states that "double-barreled questions give the subject a choice that allows them to avoid the question they want to ignore and choose the less difficult one." You can easily spot double-barreled questions by looking for conjunctions between complete questions, such as in this example: What prompted you to try this new type of cardioprotective fluid, and what side effects could it possibly have?

Every question should have a clear purpose or aim (Adams and Hicks 2009). Before asking a question, ask yourself what you would like to achieve with this question. Additionally, Adams and Hicks (2009) add a few more types of questions that you should consider, such as leading questions. Leading questions are largely frowned upon because they subliminally induce the interviewee to respond in a certain way. Hence, they can threaten the impartiality of your interview. Because leading questions can elicit short answers, Adams and Hicks (2009) consider them a sub-type of closed-ended questions. You can easily spot leading questions by answering one of the following questions with yes:

- Is the question a statement rather than a question?
- Does the statement end with *aren't you, didn't you* or *right* (or their corresponding negations)?
- Does it assume an unproven fact?
- Does it contain a prefabricated answer?
- Can it only be answered with yes or no?

Adams and Hicks (2009) further subdivide leading questions. One subcategory is the assumptive question, in which you assume facts. If you are wrong, the interviewee might have to correct you continuously, which could harm your interview's flow. But if your assumptions prove correct, such questions might provoke interesting answers. Also, you can use assumptive questions to demonstrate you have been following your interviewee's statements, so referring back to those statements can help strengthen your rapport unless you overdo it:

> Asking an assumptive question that relates back to something said at an earlier stage of the interview can flatter the interviewee, reinforcing how interesting you find what they're telling you. Referring back and getting it wrong can lead to a complicated and useful correction, but don't try this too often or they may suspect you're not as shrewd as they first thought.
>
> *(Adams and Hicks 2009:50)*

Loaded questions are biased trick questions that often contain presuppositions, emotion-laden language and emotive terms known as *loaded language*. While the presuppositions can turn out to be either true or false, the emotive language aims at triggering an immediate, emotional response from the interlocutor. For example, assume you asked a scientist the following question: Have you stopped fabricating your data? This would be a loaded question, because if she answers with yes, she has implicitly admitted that she did fabricate her data. If she answers with no, she has still not denied the alleged fabrication. If your biased presupposition annoyed her, she would appear in an unfavourable light. But if she had previously admitted the fabrication, and if this would be merely a follow-up question, the presupposition would turn true, and the question would not be loaded anymore.

Amplification and clarification questions are open-ended question subtypes. The purpose of amplification questions is to get your interviewee to expand on the details of a previous statement and "supply those all-important vivid or visual examples – the 'for instance' hooks of communication" (Adams and Hicks 2009:48). You can explicitly ask your interviewee for more details using questions that begin as follows (Adams and Hicks 2009):

- Could you tell me more . . . ?
- Could you describe . . . ?
- What/how exactly . . . ?

Clarification questions are just as important. Use them for your own understanding and for checking the facts. Clarification questions ask your interviewee to either confirm or deny specific facts. They can start as follows (Adams and Hicks 2009):

- Is that when/what/who . . . ?
- So what you're saying is . . . ?
- Would I be right to think that you . . . ?

Near the end of your interview, you should ask your interviewee whether she has anything else to add. This leads often to more interesting discourses, follow-up questions and advice as for where else you should look. Additionally, ask whom else you should talk to. Most of the time, my very last questions are:

- Do you think we left anything out that the readers should know?
- Who else could tell me more about what we discussed today?

The order in which you ask questions is also important. At the beginning of an interview, you usually have not yet an established rapport with your interviewee. Break the ice by letting your interlocutor talk; open-ended questions work well for this. Do not start an interview with tough, intrusive questions or closed-ended questions. Instead, try to create a relaxed atmosphere and ask unproblematic questions. Daniel Clery states the order in which he asks his questions:

> I always open with some sort of question that allows the interviewees to relax and get into their stride. If it's about a research project, I won't ask them about a controversial result straight away. Rather, I would ask them: "Tell me about the background of the project. How did it get started, and what is the history?" People are very comfortable about answering that sort of question. Once you have covered that – which, by the way, is also useful material that you will want to use – you get on to more difficult questions as you get along. If you have very difficult questions that are going to make them feel uncomfortable, leave those to the end.
>
> *(Clery 2015)*

Your opening question can make or break your interview. Thus, right before the interview starts, observe your interlocutor's body language: Is she nervous, annoyed or relaxed? Adapt your opening question on the fly, if needed. No matter what mood the interviewer is in, opening with an affirming question is always a safe bet (Clery 2015). First, explain why you are interviewing them and what you are looking for. Then ask about their research and about topics you know they are comfortable talking about. If they are nervous, this will allow them to warm up. Adams and Hicks (2009) confirm that you should avoid surprising your interviewee with an abrupt beginning and instead "give them a little time to collect their thoughts and get ready to answer" (Adams and Hicks 2009:37).

Leave difficult questions and accusations until the end. If your interviewee stands up and abandons the interview, you can still use the material you have gathered so far. Most important, do not adhere too closely to your catalogue but take it more as a guideline. Change the order of your questions whenever you feel it is opportune to do so. If you get the chance to follow up on one of your interviewee's answers, make sure your catalogue does not get in the way of doing so. Journalism professor Richard Craig confirms this:

> We keep going back and forth in journalism about showing up with prepared questions. I want to be able to get responses from the interviewees, listen to their responses and follow up with additional questions to them. I don't want to feel like I am holding onto this set of questions. The way that I approach interviews is to simply say "What are the most important things that I don't want to forget to ask?"
>
> *(Craig 2015)*

## More interviewing techniques

As well-prepared and focused as your questions may be, they are not the only component of an interview. You may not get good answers if you fail to establish a rapport with your sources. One of the techniques that helps is spending time with your interviewee. This may entail several lab visits or visiting your source at home or on field trips, provided she agrees to that. Talk to the interviewer a lot. Most interviews get better the more conversations you have and until you have discovered all there is to discover. All of this helps build trust, which in turn loosens the tongue.

If you know your source well enough, you can employ humour and even flattery to break the ice (Adams and Hicks 2009). This is especially efficient when the flattery is based on facts and refers to your source's achievements. This also shows that you have done your homework. The opposite sometimes works as well; when an interviewee is reluctant to confirm or deny facts, you can try to guess statistical facts and narrow down the possible answers. Unnerved, some interviewees will instantly correct you and state the real facts.

Physicist Chad Orzel of Union College in Schenectady points out in a blog post that both scientists and science journalists are responsible for the outcome of an interview, so it is not just the scientists who need to get media training. From a frequently interviewed scientist's perspective, Orzel cautions science journalists against hyping and oversimplifying the facts. He suggests four techniques that you should apply to make the most out of your interviews with scientists (Orzel 2013):

1　**Tell us what you know:** It is important to establish a common state of knowledge to avoid misunderstandings.
2　**Be as specific as you can:** If your question is vague, the answer will be broad and vague, too. For example: What do you know about this specific paper?
3　**Accept that the truth may be boring:** If a scientist gives you a tepid answer, do not automatically assume she is hiding something.
4　**Preview your paraphrases:** During editing, there is a chance you will eliminate comments the interviewee considers crucial, so whenever you can, check back and clarify. This does not mean that the interviewee should authorise your statements.

If you are an active listener, you have an edge. Let your interviewee know that you follow their deliberations by employing one or more of the following techniques while they are talking (Adams and Hicks 2009):

- Nod
- Use interjections such as *uh-huh, I see* and *right*
- Mirror the interviewee's body posture
- Tilt your head
- Lean forward.

All of these are signals that you are engaged in the interview and would like your interviewee to carry on. Adams and Hicks (2009) also note that you can overdo most of the techniques, especially the interjections. Such interjections are extremely helpful and reassuring in phone conversations, where you cannot see each other, but if you overdo it, you will interrupt your interviewee's train of thought.

These soft techniques work for most interviewees, but when you face reluctant sources, you need to apply some additional techniques. First, be fair at all times and tell your interviewees if your next questions are difficult or controversial ones. Some interviewees completely refuse to comment. Second, you can provoke them. Richard Craig states that what works is telling the reluctant source that you will write the story in any case, and he recommends you ask if they do not want to find their perspective in your article. Third, blaming somebody else for tough questions ("X commented Y about your research"), as described by Adams and Hicks (2009), is something you can frequently observe on television. This will project any hard feelings onto the people who purportedly came up with the criticism; this usually invites the interviewee to exculpate herself and address the criticism. If you still cannot get an interviewee to answer your questions, stay persistent. Try asking a few other questions, and then get back to the one she tried to avoid previously.

In science journalism, the most common problematic interviewees are media-inexperienced scientists who have difficulties expressing complex issues in graspable ways. Interviews can also become complicated when politics gets involved with science, as Siri Carpenter confirms:

> I have done some stories where the subject matter is politically sensitive, so people have been more careful about what they want to say, or they are not able to speak on the record. That is certainly a difficult conundrum to face in a story, but it happens. Obviously, this happens not so much in stories about awesome scientists doing awesome science. It tends to happen in more investigative-type stories. But I have never had anyone hang up on me.
>
> *(Carpenter 2015)*

Clery (2015) confirms that problematic interviews in science journalism are the exception rather than the rule. He states scientists are not continuously being showered with media attention but enjoy a time-limited spotlight presence.

Getting scientists to talk who are guilty of misconduct, fabrication and perhaps even bribing will be much harder. In such cases, try not to be judgmental, and be very persistent. Ask critical questions and address allegations, but avoid offending your interviewee. If she starts stonewalling, notice what topics evoked emotional responses. It is important to get the interviewee talking about anything. When people are in full spate, and especially when they are emotional, they often reveal more than they want to. Be a sensitive observer during your interviews.

## Transcribing the interview

The typical interviewing routine I followed for this book's interviews was 4 to 6 hours of preparation, 2 hours for interviewing (one of which I used for last-minute preparations prior to the actual interview) and another 4 to 6 hours for transcribing the interview. Yes, that is a lot of time just for typing, and yes, it is boring. But as you type you also read, and your understanding of the subject strengthens.

Transcribing a recorded interview is very mechanical and repetitive and does not require a lot of skills: You listen a little, and then you type a little.

Your interviewee talks faster than you can type, so at some point you will stop the playback, rewind, play again and finish your sentence. There are too many factors that influence the transcription of an interview: how fast the interlocutor talked, how fast you can type, how good the speech quality of the recording is, whether there is background noise and whether your interviewee was speaking clearly or muttering. You might have to often stop the clip, rewind it and listen to the difficult passage again, which can be time-consuming. The only software you need to transcribe is a media player (or your voice recorder) and a word processor to type the interviewee's words. Voice recognition software is just not (yet) up to the task.

If you want to turn your transcript into a profile for a newspaper or magazine, you will most certainly have to shorten and edit it, as almost no conducted interview contains only relevant questions and answers. Like the interview in the case study exhibited in the next section, profiles contain a disclaimer that states the interview has been edited and shortened.

Right after the interview is the best time to transcribe it, because you still remember what you just discussed. If you discover that your recording is damaged, you still have a chance to write down what you remember and paraphrase or simply use it as background information. You might have taken notes of the surroundings, which can capture all the visual clues that could enrich your interview. Sumner and Miller (2013) add that such handwritten notes can enliven profile articles especially: "As your recorder captures his words, your notebook becomes a receptacle of colorful but unspoken details" (171). If these notes are relevant for your story, weave them into your transcript use them at the appropriate position.

If you have handwritten notes, decipher and transcribe them as soon as possible; they could get damaged or even stolen. Adams and Hicks (2009) affirm that reading back shorthand notes is essential, as is adding additional observations:

> Shorthand interviewers who are going back to the office by train, bus, tube, car or taxi should grab the first opportunity to read back their notes, scribbling down any extra details. It's idiotic not to read back your notes the same day you do the interview. We've all made this mistake. Once.
>
> *(Adams and Hicks 2009:92)*

They also add that shorthand is not suitable for verbatim quoting, and transcribing shorthand notes involves the danger of misquoting. With longhand, you might not be able to decipher all of your own writing.

One efficient technique is to index the interview. This allows you to be selective afterwards and avoid transcribing the entire interview. In the simplest case, all you need is to prepare a spreadsheet. During the interview, every time your interviewee says something quotable, take a short note and insert a timestamp. Basically, you highlight the relevant parts. This technique is time-consuming, but less so than actually transcribing entire interviews and then using only 5 or 10 per cent of the transcript. In addition, the archive file provides a complete index of your interviews that you can search. Video editors apply similar techniques to keep track of their clips' contents, and current video editing software already provides functions to label clips accordingly. The idea for adapting and applying this technique was brought to my attention by Katia Cont, an art historian specialising in cataloguing techniques of contemporary artwork at Museion in Bolzano. If you are using a smartphone to record your interviews, you can use an app like AudioNote (science journalist David Dobbs kindly brought this to my attention). AudioNote, as shown in Figure 4.2, allows you to take notes while recording, and it automatically adds a timestamp as you type.

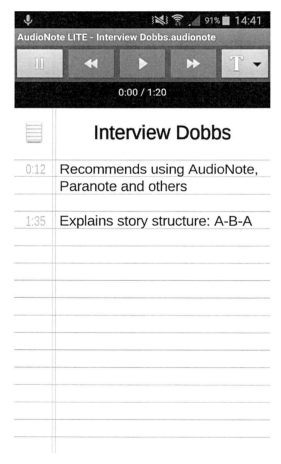

**FIGURE 4.2**  A screenshot of the audio recording software AudioNote LITE with notes and timestamps

## Best practices for citing and quoting

Over the course of your career, you will have interviews that yield quotations of varying quality. For example, for a story on how large ocean cruisers slowly destroy Venice, I once interviewed an environmental activist, a local Venetian. I had done my homework, read a lot of scientific background information and read all his articles and previous interviews. I came up with an opening question that I knew he could easily answer. But all he gave me were canned, recycled quotes that he had given to everybody else. He clearly had an agenda. The interview was difficult, and it was only at the end of the interview that I managed to get a few fresh quotes. Another time, I interviewed a cardiac surgeon who told me a lot of interesting facts on a new resuscitation technique he had just developed. Unfortunately, his statements contained considerable errors; I knew he meant one thing but accidentally said something else instead.

So, what are you supposed to do with boring or flawed quotes? Are you allowed to alter phrases or even their meaning? Can you just shuffle them around? Should you cite verbatim and accept the risk that erroneous quotes will reflect badly on your interviewee?

Let us start with empty and hollow quotes. Those add nothing interesting for your readers, so you cannot use them for direct quotes. After transcribing an interview, clean it up. Highlight the passages you cannot use as direct quotes, but do not entirely delete them. You may want to keep them for your own understanding or for later use, in case you want to follow up with your interviewees and ask them clarification questions. On the upside, this makes it immediately clear which parts of the transcribed interview make good, direct quotes. Part of this early interview housecleaning process is the ability to spot prominent statements that evoke emotions, as is confirmed by Sumner and Miller (2013).

It gets trickier if you want to quote directly. Your top priority should be to get your facts right. The *Guardian*'s former editor and owner, C.P. Scott, famously expressed this as follows: "Comment is free, but facts are sacred" (Scott 1921:35). While to its originator a quote might represent a comment, you as a journalist must treat it as a fact. As such, you must not tinker with it – with a few exceptions, that is.

If the quote contains mistakes that you intentionally want to leave as they are, you can employ the adverb *sic*, which is Latin for *sic erat scriptum*, and literally translates to "it was written exactly this way". Insert *sic* in brackets right after the mistake in the quote. This indicates that you are not accidentally misquoting the person. If used frequently in the same quote, readers might get the impression that the quote's originator is incompetent; thus, you will often find multiple occurrences of *sic* in articles on politics, predominantly in opinion pieces. The following example highlights this particular use of the adverb:

> So perhaps someone would be kind enough to lend them a dictionary, or at least a lightbulb to illuminate the room that houses the computer

they use for typing out their press releases. . . . One endearing example: "I welcome the O'Farrell governments [sic] ringing endorsement [sic] of the Gillard Governemt's [sic] first Federal Labor budge [possibly sic, but it's hard to be sure]."

*(Jeffrey 2011)*

Clearly, Jeffrey (2011) is mocking the originator of the quote.

Square brackets represent another best practice of quoting. Whenever you insert words that did not appear in the quotation, you put them in square brackets. Brackets contain your own comments and explanations. For instance, if your interlocutor used a jargon word that might not be familiar to your audience, you can briefly explain it in your own words in square brackets immediately after the jargon word. Be sure your explanation is as short as possible, such as one or two words. This way, you will preserve the quote's readability. The previous quote also contained ellipses, which indicate that you have omitted part of a quote. You can safely do this as long as you do not separate the interviewee's words from their context, which ultimately changes the quote's meaning.

Cleaning up your quotes is allowed as long as they keep their meaning. For example, if your interviewee corrects herself or starts a sentence but does not finish it, keep only the corrected wording. Also, remove all filler words such as *um, well, you know, like* or *basically*, because they distract your readers and add nothing to the quote's message. The same is true of swear words. Remove all that clutter, unless you want to show your readers that an interviewee was insecure, angry, hesitant or nervous. If in doubt, you should always get back to your commissioning editor to make sure you respect the publication's editorial policy with regard to editing quotes.

Once you have added explanations and cleaned up your quotes, how do you format them? Enclose the originator's statements between double quotation marks. If your interviewee cites another quotation in her statement, put this quotation in single quotation marks.

Once the quote ends, attribute it to its originator by using one of the many attribution verbs. There is no better word than *say* for this. It is neutral and free of emotions. Verbs such as *comment, state, confirm, affirm, explain, mention* and *note* work as well, but they are a bit more context dependent, as not everybody who is saying something necessarily *explains* or *affirms* what they are saying. Avoid value-laden verbs like *cry, sigh, curse* and *hiss*, as they imply emotions and portray the person you quote in a biased way. I would recommend leaving those verbs to the fiction writers, although even the famous fiction writer Elmore Leonard discouraged writers from using them because they threaten a writer's invisibility: "The line of dialogue belongs to the character; the verb is the writer sticking his nose in. But said is far less intrusive than grumbled, gasped, cautioned, lied" (Leonard 2001).

Be sure the paragraphs you fill with quotes are well-balanced and clear; use only one interviewee's quotes per paragraph. More voices would distract and confuse your readers, and it should always be clear whom a statement belongs to. If you are writing a long-form article, you may also want to alternate between direct and indirect speech, as too many direct quotes can clutter your text. Richard Craig tells me that his preference, whenever possible, is using direct quotes. You can overdo it to the point that it sounds like a Q&A, so sometimes an indirect quote works better. Most important, Craig says you should look at how well your interviewee explains a topic. He recommends you then pragmatically choose whether to directly quote or paraphrase your interviewee, depending on what is most appropriate for clarity (Craig 2015).

## Case study: an interview with a famous scientist

In November 2014, the Hollywood movie *Interstellar* was officially released. Scientists widely praised it for accurately depicting scientific concepts such as black holes, wormholes and time dilatation. At the same time, theoretical physicist Kip Thorne published a book to accompany the movie titled *The Science of Interstellar*. Thorne's book provides scientific explanations for the movie. Thorne's role in the production of the movie was substantial; not only had he come up with an original treatment that served as a basis of the screenplay subsequently written by Jonathan Nolan and co-written by Christopher Nolan, but he was also an executive producer of the movie and, most important, a scientific advisor to director Christopher Nolan.

One of the people who received an early copy of Thorne's book was *Science* magazine's Daniel Clery, then deputy news editor. In the run-up to the release of the movie, Clery interviewed Thorne on his initial vision and how it eventually made it into the movie. The resulting Q&A-style interview (Clery 2014) was published in *Science* one week after the official US and UK releases of the movie. The full article appears in the appendix at the end of the book.

In a personal interview, Daniel Clery (2015) talked with me about his interviewing experience with Kip Thorne and explained his interviewing techniques as well as his views on successful interviews. When asked how he prepared for the interview, Clery, who is also a theoretical physicist, responded:

> I contacted the book publisher and said "This is really interesting, I would love to interview Kip Thorne before the movie comes out." I think they went back to Kip Thorne, and then they came back to me and said "Sure, you can interview him – but you have to go and see the film first." I was only too happy to go and see the film. So they got me a ticket to the press screening, which was in an IMAX

cinema in London, and I went along to the press screening, which was on a Monday before the movie came out on Friday. So I saw the film on Monday, and then they lined up a time to speak with Kip Thorne on Tuesday. By then, I had a lot more information. I had read his interview in *WIRED*, I had the book, so I started reading the book before interviewing him, and the whole first chapter is all about the process of how he came up with this idea. There was quite a lot of background information in the book, which is very useful. By Tuesday afternoon, I had done a fair bit of research and was ready to talk to him.

Clery confirms there are four phases of setting up and conducting an interview, all of which demand a different amount of time:

1   Doing research.
2   Arranging the actual interview.
3   Conducting the interview.
4   Transcribing the interview.

Ideally, the most of the time goes into researching. Second is transcribing the interview, which can take several hours. Conducting the interview is actually quite short, as most interviewees do not grant you more than one hour. Clery subsequently explains how he allocated his time for the Thorne interview, although he acknowledges that in this instance, transcribing took relatively little time:

> For an interview like the one with Kip Thorne, you will work for a couple of days, maybe, just gathering online material and reading before you conduct the interview. The interview itself might take 45 minutes, an hour tops. Transcribing and writing it down is quite quick, compared to doing your research – maybe a couple of hours.

If you read the article in the appendix, it immediately becomes evident that all of Clery's (2014) questions are open-ended. Clery comments on how many questions he had prepared, and he also expands on why not all of them were published and how he selected the ones for publication:

> Initially, I prepared probably ten or twelve questions. In the [end], some of the answers to those questions just were not very interesting, so they got consigned to the delete box. Sometimes, I have merged answers to different questions into one answer as it were, so [I've] just taken out the question because sometimes he [Thorne] answered one of my forthcoming questions in the answer to another question.

Clery also explains why he preferred to ask open-ended questions, all of which made it made it into the article:

> I prefer to ask open-ended questions, because I would love my inter-viewees to say things that I am not expecting, to surprise me with something I didn't already know. Because you do a lot of research, you think you know what people are going to say, so it's quite nice when people are starting to tell anecdotes or informal, funny things that happened while this research was going on. That, to me, is gold dust. That's what you want people to say. You want people to say things off the cuff, in colloquial language. That is the sort of quote that makes a piece really come to life, and you get that by it being more like a con-versation than yes-or-no answers. A yes-or-no answer, to me, is a failed question: Because you don't learn anything new, you probably even know the yes or no already. But you are not looking for confirmation, you are looking for a quote.

## Summary

Journalism without interviews is unthinkable. As stated in the second chap-ter, people are the single best source for science stories. In science journal-ism, study authors can be a good starting point, but be sure to also interview independent researchers that can comment on these findings. Scientists often have their own agendas and try to advertise their work due to motivations like raising funds. Also, keep in mind that interviewing the same number of scientists from each camp does not automatically guarantee real journalistic balance, especially when one camp has substantially fewer members than the other.

Preparation is key. A catalogue of questions is helpful, but it should serve mainly as a guideline. You should listen actively and then be able to deviate from the catalogue, asking follow-up questions and going into the inter-viewee's affirmations whenever appropriate. At the time the interview starts, the technical equipment must be ready. If you use audio recorders or smart-phones, the batteries must be fully loaded and memory cards should be wiped before starting. Also, bringing extra batteries and memory cards is a must. Indexing the interview while recording pays off, as it can significantly speed up the transcription process afterward. Moreover, being able to write shorthand comes in handy when the technical equipment breaks, although taking notes consumes a lot of your concentration and may interrupt the interview flow.

Being empathic and establishing a relationship with the interviewee will most likely result in better quotes; if that is not the case, you can also directly ask for metaphors, analogies and anecdotes. Sometimes, flattery and humour work wonders. Generally, open-ended questions yield better answers than closed-ended ones, although the latter type is often helpful in confirming facts. Leading questions are to be avoided under most circumstances, and you should ask difficult and controversial questions near the end of the interview, as they may upset interviewees and lead them to abandon the interview. Whenever you can, conduct face-to-face interviews; video calls are second best, followed by phone calls. Use email interviews only as a last resort.

## Review questions

- What are the four principles of interviewing?
- What should your interview kit contain?
- What are the main types of questions and their sub-types?
- Would you rather interview someone on the phone or in person?
- Which question types should you ask your interviewees?
- When is it appropriate to ask leading or assumptive questions?
- When should you transcribe your interviews?
- When should you paraphrase someone and when should you quote directly?
- How can you get a shy person to talk?
- What are valid reasons to alter interview statements?

## Exercises

- Pick a current science paper that interests you. Find the PI and one independent expert, and research everything about them.
- Alternately, find a scientist at your university who wrote an interesting paper (again, look her up).
- Prepare a list of questions you would like to ask this person regarding the paper.
- Try to set an appointment for an interview. State the purpose, record the interview and be sure to mention that you are recording.
- Download at least one recording app (most have limited free versions) and get acquainted with it. Use it to interview a classmate; then switch roles.
- Take one profile from the Profiles in Science column (see Links) and find out which purpose each quote serves. Does it advance the scientist's personal story, or does it explain the science?
- Take that same column and extract all quotes and paraphrases. What is the ratio quotes to paraphrases?
- Take that same column and reverse-engineer all interview-obtained quotes, paraphrases and passages. Can you guess what type of question led to the answer?

## Reading list

Adams, S. and Hicks, W. (2009) *Interviewing for Journalists*. 2nd edition. London: Routledge

Blum, D., Knudson, M. and Henig, R.M. (eds.) (2006) *A Field Guide for Science Writers*. 2nd edition. New York: Oxford University Press

Bubnoff, von A. (2013) Getting the story, and getting it right, In Hayden, T. and Nijhuis, M. (eds.) *The Science Writers' Handbook*. Boston, MA: Da Capo Press, 40–52

Cartwright, M. (2009) *Teeline Gold Standard for Journalists*. Oxford: Heinemann

Mencher, M. (2011) Interviewing principles and practices, In Mencher, M. (ed.) *News Reporting and Writing*. 12th edition. New York: McGraw-Hill, 293–320

Sumner, D.E. and Miller, H.G. (2009) *Feature and Magazine Writing: Action, Angle and Anecdotes*. Chichester: John Wiley & Sons

Wilson, J. and Tucker, L. (2013) *NCTJ Shorthand Video* [Online Video] Available at: www.youtube.com/watch?v=S9_5Q1QrjeE [date accessed 11 August 2015]

## Links

BBC Academy interviewing (video series): www.bbc.co.uk/academy/journalism/skills/interviewing

The *New Yorker* profiles archive: www.newyorker.com/magazine/profiles

The *New York Times* Profiles in Science: www.nytimes.com/column/profiles-in-science

## References

Adams, S. and Hicks, W. (2009) *Interviewing for Journalists*. 2nd edition. London: Routledge

Bradshaw, P. and Rohumaa, L. (2013) Technology, In Bradshaw, P. and Rohumaa, L. (eds.) *The Online Journalism Handbook*. Harlow: Pearson, 15–28

Bubnoff, von A. (2013) Getting the story, and getting it right, In Nijhuis, M. (ed.) *The Science Writers' Handbook*. Boston, MA: Da Capo Press, 40–52

Carpenter, S. (2015) Personal phone conversation on 31 July 2015

Clery, D. (2014) The theoretical physicist behind Interstellar, *Science*, vol. 346, no. 6211, 800–801

Clery, D. (2015) Personal phone conversation on 13 August 2015

Craig, R. (2015) Personal phone conversation on 23 September 2015

Friedman, A. (2013) The art of the interview, *Columbia Journalism Review* [Online] Available at: www.cjr.org/realtalk/the_art_of_the_interview.php [date accessed 12 December 2016]

Goldacre, B. (2016) Personal phone conversation on 25 July 2016

Greenslade, R. (2010) The shortcomings of shorthand, *The Guardian* [Online] Available at: www.theguardian.com/media/greenslade/2010/dec/08/journalism-education-dailytelegraph [date accessed 11 August 2015]

Hunter, M.L. (2016) Personal Skype conversation on 13 July 2016

Jeffrey, J. (2011) Sic joke, *The Australian* [Online] Available at: www.theaustralian.com.au/opinion/strewth/sic-joke/story-e6frgdk6–1226109352225 [date accessed 29 August 2015]

Kunzig, R. (2006) Gee whiz science writing, In Blum, D., Knudson, M. and Henig, R.M. (eds.) *A Field Guide for Science Writers*. 2nd edition. New York: Oxford University Press, 126–131

Leonard, E. (2001) Writers on writing: Easy on the adverbs, exclamation points and especially hooptedoodle, *The New York Times* [Online] Available at: www.nytimes.com/2001/07/16/arts/writers-writing-easy-adverbs-exclamation-points-especially-hooptedoodle.html [date accessed 12 December 2016]

Mencher, M. (2011) Interviewing principles and practices, In Mencher, M. (ed.) *News Reporting and Writing*. 12th edition. New York: McGraw-Hill, 293–320

The New York Times (1999) How to write a profile feature article, *The New York Times (Student Voices)* [Online] Available at: www.nytimes.com/learning/students/writing/voices.html [date accessed 1 August 2015]

Orzel, C. (2013) How journalists can help the scientists they interview, *Physicsfocus.org Blog* [Online] Available at: http://physicsfocus.org/chad-orzel-how-journalists-can-help-the-scientists-they-interview/ [date accessed 24 October 2016]

Scanlan, C. (2013) How journalists can become better interviewers, *Poynter* [Online] Available at: www.poynter.org/news/media-innovation/205518/how-journalists-can-become-better-interviewers/ [date accessed 4 August 2015]

Scott, C.P. (1921) A hundred years, *The Manchester Guardian*, 5 May 1921, p. 35 [Online] Available at: https://archive.org/stream/701344-100-years-cp-scott [date accessed 29 August 2015]

Sumner, D.E. and Miller, H.G. (2013) *Feature and Magazine Writing: Action, Angle and Anecdotes*. 3rd edition. Chichester: John Wiley & Sons

White, W. (1989) Her deepness, *The New Yorker* [Online] Available at: www.newyorker.com/magazine/1989/07/03/deepness [date accessed 1 August 2015]

# 5

# WRITING ABOUT SCIENCE FOR MAGAZINES

**What you will learn in this chapter:**

- Foundations of magazine features
- Types of magazine features
- How to structure a magazine feature
- Crafting effective beginnings, endings and transitions
- Anecdotes
- Writing narrative for science features
- Magazine feature language
- Outlines
- Case study: analysing an award-winning feature

## Introduction

Feature writing is a lot of fun. It allows you to use creative structures and vivid anecdotes and expand on the issues. While there are shorter features, the longer ones allow you to do more reporting and portray science in its context. Writing hard (and especially short) news items is easier as it is much more formulaic, but this allows for less creativity. The difference between features and news stories, however, is not the length, as *Nature*'s senior physical sciences reporter Davide Castelvecchi told me:

> The primary distinction between feature story and news story is not length but structure, tone, voice and style.
>
> *(Castelvecchi 2016)*

The tone, voice and style depend on many factors: your story, the type of text, the publication you work for and, especially, you as an author. While hard news stories are supposed to be objective and hence reveal as little as possible about your voice, in magazines, your voice as a writer is actually sought after, as journalism professor David Sumner states:

> Every magazine has its own editorial personality. You have to write for the magazine, and I think magazines are expected to have a point of view. Particularly political magazines expect their writers to assume a certain point of view. It is not so much outright stating opinions, but it comes through in the sources you use and who you quote.
>
> *(Sumner 2015)*

Although news stories starkly differ from feature narrative stories in structure and style, the topics and news factors connect them. Also, their topicality makes science news items legitimate sources of inspiration and often lead to more profound stories with interesting themes. At the same time, features allow you to expand on the topics, conduct more research, interview more scientists and provide more background information and context. In terms of questions answered, news stories provide answers to the *what* of an issue, and features additionally shed light on the *why* (Nick Morris in Pape and Featherstone 2006).

The first section of this chapter covers the building blocks of good features, such as the creative anecdotal leads, back-circling endings and nutgraphs, as well as the "hard science" parts, such as explanatory blocks. In the next section, you will get to know some of the most common feature types and learn about their characteristics and when to use them.

Since I have argued how important structures are in features, you will also find a section dedicated to structuring techniques for features. The most basic structure, which alternates between an individual case example and explaining the science, works well for many features and will get you started easily. Also, hooking your reader from the beginning is crucial, so there is a section on how you can craft compelling leads. I also discuss endings, because unlike with news stories, features' endings are one of the most important parts. They sew your story together and ideally leave your readers with a satisfactory feeling that all issues are resolved.

Anecdotes are little stories within your stories that you can only get through interviews. They are so important that an entire section is dedicated to what makes good anecdotes, where you can get them and how you best put them down on paper. Structure, beginnings, endings and anecdotes are the essence of creativity in feature stories.

Even more than classically structured feature stories, narratives strongly focus on characters and their goals, conflicts and journey to achieving these goals. Your audience can remember narratives easier than bare scientific facts. Hence, if you create a blend of both worlds, your science article becomes memorable, provided the raw material you have gathered lends itself to be told in a narrative way. In order to tell such stories, you will also have to have a firm command of the English language. That is why this chapter includes another section with advice on how you can most effectively employ language to convey complex science and at the same time entice your readers.

After reviewing outlining techniques that help you put your raw material in order and select only the relevant material, I dissect part of Hillary Rosner's award-winning science story on genetics and conservation and check it for the elements discussed in the previous sections of this chapter.

## Foundations of magazine features

Feature stories allow you to expand on a topic, dig deeper and look at that topic from a specific angle while allowing your readers to see your story in a bigger context. That is why you have to do much more reporting for features than for traditional news stories. Also, you will need to structure features differently than hard news stories. Following the inverted pyramid, a typical news lead is supposed to present the most important facts upfront. This approach immediately informs the reader, but it also removes all the tension from a story. Writing a feature story using this pattern would be a mistake. This is where storytelling comes into play: Release the right amount of information at the right time, and intersperse storytelling elements with hard facts. For example, some science features revolve around a scientist in pursuit of a discovery that may change the world or our understanding of it. Others portray patients in need of a cure for an incurable illness. What most of them have in common is that they have a human element readers can relate to. In contrast to short news items, as a feature writer you will need to keep your readers interested over a long period of time. Due to all these differences, some define features as "anything that isn't news" (Pape and Featherstone 2006:2). But features are often based on a recent event to make them newsworthy, so they are inextricably tied to news. More than a century ago, Harry Harrington, a journalism professor, and Theodore Frankenberg, a journalist with the Ohio State Journal, described features' relationship to news as follows:

> To feature or play up a story is to give some element of it unusual prominence, because of its freshness, setting or breadth of appeal. The feature of a story is its most interesting detail as introduced into the first paragraph. A feature story is one in which the news element is made subordinate.
>
> *(Harrington and Frankenberg 1912:294)*

Today, this definition is mostly still valid, but the part on revealing the most interesting detail in the first paragraph is not necessarily true anymore; you usually withhold that information at the very beginning. If you revealed everything upfront, keeping your readers' attention would prove difficult, as features are typically much longer than news stories. They typically range from 600 to 2,000 words (Pape and Featherstone 2006). But there really is no upper limit, as some award-winning stories even run from 5,000 to 10,000 words.

What length works best depends on your story. The same is true of the type of feature you employ for telling it. But you can find recurring elements that work in most stories; for example, good quotes and anecdotes are necessary elements. Instead of a hard news lead, you will need to hook your reader with an enticing lead: Quote somebody, tell an anecdote, dispel a myth or cinematically describe the scenery your story unfolds in. The lead is the point where your readers decide whether they want to invest the time to read the whole story.

Endings are just as important: They have to be satisfactory, which means every open conflict or issue should be resolved to give your readers some sense of closure. If your lead introduced a scientist who fights the FDA to get a new drug accepted, your ending should take up that fight again and state whether she won or lost it.

While the lead introduces a specific instance or manifestation of a larger issue, nutgraphs (short for "in a nutshell paragraphs") are paragraphs that introduce that underlying problem and tell the reader what they can expect to read about in your feature. They also often hint at the article's relevancy. The nutgraph, which is also called the billboard paragraph, is usually the second or third paragraph and comes right after the lead. Here is an example from the May 2015 issue of *BBC Focus* magazine:

> Your last act is to open your mouth to scream, but no sound emerges. Instead, you inhale super-heated gas that shreds your windpipe and destroys your lungs.
>
> Death by volcano is not pleasant as 12,000 inhabitants of the Indonesian island of Sumbawa discovered exactly 200 years ago. In April 1815, the island's Tambora volcano tore itself apart in the largest known eruption of the historical period, and one of the biggest since the Ice Age. But what happened in the weeks and months following the eruption, and will we ever be threatened by such an event in the future?
> *(McGuire 2015:61)*

The excerpt shows the transition from lead to nutgraph. The first sentence is part of a scenic lead that puts the reader in the middle of a volcanic outburst. The next sentence connects the rather graphic lead to the hard facts, puts it in a larger context and makes it relevant to today's audience. In doing this, McGuire makes an implicit promise to the reader: Read the article, and you will find out (which was the May issue's cover story; see Figure 5.1).

**FIGURE 5.1**   Bill McGuire's feature about deadly volcanic eruptions on the cover of *BBC Focus* magazine's May 2015 issue

*Source*: *BBC Focus* magazine

At some point, you will also have to explain the actual science. Hence, you will need to boil down complex facts and scientific jargon and explain them to your audience in simple terms. This can be a tightrope walk: If you oversimplify, you risk dumbing down the science and boring your audience. However, if you bandy jargon about without explaining it, you might instantly lose your reader's attention. Keep in mind that magazine readers know the subjects in which they have a special interest quite well. Many are subscribers and regularly read about the same topics. In addition, magazines monitor their readers' interests and tailor their articles to them. That makes magazine readers more of an expert audience than newspaper readers.

Catchy, vivid quotes are an indispensable part of every well-written feature, and they help explaining otherwise lengthy and dry science passages. You can, however, exaggerate the use of quotes in features. One interviewee or point of view per paragraph is the rule of thumb, as it is rather distracting to switch back and forth within the same paragraph. Good features use quotes to advance the story and crack open lengthy verbose passages that would otherwise just be the writer's waffle. Good and well-positioned quotes also let experts explain and boil down complex scientific processes, but they never stand there just as an end in themselves.

What will make most features shine are anecdotes. The word *anecdote* means a little story, and you can weave this in as a story within your story. If you can get your interviewees to share their emotional anecdotes and also show scientific concepts, these gems will evoke emotions in your readers and hook them.

## Types of magazine features

Features come in many shapes and sizes. Unlike hard news stories, almost all types of feature stories express your thoughts as a science writer. For example, the way you select your facts, the length of your sentences, whether you employ formal or informal language, whether your tone is light-hearted or reverential – these characteristics form your voice, tone and style as a writer. But they must also fit the type of feature you are writing.

### *News-accompanying features*

The first three types of features clearly show how closely some features are tied to news stories (Pape and Featherstone 2006):

1   **News backgrounder:** Sheds more light on a hard news story; typically published the same day as its corresponding hard news story.
2   **Colour piece:** Changes the perspective of a hard news story and picks an unexpected, often offbeat or quirky angle.
3   **Follow-up feature:** Returns to a previously published story even after substantial periods of time and examines how the story has developed since the original article had been published.

In fact, many science features are (together with profiles) news backgrounders that scrutinise a topical finding and provide additional background

(McKay 2013). Also, this type of feature allows you to be flexible about finding an original angle and story idea: "There are no real restrictions to the kind of question that can be asked in a news backgrounder, giving the reporter scope to think through the implications of an event" (McKay 2013:114). Once you have pondered those implications, be sure to put down your story's core idea in one or two sentences.

Anniversaries are valid reasons to write follow-up features on non-topical issues (Pape and Featherstone 2006), and so are famous scientists' birthdays. This falls perfectly in line with the news factor anniversaries, which Graham Southorn mentioned in Chapter 2.

## Specialist features

Apart from news backgrounders, there are a number of specialist features, such as science, health and education features (Pape and Featherstone 2006). They subdivide health features into two categories. First, based on the assumption that our Western society is generally wealthy, the psychological approach focuses on our psychological problems and their physical manifestations. Second, the medical approach deals with pointing out medical problems and showing how new medical research can possibly solve these issues.

Here is an example of the medical approach: In a feature in *Scientific American* about hearing loss, M. Charles Liberman, a professor of otology and laryngology at Harvard Medical School, explains how loud noise damages not only the hair cells but also the auditory nerve fibres, which cannot be discovered by traditional diagnostic methods like an audiogram. At the end of the article, Liberman presents the prospect of finding a treatment that can restore the broken synapses even years after someone suffers noise-induced hearing loss (Liberman 2015). To the reader, this provides a nice twist, as it dispels the generally accepted belief that noise-induced hearing damage is irreversible. Such articles may prompt affected readers to try novel treatments. So, as a health writer, you have a great responsibility to them, and it is all the more important to get your facts right (Pape and Featherstone 2006).

## Interview-based feature types

Every good story needs interviews, but some feature stories are actually condensed interviews. In its simplest form, an interview-based feature is a sequence of questions and answers; such interviews are sometimes called Q&A (questions and answers).

If you want to write a good Q&A, conducting one short interview may be enough. But you will still have to ask good questions, empathise with your interlocutor and carefully select and edit the answers that you put into the final Q&A.

According to McKay (2013), profiles are another very common type of magazine feature. In contrast to Q&As, profiles are more in-depth interview-based features. Through their human factor, profiles can help raising awareness of neglected issues:

> A profile is a great way to put a "face" on an important issue and cause readers to get involved and care about a topic they might otherwise dismiss. Many magazine and newspaper writers use this tactic in preparing in-depth articles about complex issues.
>
> *(Sumner and Miller 2013:177)*

The historical origin and definition of the term *profile* date back to the launch of the *New Yorker* in the 1920s, when its editor and his staff journalists wrote profound articles on famous personalities. In contrast to those lengthy articles, nowadays there are also shorter profiles, called *snapshot profiles* (or snapshots). Snapshots focus only on specific aspects of a person's life or their comments and thoughts on topical issues, and they typically range from a single paragraph to a single page (Sumner and Miller 2013).

### Columns

At first, writing columns on science sounds repugnant. Science still carries an image of impartiality, hard facts and static truth, although often the opposite is true. Science columns are generally less opinionated than political columns or op-eds, but they still remain a perfect means for questioning and criticising science. Science column authors often single out topical issues such as new scientific discoveries. These authors often have acquired some level of expertise in the area they are writing about. Good columns always buttress their claims and opinions with well-researched facts. The best columns manage to bridge the gap between information and entertainment.

Many readers bond with their favourite science columnists. For example, in his monthly column TechnoFiles in *Scientific American*, David Pogue examines how technology ties in with our culture and lives. Over the years, he has developed a loyal readership, which is good both for him and the publication. As McKay (2013) states, columns "help to create the tone or atmosphere of the publication, and this in turn, editors believe, helps to inspire the loyalty of readers" (113).

### How it works

Another type of explainer-style feature is the aptly named *how it works* feature. You can typically find them in science magazines with a strong focus on technology; *Popular Science, Popular Mechanics* and *BBC Focus* magazine all run how it works articles that explain how gadgets or complex scientific procedures work in detail. They are rather easy to structure; just start from a gadget-user's perspective and chronologically elucidate the steps in the procedure. Accompanying infographics often substantially underpin these explanations. If you want to write your own *how it works* articles, start reading them in the relevant publications. At the end of this chapter, you will find a link to *Popular Science*'s *how it works* rubric.

## Structuring a magazine feature

You will soon find that the essential dilemma of science features is striking a balance between informing and entertaining your readers. This is reflected in how you structure your features. Human interest and stories will hook your readers, but at some point you will have to explain the actual science that initially drew your interest and prompted you to craft a pitch.

That is why most science features are also explainers. This is probably the aspect where science features differ most from other magazine features; you have to do much more explaining in a science feature than in, say, a lifestyle magazine feature in *Cosmopolitan*. Therein lies the rub: If you just explain all the time, you lose your audience's interest. In addition, entertainment has an edge over information: Only two science magazines are in the top 50 US magazines by circulation (based on data from the Alliance of Audited Media from 30 June 2016): *National Geographic* and *Smithsonian*. The most popular magazines are lifestyle magazines that target specific audiences of the population, such as retirees, gardeners, women or men.

The goal is to explain science thoroughly but to keep the explanations to a minimum. In his guide to writing science explainers published in the Open Notebook, science writer Carl Zimmer recommends finding good metaphors that wrap up scientific concepts instead of losing yourself in details: "The most important step in explaining something well is to figure out what's the minimum amount of explanation required for readers to understand your overall piece. How little explaining can you get away with?" (2015). But he also concedes that whenever you are explaining a bigger idea, "it's often a good move to disperse pieces of the explanation throughout your story."

With this in mind, one technique that you can often find in news-accompanying feature stories is alternating between story and background. It is fair to say that this technique usually works. Different authors have dubbed it differently; for example, Nijhuis (2013) calls it the layer cake structure, while Göpfert (2006) dubs it the AB structure:

> The lead is important, because it hooks your readers. Using an exemplary anecdote in the lead works particularly well. Make sure the anecdote is short enough, and use it only for illustrative purposes as it must not develop a life of its own. In the next paragraph, the story should then leap from the individual case to explaining the general

issue. Nevertheless, this structure still tells a story: That general layer shows how the issue is connected to society, and it describes the problems and presents solutions. At the end of your story, you can return to the individual case and draw your conclusions.

The individual case becomes more dramatic if the protagonist suffers a setback or behaves riskily, so perhaps you can even close the story with a trenchant ending. Then you can intertwist the narrative threads using the AB structure: The B part [the individual case; in German, *besonders*] just opens the story. The second paragraph then elevates it to the more general A part [in German, *allgemein*]. The following paragraph further develops the B story. What follows is another A part that picks up the newly introduced B developments and factually, objectively explains them. You can alternate between story and science from paragraph to paragraph, or you can occasionally intersperse longer passages of explanatory writing with B paragraphs, but this depends on your story.

*(Göpfert 2016)*

Structuring your story means also letting it flow naturally. Your readers must never notice they have just made a transition between story and explanation, so you must logically connect your paragraph's inner ideas. If you take too big a mental leap from one paragraph to the other, you distract your readers. As for writing technique, transitions help you connect your paragraphs (see the section Magazine Feature Language for details). Order your stories chronologically, if you can, as it is the most common organising principle (Mencher 2011). If somebody's action causes a result, be sure to report it that way. One way to organise your story chronologically is to use the tick-tock format, which is discussed in Box 5.1. Also look at the very popular listicle and hourglass formats (see Box 5.1), although the listicle is not chronological. You can also organise your story spatially if it lends itself to that, but choose whatever you feel logically connects the arguments and makes your text coherent.

### BOX 5.1   MORE STORY STRUCTURES

#### Listicles

Listicles are articles based around lists (as the portmanteau between list and article suggests) that have long existed in print journalism but enjoy popularity on the internet. They usually revolve around one central idea and include a lead and a closing paragraph. A number of similarly structured elements are listed that support the central idea, and they often include visual elements such as photographs, animated pictures, or videos and short descriptive text. Listicles are especially suitable for mobile consumption.

## Tick-tock

These stories detail the events from beginning to end. Not all journalistic stories can be recounted as a chronology of events. In fact, chronological order might be inappropriate for a number of reasons, as *The Atlantic's* staff writer, Megan Garber, writes: "Timeline-driven narratives are the ultimate show-don't-tell conceit, and, as such, they're particularly convenient as a format for writers who'd prefer to avoid, you know, making a point" (2006).

## Hourglass

The hourglass is another way to structure your story, and it combines the structure of a hard news story (modelled after the inverted pyramid) with a narrative. You can divide hourglass stories into three sections. First, you answer the five Ws and one H and proceed in descending order of importance, just like the inverted pyramid. This part is usually four to six paragraphs long. Second, write a transition that signals that what follows next is a narrative that is usually chronologically recounted. Third, start telling the events chronologically and show how the event unfolded. In doing so, include quotes and witnesses' accounts (Scanlan 2003).

In the sense of coherence, be sure to move your story forward as stated by Göpfert (2016): Each paragraph of your article must either move the B story forward or explain something new from the A part. In any kind of writing, stasis equals death, as in boring your readers to death. Checking for this principle helps you make better selections and sift out paragraphs that hamper a reader's train of thought. Once you have all your elements together and have assigned them either to camp story or camp science, you are ready to start writing, unless you want to create an outline first.

Some feature writers favour outlining their structure before they start writing; others cringe at the thought. If you create an outline, be prepared to throw it overboard at some point. Like writing itself, structuring your feature is a continuous process that will require you to adjust your ideas and shuffle around some paragraphs while eliminating others as you research the topic. Once you submit a finished manuscript, be prepared for structural changes from your editor, too. In trying to optimise the structure and the reading flow, editors often move around or eliminate paragraphs.

One easy way to get started structuring your features is to use the so-called *Wall Street Journal* formula (see Figure 5.2). Also described as the classic magazine-feature style, stories based on that formula start with a human-interest lead and then head over to the nutgraph, which summarises the

```
┌─────────────────────────────────────┐
│          Soft Lead                   │
│  Person, scene or event              │
│  Present tense                       │
│  Length: 1+ paragraphs               │
└─────────────────────────────────────┘

┌─────────────────────────────────────┐
│          Nutgraph                    │
│  Theme stated                        │
│  Answer some but not all of the 5 Ws │
│  Length: 1+ paragraphs               │
└─────────────────────────────────────┘

┌─────────────────────────────────────┐
│          Body (1)                    │
│  Support claims with facts, quotes   │
│  Background and context              │
│  Length: 1+ paragraphs               │
└─────────────────────────────────────┘

┌─────────────────────────────────────┐
│          Body (2)                    │
│  Answer remaining Ws/developments    │
│  Context for the remaining Ws        │
│  Length: 1+ paragraphs               │
└─────────────────────────────────────┘

┌─────────────────────────────────────┐
│          End/kicker                  │
│  Resolve issues raised in the lead   │
│  Outlook on future developments      │
│  Length: 1–2 paragraphs              │
└─────────────────────────────────────┘
```

FIGURE 5.2  The *Wall Street Journal* formula for structuring feature articles

story but also elevates the story to a scientific level, often by stating what is new and referring to researchers' findings (Nijhuis 2013). What follows is an explanatory part, the first body paragraph that throws in scientific facts. The second body paragraph (or sequence of paragraphs) then either further develops characters (in case you introduced them in the lead) or answers the remaining open questions that the nutgraph has not answered yet. The end should, as Göpfert (2016) states, be to the point and trenchant. If you can surprise your reader with an unexpected fact, event or plot twist, this will work particularly well.

## Crafting effective beginnings and endings

Leads and endings are important elements for reeling in your readers and giving them a sense of closure, respectively. Writing drafts of your lead and ending can also help you delimit your story's scope and hence become a valuable structuring tool:

> Once you have created the lead paragraph and the closing paragraph, you have established your boundaries. The next challenge is to arrange

the remaining content in logical order. This is not easy, of course, but the lead paragraph should give you a direction and the closing paragraph should give you a destination.

*(Sumner and Miller 2013:111)*

Leads and endings are the fun part of feature writing, as you can make a lot of creative choices. The only limitation is that the lead has to be connected to your story idea and your themes; other than that, you can decide whether you want to (Pape and Featherstone 2006):

- Cinematically describe the scene
- Introduce the story's characters
- Use punch lines and comments
- Ask a question.

The lead must also match your article's tone: If you want to alienate your readers, write a funny lead to a sad story. Also, beware of asking questions. Only employ them when you are sure you know how your audience will respond. This is why questions are aptly raised in opinion pieces – the writer and her readers tend to know each other quite well.

On a more formal note, the following types of leads work well for most types of features (Sumner and Miller 2013):

- **Scenario leads:** Catapult your readers right into the scene by describing the setting vividly.
- **Shock leads:** Hook the readers by confronting them with surprising facts or dispelling a myth.
- **Blind leads:** Withhold important information until later paragraphs; this excites your readers' curiosity.
- **Quote leads:** Start with direct quotes of an interviewee. This works best when you have a quote that encapsulates your story idea or one of the themes.
- **Direct-address leads:** Drag the readers right into the article by approaching them directly. Using the pronoun *you* achieves this effect.

Look at how Ed Yong starts his article on salmons' ability to develop night vision with a scenario lead. His description of the surroundings and the fish make the readers feel like they are right in the middle of the scenery:

It's November, and salmon are currently leaving the oceans and returning to the rivers where they were born. During these epic waterfall-leaping, bear-dodging migrations, their bodies change. Their color darkens and reddens. The males develop hooked jaws, and sometimes humps.

*(Yong 2015)*

Such leads contain graspable details. With this in mind, you should generally avoid hypothetical leads (Sumner and Miller 2013). In fact, some leads can be completely based on facts and add an element of surprise: If your lead can dispel a myth or a widely held belief, you immediately have the news factor of unexpectedness in your story. That said, what makes most leads work is the aforementioned human element, as David Sumner, professor emeritus in journalism, says:

> There is one rule: Put a person in the lead. If you can put an anecdote, a story or a quote in the first paragraph, it is going to be more interesting than if you just put facts in a story. Overall, I would say that in most American consumer magazines, you see a person in the lead in some way or another. The best magazine leads are anecdotal leads, which are little, fresh stories that illustrate the larger point that you want to make. But anecdotes are difficult to get. The only way you are getting them is through good interviewing and directly asking your sources for stories and anecdotes. You can't always get a good anecdote, but sometimes you can get a good quote or some good fact. Either way, your lead has to point in the direction of the story.
>
> *(Sumner 2015)*

Endings should be specific, too. Resolve open issues that you introduced in your lead or throughout your story. If you raised a question in the lead, answer it in the ending. If your story portrays a scientist who faces difficulties getting a novel treatment approved by the FDA, tell your readers whether she succeeds at the end. Tell them something they did not know yet. That is why interviewing people is important: It yields the most original material for crafting good beginnings and endings. But an effective ending can also be an insight you have gained over the course of writing the article – the logical consequence of all of your arguments and ideas. Just be sure to buttress personal opinions and general remarks with hard facts. In addition, one technique that almost always works is tying in with the lead:

> A good ending has to lead to an emotional conclusion. You have to have a sense of finality, that you have summed up everything there is to say about it. It also gives the reader some emotional satisfaction. You can't leave facts or questions hanging in the air. Sometimes, a good zinger quote will work, and sometimes a good anecdote will work in the ending – just like it does in the lead. Use the circle technique if possible: Circle back to where you originally began in the lead, and tell your readers more of the same story or give them another quote

from the same person. That gives the stories more of a sense of unity and wholeness.

*(Sumner 2015)*

Like leads, endings allow you to be creative. You can also try to be scenic in the ending, if it is appropriate, as freelance science writer Robin Meadows shows by analysing an article on salmon runs. In that same article for the Open Notebook (see the Reading List), she interviews science writer Steve Volk who says when choosing the scenes for his beginnings and endings, he picks the most emotional scenes.

If you want to create a tension-fraught combination of a beginning and an ending, you can withhold part of an anecdote from your interviewee. Start it in the lead, but only resolve it at the end of your article. This will stimulate your readers to read on until the end.

## Anecdotes

Anecdotes are little stories within your story. They are effective devices that help you give complex scientific issues a human face. This can prompt your readers to care about your story's characters and relate better to the story. Good anecdotes are short and to the point, and they frequently evoke emotions. The Oxford English Dictionary (2016) has two trenchant definitions of *anecdote*: "Secret, private, or hitherto unpublished narratives or details of history" and "the narrative of a detached incident, or of a single event, told as being in itself interesting or striking."

Anecdotes are popular because of the human touch they lend to the stories, and there are researchers who claim that human touch and its associated emotions are an essential ingredient of award-winning, outstanding journalism. In an article for *Pacific Standard*, Weldon (2014) claims that, as humans, we are inevitably wired for story. She argues that the brain's connectivity increases after reading a narrative story. This augmented connectivity then persists for days. Knowing about the effectiveness of anecdotes has its downsides, too: "The flip side is that the drive to find compelling stories is so strong and the rewards so great, that it lures some journalists to become fabulists, plagiarizing and fabricating their way into false stories" (Weldon 2014). Weldon then names three journalists who fabricated anecdotes and states that the effectiveness of anecdote-based stories also reflects in how often they win high-profile prizes: "Yes, personal narrative stories are at the core of stories that win Pulitzer Prizes for journalists, this year, and for the past several years."

In science journalism, you can use anecdotes to capture scientists' eureka moments. Some will tell you personal stories of why they became experts in their fields; others will tell you when they first encountered a particular scientific problem. Anecdotes are always personal, which is why they are almost always fresh and original. For example, in her award-winning *Nature* feature about two siblings exploring the science of Pluto, science journalist Alexandra Witze (2015) tells an anecdote that spills the backstory on how the two joined up professionally: "One day, she [Jim Elliot's sister] stopped in at his lab to show him a piece of computer coding she had done. Even though she was still an undergraduate at nearby Harvard University, Jim Elliot was impressed enough to offer her a job working on software."

Getting this good material requires hard work. If you want to educe vivid anecdotes from your interviewees, you need to sensitively lead them there and not just vaguely ask them whether they have a good anecdote for you. It is possible that a question such as "How is it possible that you both share a passion for the same planet?" led to the aforementioned anecdote in Witze's article. Ask open but informed and specific questions, and also ask your interviewees how they felt in certain situations; if the story allows for it, you can also draw on your own anecdotes: "Some of the best anecdotes surface during the interview process when the interviewer presses his interviewee for specific details about a key moment or event. Another good source for memorable anecdotes is a writer's personal experience" (Sumner and Miller 2013:139).

Not using anecdotes is one of the five major mistakes you can make in feature writing. Since anecdotes illustrate larger, general concepts by using very specific actors, places and actions, you should use them in your beginnings and endings. Figures and facts are important to buttress science stories, but what your readers will remember are the anecdotes and not the bare numbers (Sumner and Miller 2013). The best stories and anecdotes implant the hard science into your readers' minds without them explicitly noticing. They also evoke emotions. Look at how science writer Kathryn Schulz uses an anecdote to open her article on a possible earthquake in the US:

> When the 2011 earthquake and tsunami struck Tohoku, Japan, Chris Goldfinger was two hundred miles away, in the city of Kashiwa, at an international meeting on seismology. . . . Everyone in the room began to laugh. Earthquakes are common in Japan. . . . Then everyone in the room checked the time.
>
> *(Schulz 2015)*

Schulz's lead is masterful on many levels. First, it tells the personal anecdote of one seismologist and drags the reader right into the story. Second, the anecdote is ironic because of the clueless laughter when the catastrophe happens. This irony evokes emotion because readers already know what happened. Third, she does not tell the entire anecdote in the lead, which creates tension. Readers start asking themselves: What happened then? Were the scientists harmed? When and how did they discover the real extent of the event? Schulz then gradually intersperses her story with the remaining anecdote. No wonder her masterpiece for the *New Yorker* won her the 2016 Pulitzer Prize in feature writing. Schulz's technique also shows the importance of getting close to your interviewee: She writes in her article that she visited Goldfinger in his laboratory. Where else could she have gotten that personal story if not directly from Goldfinger?

While the scientist will tell you his anecdotes during an interview, you have to put them down on paper. Some scientists will give you interesting raw material that you have to rearrange and mould into good anecdotes for your readers. In doing so, be selective and watch out for the following characteristics (Sumner and Miller 2013):

- **Brevity:** Write short anecdotes. Re-read them several times and eliminate all adjectives and adverbs that are not needed. Anecdotes should never upstage the underlying story but rather support it.
- **Relevance:** Your anecdotes should serve a purpose, such as introducing the topic in a compelling way, establishing your feature's tone or connecting with your audience.
- **Real people and real events:** Hypothetical leads have less impact and are more likely to lose the readers' interest.
- **Specificity:** Be sure to include verifiable, measurable and graspable details. This is your main device for creating images in your readers' heads.
- **Structure:** In its most basic form (and in the Aristotelian sense), every story has to have a beginning, a middle and an end. Anecdotes are not different.

## Writing narrative for science features

A story consists of a beginning, a middle and an end. By itself, this might not be much of an instruction to write compelling narrative, but it hints at how important chronology is for telling narratives. What is a narrative, after all? The following is a definition of what Dahlstrom calls the "triumvirate of causality, temporality, and character" (2014:13, 614): "Narratives follow a particular structure that describes the cause-and-effect relationships between events that take place over a particular time period that impact particular characters."

Jamie Shreeve (2006), executive editor for science at *National Geographic*, claims that stories can be broken down into a series of events that connect the three parts of a story. That alone is not enough. Most important, you will need to logically order these events. What narratives do is make your readers want to know what happens next. It is your story's human factor that makes readers relate to it, so narratives benefit from tangible characters, good dialogue, the characters' conflicts and the resulting tension

(Shreeve 2006). You can also find these elements in screenplays, novels and short stories.

Science naturally lends itself to being told as narratives: It is a process (with obstacles and conflict) that unfolds over time, it consists of specific events and it involves intriguing characters and dialogue. In fact, you can discover narrative threads in many scientific procedures, phenomena and discoveries. Sometimes this is sufficient to roughly structure a story (Shreeve 2006).

That said, we absorb science and narratives in different ways. Logical-scientific communication is not as coherent as a science narrative, which allows readers to understand particular bits of information without providing context (Dahlstrom 2014). Narratives are easier to comprehend as they are part of who we are; specifically, "narrative cognition is thought to represent the default mode of human thought, proving structure to reality and serving as the underlying foundation for memory" (Dahlstrom 2014:13615). Thus, narratives can help your readers better grasp complex scientific issues and recall them. On the downside, skilful narrators may persuade readers by relying solely on narrative and less on the actual science. This works even when readers know that some elements are purely fictional (Dahlstrom 2014).

So, how do you get these narratives? Shreeve (2006) recommends you either directly observe the events as they unfold or you ask scientists for first-hand accounts of such events. As you go, think in scenes and identify key moments and the story's climax (Shreeve 2006). The key moments are the moments of change. In fiction writing, these moments are called *turning points* because they give your story a new, often unexpected direction. That is exactly the device that forces your readers to continue. Remember: Stasis equals death.

Equipped with such a set of scenes and turning points, you can later easily re-arrange your article's structure. You re-arrange because you do not want to give away all the key information at the beginning. Keep your readers in suspense until the climax happens near the end of the story. That is a narrative technique borrowed from fiction, as is intertwining different threads, in which you alternate the narrative B story (see Göpfert 2016) with the explanatory science writing. Connect those paragraphs or passages by tying them in with each other, so the readers will not notice the change from narration to explanation.

The four ingredients of a good narrative are one or two sympathetic characters, a plot (obstacles characters face and goals they pursue), a resolution and a clear temporal demarcation of the story's beginning and end. Your story gets better the more your readers can relate to your characters' conflicts. Also, these conflicts must force the characters into action. Every conflict needs to come to a satisfactory resolution or your readers will feel left behind. If you want to chronologically arrange the series of events (which is preferable), you have to be specific about dates and times (Sumner and Miller 2013).

To get started, you may also want to consider using one of the typical plot types that many stories are built around (Sumner and Miller 2013):

- **Rising to the challenge:** Such stories typically involve a character that discovers and accepts a new challenge (and, in most cases, achieves this goal).
- **Failure to achievement:** The clue is in the name; usually these are not success stories, but they can end with a character who has failed to achieve the goal achieving an alternative goal.
- **Victim to survivor:** Such stories can be an unfortunate series of events that at first harm the character but eventually lead her out of her misery.
- **Chaos to meaning:** These are typically stories that portray characters who suffer major setbacks such as the death of a family member.
- **Saving the world:** These are success stories that often focus on a single character and how that character changes over the course of the story, usually for the better.
- **Love conquers all:** As the name implies, these are typical reunion stories.

These plot types can all be perfectly applied to science writing for magazines. Reading science news is a good way to find the key points (and sometimes even some turning points) of a potential science narrative. Short news almost never touches upon a scientist's motivations and struggles, but you can often recognise some of the traits that make a good story and evaluate whether it is worth following up with a scientist to talk with her and perhaps unveil a good story behind the news.

## Magazine feature language

Once you have put together a preliminary story structure and identified the events, you need to depict them on paper and glue them together so your feature flows. For that, you need a firm command of the English language. Write compelling passages and create powerful images in your readers' heads, which in turn can evoke their emotions. Leave nothing to chance: Every sentence and every word should serve a clear purpose. If a sentence does not advance your story or add background information, toss it away.

It all starts with the right words. No one likes to read a conglomeration of jargon words. Whenever you can, choose simple and succinct nouns and verbs, and avoid overuse of adverbs and adjectives. Scientific jargon words are never simple, but you cannot avoid them entirely, so be sure you introduce and explain them well:

> The subject might be medical, scientific or technical in nature but this should not be an excuse to litter your copy with words and phrases that

> are not in everyday use – and, if you have to throw in the occasional med-
> ical, scientific or technical term, make sure you explain what it means.
>
> *(Pape and Featherstone 2006:125)*

With respect for language, there are a number of techniques that will help your explanatory writing become more appealing and lose some of its dryness. Dunwoody (in Blum et al. 2006) suggests using the following techniques to explain science in a way that it seamlessly ties in with your story:

- Use active verbs.
- Use analogies and metaphors.
- Explain before labelling a term.
- Explain processes by picking out only the vital steps.
- Avoid too many details.

Whenever possible, use active verbs. Use passive language only when you cannot express who did something. In some cases, using the passive becomes absurd; for example, "Radium was discovered by Marie and Pierre Curie." Why use the passive form if you know who discovered radium? Instead, you could reshuffle the sentence: "Marie and Pierre Curie discovered Radium." That said, if you wanted to put an emphasis on the word *Radium* and not on the researchers, the passive form would be a valid way of doing this.

The passive form is not the only linguistic crime you can commit. *New York Times* science journalist Natalie Angier (2015) says that she avoids writing the obvious (truism) and clichés, as that is really bad style. Your job as a science writer is not writing any of these automatic, empty statements; you should rather leave that to the bureaucrats. Her stance overlaps with that of award-winning science journalist and educator Deborah Blum, who suggests you should instead use analogies and metaphors to bring science stories to life. In her book *A Field Guide for Science Writers*, Blum gives an account of how she grades cliché-laden stories:

> Never, never, never use clichés. If you want to write in your voice, generic language will not do. In my class, there are no silver linings, no cats let out of bags, no nights as black as pitch. A student who uses three clichés in a story gets an automatic C from me.
>
> *(Blum et al. 2006)*

Most important, be an economical writer. If a word does not illustrate or explain the science, if it does not create images in your reader's mind. If a word contributes nothing to understanding the idea your sentence conveys, toss it away. With this in mind, delete all expletives and replace vague nouns with strong, concrete ones. Similarly, remove phrases like *there is* and *there are*. Moreover, she suggests you scan your text for superfluous *thes* and *verys* and remove those as well. Finally, limit the use of adverbs (Ann Fink-beiner in Blum et al. 2006). This matches David Sumner's recommendation; he prefers to avoid both adverbs and adjectives:

> You have to use as many nouns and verbs as possible, because nouns and verbs do more than 50 percent of the work in making an interesting story. I stress really clean, narrow and precise writing. Every time I write, I am looking to eliminate a word here and there: You can often eliminate the adjectives and the adverbs. They are two of the least essential parts of speech, because if you are using good, strong verbs and colorful nouns, you are not going to have to prop them up with a lot of adjectives or adverbs.
>
> *(Sumner 2015)*

If you want to make your text flow, you have to balance the length of your sentences, too. This is also known as *rhythm*. The longer your sentences are, the more your readers have to work to understand them. For example, an eight-word or less sentence is very easy to read compared to a twenty-nine-word sentence. The average sentence length is seventeen words (Mencher 2011). Mencher also suggests you find the right balance between the two extremes: "One sentence after another under 17 words would make readers and listeners feel as though they were being peppered with bird shot. The key to good writing is variety, rhythm, balance. Short and long sentences are balanced" (Mencher 2011:161). Magazine features allow more creativity when it comes to the rhythm of your sentences, as David Sumner confirms:

> In feature stories, you can use longer sentences, and you can have more variety in your sentences. News stories frequently have ten to fifteen words per sentence. In magazine writing, the sentences can be longer; in fact, it is even better when there is a lot of variety. Sometimes, I use a two- or three-word sentence – and the next time, I may write a twenty-five- or thirty-word sentence. That creates more rhythm and pace in the writings. News stories just have much more monotonous rhythms.
>
> *(Sumner 2015)*

Some reporters struggle to write adequate-length sentences because they struggle with transitions (Mencher 2011). Mencher attributes this flaw to a lack of command of language, particularly regarding transitional words. Use transitions from the following four major categories, as they will help you connect your sentences and paragraphs (Mencher 2011):

- **Pronouns:** Use them to refer to nouns in previous sentences.
- **Key words and ideas:** Using pronouns, repeat your key ideas throughout sentences and paragraphs.

- **Transitional expressions:** Use them to connect sentences and link paragraphs. Categories are: additives (*moreover, also, again*), contrasts (*however, but, nevertheless*), comparisons (*likewise, similarly*), place (*here, there, beyond*) and time (*meanwhile, later, soon*).
- **Parallelisms:** Use these rhetorical devices to help you link sentences. Start each sentence in a sequence with similar or identical expressions, such as "No one. . . . No one. . . . No one. . . ."

Once you have written a sequence of paragraphs, you can easily test how well they flow by reading them aloud: "You will be able to hear rhythm and flow of language this way, and you really cannot hear it when reading silently" (Blum et al. 2006:26). And, most important, be sure you never condescend your readers.

## Outlines

Most seasoned science journalists do not put much time and effort into planning their features. Over the course of their careers, they have developed an intrinsic sense of what structures fit a story. The more experience you have, the less planning seems to go into outlining articles. The longer an article is, however, the more an outline can help you, even if it is only a basic one that you later discard. It helps you organise your ideas and put the events in the right order, at least initially.

Award-winning freelance science journalist Hillary Rosner writes a multitude of science stories per month. At the time we talked, she was working on six different stories, most of which were features. Her approach to outlining is a bit reminiscent of a screenwriter's method of using index cards to briefly describe scenes and characters' actions:

> I do have some sense of structure in my head. People often ask me, "Do you make an outline or something?" Yes, I make just the most basic outline. For example, I might make a list of the six sections I want to include, but just one sentence per section. This could be something like: "Intro section – in the field with the pupfish". Once I have that list, I try to just write and get in the flow of it. I will worry only later if these sections make sense.
>
> *(Rosner 2015)*

Because Rosner and her editor at *WIRED* know each other very well, they continuously work on and shuffle around the outlined sections until the story works for both of them. Whether you want to outline using lists of scenes, mind maps or a structured outline containing the key idea of each paragraph is entirely up to you. You can also use the *Wall Street Journal* formula (see Figure 5.2) and organise and order your raw material around it. Each section can contain one or more paragraphs, and each paragraph should essentially contain one idea you want to convey. Outlines are an effective tool for selecting information, not for actually writing the finished article. This means you can only create an outline after you have done sufficient reporting.

Investigative journalist Mark Lee Hunter claims that he dislikes creating outlines. What Hunter proposes as part of his process is creating a master file that contains all your research: sources, documents (as links, if necessary), interview transcripts, bibliographical information. Also, you should preliminarily order your data chronologically. You should also look for connections between your files (Hunter 2012).

That basic chronological structure follows the present-past-future pattern but is flexible enough to be reordered. When outlining, you should start with the lead scene, as it is most powerful for the reader, and you should also avoid leaping back and forth in time, as this will only distract readers (Hunter 2012). With this in mind, Hunter provides a step-by-step guide for how you can turn your master file into a provisional outline (2012:68):

1   First, open the master file and read it through.
2   Then, save a version for editing.
3   Now, read it through again.
4   This time, cut material that you will not use.
5   Read it through yet again.
6   This time, cut and paste the material into the order in which you think it should be used, on a chronological or picaresque basis.
7   Repeat the above two steps until you feel you have the material you like best, ordered for use.

You can then start writing the article by sequentially going through your preliminary outline and turning the facts in the master file into written text. If instead of a chronological order you want to use picaresque structure, identify the scenes you want to use in your article, write proper headings and extract the information from the master file. Make sure that each scene propels your story and contains key moments. Also, it should be clear how these scenes transition from one to another (Hunter 2012).

While Hunter's organising method starts with the beginning, other writers start with the ending. Science journalists like David Sumner and David Dobbs prefer defining the end early in the process because they want to know where the story is going. In a personal conversation, Dobbs tells me why he figured out the end of one of his award-winning science stories early in the process:

> I try to identify the end as early as possible. When I finish my reporting, I like to know, or at least think I know, what I am going to end it

with, and write toward that in the piece. Probably 25 to 30 per cent of the time, I end up using something else at the end, but it is useful to know your target. It makes it easier to write and organise things around it. The scene I knew all along I wanted the piece ["A Depression Switch?"] to end with was the scene where they drive to the hospital that I had already mentioned she stayed in. I had to get that out of the way early, because the closer you get to the end of any narrative piece, the less you should have to explain. The context should all be in the story by the time you are three quarters through. There should be almost nothing left to explain.

*(Dobbs 2016)*

You can read an interview with Dobbs on this story in Chapter 8.

## Case study: analysing an award-winning feature

You can benefit from this section most if you read Hillary Rosner's *WIRED* article "Attack of the Mutant Pupfish" (see the Reading List) first. In this article, Rosner describes how one biologist attempts to save an endangered species, the Devil's Hole pupfish from going extinct: He introduces genes not from a congeneric subspecies but from a different species which reproduces at a much higher rate. His approach drew the criticism of some biologists and conservationists, whereas others supported the idea. Rosner's feature won the magazine category of the AAAS Kavli Science Journalism Awards in 2013.

Rosner explained to me how the story came about: She knew she wanted to write about hybrid species and which role genetics played in our understanding of the species, but also about using genetics in conservation. With these topics in mind, Rosner then approached two universities in her vicinity and eventually found her story's protagonist:

I was trying to do a story about the intersection of climate change and evolution, and I was actually trying to do it without having to travel, because I was sick to death of travelling. So I searched the evolutionary biology department pages of the University of Colorado in Boulder and then Colorado State University, which is only an hour away from me. I looked through the entire department faculty in both universities and identified a dozen people who were doing work that looked like it might be in this broad topic that I was looking for. Then I just emailed them all and said: "Can I call you for a chat, or can we meet up for a coffee?" It turned out that I got at least four different stories from just doing that. One of the people that I met with was Andy Martin, who is the protagonist of this story. As it turned out, his research was in Nevada, so I did have to travel. We sat down and I just started talking about this topic, and he started talking about his research. So I had my topic, and then I narrowed it down to a story after talking with Andy.

He told me about this pupfish project he was working on, and I just thought, this is a really terrific story.

*(Rosner 2015)*

I will now analyse the first part of Rosner's article paragraph by paragraph. The lead is very scenic and describes the Devil's Hole pupfish's habitat: an aquifer located in the desert. This is a contradiction and is such a great way to hook the readers. Rosner then immediately brings up a bit of conflict in the next paragraph: This fish species is rare and has survived several dangers. In the second paragraph, she further substantiates the existential threat the pupfish is facing and packs the paragraph with facts that underpin the pupfish's resilience.

The transition from the second to the third paragraph is textbook, as Rosner picks up almost the same line and extends it:

It's hard enough being endangered; being endangered and picky is a deadly combination.
Endangered, picky, and unlucky? Even worse.

*(Rosner 2012)*

In the third paragraph, she then introduces the story's protagonist, biologist Andy Martin, and discusses how he came up with the idea of saving the endangered fish. That paragraph is longer than the previous ones, which is typical for explanatory passages. Whenever experiments are described and science is explained, the paragraphs are longer. What is important is that you vary the length of paragraphs, which induces a change in your story's rhythm. Rosner does this perfectly: The fourth paragraph is rather short but manages to create tension at the end by showing there are opposing forces.

In paragraphs five and six, Rosner moves on to detail how conservationists think endangered species should be protected and how Martin would protect them: by altering their genome, which the conservationists frown upon. Paragraph six clearly exhibits one of the story's main themes: Which role do we play in the conservation of nature?

In paragraph seven, Rosner then adds more context (a panther crossbreeding project in Florida) to the discussion. In doing so, she also makes a point for why Martin's proposal could be valid.

She then draws a distinction between the two projects in paragraph eight. More background information follows, and Rosner explains how a species can be defined in only one short paragraph. In citing Darwin and several other evolutionary biologists, Rosner provides historical background and touches upon the traits that distinguish species.

Paragraph nine shows another theme of the article: What is a species? Instead of raising the question herself, she lets a scientist pose it and she quotes him directly. Also, the quotes loosen the reading flow. Again, Rosner elegantly connects paragraphs eight and nine by directly referencing the information provided in the previous paragraph. This ensures a steady reading flow.

How does Rosner craft such transitions? She tells me her number one technique to ensure her story flows well: She uses her ears to tell what works and what does not:

> The one rule that I do have is: I read everything out loud. That is so helpful, because you can read it to yourself in your head a million times over, and then you read it out lout and you are like: "Wow, that is one awkward sentence." That is really important for me.
>
> *(Rosner 2015)*

Larger projects can be intimidating, she concedes. Rosner generally rejects including classical nutgraphs in her feature stories. She points out that especially in the beginning, the nutgraph can help you pinpoint what your story is about, and it can help you find your way back into the story should you ever deviate too much over the course of writing it. Also, Rosner has one more specific piece of advice for you about how you can create good transitions between paragraphs:

> Don't use section breaks when you are writing. I think a lot of students will lean on section breaks as like a crutch. If you don't write with section breaks, then you need to weave all your material together. For example, imagine you have just taken the reader to this desert in Nevada. Now you are taking a step back and take your readers back to a political battle that happened fifty years ago. But you have to do it in the next paragraph, and you have to write a smooth transition. Only put in the section breaks afterwards. Once you get better at it, you just start using them again. This helps you see that it should really be seamless, instead thinking of sections like chapters in a book, which I think is how people tend to look at it. You should think of them as book chapters only when you organize the structure in your outline.
>
> *(Rosner 2015)*

## Summary

Unlike news stories, magazine features do not just point out the topical part of a story; they also provide context information, a wider range of interviews and a differing structure. Nevertheless, magazine features are often closely tied to news stories, as many have a news peg. In fact, magazine features can be subdivided into news-accompanying (explainers), specialist and interview-based features. Columns are also a type of feature, and they are often based on topical events.

Magazine features often start with leads that either immerse the reader in the scenery or add a human touch. What follows is often a nutgraph that prepares the reader for what will follow. One way to structure magazine features is to alternate story-propelling passages (such as in the lead) with background passages that explain the larger context and the science. If you follow such layer-cake structures, you will need to vary the lengths of the paragraphs to add rhythm to the article and make it flow. Another tool for achieving a smoothly flowing article is using proper transitions between paragraphs. Adding in-paragraph rhythm by varying the length of the sentences and adding colourful anecdotes, analogies and metaphors further enriches the piece.

For complex and longer features, outlining the basic skeleton may pay off, as can establishing the lead and closing paragraph early in the process. As you start writing, don't stick too rigidly to that structure; shuffle the structure as you write. Magazine features allow for a more creative use of language, but always choose concise terms and active verbs that paint pictures in readers' minds. Overall, science features are probably the clearest incarnation of science journalism's dualistic task to both entertain and educate.

## Review questions

- What building blocks are essential for good features?
- What structures can you use to model your features?
- Can you name at least four different types of feature leads?
- What is the most important factor in a successful lead?
- Which technique is most popular for writing an ending?
- Which characteristics does a good anecdote have?
- What should you pay attention to when formulating anecdotes?
- How do classical feature structures differ from narratives?
- What are the four ingredients of a good narrative?
- What does *rhythm* mean in writing?
- What is a master file, and how can you use it to outline a story?

## Exercises

- Read at least three science features and try to identify the nutgraph.
- Using the same features, identify which paragraphs advance the B story and which ones advance the A story (explanation). Compare their quantities.
- Interview a scientist at your university on a current research project and try to get an anecdote.
- Based on that material, write a lead using one of the lead types mentioned in this chapter.
- Find at least one science feature for each type of plot and present it to your classmates.
- Analyse the remaining paragraphs in "Attack of the Mutant Pupfish" with regard to ideas per paragraph, length, rhythm and transitions.

- Pick a science press release and write a nutgraph about its main finding. Then, write an explanatory paragraph to back the nutgraph, and write a transition between the two.

## Reading list

Blum, D., Knudson, M. and Henig, R.M. (eds.) (2006) *A Field Guide for Science Writers*. 2nd edition. New York: Oxford University Press

Meadows, R. (2015) Good endings: How to write a kicker your editor – and your readers – will love, *The Open Notebook* [Online] Available at: www.theopen notebook.com/2015/11/24/good-endings-how-to-write-a-kicker-your-editor-and-your-readers-will-love/ [date accessed 25 November 2015]

Mencher, M. (2011) Features, long stories and series, In Mencher, M. (ed.) *News Reporting and Writing*. 12th edition. New York: McGraw-Hill, 169–192

Mencher, M. (2011) The writer's art, In Mencher, M. (ed.) *News Reporting and Writing*. 12th edition. New York: McGraw-Hill, 140–168

Nijhuis, M. (2013) Sculpting the story, and getting it right, In Hayden, T. and Nijhuis, M. (eds.) *The Science Writers' Handbook*. Boston, MA: Da Capo Press, 75–86

Rosner, H. (2012) Attack of the Mutant Pupfish, *WIRED Magazine*, vol. 20, no. 12 [Online] Available at: www.wired.com/2012/11/mf-mutant-pupfish/ [date accessed 12 September 2015]

Sumner, D.E. and Miller, H.G. (2009) *Feature and Magazine Writing: Action, Angle and Anecdotes*. Chichester: John Wiley & Sons

## Links

Alliance for Audited Media, US magazine circulation: http://abcas3.auditedmedia. com/ecirc/

Nieman Labs, Nieman Storyboard: www.niemanstoryboard.org

*Popular Science* How It Works: www.popsci.com/tags/hiwReferences

*WIRED,* Writing Narratives about Science: Advice from People Who Do It Well: www.wired.com/2013/06/wcsj2013-narrative/

## References

Angier, N. (2015) Personal phone call on 9 October 2015

Blum, D., Knudson, M., Levy Guyer, R., Dunwoody, S., Finkbeiner, A. and Wilkes, J. (2006) Writing well about science: Techniques from teachers of science writing, In Blum, D., Knudson, M. and Henig, R.M. (eds.) *A Field Guide for Science Writers*. 2nd edition. New York: Oxford University Press, 26–33

Castelvecchi, D. (2016) Personal phone conversation on 20 September 2016

Dahlstrom, M.F. (2014) Using narratives and storytelling to communicate science with nonexpert audiences, *Proceedings of the National Academy of Sciences*, vol. 111, suppl. 4, 13614–13620

Dobbs, D. (2016) Personal Skype conversation on 6 May 2016

Garber, M. (2006) A time for tick-tock, *Columbia Journalism Review* [Online] Available at: http://archives.cjr.org/the_kicker/a_time_for_ticktock.php [date accessed 9 March 2017]

Göpfert, W. (ed.) (2006) *Wissenschaftsjournalismus: Ein Handbuch für Ausbildung und Praxis*. Berlin: Econ

Göpfert, W. (2016) Personal email conversation on 21 March 2016

Harrington, H.F. and Frankenberg, T.T. (1912) *Essentials in Journalism: A Manual in Newspaper Making for College Classes*. Boston, MA: Ginn and Company

Hunter, M.L. (ed.) (2012) *The Global Investigative Journalism Casebook*. Paris: UNESCO [Online] Available at: http://unesdoc.unesco.org/images/0021/002176/217636e.pdf [date accessed 14 September 2016]

Liberman, C. (2015) Hidden hearing loss from everyday noise, *Scientific American*, vol. 313, no. 2, 48–53

McGuire, B. (2015) Deadly mega eruption, *BBC Focus Magazine*, May 2015 issue

McKay, J. (2013) *The Magazines Handbook*. 3rd edition. London: Routledge

Mencher, M. (2011) *News Reporting and Writing*. 12th edition. New York: McGraw-Hill

Nijhuis, M. (2013) Sculpting the story, In Hayden, T. and Nijhuis, M. (eds.) *The Science Writers' Handbook*. Boston, MA: Da Capo Press, 75–86

Oxford English Dictionary (2016) "anecdote, n.", *OED Online*, Oxford University Press [Online] Available at: www.oed.com/view/Entry/7367?rskey=6eZD0v&result=1&isAdvanced=false#eid [date accessed 27 October 2016]

Pape, S. and Featherstone, S. (2006) *Feature Writing: A Practical Introduction*. London: Sage

Rosen, J. (2015) Narrative X-Rays: Looking at stories' structural skeletons, *The Open Notebook* [Online] Available at: www.theopennotebook.com/2015/10/20/narrative-x-rays-stories-structural-skeletons/ [date accessed 24 October 2015]

Rosner, H. (2012) Attack of the Mutant Pupfish, *WIRED Magazine*, vol. 20, no. 12 [Online] Available at: www.wired.com/2012/11/mf-mutant-pupfish/ [date accessed 12 September 2015]

Rosner, H. (2015) Personal Skype conversation on 29 September 2015

Scanlan, C. (2003) The hourglass: Serving the news, serving the reader, *Poynter* [Online] Available at: www.poynter.org/2003/the-hourglass-serving-the-news-serving-the-reader/12624/ [date accessed 10 March 2017]

Schulz, K. (2015) The really big one, *The New Yorker* [Online] Available at: www.newyorker.com/magazine/2015/07/20/the-really-big-one [date accessed 28 October 2016]

Shreeve, J. (2006) Narrative writing, In Blum, D., Knudson, M. and Henig, R.M. (eds.) *A Field Guide for Science Writers*. 2nd edition. New York: Oxford University Press, 138–144

Sumner, D. (2015) Personal phone conversation on 26 September 2015

Sumner, D.E. and Miller, H.G. (2013) *Feature and Magazine Writing: Action, Angle and Anecdotes*. 3rd edition. Chichester: John Wiley & Sons

Weldon, M. (2014) Your brain on story: Why narratives win our hearts and minds, *Pacific Standard* [Online] Available at: www.psmag.com/books-and-culture/pulitzer-prizes-journalism-reporting-your-brain-on-story-why-narratives-win-our-hearts-and-minds-79824 [date accessed 18 November 2015]

Witze, A. (2015) Planetary science: The Pluto siblings, *Nature* [Online] Available at: www.nature.com/news/planetary-science-the-pluto-siblings-1.16987 [date accessed 18 November 2015]

Yong, E. (2015) How salmon switch on infrared vision when swimming upstream, *The Atlantic* [Online] Available at: www.theatlantic.com/science/archive/2015/11/how-salmon-gain-infrared-vision-when-swimming-upstream/415368/ [date accessed 14 November 2015]

Zimmer, C. (2015) Carl Zimmer's brief guide to writing explainers, *The Open Notebook* [Online] Available at: www.theopennotebook.com/2015/07/07/zimmers-guide-to-explainers/ [date accessed 19 October 2015]

# 6

# WRITING ABOUT SCIENCE FOR NEWSPAPERS

What you will learn in this chapter:

- Structure and building blocks of news stories
- Science stories in newspapers
- Crafting effective news story intros
- Accuracy in news stories
- News language
- Writing short-form science news
- Case study: analysing an award-winning newspaper story
- Common pitfalls in news story writing

## Introduction

Guess what? Writing about science for newspapers is fun, too. Like magazine feature writing it hones unique skills, such as being able to boil down complex issues in as few words as possible. It is true that in short news stories you cannot expand on context and background as much as you can in a magazine. Also, there is not much room for storytelling when writing short news stories. But newspapers also run feature stories, although their tone is often more serious compared to magazine features.

Especially when you are just starting out, writing shorter news stories can be fun as there is a proven structure that you can mould your story into. That structure, the inverted pyramid, provides the most important information upfront and provides almost no room for storytelling techniques. In this chapter you will find a dedicated section on structuring your news stories using this technique and a list of crucial elements every news story needs to contain.

The key element among these in hard news stories is the lead. In fact, your audience could stop reading after the lead and still grasp the whole story. Writing good leads means you need to be able to answer the basic journalistic questions in a nutshell while writing in a clear, unambiguous way. That is why there are two dedicated sections on leads in this chapter: One on crafting different types of news leads and another on accuracy, brevity and clarity – the ABCs of journalism. The latter section also contains advice on how you can correctly attribute quotes to their sources.

A section on news language follows. Drawing on the experiences of established science writers, that section contains advice on how you can employ active language, avoid euphemisms and jargon and use colourful verbs and nouns. Using too many adjectives and adverbs is frowned upon, and "a cliché is the enemy of good writing, always", as the *Guardian*'s Tim Radford (2016) tells me. The bottom line is: Keep it simple and concrete.

The next section provides different science writers' approaches to and advice on structuring and writing short news stories. That section shows that not every science journalist happily applies the inverted pyramid scheme. In fact, one science journalist will show you a structure he uses to write news features of varying length; his structure is specifically tailored to covering science. Another science writer has transformed his workflow of writing short science news into a provided list of steps.

The penultimate section contains an analysis of an award-winning *New York Times* essay. I will look into its structure and language and how the author manages to make smooth transitions while he masters the techniques that, by then, you will have learnt in the previous sections. Finally, the last section shows some of the most common pitfalls. It also provides a list of questions you should ask yourself before submitting a finished article. These questions address the research, structure and style of your article. Use it not only to avoid the most common pitfalls but also whenever you feel stuck during researching or writing a story.

## Structure and building blocks of news stories

News story writing is perhaps the area where it becomes most evident that journalistic writing is indeed a craft. Structures are much more rigid than in feature writing. What counts especially in short news writing is your ability to boil down the most important facts right at the beginning. If you write for newspapers, you have only little time to write your stories as they are published either daily or weekly; therefore, prefabricated, formulaic structures are useful in quickly producing a publishable news story. In fact, these structures are a bit like moulds that you can pour your reported facts into.

But before you do this, your journalistic homework is due: You should find the facts, interview people and clearly know the themes and main idea.

What you are trying to say? Forget about narratives, turning points, climaxes and characters who pursue their goals. A human element does help in news story leads, but it is of very limited use; as opposed to feature stories and narratives, news stories do not have interwoven B story threads but instead focus on the expository part – describing events and facts.

If your news story gets straight to the point at the beginning, this is called a *direct lead*. If instead your lead is an anecdote that ties in with your main story idea but does not give away the crucial facts right away (the subsequent paragraph will), then you are using a *delayed lead*. Either way, in its simplest form, a news story consists of the following elements (Mencher 2011:130):

- Lead
- Explaining or lead-amplifying material
- Background
- Secondary material.

Here is a possible workflow for writing news stories using this structure (adapted from Mencher 2011): First, extract your main idea from your preliminary material. In science writing, that initial material is often a published paper plus some background material, such as related studies. Think about your main idea as a thesis you want to prove to your audience. Good theses often arise from pondering the implications or limitations of a research paper. Next, carry out additional research that explains and supports your main idea. Order this secondary material in descending order of importance. Now, settle for either a direct or delayed lead. Start writing the story using the aforementioned elements and continuously check for correctness and style. Most important, rewrite your story. Writing is an incremental process.

Obviously, this structure is a derivative of one of journalism's most famous structural devices: the inverted pyramid (see Figure 6.1). With the inverted pyramid, a delayed lead is the only way to create a little tension. The direct lead (or *summary lead*) immediately answers the five Ws (who, what, when, where, why) and one H (how) of journalism, leaving no questions open. If context information is provided at all, it ends up near the bottom of the article, so it can be painlessly trimmed away without losing its main theme. As rigid as it is, the inverted pyramid is still a valid tool because it facilitates editors' work and it meets the readers' demands (Mencher 2011). Now more than ever, readers have decreasing attention spans.

Natalie Angier, an award-winning science journalist at the *New York Times*, has a clear structure in mind when she writes her science articles. Although she emphasises that this structure is not canonical and can and should be altered where appropriate, she also says that, eventually, all stories

**FIGURE 6.1**   Use the inverted pyramid to structure short news stories

should have a lead and a billboard in order to hook the reader and make a number of initial promises:

> I always like to have an interesting lead. The lead is not only where you are trying to seduce the reader, but it is also the part of the story where you get to be the most creative. It's your opportunity to come to your story and think of it as a creative act as opposed to something functional. Try to come up with something offbeat. That is my approach. This is why I object to a lot of ways in which people start stories, like formulaic ways. I hate question leads – it is as though they completely shrugged off the responsibility that writers have to be creative. It is important to have a creative lead. The second part of the story is the nut[graph]: You had a little bit of fun in the lead, and now, in the nut, you are going to tell people what the story is about. The lead is hard, and the nut is hard. So that is when you have to get clear in your mind: What is your story about? Clearly lay it out to the reader: Here is the fun, and here is what it means and why you should care. Basically it's the nut and the billboard. So you are putting everything into those two or three paragraphs, what the story is about and a quick summary of what you are going to tell them. Just one sentence for each.
>
> *(Angier 2015)*

This is your outline, and Angier tells me the technique works with both news stories and features. She then proceeds to show how she fleshes out the structure and connecting ideas and paragraphs, which is how she keeps her articles organised:

> Laying out your lead and your nut is 75 to 80 per cent of your work. Once you have done that, then you make good on what you have just promised the reader. After that, usually you give a bit of background, a history part, and then, from there you are going to then expand on the nut and the billboard. Each subsequent paragraph will be an expansion of what you already promised earlier, and that is a story. If you can master that basic structure, you can apply that to anything, including a profile, including a news story, too. With a news story, you may have to say right at the beginning what the news is, and sometimes you can also have a delayed lead. But then, you have to do exactly as I described: Follow up on that with your nut and your billboard, and then present that in a more expanded format for the rest of your story. At the beginning of each paragraph, either have a very good transition from the previous paragraph or just a good introduction. Each paragraph is basically one idea, and you have a good initial sentence that kind of lays that out. When you are able to do that, your story will seem very organised and it will seem very put together as opposed to just randomly copy-and-pasted together. If you can master that form, you can write anything. These are the tools of writing an article.
>
> *(Angier 2015)*

Another important structural element is the headline. This is the most condensed form of your article that will draw the reader into your piece. It also helps distinguish science news stories from feature stories, as the former often start with "Scientists find that . . ." or "New study shows . . ." or end with ". . . new research suggests". Such headlines suggest that science news stories focus on a specific scientific achievement and providing context is not a priority. Apart from these straight news headlines, the *Guardian*'s former science editor, Tim Radford, has very concrete advice as to how you should craft your headlines (see Box 6.1). With straight news stories, the headline often summarises the main idea; feature headlines are often vaguer and less on-the-nose. They do not tell the story by themselves but are generally complemented by standfirsts or decks, which narrow down the title and reveal a bit more by hinting at the story without giving away all the essential information.

What follows is an example of a straight science news headline from *New Scientist*. It clearly gives away the story's gist: A causes B.

> Honeycomb-shaped streets would stop traffic from getting sticky
>
> *(Young 2016)*

## BOX 6.1 TIM RADFORD: WRITE POETIC HEADLINES

In English, if you are going to write a headline, it better be an iambic pentameter. This is the rhythm that is characteristic of the sonnets and of Shakespeare. If you look at almost any poetry, there is a natural drift into iambic. It has got to have a certain rhythm. Headlines become memorable because they are like lines of poetry. A headline is a poem in one phrase. It nearly always incorporates some kind of literary imagery. There is a metabole or alliteration or some other figure of speech involved in most headlines. In English, perhaps a double meaning, but certainly puns appear in headlines. Also, you would always use an active verb rather than a passive verb, and you would try never to use a gerund or a participle. Corporations and research agencies are very fond of using participles. They make these sententious statements that suggest that they are nourishing science and feeding the world. But the answer is no, they are just destroying meaning by using truly weak language. If you have to say: "He said laconically", then you are not helping the reader at all. You have always to be able to get your message across without labouring the point by pasting on an adjective as if it was a kind of poster stuck on a wall.

*(Radford 2016)*

In contrast, in her feature article for *New Scientist*, author Chloe Lambert does not give the entire cause-and-effect relationship away. The headline is a teaser that whets the readers' appetite, and the standfirst shows a bit more and presents the prospect that this article could show readers how to improve their eating habits:

> Craving control: how food messes with your mind
> There are strange forces at work behind our food desires. And unpicking the reasons why we reach for the wrong foods could lead to new ways to eat better

*(Lambert 2015)*

## Science stories in newspapers

You can find all the types of science stories that you read in popular science magazines in newspapers. What differs greatly is the audience for these stories, the degree to which editors know that science audience, the number of stories published in each category, the frequency at which these stories are published and which news values editors consider.

If you worked for a daily newspaper, you would produce more short science news stories than if you worked for a monthly science magazine.

Topicality is an important news factor for both, but magazines mostly use trending or topical developments as a news peg for features that cover these issues in depth and from different angles. In contrast, newspapers rely greatly on topical science stories and publish them as they pop up. Online science magazines are increasingly blurring this distinction; most of them publish a set number of short news stories per day as well as longer features every other day.

Karen Kaplan, science editor at the *Los Angeles Times*, confirms the prevalence of news items in print and explained to me how fast-paced the production of science news is for her staff of four to five science journalists:

> In our case, the first priority is to make sure you have got the news covered. Some weeks, there is a lot of news, and some weeks there is not that much that truly must be covered. Then we try to take advantage of a "quiet" week and put time toward enterprise stories – that is what we call our feature stories. You don't always know what is coming. One of the nice aspects about science journalism is that we get the tip sheets from big journals in advance, so we can really plan and prioritize our stories. . . . We get most news stories done in about a day.
>
> *(Kaplan 2015)*

When Kaplan's team has covered all the important, topical news stories, they take turns writing enterprise stories of varying lengths:

> Some of those features are short and sweet. Just because something is interesting, that doesn't mean it has to be a fifteen-inch story.

Due to the high volume and fast pace of shorter news stories produced, it is important to be able to set some time aside for such stories, Kaplan adds:

> Everybody gets an equal chance to be out of the regular news treadmill for a week or so. It's not really a mental vacation, but it's just a change of pace.

If you write for a newspaper, you must be aware that your readers are generalists. Most of them pick up a newspaper and read the articles that most interest them. Science stories are vying with other desks' stories for the best positions in a newspaper, and they frequently lose. Political stories are always better positioned and generally end up on page one. So, readers get to read the science stories after they have already read the breaking news and the politics sections. Newspaper readers do not have the same inter-est in science stories as subscribers to popular science magazines, who are inherently interested in science. Bandying about facts and figures alone is not enough to entice a smart audience. That is why all of her staff, including the interns, know that they have to:

> Explain why these numbers and the data support the conclusion that they make, and also explain what are the implications of that research, and answer the question: Why would you care?
>
> *(Kaplan 2015)*

With this in mind, Kaplan demands that all science stories answer at least the following three questions:

1   What is the finding – the claims that the study is making?
2   What is the evidence that supports these claims?
3   Where did this evidence come from?

Note there are no clear storytelling or human elements involved; science news stories in newspapers are more educational than entertaining in nature. This willingness to read expository writing and even learn from it suits the audience well, as George Johnson, a science journalist at the *New York Times,* confirms:

> With the *New York Times*, we assume we are writing for an intelligent audience that is eager to learn new things without assuming that they have the actual background knowledge – although they probably have a background. I mean, they are used to thinking analytically and they are used to absorbing new information. So you know you are writing for really smart people. They are willing to learn some things within the course of an article.
>
> *(Johnson 2015)*

In his longer newspaper science features, Johnson applies a technique of zooming in and out of details, that is, alternating between the general, background information and describing concrete events in meticulous detail. Johnson's technique is reminiscent of the AB or layer cake structure discussed Chapter 5. He also warns that you should not get lost in the details when zooming in:

> I usually think of it as like the view of the earth from an airplane, and you can write at this very high altitude where you are just talking in kind of general terms and large brushstrokes. But when you need to, you can descend a little lower and get into more details and make something come alive and really seem real and more understandable.

But you don't want to descend too much into the details, or you will just lose the reader. I think that is kind of an instinct that you develop over the years from doing it. Of course, the editors that you work with are invaluable as far as giving you feedback. You can figure, if your editor doesn't understand, and if they think you are going off on an interesting but overly detailed tangent, then probably most of your readers are going to feel the same way.

*(Johnson 2015)*

You can see George Johnson's technique in action in this chapter's penultimate section, in which I discuss one of his award-winning stories for the *New York Times*.

## Crafting effective news story leads

The purpose of a direct lead is to hook the readers and provide them with the most important information. You will need to address the five Ws and one H in your lead. In practice, many news stories answer all of them. In fact, how many of those questions you answer in your lead depends on your story. At the very minimum, it should follow the formula of who did what (Hicks et al. 2008). In science news stories, this formula provides a stencil that you can readily fill with almost any type of story. You can distinguish between a number of science news story categories that will dictate the headline, standfirst and lead style of your article. The most common categories and their typical introductory phrases are:

- **Scientific discovery:** Scientists find . . .; research suggests . . .
- **Empirically verifiable phenomena:** A happened because of B; half of the population of X has died

You can apply the who did what formula to news headlines as well, but beware that headlines are even shorter than the already-short leads. That is why you need to keep your leads clean and short by following these guidelines:

- Use imaginable nouns and verbs
- Avoid adjectives and adverbs
- Avoid conjoined sentences and limit them to one clause
- Use subject-verb-object sentences
- Avoid overly detailed attribution (with science, simply choose *scientists* or *researchers* to answer *who*)
- Avoid precise dates
- Keep your lead to between twenty-five and thirty-five words

Here is one example of the first category of science news lead styles (scientific discovery). Note that the story's main idea is that inhaling e-cigarette vapours has potentially harmful effects, as its author Doug Bolton writes in his article for the *Independent* in 2015:

> New research from Harvard University has found that a chemical in some liquids used in electronic cigarettes can cause a rare condition called "popcorn lung", an irreversible and life-threatening disease in which airways in the lungs are narrowed and weakened by scarring or inflammation.
>
> *(Bolton 2015)*

Note how Bolton answers the questions who (Harvard researchers), what (e-cigarettes cause the popcorn lung) and where (at Harvard University) in the lead. In addition, he expands on the what by explaining what popcorn lung means. He does not, however, answer the when, why and how. While he addresses the latter two questions in the course of the article, he omits the when entirely. Given that the *Independent* is a daily newspaper, and given that the article is based on a single study, readers usually can assume the article is being published shortly after the study has been published.

While it is true that a lead should answer the who and what, you should figure out on which question you want to put your lead's focus (Hicks et al. 2008). Knowing your audience is key for this step. Is the action more important or is the character? In science journalism, the action's importance usually outweighs the character's. Bolton's (2015) example clearly shows this, as the researchers remain unnamed and the actual scientific discovery is the article's main focus. There are obvious exceptions to this rule, such as when the scientists are celebrities like Neil deGrasse Tyson or Stephen Hawking. In such cases, beginning the lead with the name of the scientists is a safe way to start your article because you can assume your readers know their names.

Starting with the when does usually not work well with news leads unless the timing of a discovery is crucial to the finding (Hicks et al. 2008). There are rare exceptions, though. Consider the following fictitious example that addresses a neuroscientist's claims to be able to carry out a full human head transplant:

> Two years after announcing the first human head transplant, an Italian neurosurgeon claims yet again he will cut off a dying patient's head and reattach it to a donor's body.

This kind of lead works well if you want to follow up with, compare or revisit scientists' claims. In the case at hand, the main story idea is not to simply present the neurosurgeon's approach but also to criticise him and alert the audience that this is not the first time he has announced carrying out a human head transplant. With this in mind, the action supersedes the character's importance. It answers the questions when (now and two years ago), what (transplanting a head), who (an Italian neurosurgeon) and (roughly) how (cutting the head off and reattaching it). It does not explicitly address the why and where, although you probably can intuit the motivation for such an operation. By starting with the when, this lead implicitly levels criticism at the surgeon's claim, and the phrase *yet again* amplifies this effect. It would be hard to achieve this without starting the lead with the when.

The example also illustrates the basic stylistic features of traditional news leads within a scientific context. A good lead gives the reader the gist of the story without fancy embellishments such as quotes and certainly without being overloaded with jargon, acronyms and terms that need explanation. With this in mind, add the following guidelines to your checklist for a good lead (adapted from Hicks et al. 2008):

- Avoid posing questions
- Avoid using quotes and figures
- Avoid abbreviations and acronyms
- Read your lead aloud: Is it easy to grasp?
- Revise and rewrite the lead after finishing the article

While these rules work well in most cases, none of them is carved in stone. You can ask a question in the lead, but you have to be sure it suits your main idea, and you should also be able to anticipate how your audience will respond to it. Most important, be sure to answer the question in your article. Also, it is perfectly fine to use acronyms in a lead if they are common knowledge, like WWF or the UN. As a general rule, do not use words that are too long or ones that need explanation; there is simply not enough room in the news lead for much expository writing. Make every word count, and if you can replace one word with a more trenchant one, do it.

## The ABCs of journalism and attribution

As a journalist, you need to convey correct information, and you need to convey it in the most trenchant words. Also, you need to do so without wasting space or the readers' time. Failure to do so has consequences: In the most benign yet unacceptable case, you have only misinformed the readers or wasted their time. But in the worst case, readers take actions – for example, based on a health-advice article you wrote – and possibly make the wrong decisions and put their lives in jeopardy. That is why you have to write with *accuracy, brevity* and *clarity* (the ABCs of journalism) at all times.

Clarity means you convey a clear and unambiguous idea. This entails using simple but striking expressions. The benefits of writing with clarity are twofold. First, if you pick the most trenchant terms, the readers will immediately grasp what you mean. This helps prevent misunderstandings and disappointing your readers. If you write *laboratory mouse*, there is no misunderstanding. If you write *rodent*, will the readers imagine a hamster, guinea pig or rat? Who knows. Second, if you write accurately, readers will never feel like you lied to them. This is often the case when gee whiz-style headlines suggest causation but the study points out a correlation.

Newspaper writing, even more than magazine writing, entails being economical about the words you employ to show your readers scientific advances. This ensures your text maintains brevity, as trenchant words will need no further explanations and are often shorter than less precise nouns that you need to embellish with adjectives or vague verbs that demand adverbs to get your message across.

Accuracy is probably the most important of the three principles. Above all, as a journalist, you have to report facts and verify them before you do so. This is indeed another point where science writing and science intersect: Scientifically verifiable facts and processes ideally are the cornerstone of all research. In order to be accurate, you must very all facts before publishing them. Scan your text over and over again for your own or somebody else's assumptions, as they are the most common error sources. The same is true of interviewees' claims (Mencher 2011). Leave no doubt as to what is a fact and what is somebody's opinion. Your readers should not have to guess that. You can quickly fact-check interviewees' claims by recording them, transcribing them, and contacting independent experts who can either confirm or deny them. Bear in mind that their comments alone are not a formal verification, though; you can find more fact-checking techniques in Chapter 9. To make sure you get facts in the first place and not just opinions, you need to develop a critical mindset. Never be gullible, and never take people's claims at face value without verifying them. Question everything, even if it seems a sacrosanct truth. Most important, disavow and question sensationalist claims such as breakthroughs or predictions.

That said, at some point factual mistakes will happen. If they happen, it is important that the publications acknowledge them and publish corrections. "When mistakes are made, corrections follow so the record is accurate" (Mencher 2011:32). Print publications typically publish their corrections in the issue following the one containing the flaw. Online publications typically update their articles by adding a paragraph below the original text clearly stating the time and date of the correction. Corrections clearly point out the errors committed along with the verifiable, corrected facts. In doing so, they are brief and to the point. For example, the *Christian Science Monitor* keeps a page for corrections, and one of its corrections is shown in Box 6.2. You can find a link to the *Christian Science Monitor*'s corrections in the Links section at the end of this chapter.

---

**BOX 6.2 EXAMPLE OF A CORRECTION POSTED ONLINE BY THE *CHRISTIAN SCIENCE MONITOR***

Correction posted 25 August 2015

*Duke Kahanamoku and the one mile-long wave that made him a legend*

The original version of this story misstated that Hawaii won statehood in 1950 instead of 1959.

---

Even if you are self-publishing your articles on a blog, be sure to post corrections. Many blog readers provide valuable thoughts and propose corrections, so be sure to read through comments and post corrections, if necessary, and clearly indicate what you corrected and when. If a publication does not correct obvious mistakes, you can safely dismiss it as non-reputable. In science journalism, this process can become interactive, as many readers are scientists who can often contribute to fact-checking and correcting the science of your articles.

Apart from fact-checked assumptions and second opinions, the best way to obtain verified information is to observe and experience events first-hand, as Mencher (2011) confirms. First-hand accounts are always preferable, but you do not always have a chance to witness science as it happens in the laboratories or in the field. If instead you have to rely on observers' statements, your story is a second-hand account. If you base your story on somebody's account of somebody else's account, this is a third-hand account (Mencher 2011). This filtering of news poses a threat to the accuracy of your facts. The principle of accuracy dictates that in these cases, you should provide the proper attribution.

You should attribute every piece of information that you have not observed first-hand to the information's source. How you do that depends on the agreement you have find with your sources; in addition, be sure to check your publication's editorial policy so your attribution falls in line with it. For example, attributing to anonymous sources is usually not allowed, as the following excerpt from the Associated Press (AP) confirms:

> We should give the full name of a source and as much information as needed to identify the source and explain why he or she is credible. . . .
>
> If we quote someone from a written document – a report, e-mail or news release – we should say so.
>
> *(www.ap.org/about/our-story/news-values)*

Furthermore, the AP defines the following four types of attribution and states that the clearer the attribution is, the better. Please note that the AP states not to accept anonymous sources unless they are essential to a story.

1    **On the record:** You can quote the source by name.
2    **Off the record:** You cannot quote the source at all nor can you publish any of the obtained information.
3    **Background:** How you quote your source is subject to negotiation. Usually, they will ask you to publish their role rather than their name.
4    **Deep background:** You may not publish the source's name nor any of its affiliations. This is tantamount to publication without attribution.

Be sure to read the rest of the AP guide for news values and principles, as it contains precise instructions for how to deal with anonymous sources. You can find a link to it in the Links section at the end of this chapter.

You can easily spot attribution due to the language used to initiate them, such as *according to* or *a neuroscientist states*. Note that most scientists stand by their claims, so the most common cases of attribution you will have to deal with are either on- or off-the-record attributions. You can expect to employ background and deep background attributions whenever you unearth an investigative story and people could lose money or their reputations.

## News language

Language is your primary device to convey facts and ideas and to prove the point you are trying to make – your main idea. As news stories are often shorter than magazine features, you must make every word count. The first rule is to write accurately and concisely. This is no simple task, as Mencher (2011) confirms, so he recommends using only concrete words that your readers can understand. Be as specific as possible without exaggerating. For example, you could describe a surgeon's operating routine by stating it in one of these ways:

> The surgeon opens the patient with one of his instruments.
>
> or
>
> The surgeon grabs his scalpel and makes a two-inch-long, horizontal incision right above the patient's navel.

The former sentence is not factually wrong, but it is not as precise as possible. *Instrument* is too general and vague a term, so it leaves readers wondering what exactly the surgeon used. The second sentence is much more visual, and it is quite easy to imagine what the surgeon did. Refrain from using hollow and vague terms. Instead, use colourful and concrete nouns and verbs. But how much is too much? There are two rules: First, every word needs to have a purpose. Be rigorous, especially with adjectives and adverbs. For example, the aforementioned two-inch incision might be relevant if you are also describing how the surgeon snakes an endoscope into the patient's abdomen. Second, eliminate emotion- or opinion-laden words or replace them with facts. For example, instead of saying "after his death, the patient's relatives were sad," you could write that "the patient's mother and siblings stood in tears." The former expression could be a guess, while the latter is a fact. Incidentally, this way of recounting also follows the narrative principle of show don't tell.

Euphemisms also dilute your writing. Mostly employed by politicians and public officials, euphemisms have no place in journalism. Mencher (2011) encapsulates this thought very well:

> Actually, [euphemisms] do damage us because they turn us away from reality. If the journalist's task can be reduced to a single idea, it is to point to reality. Words should describe the real, not blunt, blur or distort it.
>
> *(157)*

Whether your article reads easily and comprehensibly depends on the words you use. Words with fewer syllables are preferable since they read easier. You should avoid loanwords whenever possible, as Tim Radford recommends:

> In English, as a bastard language, we have a lot of words which were once German and a lot of words which were once Latin. Go for the English or Anglo-Saxon or the Saxon word every time, if you have a choice, because Latinate words tend to have three syllables, and Germanic or English words tend to have one or two. That is the language of newspapers: It is simple and direct. It's a very bad idea to use the words of another language, unless you are doing it for some very specific effect. I will always try to write in English and use the words that are as short and potent as possible.
>
> *(Radford 2016)*

Radford (2016) also states that one of the most common pitfalls he observes in science writing is the use of too much jargon. As a science journalist, you will read and hear a lot of jargon that you cannot possibly expect your audience to put up with. It is your job to understand the jargon, translate it and simplify it in a meaningful way for your audience.

All journalists interviewed for this chapter unanimously agree that over-using jargon is a tell-tale sign that the writer herself has not understood the science. The *Los Angeles Times*' Karen Kaplan adds:

> What would make you stop reading is when the story gets bogged down in jargon. So we try not to use jargon if we can avoid it. Often I find, like with interns, if you see jargon, it's a sign that the reporters really don't understand what they are writing about. If they understood, they would translate it into plain English. It's really hard to do it. If you're not sure, you just use the scientists's words – that way you know you are not making a mistake, because you are saying it just like they said it. So it's not an error, but it's not really helpful to the readers if it doesn't make sense to them.
>
> *(Kaplan 2015)*

The following definition from Oxford English Dictionary (2015) is worth considering, as it specifically pays tribute to the distracting effects jargon has: "Unintelligible or meaningless talk or writing; nonsense, gibberish. (Often a term of contempt for something the speaker does not understand.)"

Correct grammar and spelling are important and clearly fall under accuracy. That said, spelling mistakes can and will occur. Using spell-checker software is one thing, but putting correctly written words in their appropriate place is another (Mencher 2011). In some cases, spell-checkers may correct an orthographical mistake but change the semantics of the corrected word for the worse. Consider the following example:

> Just before hitting the dummy, the car breaks.

In this case, the intention was not to write that the car breaks down right in front of the dummy. *Breaks* is spelled correctly, but the author obviously meant *brakes*.

Your main tool for writing accurately will be the good old dictionary. As Mencher (2011) contends, a dictionary can also help you build a good vocabulary, which ideally results in you being able to select the most trenchant term.

Try not to use all the synonyms of a word in a text. On a structural level, you should avoid repetition; every bit of information you feed the reader needs to be fresh and new. However, using synonyms will only confuse your readers, as varying the terms can weaken their meaning. For example, if you discussed *blood* in the first paragraph and then mentioned a *body fluid* in the second, just for the sake of variation, this may leave your readers wondering whether you mean blood, urine or semen.

One of the worst news-writing habits you can acquire is to avoid calling a spade a spade – or rather, having called it a spade in the intro, to insist on calling it a gardening tool, a digging device and then a horti-cultural implement in the pars that follow.

This practice is based on two false assumptions: one, that the rep-etition of words like spade is always a bad idea; two, that attentive readers enjoy these variation words for their own sake.

*(Hicks et al. 2008:37)*

Be pragmatic and carefully choose the words that best convey your idea. Like every part of the journalistic process, writing is highly selective. Using too many variations of the same term or using loanwords when they add nothing is a sure sign that you just want to show off your elitist vocabulary. This, in turn, would alienate many readers, which most publications (and you) do not want. The simpler you keep your vocabulary, the more readers you reach and the easier you can repeat terms. That is why *say* in attribu-tions doesn't get annoying.

What does annoy readers are double negatives. Double negatives are less clear and they potentially confuse readers. Misleading double negatives are quite common, such as "cannot help but" to express a negative statement (the inability to do something). The adversative conjunction *but* should be omitted. In the case of litotes, the double negation is an understatement that affirms the positive; for example, "this is not a bad idea" actually means "this is a good idea."

It is a good idea to maintain your tone once you have established it in your lead. Whether your article is light-hearted or serious, be sure it stays the same. More often than not, your tone will be serious in news stories, but that should not keep you from writing vividly and addressing all of your readers' senses, as Natalie Angier suggests:

We understand the world through our five senses. So whenever you are describing something, to the extent that you can appeal to any of those five senses, do it, because then people will feel that they are getting the material. You can say what it sounds like, what it feels like, what it looks like, to the extent that you can use all these very embodied images, it makes for a much livelier story. Use very active verbs and do not use cli-chés. At every step, ask yourself: Are you writing on automatic power? The writing process to me is always getting forth and back between let-ting my mind expand and then bringing it back and narrowing it down. So it is kind of expanding and narrowing. Also, you are never just saying the obvious. This is why I can't stand it when people say: "This horrific event". Every event is horrific. Using automatic phrases? Your job as a writer is to not do that. Leave that to the bureaucrats. You are supposed to make this new and make people think again. If you can master these few techniques, I think you can write a good story.

*(Angier 2015)*

## Writing short-form science news

Much of the short-form output in science journalism is based on or inspired by press releases. The upside of using press releases to write short news is that you can easily identify the main idea and angle; somebody else has done half the work for you. While this does not mean that you can skip reading the actual study or interviewing the study's authors and independent sources, the reality often looks different. As a consequence of massive lay-offs of staff journalists at newspapers, fewer journalists need to cover more topics and produce more stories in shorter amounts of time. In Australia, there are not many dedicated science journalists. Joan Leach, director of the Australian National Centre for the Public Awareness of Science (CPAS), observes how the science media landscape has changed in Australia. Leach (2016) tells me that due to the lack of science desks, many science journalists have joined scientific institutions and become public relations writers, which in turn forces lots of PR science writers out of business.

John Ross, a science journalist for *The Australian*, used to write about higher education and was then recruited as the newspaper's science writer. He now writes for both sections. Every day, Ross writes one to two science stories for the news section and another one for the world section. The topics he covers are medical science, including potential new cancer treatments and mental health topics, but also "blue skies research of medical-technological potential, genomics, stem-cell technology and antibiotic resistance, as this is an enormous issue" (Ross 2015). He also covers astronomy, quantum cryptography and palaeontology. Ross's short-form stories span 400 words and are mostly based on journal papers:

> Most of the material I write is based on fresh papers that are being published in some of the most reputable journals, which I can access through science media centres or services like *EurekAlert*.
>
> *(Ross 2015)*

He then reads the study and calls the study's author and other experts. For controversial articles, for example, on science policy and funding of science media centres, he sometimes interviews more, up to four or five sources for a 400-word article.

Ross explains that he does not strictly follow the inverted pyramid for structuring his stories:

> I don't really follow the inverted pyramid. . . . You first try and get the gist of the story into the first few paragraphs and then go back and fill in some of the detail. I do have an idea of the length, but I don't really have any particular blueprint for writing these stories. What I also try is to write in a way that makes clear this story is about claims that are

being made, as opposed to some sort of objective truth – although it is hopefully peer-reviewed and solid science.

*(Ross 2015)*

As you can see, although Ross has no particular blueprint, he intuitively relies on a simplified version of the technique described by Angier (2015) in this chapter's section on structure. Writing short-form news is all about economic choices, Ross (2015) adds, especially because there is little time and space. This economy should be reflected in your article, beginning with the first paragraph:

> Structurally, the first paragraph is a choice about whether it is very straight and you just try to summarize very briefly what the study is about or whether you go for a more lateral introduction which is still relevant but also fun.
>
> *(Ross 2015)*

Being economical should also reflect in your process, especially when you are a science journalist tasked with writing short news. Ross claims his process has improved over time and he has become more efficient compared to when he first started crafting short-form science news. Initially, he invested much time into hoarding material he never actually used, but he has become more selective over time. For example, Ross too uses the technique of indexing interviews and then picking and transcribing only the quotes that will make it into the story:

> When I started, I had a tendency to gather all the pertinent material. I often transcribed entire interviews and only then put it all together and distilled it to the length of the story that I wanted. That is a very inefficient way of doing it if you are running only 400 words. Now, I think of it more as building from the ground up. Ask yourself: What is this piece about? What points have to be part of this story? What quote from the interviews I just made illustrate that? If you think this is a very good quote or this is a very good point, make notes about those and put down the time so you know where to find them rather than transcribing the entire interview.
>
> *(Ross 2015)*

Ross is not the only science journalist who does not use the inverted pyramid. *Nature*'s senior physical science reporter Davide Castelvecchi tells me he uses a different structure for writing science news features (also see Figure 6.2):

> I don't use the inverted pyramid. For articles that describe research findings, I find it useful to use a structure that is a standard for science

```
┌─────────────────────────────────────┐
│              Lead                    │
│ Introduce the scientific problem     │
│ Hint at the status quo               │
│ Human interest: Good but not a must  │
└─────────────────────────────────────┘

┌─────────────────────────────────────┐
│           Background                 │
│ What was known before?               │
│ Explain essentials                   │
│ Show previous studies                │
└─────────────────────────────────────┘

┌─────────────────────────────────────┐
│            Findings                  │
│ Describe findings                    │
│ Explain methods                      │
│ Interpret results                    │
└─────────────────────────────────────┘

┌─────────────────────────────────────┐
│            Comments                  │
│ Put findings in larger context       │
│ Address implications                 │
│ Interview independent scientists     │
└─────────────────────────────────────┘

┌─────────────────────────────────────┐
│             Outlook                  │
│ Where do we go from here?            │
│ What is next in related research?    │
│ Are there unresolved questions?      │
└─────────────────────────────────────┘
```

**FIGURE 6.2**  Use this template to structure science news features

*Source*: Based on an interview with Davide Castelvecchi

publications, which consists of five parts: First comes the lead (or introduction); then there is a background section which says what was known before about this particular topic; number three is the description of the findings, including the methods and results; number four is the comments, putting the findings in a larger context, talking about the implications and including comments from people who are not connected to the authors of the study; number five is the forward-looking part: Where do we go from here, and what is next? That is the structure for covering research news that I learnt during my science writing training. You cannot go wrong with it. If you look at such articles in *Science* or *New Scientist*, you will find they have the same structure.

*(Castelvecchi 2016)*

Ian Sample, science editor of the *Guardian*, provides ten guidelines for successfully putting together a short-form science news article. He explains them in an article that was part of the series "The *Guardian*'s Secrets of Good Science Writing", acknowledging that most science stories you will write are probably based on research papers (Sample 2014):

1 **Find a good paper:** You can discard most papers, as the lion's share are not newsworthy. Instead focus on news values and consider what appeals to the reader.
2 **Read the paper:** Focus on how the scientists accomplished their findings. Are their methods sound and their conclusions expressive?
3 **Check for conflicts of interest:** Double-check potential conflicts of interest and do your own research on scientists' ties to the industry.
4 **Research background and context:** Read related studies so you can provide the reader with the appropriate context.
5 **Interview the study authors:** Explain scientists' findings in plain English. Check your own phrasings for correctness.
6 **Interview independent scientists:** Give independent sources enough time to read the paper. Comments from other scientists will always improve your story.
7 **Identify the main point:** Sift through your interviews and recall what sparked your interest in the paper in the first place.
8 **Write with the reader in mind:** Explain complex science in simple terms. Never talk to your readers in a condescending way.
9 **Fact-check:** Check your own claims, as science papers already contain enough errors.
10 **Write well:** Connect paragraphs logically. Write one idea per paragraph. Also, make sure you actually add something to the discussion.

What is interesting about Sample's (2014) process is that he manages to squeeze in a few investigative elements, such as scrutinising scientists' ties to companies, questioning studies' methods and results and fact-checking all claims. As you have seen in this chapter, the actual process of writing short-form science news differs only marginally from writer to writer. You will always have to identify a study's main findings and implications, you will have to talk with the authors and a number of independent sources, and you will have to give the reader the most important details upfront. As a science journalist, reading the paper you are writing about is a must. In that sense, short science news stories may be shallower than features and perhaps sometimes lack context. But due to their brevity, you can use them as an excellent training method to learn how to boil down complex material.

## Case study: analysing an award-winning newspaper story

Here I will analyse an award-winning science essay written by George Johnson. This article was part of a series of three health essays that dispel common myths and misconceptions about cancer that won the 2014 AAAS Kavli

Science Journalism Award (in the category for large newspaper – circulation of 100,000 or more). All three essays appeared in the *New York Times*. The first one, "Why Everyone Seems to Have Cancer" (Johnson 2014), was published 2 weeks after a report on US cancer statistics. You can find a link to the full article in the Reading List at the end of this chapter. The publication of the cancer report constitutes Johnson's news peg, as you can see in his opening paragraph: "Every New Year when the government publishes its Report to the Nation on the Status of Cancer, it is followed by a familiar lament. We are losing the war against cancer."

In the next paragraph, Johnson compares cancer with heart disease but still withholds his essay's main idea, which he states in the third paragraph, where he calls cancer a "condition deeply ingrained in the nature of evolution and multicellular life". Next, he concedes that there are battles cancer research can win, but when it comes to elderly people, there is not much that can be done. Johnson does not explain it further in that paragraph but waits until the next two paragraphs to buttress his claim.

The fourth paragraph contains two main points. First, Johnson criticises the rhetoric of cancer research in the sense that it creates a false image: Enough money and research will cure cancer for good. He closes with another claim: Most people will die either from cardiac disease or cancer, provided they live long enough.

The next four paragraphs contain a reasonable amount of facts and figures to substantiate Johnson's ideas. First, he refers back to the report from the beginning, stating that cancer mortality is on a slow decline that is much less prominent than heart disease mortality's steeper decline. Johnson buttresses this by citing a timeline from the CDC. He closes paragraph seven by correctly pointing out the exception (the complications of Alzheimer's disease) without losing himself in the details. Instead, he leaves the digression to the reader by merely putting a link. Johnson explained to me how he approaches this interplay between general and specific information (see his analogy of viewing the earth from an airplane earlier in the chapter). In paragraph eight, Johnson hints at the ever-increasing life expectancy and (together with the second to last sentence from the previous paragraph) makes it clear that cancer death occurs at a rather late age: "The median age of cancer death is 72. We live long enough for it to get us." (Note how he correctly makes use of *median* not *average*. Also note how some of his paragraphs contain one or two clear ideas, while other paragraphs substantiate these ideas with hard facts.)

In the next two paragraphs, ten and eleven, Johnson states that other diseases have been relatively easy to eradicate compared to heart disease. He also seamlessly progresses from paragraph eleven to twelve: He ends paragraph eleven by claiming that heart failures such as clogged vessels and malfunctioning valves can be accounted for. Next, he starts paragraph twelve with a because clause that picks up the aforementioned interventions; this clause marks the transition and makes the text logically flow from one paragraph to the next.

Immediately after the transition, Johnson puts in a twist: Cancer replaces heart disease because of the improved medical treatment of the latter. Next, he explains the how and why of his findings. First, he claims that cancer is not exactly a disease but rather a natural phenomenon. To substantiate this claim, he explains the basic DNA-copying mechanism of body cells.

He then progresses to explaining that most cells can fix any errors that occur during the DNA-copying process. In doing so, he uses metaphors such as "mutations are the engine of evolution" and draws analogies such as "like a new species thriving in an ecosystem, [a cell] grows into a cancerous tumor". He closes with a clear and simple statement that substantiates the idea that this innate mechanism is the crux of the cancer development.

In paragraph fourteen, Johnson again employs a simple metaphor, "these microscopic rebellions", to visualise a rather complex scientific process. Note how he uses one or two metaphors or analogies per paragraph. In addition, Johnson explains complex scientific flows in a vivid way. These paragraphs may seem like pure background information, but all of them affirm the essay's basic message. He almost seems to sympathise with cancer cells.

The next, shorter paragraph serves as a reminder that cancer is inevitable and that, all other diseases ignored, everybody would get it eventually. While structural repetition is generally not a good idea, in a 1,500-word essay like Johnson's, occasionally bringing up the article's main idea can be used as a stylistic device. The last sentence of paragraph fifteen serves as a thematic transition to the ideas of the following three paragraphs: Johnson hints at the prospect that getting cancer is inevitable, even if we could cure most diseases and if there were no carcinogens.

The subsequent four paragraphs then expand on a thought these two sentences induced: Even though resistance is futile, the progress in medical research has achieved some impressive results, too. In chronological order, the following paragraphs' statements are:

- Cancer can be more easily cured if it occurs in the childhood (provided it is not particularly aggressive).
- Roughly one-fifth of cancers are possibly caused by infections.
- Obesity and diabetes foster cancer.

All four paragraphs buttress Johnson's claim that prevention is the most effective countermeasure for cancer, if that. He "proves" this affirmation by enumerating the aforementioned examples and cementing them with facts and figures.

Paragraph twenty raises two ethical questions, wealth and race issues, without addressing them in-depth. A digression this late into the essay would have been rather a distraction than a service to the reader. However, pointing the reader to links to secondary information would have been desirable.

The same is true of the penultimate paragraph, which provides an outlook to promising research that might contribute to solving the problem – as far as is possible (remember the essay's main idea). Again, no details are given, and the article is coming to an end. Clearly, the last two paragraphs are less important than the previous ones. Rather, they contain accompanying information that strengthens the readers' understanding of the topic, but it is not vital.

Finally, the last paragraph provides a quick roundup of the presented facts. The last sentence is always your final chance to equip your readers with a final thought and give them a key takeaway. Johnson clearly uses this chance to once again emphasise that there will be no definitive cure for cancer, no matter our efforts and scientific achievements: If heart failure is not going to kill you, cancer likely will.

As such, the end is satisfactory, even though it is not exactly good news. Taking up initial claims or examples is generally a good idea for concluding every story because it lends to your texts a sense of closure that will satisfy your readers.

## Common pitfalls in news story writing

Science writing is a tough job; starting with understanding the scientific discipline you are reporting about, opportunities to make errors are scattered all over the road to a published science article. Are you referring to a study? It might contain errors. Are your sources telling the truth? Is the industry paying them as promoters? Are their conclusions correct? Are yours? Are the synonyms you use correct? Do you correctly write your sources' names and roles within their institutions? Do your headline and your main point in the nutgraph dumb down the actual findings? Do you falsely declare or merely suggest that a cure for a disease in humans has been found, when in reality it has only been tested under limited circumstances in a specific type of tissue in rats?

All of these problems can happen independently from the type of science story you are writing. Mistakes are more likely to happen when you have little time to research and write your article. That is why in this section, you will find a list of dos that you can use as a checklist before completing an article and submitting it to an editor or publishing it online. I have subdivided this into the categories of research, structure and style so you can use the list based on where you currently are in your journalistic workflow.

### Research

Did you . . .

- Read the entire paper?
- Read related papers and additional literature?

- Interview the study authors?
- Interview independent sources?
- Identify the main point?
- Check for conflicts of interest?
- Disclose potential conflicts of interest of your own?
- Check your own claims and phrasings with scientists?
- Double-check any synonyms you introduced and your interpretations?
- Separate correlation from causation?

### Structure

Did you . . .

- Write a relevant yet entertaining lead?
- Get to the main point early in the first few paragraphs?
- Order the facts in a top-down manner?
- Write paragraphs with no more than one idea?
- Quote no more than one interviewee per paragraph?
- Order your paragraphs (chronologically often works)?
- Eliminate all paragraphs that contain far-fetched, unrelated ideas?
- Alternate between quotes and running text?
- Connect paragraphs using transitions?
- Connect sentences using transition words?
- Close your article in a satisfying way?
- Check whether your article logically flows from one argument to the next?
- Read your article aloud?

### Style

Did you . . .

- Employ but limit the use of metaphors and analogies?
- Use active verbs?
- Prefer nouns and verbs that elicit pictures in readers' minds?
- Alternate between longer and shorter sentences and paragraphs?
- Eliminate all truisms?
- Eliminate all clichés?
- Eliminate all adverbs?
- Eliminate all jargon?
- Eliminate all structural repetitions?
- Explain acronyms before using them?
- Edit and rewrite your article?

If your answer to more than just a couple of these questions is no, you should probably review your article. You can often fix the style-related issues in a short time. As suggested in previous chapters, read your work aloud to discover what reads well and what does not. Here is another technique that works: Review the material you have gathered while reporting the story. Have you prioritised events and facts and only distilled the ones that encapsulate your story's main idea? Also, does that mean you have discarded 90 per cent or more of the raw material you had gathered? Another piece of advice: Never submit the first draft of your text. While texts can be over-edited, a number of rounds of editing will improve it for certain.

Finally, never overhype your story. The readers should decide how they feel about a particular scientific advance. They are intelligent creatures that do not need you to spoon-feed them emotions or judgments. With this in mind, Tim Radford recalls an episode from when he was working as a sub-editor:

> I can remember when I was trying to explain a story to a news editor. He turned to me and said: "Is this a revolutionary breakthrough?" The answer is: If you have to put a label like that on a story, it's ridiculous then. Clichés and careless writing are just bad. What I look for when I'm editing is a sentence that will make you read the next sentence. The whole purpose of a good first sentence is to make you read the second sentence.
>
> *(Radford 2016)*

## Summary

There is not much room for storytelling in science news stories. The classic way to structure a short news story is the inverted pyramid. That structure provides the reader with the most important information upfront: the five Ws (who, what, when, where, why) and one H (how). As news stories are vying for newspaper space, this structure also allows the editor to delete paragraphs from the bottom up without substantially mutilating the story. Also, the reader can grasp at a glance the most important aspects of the story; in fact, she could stop reading after the lead and would still have absorbed the whole story in a nutshell. On the downside, the inverted pyramid is not a tool for building suspense or tension, as the lead gives away the entire story.

The following paragraphs further expand on the facts and add more details that could not fit in the lead. Moreover, the lead does not always answer all of the five Ws and one H. In fact, sometimes only the who and what (and rarely the when) are answered. If that is the case, the following paragraphs need to address the open questions. The final one or two paragraphs add secondary material, such as background information on what happened. Although this additional information further informs the reader about the context of what happened, it is expendable without mutilating the core story.

The ABCs of journalism – accuracy, brevity and clarity – play a key role in news writing. There is no room for flowery writing and euphemisms that only take up space while watering down the article's message. When quoting sources, make sure you establish whether they are on-the-record, off-the-record, background or deep-background quotes. There is no reason you should use any other verb than *say* for attributing the quotes. Neither should you consider using adverbs when quoting your sources. Also, showing off your vocabulary by replacing every instance of the same word with one of its synonyms only confuses the reader and violates the rule of being accurate.

## Review questions

- Why is the inverted pyramid still a valid tool for structuring news stories?
- Which important elements must every news story contain?
- Which other, science-specific structure could you use? How do they differ?
- Linguistically speaking, what should a news lead look like?
- How should the ABCs of journalism be reflected in your writing?
- What types of attribution exist, and how should you put them down on paper?
- What are the dangers of using too many synonyms?
- Which investigative techniques should you apply for writing short news?
- What type of lead does Johnson (2014) use in his article on cancer?

## Exercises

For the sake of simplicity, you can use a press release on a recent scientific finding for the following exercises.

- Identify the story's main idea and the five Ws and one H.
- Find and briefly interview an independent scientist on the story's findings.
- Read the associated paper and lay out a preliminary structure using the inverted pyramid.
- Lay out an alternative structure using Castelvecchi's formula.
- Write both a direct and a delayed lead for the story.
- Based on the previous exercises, take the initial press release and rewrite it as a short science news item (based on the inverted pyramid structure).
- Rewrite the story. This time, use Castelvecchi's structure for writing the news item.
- Write second drafts of both stories, this time focusing on the ABCs of journalism.

## Reading list

Hicks, W. (2007) *English for Journalists*. 3rd edition. London: Routledge

Hicks, W. (2008) News writing, In Hicks, W., Adams, S., Gilbert, H. and Holmes, T. (eds.) *Writing for Journalists*. 2nd edition. London: Routledge, 10–44

Johnson, G. (2014) Why everyone seems to have cancer, *New York Times* [Online] Available at: www.nytimes.com/2014/01/05/sunday-review/why-everyone-seems-to-have-cancer.html [date accessed 7 October 2015]

McKane, A. (2013) *News Writing*. 2nd edition. London: SAGE

Mencher, M. (2011) Features, long stories and series, In Mencher, M. (ed.) *News Reporting and Writing*. 12th edition. New York: McGraw-Hill, 169–192

Radford, T. (2011) A manifest for the simple scribe – My 25 commandments for journalists, *The Guardian* [Online] Available at: www.theguardian.com/science/blog/2011/jan/19/manifesto-simple-scribe-commandments-journalists [date accessed 10 October 2016]

## Links

Associated Press, News Values and Principles: www.ap.org/about/our-story/news-values

*Christian Science Monitor* corrections: www.csmonitor.com/About/Corrections

## References

Angier, N. (2015) Personal phone call on 9 October 2015

Associated Press, *News and Values* [Online] Available at: https://www.ap.org/about/our-story/news-values [date accessed 5 December 2015]

Bolton, D. (2015) E-cigarette users could be at risk from dangerous 'popcorn lung' disease, Harvard research finds, *The Independent* [Online] Available at: www.independent.co.uk/news/science/e-cigarettes-popcorn-lung-diacetyl-dangerous-a6767841.html [date accessed 11 December 2015]

Castelvecchi, D. (2016) Personal phone conversation on 20 September 2016

Hicks, W., Adams, S., Gilbert, H. and Holmes, T. (2008) *Writing for Journalists*. 2nd edition. London: Routledge

Johnson, G. (2014) Why everyone seems to have cancer, *New York Times* [Online] Available at: www.nytimes.com/2014/01/05/sunday-review/why-everyone-seems-to-have-cancer.html [date accessed 7 October 2015]

Johnson, G. (2015) Personal phone conversation on 8 October 2015

Kaplan, K. (2015) Personal phone conversation on 9 October 2015

Lambert, C. (2015) Craving control: How food messes with your mind, *New Scientist* [Online] Available at: www.newscientist.com/article/mg22830483–300-craving-control-how-food-messes-with-your-mind/ [date accessed 30 October 2016]

Leach, J. (2016) Personal phone conversation on 6 September 2016

Mencher, M. (2011) Features, long stories and series, In Mencher, M. (ed.) *News Reporting and Writing*. 12th edition. New York: McGraw-Hill, 169–192

Oxford English Dictionary (2015) "jargon, n.1", *OED Online*, Oxford University Press [Online] Available at: www.oed.com/view/Entry/100808?rskey=iyFwix&result=1&isAdvanced=false#eid [date accessed 3 December 2015]

Radford, T. (2016) Personal phone conversation on 12 April 2016

Ross, J. (2015) Personal phone conversation on 9 October 2015

Sample, I. (2014) How to write on a science news story based on a research paper, *The Guardian* [Online] Available at: www.theguardian.com/science/2014/mar/28/news-story-research-paper-wellcome-trust-science-writing-prize [date accessed 28 November 2015]

Young, M. (2016) Honeycomb-shaped streets would stop traffic from getting sticky, *New Scientist* [Online] Available at: www.newscientist.com/article/2110821-honeycomb-shaped-streets-would-stop-traffic-from-getting-sticky/ [date accessed 29 October 2016]

# 7

# WRITING ABOUT SCIENCE ONLINE

**What you will learn in this chapter:**

- Building blocks of online science writing
- Science blog networks
- Blogging 101 for science writers
- Understanding your audience
- Starting a science blog
- Writing for SEO
- Sourcing images
- Case study: analysing a science news post
- Case study: analysing an award-winning, long-form online science article

## Introduction

Online, your most important asset is still knowing how to write a good story. But unlike immutable print pages, websites and blogs open a lot of new possibilities for how you can tell these stories. Also, the internet allows you to get to your audience even better and tailor story formats, topics, voice and tone to their demands. Competition is rough online, as the internet is awash with science news of varying formats and quality.

That is why you need to add web, and perhaps even programming, skills to your journalistic toolbox. Those skills help you harness the web's capabilities to tell stories in interactive ways that are impossible in print. Web journalist and journalism professor Robert Hernandez tells me that knowing how to code is not about turning journalists into programmers but rather turning them into creative thinkers by letting them programmatically solve problems; this resulting creativity influences how they tell stories:

> I'm a journalist first, but I'm also a technologist or a geek, so I'm constantly tinkering and playing with technology, trying to find out how I can hack it and hijack it for journalism.
>
> *(Hernandez 2014)*

This chapter's aim is not to show you how to write source code. You will need a basic understanding of what distinguishes online writing from print publications and how readers interact with online articles; this is what the first section covers. I will then discuss how the science blog networks can help you increase your reach and develop relationships with fellow science bloggers, which often leads to interesting scientific discourses and cross-posts.

Science bloggers' style is more conversational than that of print writers, and they often have a deliberately more opinionated voice. Hence, you will also find intuitive advice on how to style your paragraphs and how you can use language to write suitable stories for the web.

You also need a thorough understanding of who reads these stories. Fortunately, the web provides a myriad of tools to tell you which posts are the most popular, who reads them, where those readers come from and how they engage with your online articles. Some blog networks, like the one hosted on Forbes.com, pay their bloggers a set amount per unique visitor. If you blog for such networks, maximising your blog's reach must be one of your goals, so be sure to read about this in the section dedicated to understanding your audience.

Starting your own science blog is a straightforward way to apply all the techniques and experiment with different formats. Although it seems easy to set up your own blog, you still need to find your niche, think about your future audience and plan what you want to blog about and how often; therefore, there is a section dedicated to those deliberations. You will also have to consider image sources, so a later section focuses on where you can find paid and free images and avoid legal trouble.

The more you enrich your blog posts using the web's capabilities, such as images, videos, maps, charts and interactive visualisations, the more you become a journalist not just on but of the web (Hernandez 2014). Being a web-native writer also means that you know how to employ search engine optimisation (SEO) techniques that ensure your articles are properly indexed by search engines and ranked as highly as possible. As writing for SEO greatly influences your article's language, structure and length, this chapter dedicates an entire section to it.

Finally, you will find two case studies of online science journalism in this chapter. The first is a short, news story-like blog post that is based on a press release. I will analyse its structure. In contrast, the second is a long-form, award-winning science story whose author beautifully employs narrative techniques to both tell the story and convey the science behind it.

## Building blocks of online science writing

Science writing for an online audience is different from print in many ways. The immediacy of online journalism is both striking and intriguing. It can take a monthly magazine 3 to 6 months to fact-check and finally publish your feature. A daily newspaper is much faster, but nothing beats blogs and online magazines for speed; as soon as the sub-editor has finished editing your story, she can publish it online. Reader feedback is also immediate and interactive. Readers can comment on your articles, point out factual errors or express whether they like your story or not. They can post follow-up questions, and you can answer those if you wish. In the print-only era, the only way readers could provide feedback was the comparatively static letter to the editor.

This openness and speed of online publishing comes at a cost. First, anybody can set up a blog and start publishing in a matter of minutes. This is good news for the readers, who can enjoy more stories (often for free). This is also bad news for the readers, because the high volume reduces the overall quality of online stories. Sub-editors have less time to fact-check stories, as you will read in Chapter 10. Readers get inundated with online science news stories via newsletters and social media. This inundation makes it difficult for them to decide which stories are relevant.

The effect of this information overload is that many readers now have shorter attention spans (Weatherhead 2014). The way you structure your articles, the way you craft your headlines and the length of your paragraphs and sentences will have to cater to this phenomenon. Also, you will have to acquire technical skills, such as SEO-optimised writing, to be sure your articles get the attention of search engines. Moreover, you will need to harness the internet's tools to produce attention-grabbing stories.

Hooking your audience starts with your headline, your lead and how you structure your texts. Most important, get right to the point. Every paragraph that follows your lead must support your main idea. As a general rule, keep paragraphs short and do not clutter them with too many ideas or opinions. Neuroscientist, comedian and science blogger Dean Burnett tells me his blog posts all run from 800 to 1,200 words because longer blog posts are harder to sell. Also, most online readers are looking for something to keep them briefly amused, for example, while they are on a commute. But Burnett's number one piece of advice is to keep it simple and break down complex, lengthy passages into digestible bites:

In terms of structure, long blocks of text are generally discouraged, because they look like intimidating, big chunks of words. Most of the news websites haven't got these big, bold paragraphs. They are only four or five lines each. That doesn't mean that you can't explain complex science. It's just breaking it down to chunks.

*(Burnett 2016)*

In fact, you can apply most of the short news-writing techniques to produce compelling and snappy online texts, but there are exceptions. For example, while large chunks of text are readable in print, readers expect more navigability online; you have to loosen up long passages by interspersing them with images, videos or subheadings. Subheadings cause your readers to perceive passages as standalone modules (Boyle 2006).

If you want your article to pop up in readers' search engines, on Facebook and on Twitter, you will have to write headlines that help these services find and index your article. This is more difficult than in print, as your headlines have to appeal to both humans and algorithms. What works well for humans does not always work well for machines, which is why sometimes you will find quirky headlines that rank highly in search engines but are terrible to read. Headlines are perhaps more important than leads in the online realm; they determine whether readers click on an article to open and read it, which causes the number of page visualisations and unique visits to rise.

Here are a few ideas for crafting online headlines. If your article is about a specific question, pose that question in the headline (some editors strongly oppose this technique). You can also use wordplays and puns to attract readers, but be sure not to do so just for the sake of it. In any case, if your headline does not contain your article's key words, it is an ineffective online heading (Marsh 2014).

Once you have bagged that click, what happens next? The page opens, and your readers start scanning the lead. This is another decisive moment: Is your lead to the point, or is it at least shocking or catchy? If not, readers may swiftly turn away and close the article. Too short a visit does not count as a proper page view but as a bounce. High bounce rates, in turn, lower the overall search engine ranking of the publication and make it less likely that its articles are found on the internet. Translated to business speak, this means bad headlines and leads equal short visits, which equal loss of advertising money.

Also, write short and direct leads that introduce your article's main idea right away. Avoid writing delayed leads as you would normally do in print magazines (Boyle 2006). Good leads also contain search-engine friendly words. That is why most blogging systems let you define separate search engine leads which appear in search engine results right below the headline. These excerpts help readers determine which search result is most relevant for them and whether they should further explore it by clicking on the headline. By now, you can probably see where this is going: There is a technical aspect of writing online and there is a journalistic aspect. The two complement each other, as "the medium does shape the message, as well as the qualities that each medium considers most important" (Boyle 2006:91).

## Science blog networks

Science blogging has become more than just a playground for aspiring science writers. Science blogs have become an established publication format due to their immediacy, interactivity and the proximity to the audience. People want to be informed and entertained as the news breaks. Many want to discuss the implications of scientific findings and become part of the discourse. In doing so, readers often fact-check the articles and suggest corrections. This form of interaction is a strong suit of science blogs. Another key aspect for the success of science blogs is that they are often written by scientists. For example, *Scientific American*'s science bloggers are mostly scientists, as its former blogs editor Curtis Brainard (2015) confirms: "The ratio scientists to science writers is 60 to 40 or maybe even 65 to 35 per cent." This approach ensures readers get fresh information right off the lab bench. Blogging scientists have unique access to scientific topics and provide angles and insights into academic issues before they are published in the mainstream media. Major science publications now realise the potential of science blogs, hire bloggers and let them write exclusively for their in-house science blogging networks.

The typical science blogger has either a background in humanities or in science and sometimes in both. There are also paid and unpaid bloggers. How much money paid bloggers earn varies greatly; some networks offer flat fee payments, others provide paid bonuses and still others use a pay-per-click model. Many paid science bloggers are not blogging full time and have to produce a set number of articles per week or month. But even then, science blogging generally pays significantly less than print:

> The blogs do not pay much, unfortunately. They certainly do not pay as much as the print issues or even the news areas of the [*Scientific American*] website. Most science writers and journalists know that, and they will seek to pitch higher-paying areas of the publication first, before they will pitch a blog post.
>
> *(Brainard 2015)*

Money aside, a major advantage of joining a science blogging network rather than running an independent science blog is reach: You profit from the publication's well-indexed website, which in turn ensures your blog will rank highly in the most popular search engine results. In addition, blog networks have editors who offer can offer some level of editorial advice. Most blog editors do not edit every single blog post. But if you propose a new blog, they will make sure the idea behind your blog is sound and will attract a certain audience. You will have to find your own niche that you sufficiently narrow down to attract a particular audience. You should also establish your own voice and style. To demonstrate this, you should have successfully blogged somewhere else before. Science blogging networks love it when you bring your own loyal audience with you. Running your own blog, even within a network, means running your own business. You must know whom you are blogging for, what you are blogging about, how often you are blogging and how much feedback you can expect. Persuading even large networks then comes within reach.

In 2011, *Scientific American* started one of the first larger networks. The network soon grew to sixty blogs written by scientists, editorial staff members and science writers. Part of the network was a guest blog where budding science journalists could publish their blog posts. Today, Curtis Brainard manages the blog network which now comprises thirty-nine blogs, two of which are guest blogs. Breaking into the network remains difficult unless you have a unique idea and a proven record of success. If you want to establish yourself as a science writer, you should consider writing for one of the science guest blogs. This will allow you to work with an editor and gain exposure once your post is online.

*National Geographic's* blog network, Phenomena, has taken an all-star approach and assembled a squad of established science writers that were part of other science blogging networks. The advantage of that approach is that established science bloggers such as Carl Zimmer, Ed Yong, Maryn McKenna and Robert Krulwich brought their own, loyal audience with them when they joined. In fact, their reputation as established science journalists is key to the blog network's success. *National Geographic* incorporated science blogging into its news section in 2016.

The *Guardian* has also obtained popular science writers from unpaid networks. For example, in 2012, Bristolian psychologist Pete Etchells started a blog at the unpaid (and now defunct) science blogging network SciLogs. com. In 2013, the *Guardian* approached Etchells and asked him to blog for their network. Etchells agreed and has since become the coordinator of the science blog for network. Occasionally, the *Guardian* network recruits new bloggers. When they do, they prefer established writers that cover specific niches (Etchells 2015).

One of these established science bloggers is molecular biologist and science writer Christie Wilcox, who writes the blog Science Sushi for *Discover* magazine's science blogging network. She confirms the benefits of being part of such networks, but only if you commit to it:

> If you are going for a career in writing, then joining a major science blogging network is beneficial – but only if you don't see it as a side job. That is because the major networks require a certain number of posts or a certain level of activity. If you are not ready to commit to, for example, four posts a month, then you are going to be in trouble.
>
> *(Wilcox 2016)*

Wilcox also tells me that her contract requires her to write a minimum number of blog posts per month. In fact, the more posts she publishes, and the more readers those posts attracts, the more she is paid.

In addition to science blogging networks run by popular science magazines and newspapers, scientific journals also run their own blogging networks, such as *Nature* and *PLOS ONE*. Again, it is mostly scientists who blog there, so the science presented on such blogs is mostly previously unpublished, fresh material. Even if you do not intend to blog yourself, these blogs can provide you with lots of useful material for science story ideas. With this in mind, subscribe to the science blogs that interest you most and read them regularly.

## Blogging 101 for science writers

If you want your readers to stay focused on your article, you have to write it in an accessible way. Distractions like email or Facebook notifications will pop up and make your readers lose focus. When they lose attention, you must provide them with an easy way to resume reading without entirely losing their train of thought. Hence, you need to first visually break up your article by providing short, one-idea paragraphs. Anywhere between 30 and 100 words is short enough. Single-sentence paragraphs also work well. Most important, alternate paragraph lengths. Rhythm is very important to keep your reader's attention.

You can use subheadings to logically group paragraphs into modules (Boyle 2006). Recalling his experience at *MSNBC*, Boyle (2006) argues that contributions running longer than 1,200 were likely to be split up into chunks of 300 to 600 words. They then used subheadings to mark the single modules. Using subheadings also "improves readability on the Web, because the story doesn't look so daunting, and readers can skim past modules if they want to" (Boyle 2006:93). In addition, subheadings provide an easy point of re-entry for readers if something distracts them. You can use short summaries taken from the text or quotes as subheadings.

Science needs explanation, but long expository passages and online writing do not go well together. The AB structure (see Chapter 5) works well in print and for long-form online pieces, but it requires readers to linearly read through the text. The internet is a non-linear medium, so this does not work as well as in print. This is one of the points where you can harness the web's capabilities to weave in context and background without artificially inflating the entire article: If it is not essential to understanding the story, add links to additional explanatory material instead of writing out that background information in full. The same works with jargon terms and acronyms if they are non-essential to the text; you can simply incorporate links to these definitions so your readers can decide whether and when they want to consult them. Be pragmatic in deciding which passages and definitions you can outsource. Here is a simple test: If your readers cannot understand your article without an explanation or definition, explain it yourself rather than linking to it. Many blogs and content management systems (CMS) also allow you to incorporate foldout paragraphs that hide background passages. If your readers want to read them, they can click on the section to expand it and afterwards tuck it away.

Structural differences between online and print writing aside, blogs allow a different tone, voice and style than, for example, an established newspaper. Blogs have a more personal and light-hearted tone, and they allow you perfectly to express your own voice, much like a column. This is especially true for individual, independent blogs; however, many blog networks have editorial policies and style guides that you will need to follow.

If you plan to write for online magazines and science websites, first, analytically read their articles and pay attention to their writers' styles. Second, many print and online publications, such as the *Guardian* and the *Economist*, publish their style guides. These style guides contain specific requirements on punctuation, grammar and spelling, and they often also state what the publication demands from its writers and how it perceives its audience. For example, *VICE* magazine's online technology and science magazine, *Motherboard*, is (just like the entire brand) known for its conversational style, which allows its authors to express personal opinions and report about personal experiences in a rather colloquial way. But similar to column writing, the writers support their opinions and anecdotes with facts or additional arguments. Here is an example of one passage that demonstrates this:

> It's a four-step, multi-minute long process emotionally equivalent only to having to endure . . . watching your Dad clip his toenails over the toilet. So why the hell do we still use it?
> Well, increasingly, we don't. . . . Businesses from JPMorgan to Coke have started scrapping voicemail to cut costs.
>
> *(Rogers 2016)*

Rogers's style becomes immediately apparent: By using vivid analogies ("watching your dad clip his toenails"), she evokes pictures in her readers' minds, which is a guaranteed attention-grabber. Her colloquial diction ("why the hell") reflects that she is addressing a younger audience that likes reading straightforward statements rather than digressive discourses and politically correct euphemisms. Most of all, her article is opinionated (she later says, "If you're like me, though, and loathe the anachronistic timewaster . . ."). Also, her use of personal pronouns like *you* and *we* is typical for *VICE*'s publications. Directly addressing the reader is a great way to bond with her. It works particularly well in leads. What follows in Rogers's article is a logical line of argumentation, a quote from an MIT scientist and information that supports her thesis. This is the quality that online writing ideally shares with columns: It is personal but fact-based.

## BOX 7.1 LISTICLES AND HEADLINES

Buzzfeed UK's science editor, Kelly Oakes, tells me that listicles are Buzzfeed's most successful type of online science article. You can easily recognise these short, list-style articles by their headlines: "The X most important Y" or "X things you need to know about Y" or "X surprising pictures that will make you Y."

Oakes adds that it is a listicle's content that makes it successful, not the format:

> You can't just take a 500-word news story, put it in a list and expect it to reach 300,000 people. That's not going to happen. What you are writing in the format of a list is what people want to read anyway. So we write a lot of identity posts, as we call them. People read the list and they are like, "Oh, I identify with all of this, this is totally me." And then they share it with their friends.
>
> *(Oakes 2016)*

Part of why Buzzfeed's listicles draw readers' attention is their headlines. Oakes's advice for writing effective headlines is:

> Write them in a conversational way – in the same way that you would tell the story to your friends. Also, as for the number of items, use specific, odd numbers like twenty-seven, because then it means that all twenty-seven items really deserve their place on the list, whereas, if we wrote a list of ten new things that we just found, it sounds like we have chosen to write ten things and then gone and found those ten things.
>
> *(Oakes 2016)*

Finally, Dean Burnett tells me what he thinks you should consider when blogging about science. Get to the point, be credible and beware of showing fake authority:

> My advice is to put the main point of what you want to get across in the first one or two paragraphs. It is often tempting to build up to a big reveal. But people increasingly find the whole clickbait approach annoying. . . . It comes across as manipulation, and it really is. There is also a mistake that students often make in submissions for academic assignments: They try to sound clever to convey authority or to seem like they know what they're talking about. That's a very risky move to make, because if you say something that you don't understand but which you think sounds right, someone will come along and say "That's not right, what are you talking about?" That sort of undermines everything else you said.
>
> *(Burnett 2016)*

## Understanding your audience

If you are a paid science blogger, your earnings typically depend on how much traffic you drive to a publication's science blogging network. This makes perfect sense: Online publications still mainly generate profit via advertising. Your audience's clicks translate to money. It is important to know whom you are writing for and to take into consideration those people that are not yet your regular readers. Science blogger Christie Wilcox confirms that she has a clear idea of who her target audience is:

> I like to think I know my audience pretty well. My target audience is anyone who is interested in science but does not really know it yet. They have at least a high school-level education but may not be working in science. They could be nurses or electricians, so not exactly scientific researchers. That is what I aim for: A skilled, intelligent audience, but not necessarily scientists. But I would also include in my audience a psychologist [who] would want to read about marine animals.
>
> *(Wilcox 2016)*

Wilcox concedes that when she started blogging, she was unaware of developing a concept or analysing a potential audience beforehand. In retrospect, however, she affirms that thinking about your audience, developing a proper blog concept and finding your own niche is great advice (Wilcox 2016).

If you are going for an individual blog, you should carry out market research on your future audience. For instance, you can investigate existing blogs that cover similar topic areas and analyse their posts for topics covered and number and quality of comments. How emotionally does those blogs' audience react to the posts? You should also analyse these blogs' social media impact. Which topics, which stories, which formats do people share most and recommend to their friends? That is how audiences grow: through recommendations. You can monitor the social media impact of stories by inserting post URLs into online tools such as Like Explorer (see the Links section). Like Explorer then shows you how many times readers have liked or shared a blog post on platforms such as Facebook, Twitter or Pinterest. Media companies also use professional tools like Hootsuite Insights (see Figure 7.1) or Brandwatch's PeerIndex. These provide a demographic breakdown of your audience and present the data in infographic-style dashboards. However, as an individual science blogger, you will most probably rely on Google Analytics or similar analytical services, even when you are part of a blog network.

Was your last story on gene editing highly unpopular? Then maybe that topic did not resonate well with your readers. Or perhaps you published it at the wrong time, when everybody still was at work. If you want to quickly respond to increases or decreases in your writing's popularity, you will need to employ web analytics tools. They allow you to dissect your readers' demographics, location and surfing behaviour. By providing powerful

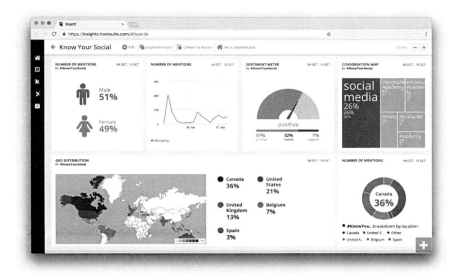

**FIGURE 7.1**   The dashboard of Hootsuite Insights allows you to analyse your audience's demographics

*Source*: Hootsuite (2016)

statistics, these tools allow you to see when your audience opens your blog posts, how long they read a particular post and, quite importantly, which platform they came from. Box 7.2 shows a list of the basic metrics you should consider and what they mean. Christie Wilcox tells me that about 75 per cent of her blog's traffic comes from social media, predominantly Facebook and Twitter, because *Discover* promotes its bloggers via their social media accounts, which guarantees a certain reach (Wilcox 2016). Wilcox also uses Google Analytics to analyse her traffic as her blogging network gives her direct access to her blog's statistics.

If you want to understand how audiences develop, you should also consult the reports created by measurement companies such as Nielsen or comScore (Media Matrix) or journalistic research institutions like the Pew Research Center. They regularly analyse audiences and publish reports that you can often access for free. These reports often reveal trending topics and formats and let you extrapolate from similar audiences to your own audience.

If you want a slice of that shared audience pie, you must establish yourself as an expert in your chosen field. That is why finding your own niche is important. The more specific, the better it is when you are just starting out. You need to brand yourself as a go-to person for very specific topics, as journalism educator Liisa Rohumaa put it during a coaching session at Edinburgh Napier University in February 2014.

Apparently people with advanced science backgrounds also have a keen interest in reading science blogs. In a study on how science blogs facilitate

---

## BOX 7.2 METRICS

Here are a few basic metrics that help you understand how well your blog posts are doing:

- **Pageviews**: How many visitors have opened a particular page or all pages? This includes multiple views from the same readers.
- **Unique visitors**: How many people have visited your website? This is the number of unique people (not repeat visits).
- **Bounce rate**: How many of your website's visitors left your site without opening or reading anything?
- **Average session duration**: How long does a reader typically interact with your website before turning away?
- **Pages per session**: How many pages does a reader open during one session?

While most website analytics tools will let you track this data, they will not tell you your social media metrics, such as the numbers of shares, likes and re-tweets, but those are also important indicators that help you understand your audience's engagement. Here you can find a few social media analysis tools (most are commercial, but many offer limited trials and/or demos of their functionalities):

- Buffer.com
- Buzzsumo.com
- Hootsuite Insights
- Keycole.co
- TweetReach (Twitter only).

---

or hamper public engagement with science, Kouper (2010) analysed eleven blogs, including blogs from the *WIRED*, *Discover*, and *ScienceBlogs* networks. Kouper's findings indicate that most of readers of the analysed blogs are more connected to science than some of this chapter's bloggers estimate:

> Readers of science blogs also had some relationship with science, i.e., they were not exactly non-scientists or lay persons. One author posted a message titled "Who are you?" and asked his readers for information about themselves and their background. The answers to this post as well as the overall analysis of readers' comments demonstrate that those readers who engage in commenting are almost always associated with science one way or another. They are graduate students, postdoctoral associates, faculty members, and researchers from a variety of scientific and research fields including biology, physics, neuroscience, and medicine.
>
> *(Kouper 2010:6)*

As the only exception, she argues that "*Wired* Science was probably the only blog in the sample where non-scientists formed a considerable portion of the commenting audience" (6). The commenting audience of the latter, she argues, is inclined to appear as experts in the field through their comments. She also adds that the readers "offer quick personal judgments, insulting and sarcastic remarks, and personal details" (89). Christie Wilcox confirms that you need to quickly develop a thick skin to digest insulting and destructive comments if you want to survive as a science blogger. Additionally, you should never forget that if it is your personal blog, you decide what level of comment quality you will tolerate (Wilcox 2016).

## Starting a science blog

Blogging regularly is excellent writing training. You can write and post frequently because you do not have to wait for editors' commissions. This intensive training character of blogging will also help find your own voice and develop your style, as Christie Wilcox confirms:

> Because a blog is "low stakes" – without it being edited, without you having to pitch every article and get it accepted – you can write about what you want, you can play around with styles, different tones and different structures.
>
> *(Wilcox 2016)*

But the sheer fact that blogs are writing incubators does not attract your readers. The crux is: If nobody reads your blog, your motivation declines and you probably post less or sporadically, which will result in less reader engagement.

Prior to launching a blog using one of the popular platforms, you will have to consider the following questions:

- Why do you want to blog?
- What is your niche?
- What is your area of expertise?
- Who will want to read your stories?
- Who else blogs about the same subject area?
- What types of posts will you publish?
- How often will you publish new stories?
- How will you advertise your blog?

In addition, you need to know how to structure blog posts, how to analyse and read your audience and how to promote your blog using SEO techniques to increase your blog's reach. Most important, you should ask yourself why you want to blog. Are you a scientist whose goal is to disseminate her research? Are you trying to gain a reputation as a science blogger, and is your ultimate goal to become part of a major science blog network? Do you simply want to become a better science writer? Blogging can cater to many of these aspirations at the same time: "It's not just a matter of a personal portfolio: blogging develops and improves your journalism; blogging develops your expertise in a specialist area; and blogging builds contacts and networks in your areas of interest" (Bradshaw and Rohumaa 2013:78). Christie Wilcox (2016) agrees that blogging is a good exercise in writing and tells me that it is like any other skill: the more you do it, the better you will get at it. In addition, running a successful science blog may even draw editors' attention and subsequently lead to getting commissions from print publications:

> The core reasons to start a blog have to do with professional development. It can serve to help curate your online profile. Especially if you have a prolific blog, if someone Googles and finds you and reads how you write, they might say, "I'm a magazine editor, and we are looking for an article on this particular topic. You know the topic well, I have read your blogs on it, and I like your style of writing. Would you be interested in writing an article?" That has happened to me a number of times. About half of the freelance writing I do now is pitched to me, versus me pitching.
>
> *(Wilcox 2016)*

On a broader level, you should follow the following three-step workflow to get started blogging (Bradshaw and Rohumaa 2013):

1    Choose your focus
2    Start posting
3    Comment and link.

Choosing your focus is the crucial factor that will determine your blog's success or failure. Without knowing what your blog is about, all subsequent steps will fail. In doing so, you have to settle for a narrow overarching theme:

> Successful blogs tend to have a specific and clear focus, one that is narrower than those used within traditional media organisations aimed at mass markets. Blogging about solar energy, for example, is likely to be more effective than trying to blog about "environmental news".
>
> *(Bradshaw and Rohumaa 2013)*

You can subdivide blogs into three types: the niche blog, the behind-the-scenes blog and the running story blog. As an aspiring blogger, you should consider starting with a niche blog (Bradshaw and Rohuma 2013). The final step, commenting and linking, is a clear reference to outreach. When you start blogging, you will start to get noticed. Include other blogs that you read in your blogroll (a list of links to other blogs), and be sure to constructively comment on other bloggers' posts to be part of the scientific discussion.

Buzzfeed UK's science editor, Kelly Oakes, confirms that you need to find a niche. In an article that is part of the *Guardian*'s online series "Secrets of Good Science Writing", Oakes mentions ten successful strategies for establishing a science blog, including choose a blog platform like WordPress if you want to write longer posts or Tumblr if you prefer short, image-based posts, and you should regularly post new articles and engage with your audience via comments and links (Oakes 2014). You can extend your blog's reach by joining blog aggregators like ScienceSeeker (see the Links section), which will index your blog and provide it with further visibility on the internet. If you have an established blog, you should consider joining a blog network: "You'll get colleagues to help you out, a boost in traffic and a whole new potential audience" (Oakes 2014).

If joining a network is not yet possible, Oakes suggests joining one of the many existing publishing platforms and leveraging their communities and sharing tools to get noticed:

> Don't set up the blog as an independent website. Rather, set it up on a platform that has built-in sharing mechanisms, because that makes it much easier to be found. That is also the way people are increasingly consuming media: Not by going to individual websites but by looking through their Facebook and Instagram feeds. "I Fucking Love Science" on Facebook is one of the most successful science blogs, so now they have their own website. They gained that popularity through Facebook, and I'm sure Facebook and all its sharing capabilities really helped them get off the ground. Also, set up your blog on a website that already exists, and then you should follow all the people in that community. Don't tweet at them to annoy them, but engage in conversations that are going on.
>
> *(Oakes 2016)*

## Writing for SEO

If you want search engines such as Google or Bing to find and index your article, you will need to improve it for search engine optimisation by properly structuring it, inserting keywords and subheadings, tagging and categorising it and writing SEO-friendly headlines. The goal of SEO is to achieve the highest possible rank in users' search results. Google is the globally leading search engine (Statista 2016), so it is safe to say you should primarily focus your attention on optimising your article's search rank for that engine.

Search engines determine a page's rank using a myriad of factors. Some you cannot influence at all and some you can influence directly or implicitly. For example, the more links that refer to your article (backlinks), the higher most search engines rank that page. Also, the length of your domain name (shorter is better), how fast your website loads, and the number of links tweeted or posted on Facebook do count. One (if not the primary) way of directly improving an article's ranking is properly using the SEO title tag. It is a hidden HTML tag (that is, it does not show up on your article's webpage) that free tools like Yoast SEO for WordPress generate. The title tag is what Google and other search engines display as the clickable link in their search results.

In a video for BBC Academy, former digital editor at BBC Arabic, Martin Asser, explains how the BBC employs SEO-friendly headlines to get its audience to click on links and proceed to their online articles. The goal of search-friendly writing is not to lure readers into clicking on your links by using "heavily searched keywords like 'sex' or 'football' ", when they were looking for something else, but "the aim is to ensure people can find information on *BBC* websites when they go looking for it on a search engine" (Asser no date). Asser also explains his four golden rules, which you should follow when crafting headlines for SEO:

1  Include keywords in your headline.
2  Eliminate unspecific non-keywords as far as possible.
3  Put the most significant keywords first.
4  Use proper names in your headline; this will often be your story's protagonist.

There is a special variation of rule number three, which is called a *kicker*. A kicker consists of the two most important keywords followed by a colon. The resulting headline is keyword-rich and will improve the odds your article can actually be found by search engine users. Also, your headline should not exceed 55 characters.

There is a very practical reason behind this rule: Each search result has limited space on the results page. If your headline is too long, the browser will only display part of the title. Lengthy headlines risk being cut off and thus become opaque. Another problem is that most browsers use proportional fonts with a varying character width. That means that a capital *W* occupies more space than a lowercase *i*, so choose your headline's characters wisely.

Put your most important keywords first whenever you can, because Google might truncate the headline. All three results in Figure 7.2 appeared on the first page of search results for "CRISPR and ethics" using a Google UK search that was limited to results from the *Guardian*'s website. As you can see, the third search result is the least expressive; the truncated title is

Scientists genetically modify human embryos in ...
www.theguardian.com › Science › Genetics ▾
23 Apr 2015 - The Chinese group used a genome editing procedure called Crispr to ...
of human embryos, citing "grave concerns" over the ethics and safety.

Genome editing: how to modify genetic faults – and the human
www.theguardian.com › Science › Genetics ▾
2 Sep 2015 - Scientists believe that a debate should be had about the ethics of
modifying human embryos, ... **Crispr**: is it a good idea to 'upgrade' our DNA?

Scientists must be part of the ethical debate on human ...
www.theguardian.com › Opinion › Genetics ▾
21 Sep 2015 - If that were to be done, the **ethical** issues are more complex than they ...
medical applications justifying the use of **Crispr**/Cas9 in embryos".

FIGURE 7.2   Search engines may trim blog posts' titles if they exceed a certain
length or if they use too many wide characters

*Source*: Google

"Scientists must be part of the ethical debate on human . . .". This does not
invite readers to open the article, as it fails to mention what the article is
about. Had the editor avoided using "must be part of the", he could have
reclaimed 35 per cent of the allowed 55 characters and filled the gained
space with keywords. Also, note that none of the displayed search results
contains the actual search term CRISPR, despite it being very popular.

Apart from that, use categories and tags from your CMS to improve the
chances your article pops up in readers' search results when they look for
those specific terms: "Categories tend to be broad 'sections' that you cover
regularly, such as 'boxing' or 'health'; tags tend to be specific people, locations or organisations mentioned in the article such as 'diabetes' " (Bradshaw
and Rohumaa 2013:36).

Also, enrich your online article with subheadings, links, bullet points and
images, and add keyword-rich captions to your images. This helps people
and search engines scan your text, especially because Western readers tend
to scan articles in an *F* pattern (Bradshaw and Rohumaa 2013): They read
your articles from left to right using a top-down approach, and their attention diminishes as they approach the end of the text.

Subheadings also improve the ranking of your article in the search results.
Use HTML tags, namely <h1> for your article title and <h2> for any subheadings you write. Search engines recognise these tags and assign a higher
importance to the enclosed terms. The respective standard formats, called
heading 1 and heading 2, of most CMS take care of inserting these tags for
you. How you format your keywords in the running text also makes a difference; search engines prefer bold and italicised keywords. But beware that
overdoing this can ruin the readability of your text. A good search rank is
useless if nobody wants to read your article.

The good news is, you do not have to be a programmer to use these techniques. Tools like the Yoast SEO plugin for WordPress allow you to insert the relevant SEO title and provide an excerpt that pops up on the results page as a search lead. Yoast also assesses the length of your title and the quality of your keywords and correlates them with your actual article text. Additionally, Yoast generates a preview that lets you check your search results before you publish. You can see these features in Figure 7.3.

A final note: Do write SEO-friendly texts, but beware of overdoing it. You are primarily writing for human readers. Search engines come second. As backlinks are one of the best ways to improve your articles' rankings, be sure to write compelling stories that your readers can relate to, because then they will spread them.

## Sourcing images

Visualisations are one of the most powerful ways to convey science. Charts, maps, infographics, historic photographs and all sorts of embeddable multimedia content spice up long text passages and help your readers understand complex issues in a nutshell. After all, we are visual creatures. Hence, at the very minimum, you should equip every online science article with an image that symbolises the article's main idea and helps your readers choose it from the list of articles. Kristin Sainani, clinical assistant professor at Stanford

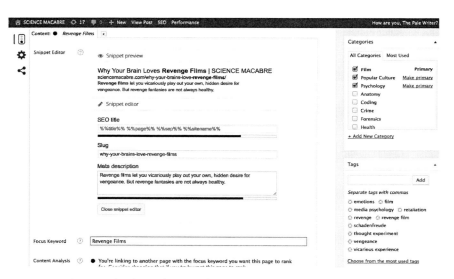

**FIGURE 7.3** Setting the focus keyword, SEO title and meta description using the Yoast SEO plugin on the Science Macabre blog

*Source*: sciencemacabre.com, 2016

University and science writer who also teaches a massive open online course on science writing (see the Links section), confirms that:

> I do think that when you are writing for the web, you have to think beyond the prose. There is so much you can add to an online story – like visuals, interactive graphs, videos, and links – so you have to be thinking about all these elements as you craft your story.
>
> *(Sainani 2016)*

If you submit an article to an online publication, your editors will probably choose the images that complement your article, so they will attend to the images' terms of use. If you are part of a science blogging network, the network's publisher usually subscribes to photo agency image databanks and will either choose the images for you or grant you access to those image databases so you can select and insert the images into your post and correctly cite them. If you are an independent blogger, you have to select the images you want to use and clear the rights before using them. Given the abundance of images on the web, it is tempting to take an image, publish it and give credit to the source. In most cases, that is a copyright infringement.

Copyright laws for using images, video, text or music vary from country to country, but as soon somebody creates original content, that content is protected by copyright. Hence, scraping images from the internet and publishing them on your blog can get you into legal trouble. This is also true of social media photographs, which you cannot freely reuse without the consent of the person who took them:

> Content that has been uploaded or exchanged online is subject to the same copyright laws as print and broadcast material. Just because someone has uploaded their photo or video to Facebook does not mean that they have given permission for you to republish it on your website, magazine or television bulletin.
>
> *(Bradshaw and Rohumaa 2013:154)*

Whoever holds the rights is entitled to decide if and how you can reuse her pictures on your website or blog. Sometimes, simply asking the owners for their written permission is sufficient to get that permission and republish the image. Others attach licenses to their images that dictate how you can reuse them. For example, these license terms could require you to not alter the image, to name the author in full or to not use their images for commercial purposes. You will often find attached licenses with images on public photo-sharing platforms like Flickr or 500px. Beware that you are not free to use images that lack such a license; they are still protected by the owner's copyright.

Luckily, you can find many images in royalty-free image databases or by browsing public domain images. Dedicated websites let you search for and download such images (see the Links section). Wikimedia Commons is one such repository. Public domain images are works for which the copyright has expired or work made publicly available by their creators. You do not have to attribute public domain images, but it is certainly good practice to do so. Beware that you can use some public domain images only in specific countries. Hence, always consult the notes that are attached to an image.

Creative Commons (CC) licenses are more flexible because they let image producers decide what you can do with their images. For example, the CC BY license requires you to correctly name the author when you reuse the image. The more restrictive CC BY-NC license prohibits using the image for commercial purposes. Many image-sharing platforms like Flickr contain images whose authors have placed them under one of the CC licenses. This makes using the images all the easier, as the license tells you how you can reuse the content. If you encounter no license but an All Rights Reserved statement, that image is protected most restrictively: You cannot use it unless its owner has explicitly given you the rights to do so. In that case, contact the owner and negotiate the terms of reuse.

Never reuse images from media companies unless you have their written permission to do so. Most of the major companies have complex clearance processes that require you to state your publication's circulation, how long you want to use the image, where you want to display it and many more parameters. Dedicated copyright clearance centres will then determine the (often considerable) fees you will have to pay to use these images under the negotiated terms.

Using a stock photo agency is another option. Many of them require you to subscribe and let you download and reuse a set number of images under defined conditions. Be aware that such subscriptions can also be expensive, so you might want to resort to CC-licensed or public domain images.

There are some very good image archives that contain free-to-use photographs and illustrations (some of which have CC licenses). Some of these archives belong to government agencies, are independent or belong privately held companies. The Creative Commons search hub (see the Links section) is an excellent starting point for finding images you can use on your blog, as it allows you to search using some of the most popular platforms like Google Images, Pixabay, Flickr and Wikimedia Commons. Even some of the premium photo agencies, such as Getty Images, have recently made some of their photos available for use on websites and blogs, provided you credit them correctly and do not reuse them commercially. Other important sources are government agency databases such as NASA, ESA, the US National Library of Medicine, the CDC's public health image library (PHIL) and others, which have a wealth of images that are mostly in the public domain. The Library of Congress has a long list of links to databases of science images that are in the public domain and cover disciplines such as agriculture, astronomy, biology, engineering and medicine (see the Links section).

### Case study: analysing a science news post

When you write your first blog post, you have to decide what story you want to tell and which format works best for telling it. The majority of science blog posts are short science news items. In fact, due to their simple, inverted pyramid-style structure, this format is easy to start with, as "covering the basics of new scientific research papers seems to be a good starting point for many science bloggers" (Jarreau 2014).

In this section, I will dissect a news-style science blog post and scrutinise the structure and language. This may not be an award-winning science blog post, but it certainly has its merits. Like print news stories, short news posts give readers the gist of a new scientific discovery, and they help you quickly and regularly fill your blog. There is almost nothing worse than a blog whose author does not frequently populate it with fresh posts. The blog post is titled "Giraffe Genetics Reveal Four Separate (and Threatened) Species". Its author is John R. Platt (2016), who writes the blog Extinction Countdown for *Scientific American*'s blog network. Before you read on, open the blog post (see the Links section).

Platt's structure is modelled after a short news article, especially at the beginning of the post. He starts with a one-sentence lead without bells and whistles. In screenwriting, this could be called an *inciting incident* (although a very minimalistic one):

> The world of giraffe conservation just got turned upside down.

That sentence creates a bit of tension and makes readers wonder what happened next. In a news story style, Platt then proceeds in descending order of importance. The first sentence of the second paragraph summarises the paper's findings: new genetic tests show that not all African giraffes belong to the same species. Platt then briefly expands on the finding and names a few important numbers: How many species have been found (four) and how many of the giraffes exist (90,000) and, most important, he implies that subdividing them means that each single species is threatened. Platt then further substantiates his claims by comparing the numbers of giraffes against those of African elephants. In only three sentences, Platt answers the following questions: What is new, whom does it affect (giraffes) and what do these findings mean?

He then progresses without any kind of transition to the next paragraph, which is again three sentences long. There, Platt details in which paper (he includes a link to it) the results appeared, and he shows the secondary facts, namely that there are several subspecies. He closes the paragraph with a sentence that ties in with the lead and answers the question that the readers had after reading it: What has changed?

> Giraffes were previous [sic] recognized as one species with up to eleven different subspecies, some of which were already contentious.

Platt then proceeds to listing the newly categorised African giraffe species and subspecies, which may be less interesting to the lay reader. What the blog post is lacking so far is a quote from the study authors and/or independent experts.

The subsequent paragraph focuses on the idea that giraffes have become more endangered than previously thought, quoting the conservationist Fennessy first indirectly and then directly and at length from the press release. If you write your own blog post, this is the latest point where you should put your first quotes from interviews (not press releases). In the case at hand, the quote adds a few concrete numbers, and the conservationist states which of the named giraffe species/subspecies are the most endangered. Because of the lengthy quote of forty-seven words, this is one of the longer paragraphs of the post.

The following paragraph is a shorter one that contains only three very short sentences with more figures taken from the press release. This is probably the least important paragraph, as Platt previously made the point that two out of four giraffe species are endangered.

He then closes the blog post by raising the speculative question of whether these findings will fuel according conservation efforts. Although the paragraph is coherent in itself, style-wise it feels a bit off, as it zealously tries to add a personal note by suddenly introducing the pronoun *we*, in the final sentence:

> Now we know more than we expected, and that can only help in the long run.

Overall, the blog post leaves the impression that it is entirely based on the press release he links to. Seemingly, Platt conducted no interviews with the study authors or independent experts (or at least nothing in the text hints at this). Nevertheless, as it is, it could almost be published as a newspaper story, with the limitation that the following key elements are not addressed:

- Who conducted the research, and where do they work?
- The "new genetic tests" are never explained.
- How did the scientists conduct the research?
- The author apparently conducted no interviews.
- The point that giraffes are endangered is over-repeated.
- The ending is a speculative deliberation.

This blog post is certainly a minimalistic example of what you can post online, and it contains a few points that could have been done better. I chose this as an example because of its simplicity and easy reproducibility; following this basic structure can help you construct your first blog using a press release. Such blog posts, however, are of little journalistic value (other than shortening a press release), and they will hardly keep your audience interested in the long run. I encourage you to write your own example following a similar structure, but consider the aforementioned points of criticism and eliminate these flaws in your own post. Finally, write an ending that references the lead or adds a meaningful conclusion.

## Case study: analysing an award-winning, long-form online science article

Online science writing is not just about catering to short attention spans. Long-form journalism can and does work, as you will see in this section. As Kristin Sainani points out, you do not need to obey formulaic word or time limits all the time:

> There are no word limits online, so you can write much longer, more in-depth pieces than you would for print. For the MOOC ["Writing in the Sciences"], I was told you could only make modules 6 minutes long or you would lose people's attention. I did not stick to this rule of thumb, and I still had plenty of viewers. I don't think we should assume that all readers on the web have short attention spans.
>
> *(Sainani 2016)*

Long-form online journalism can be successful if you can keep the readers' attention. Mere facts are not enough to do this; what you need is a compelling narrative that is interwoven with the actual science. One prime example of how you can achieve this is Phil McKenna's long-form online science article "Uprising: The Environmental Scandal That's Happening Right Beneath Your Feet" (McKenna 2013). McKenna's article won the 2013 AAAS Kavli Science Award (online category). It runs 6,500 words, which is incredible for an online science story. McKenna tells the story of gas-sniffer Bob Ackley, who used to work for major gas utilities but eventually became an environmental activist. Ackley now fights the very companies he previously worked for; in doing so, he eventually teamed up with Nathan Phillips, a professor at Boston University. Together they investigate the gas leaks and their harmful effects on the environment and the gas companies' agendas.

Examining the visual structure of the article, it is immediately evident that the dominant element is text. The article is complemented by sixteen images, most of which are reporter-style photographs. There are two infographic-style images that show the distribution of gas leaks in Boston, and there is one figure that shows predictions of the world's gas production. In addition, McKenna embeds one video. Other than that, there is no attempt to use multimedia content; there are not even links to the papers cited. Also, the writing is not particularly SEO-optimised.

As for the text structure, the paragraph length varies between roughly 50 and 120 words, with a tendency to put short paragraphs at the beginning and the end of the article. The longer paragraphs, some of which provide background information, are in the centre of the article. McKenna does intersperse his text with about half a dozen subheadings, which are catchy phrases that draw the reader's attention. However, unlike traditional subheadings, these phrases are highlights rather than true subheadings, as they do not summarise the paragraphs. Overall, the text consists of ninety-five paragraphs (including the subheadings), the shortest of which is one sentence.

With this many paragraphs, the author needed to ensure smooth transitions, and he writes in a very descriptive and vivid way. For instance, McKenna describes an inciting moment in Bob Ackley's history:

> A Norway maple stood in a patch of dead grass by the side of the road. The tree was also dying, its top branches barren twigs. The air held the foul odour of rotten eggs – mercaptan, a chemical added to natural gas to make it easier to detect leaks.

This was when Ackley learnt how to detect gas leaks by looking at the environment. From a storytelling perspective, McKenna took a cinematic or scenic approach to writing. Just like in a movie, this is the key factor that allowed him to hold the readers' attention and urged them to read on. McKenna explained to me why he took this approach for telling his story about natural gas leaks and how they influence climate change:

> My editor Dan Baum urged me to really think of the story as scenes in a movie and to focus on key turning points in Bob Ackley's story. For example, there was a point where Bob first discovered that you look for leaks by finding dead trees and dead grass. So, I would try to find that point and really drill down into it, to set up this key turning point as a scene. A lot of my reporting was getting back to these two guys and have them tell me more details about such key moments.
>
> *(McKenna 2016)*

The way McKenna writes his descriptive paragraphs is also reminiscent of fiction writing in that many of them contain characters, action and dialogue. His writing is rarely passive, and he lets his story's characters advance the story. In doing so, McKenna applies a well-known and established storytelling principle: Show don't tell. For example, he could have introduced Nathan Phillips in one lapidary sentence as an environment professor who is an idealist by definition. Instead, he chose to let Phillips's actions speak for him by devoting an entire paragraph to paint a picture of him:

> Phillips obsesses about his work, and tries to reduce his own carbon footprint in every way he can. Every morning he cycles nearly 15km

to his office, sometimes hauling unused food from his son's school to a local food charity. When he arrives at his building on campus, he walks the four stories up to his office. Inside sits a bike connected to an electric generator; his slow and steady pedaling produces enough energy to light the room and power his laptop. Next to his desk is a handcrank generator, which he sometimes uses to charge his mobile phone.

Clearly, the best way to gain such personal insights into your characters is to observe them in the field. This falls into line with what McKenna's editor at the time, Dan Baum, told him; McKenna points out that it is crucial for aspiring science writers to be good observers:

> Observe as much as you can. Write down as much as you can. Take pictures while you are reporting – not pictures that will ever be used in the publication but that you can look at the next day or over the next weeks as you are writing the story.
>
> *(McKenna 2016)*

Most importantly, McKenna explained to me the key ingredients that enabled the success of his award-winning story: He found compelling characters through which he could tell the bigger science story about how natural gas leaks induce climate change; he had two life stories that got intertwined mid-story; and he had change and conflict as in fiction writing.

## Summary

In a way, breaking into online science journalism is a lot easier than getting a foot in the door of print publications. Landing your first writing gig as a guest blogger on an established blog can be beneficial for your career, as you can easily get exposure. On the downside, online publications pay less, and most guest blogging opportunities are unpaid. But major publications have established science blogging networks and gather known science bloggers to write for these outlets. Such opportunities are generally paid, but again, less than in print. In addition, in order to break into such networks, you need to prove that you are able to write about a chosen topic and know whom you are writing for. This is best practiced by setting up your own blog, which requires a number of considerations.

If you want to build a successful science blog, finding a unique niche that no one else covers is a good idea. Also, you need to find out whom you are writing for. There are of course also some very talented generalists out there, but if you are starting out, narrowing down the topics you cover and hence the audience can prove helpful. Writing online can be very different from writing in print: You have to cater to online readers' short attention spans. If you fail to entertain them or do not quickly get to the point, they will stop reading your article. Your text, including your headlines, has to be easily indexable by search engines so it can be found. While the style and voice of online writing, even for science articles, is often more informal, proven narrative structures and transitions improve the readability of your texts.

There are also several legal aspects you need to consider. Simply reusing images from other websites or publications will earn you a lawsuit sooner or later. If in doubt, seek the permission of the author or company that holds the copyright. Most important, do not forget that simply publishing print content online is not sufficient to succeed. It must be specifically tailored to the online medium; you need to add value and leverage the technical possibilities, such as multimedia content and interactivity, in order to entice your audience and better convey complex scientific issues.

## Review questions

- How do online articles differ from their print counterparts in terms of structure, style and topics?
- What is the natural way to break into a science blogging network?
- How should you structure your paragraphs on a science blog in terms of paragraph length, ideas and post length?
- How can you incorporate non-essential background information into an online article?
- How can you find out who reads your science blog?
- Which aspects do you need to plan for before starting your own science blog?
- Under which circumstances can you reuse images from the web in a blog post?
- How can you structure a short science news blog post?

## Exercises

- Read Phil McKenna's 2013 article "Uprising" in *Matter*; then, identify and write down the key turning points.
- Make a plan for a science blog. Make a list of topics, and then narrow it down to find a niche. Find similar blogs and describe who your audience would be.
- Complement the previous exercise's plan with a schedule of how often you would post, which types of articles you would run and how you would promote them.
- Take three recent print science articles and rewrite their headlines in SEO-friendly ways.
- Take the same articles and rewrite their leads in SEO-friendly ways.
- Pick a recent press release and write a 400-word blog post about it. Address the shortcomings of the example in the first case study.
- Search the web and find apt images you could publish with the blog post from the previous exercise.

## Reading list

Blum, D., Knudson, M. and Henig, R.M. (eds.) (2006) *A Field Guide for Science Writers*. 2nd edition. New York: Oxford University Press
Bradshaw, P. and Rohumaa, L. (2013) Writing for the web, In Bradshaw, P. and Rohumaa, L. (eds.) *The Online Journalism Handbook*. Harlow: Pearson, 29–46
Bradshaw, P. and Rohumaa, L. (2013) How to blog, In Bradshaw, P. and Rohumaa, L. (eds.) *The Online Journalism Handbook*. Harlow: Pearson, 73–91
Reid, A. (2014) 9 ways to hone a headline to perfection, *Journalism.co.uk* [Online] Available at: www.journalism.co.uk/news/9-ways-to-hone-the-perfect-headline/s2/a555848/ [date accessed 23 February 2016]
Wilcox, C., Brookshire, B. and Goldman, J.G. (2016) *Science Blogging: The Essential Guide*. New Haven, CT: Yale University Press

## Links

BBC Academy search engine optimisation (SEO): www.bbc.co.uk/academy/journalism/article/art20130702112133608
Buzzfeed, Using Triggers to Know What the ?$# is Going on at Buzzfeed (SlideShare presentation by Jane Kelly): www.slideshare.net/dominodatalab/realtime-learning-using-triggers-to-know-what-the-is-going-on
Creative Commons search hub: https://search.creativecommons.org/
Daniel Bailey, Like Explorer: www.likeexplorer.com
The *Guardian* science blog network: www.theguardian.com/science/series/science-blog-network
Library of Congress, Government Resources for Science Images and Video: www.loc.gov/rr/scitech/selected-internet/imagesources.html
*National Geographic* blog network: www.nationalgeographic.com/ng-blogs/
The Open Network, Science Blogging – The Resources: www.theopennotebook.com/science-blogging-essential-guide/resources
Poynter News University, Online Media Law: www.newsu.org/courses/online-media-law-basics-bloggers-and-other-publish
ScienceSeeker (blog aggregator): www.scienceseeker.org
Stanford University, Writing in the Sciences (self-paced MOOC): https://lagunita.stanford.edu/courses/Medicine/SciWrite-SP/SelfPaced/

## References

Asser, M. (no date) Search engine optimisation (SEO), *BBC Academy* [Online Video] Available at: www.bbc.co.uk/academy/journalism/article/art201307021121 33608 [date accessed 23 February 2016]
Bradshaw, P. and Rohumaa, L. (2013) *The Online Journalism Handbook*. Harlow: Pearson
Brainard, C. (2015) Personal phone conversation on 26 June 2015
Boyle, A. (2006) Popular audiences on the web, In Blum, D., Knudson, M. and Henig, R.M. (eds.) *A Field Guide for Science Writers*. 2nd edition. New York: Oxford University Press, 90–96
Burnett, D. (2016) Personal Skype conversation on 3 March 2016
Etchells, P. (2015) Calling all paleo bloggers! Do you want to write for the Guardian science blog network? *The Guardian* [Online] Available at: www.theguardian.

com/science/blog/2015/oct/02/calling-all-palaeo-bloggers-do-you-want-to-write-for-the-guardian-science-blog-network [date accessed 30 November 2015]

Hernandez, R. (2014) Personal Skype conversation on 15 October 2014

Jarreau, P. (2014) Blogging tips for science bloggers, from science bloggers, *From the Lab Bench Blog (Scilogs.com)* [Online] Available at: www.fromthelabbench.com/blogging-tips-for-science-bloggers-from-science-bloggers/ [date accessed 10 December 2016]

Kouper, I. (2010) Science blogs and public engagement with science: Practices, challenges, and opportunities, *Journal of Science Communication*, vol. 9, no. 1 [Online] Available at: www.researchgate.net/profile/Inna_Kouper/publication/44279727_Science_blogs_and_public_engagement_with_science_practices_challenges_and_opportunities/links/00b7d51e821ea99cbe000000.pdf [date accessed 27 February 2016]

McKenna, P. (2016) Personal phone conversation on 18 February 2016

McKenna, P. (2013) Uprising: The environmental scandal that's happening right beneath your feet, *Matter (Medium.com)* [Online] Available at: https://medium.com/matter/the-environmental-scandal-thats-happening-right-beneath-your-feet-406a9f0d4166#.qly9j41ya [date accessed 12 February 2016]

Marsh, D. (2014) Secrets of great headline writing, *The Guardian* [Online] Available at: www.theguardian.com/commentisfree/2014/jan/09/secrets-great-headline-writing [date accessed 10 February 2016]

Oakes, K. (2014) How to create a successful science blog, *The Guardian* [Online] Available at: www.theguardian.com/science/2014/apr/17/science-blog-wellcome-trust-writing-prize [date accessed 12 February 2016]

Oakes, K. (2016) Personal phone conversation on 23 March 2016

Platt, J.R. (2016) Giraffe genetics reveal four separate (and threatened) species, *Extinction Countdown Blog (Scientific American)* [Online] Available at: http://blogs.scientificamerican.com/extinction-countdown/giraffe-genetics/ [date accessed 10 September 2016]

Rogers, K. (2016) Why is voicemail still a thing? *Motherboard* [Online] Available at: http://motherboard.vice.com/en_uk/read/why-is-voicemail-still-a-thing-technology-outdated-messaging [date accessed 12 February 2016]

Sainani, K.L. (2016) Personal email conversation on 3 March 2016

Statista (2016) Worldwide market share of leading search engines from January 2010 to October 2015, *Statista.com* [Online] Available at: www.statista.com/statistics/216573/worldwide-market-share-of-search-engines/ [date accessed 23 February 2016]

Weatherhead, R. (2014) Say it quick, say it well – The attention span of a modern internet consumer, *The Guardian* [Online] Available at: www.theguardian.com/media-network/media-network-blog/2012/mar/19/attention-span-internet-consumer [date accessed 20 February 2016]

Wilcox (2016) Personal Skype conversation on 25 February 2016

# 8

# STORYTELLING FOR SCIENCE JOURNALISTS

**What you will learn in this chapter:**

- Storytelling in journalism
- Narratives in science writing
- Categories of science stories
- Employing literary techniques in science stories
- The three-act structure for science storytelling
- Identifying narratives in science writing
- Case study: a debate over storytelling in science
- Case study: understanding long-form storytelling

## Introduction

Writing about science has a number of advantages. You will probably never run out of ideas and raw material, because there is an infinite pool of stories waiting to be told. Also, science has a potential to enthral readers. But science is also complex and often difficult to understand, which can scare many readers away. In fact, it is quite easy to write dry and boring science stories by simply enumerating the facts without a seeming connection. If that is not what you want, narrative structures and stories can help you carry the science and make your readers absorb even complex topics.

"Storytelling is the most seductive art of all," says Tim Radford in a video produced for the Wellcome Trust (*Guardian* 2013). In contrast to hard science, storytelling may seem like a creative but vague and often arbitrary mechanism to convey facts. But a good story is no accident. Rather, it employs techniques and tools that you can learn. That is why the first section of this chapter provides a primer on the basic elements of good stories such as character, dialogue and action. Every good character has her own agenda. In its most basic form, a story should contain at least one protagonist who wants to achieve a goal and opposing forces (antagonists with their own agenda) that try to hinder her from doing so. This formula sometimes can be perfectly applied to scientists:

> A good science story is like any other good story: it has tension and movement; it has conflicts the reader can relate to; it's usually about someone who wants something badly and faces obstacles trying to get it. What does this palaeontologist want to figure out or prove, and why? What stands in the way of her doing so?
>
> *(Dobbs 2013)*

Great stories also convey and evoke emotions. There are various techniques for achieving this, but in a nutshell, it is always better to let your characters express their emotions through their actions or statements than you just telling the readers. If you can connect facts to these emotions, your audience is quite likely to remember those facts. In fact, many Pulitzer Prize-winning stories consciously draw on emotions.

The next section picks up this thought and shows that such emotions and great narratives are usually found through extensive reporting. Carefully researched stories have the power to persuade your readers in and of themselves, regardless of factual errors. Hence, it is no wonder that scientists sometimes harshly critique storytellers who inaccurately depict science despite telling compelling stories. Also, you will find some basic story stencils that you can use to shape your own stories.

Narrative journalism makes extensive use of literature's arsenal of structural and linguistic elements. That is why in this chapter you will find a section on which literary devices you can employ to convey science, such as metaphors. The three-act structure is a narrative building block that dates back to the ancient Greeks; a dedicated section on that structure outlines how you can subdivide it and apply it to writing about science. That section contains also a number of tools that help you find your story.

Once you have written your story, you may want to check it for narrative soundness. The subsequent section points out a number of criteria that help you identify crucial narrative elements in stories. One of those techniques will also help you improve your literacy when reading about science. The penultimate section shows a debate between a scientist and a visual journalism professor over whether scientists should use storytelling elements to convey their findings.

Finally, award-winning science journalist David Dobbs discusses one of his best works and explains how he applied a classical music work's structure to write an emotional science story about depression. He explains how he changes rhythm, how you can seamlessly weave background information into your narratives and how he handled multiple narratives and protagonists in his story.

## Storytelling techniques in journalism

Applying fiction-writing techniques to journalistic stories at first sounds like a contradiction. But stories will help you make even complex science stick. At the heart of every good story lie emotions. As you will see in this chapter, this is no different for Pulitzer Prize-winning stories. In fact, it is the basic job of storytelling to make the audience feel something, says Garry Linnell, former editor-in-chief of the Australian magazine *The Bulletin* (Linnell 2014). Linnell suggests journalists could learn a thing or two from fiction writers:

> At the heart of great storytelling lies great reporting: picking up the nuances of the subject, having a great ear for dialogue. We read things every day, and sometimes we journalists are bad at quoting people, running long slabs that are meaningless. Our journalists have to get better – they have to develop a better ear for dialogue, like novelists.
>
> *(Linnell 2014:113–114)*

In fact, what novelists and other fiction writers employ when they spin narrative yarns are characters, dialogue, conflict, and obviously beautiful prose. The idea to borrow fiction writers' literary devices is not new: One of the precursors of today's narrative journalism was New Journalism, which dates back to the 1960s. Famous writers like Tom Wolfe, Hunter S. Thompson and Gay Talese advocated utilising literary devices and tell in-depth stories from a subjective point of view:

> The New Journalism has been succeeded by narrative writing, storytelling that takes some of its components from the techniques of fiction writers, as Wolfe recommended. These tools include emphasis on individuals through whom the action is advanced, dialogue, scene-setting, suspense. It takes to the outer limit the injunction "show me, don't tell me."
>
> *(Mencher 2011b:153)*

Mencher enumerates the three essentials of good fiction writing: character, action and dialogue. Do you remember Phil McKenna's story on the gas-sniffer from the previous chapter? It contains all of these ingredients. Another important element is plot (see Chapter 5). Your story's plot determines the order in which the events unfold. A classical story could portray a single protagonist who is pursuing a goal and encounters obstacles along the way (conflict) that keep her from reaching that goal; moreover, a story needs a climax that shows whether the protagonist reaches her goal. By all means, resolve any issues you have raised, because unresolved issues do not resonate well with most readers.

One rather formulaic story structure is the monomyth or hero's journey, as defined by Joseph Campbell: A protagonist goes on a quest, faces obstacles, masters a major crisis and returns changed and improved. Sometimes, no such structure may fit. Not all events lend themselves to storytelling; sometimes a news story is just a news story. In that case, narrative writing is not appropriate, and you should stick to the inverted pyramid instead Mencher (2011a).

Most writers agree (including this book's interviewees) that a chronological approach often works for writing narratives. In an essay for the *New Yorker*, legendary journalist John McPhee (2013) states that "almost always there is considerable tension between chronology and theme, and chronology traditionally wins"; he adds that this is not always desirable. Incidentally, chronology does not necessarily mean you have to rattle down your story exactly as it unfolded in reality. When you apply structures like the AB structure that alternates between story and context, be sure to digress from the story at the right time: "Good storytellers often digress at moments when especially interesting action is pending, and not at the completion of action" (Kramer 1995).

What good storytellers also do is evoke their readers' emotions. In fact, the most successful journalistic stories draw on human emotions. In a study, Karin Wahl-Jorgensen (2013) scrutinised 101 Pulitzer Prize-winning articles for their use of emotionality. She found that journalists showcase emotions to engage readers, especially in their articles' leads, but the emotions expressed are not their own:

> Even if journalists are restricted in their own emotional expression, journalistic genres remain infused by emotion because of a neat trick: journalists rely on the outsourcing of emotional labor to non-journalists – the story protagonists and other sources, who are (a) authorized to express emotions in public, and (b) whose emotions journalists can authoritatively describe without implicating themselves.
> *(Wahl-Jorgensen 2013:130)*

Emotionality and objectivity do not mutually exclude each other. Rather, they complement each other: Objective qualities, like accuracy, balance, fairness and impartiality alone are not sufficient for producing award-winning stories (Wahl-Jorgensen 2013).

In her study, anecdotal leads account for more than 60 per cent of the 101 examined stories across all genres (feature, explanatory, international, national, public service, investigative), while inverted pyramid leads are used for less than 20 per cent. When specifically examining the feature genre, the predominant type of lead within the examined feature articles is the anecdotal lead, with a share of almost 94 per cent (Wahl-Jorgensen 2013). For the most part, the leads she found draw on negative emotions, which falls perfectly into line with the according news value (see Chapter 2).

Finally, Wahl-Jorgensen (2013) contends that emotion does not necessarily have to be explicitly expressed, although this is the most common form.

Sometimes, journalists can draw on presuppositions (for example, that the death of children is always tragic) to evoke emotional responses in their audience. Journalists almost never express their own feelings but instead let the protagonists talk about their emotions, which she calls *outsourcing of emotions*. Not only is this ability of emotional storytelling highly valued but it also "is explicitly recognized as a criterion in the selection of winning stories" (Wahl-Jorgensen 2013:141).

Apart from filling your narratives with emotions, you can apply the following storytelling techniques to craft your narratives (Lillie 2016):

- **Begin in the middle:** Start with an important moment that is relevant to the story, and make sure it contains action.
- **End at the end:** After achieving closure to the initial problem, the article should end or your audience will be bored.
- **Don't give away the end:** Even if you feel the urge to tell your readers where your story is going, do not tell them. This is key to suspense.
- **Set things up ahead of time:** Important elements of your story, especially regarding scientific concepts, should be explained early enough that your audience knows how they function once they come into action.
- **Know what the narrative arc is:** Know how your characters change over the course of your story (even though you should not give it away to your audience yet).
- **Make sure we know how you're feeling:** You cannot force your audience to empathise with potentially dry and boring concepts, but you can show them how you feel about these concepts and why they are of importance to you, which in turn raises their interest.

## Narratives in science writing

Narrative journalism (also called literary or storytelling journalism) is a subset of narrative non-fiction writing, such as biographies or encyclopaedias. Before I discuss narratives in science, I will briefly recap and define what a narrative is. Many confuse narratives with plot, but plot is just the chronological or cause-and-effect sequence of events; as such, it is one of many components of a good narrative. The other components are character, action, dialogue, scenes and a narrator and her voice. Narrative journalism uses literary techniques but still adheres to journalism's core values, such as accuracy (not necessarily brevity) and clarity. As a narrative journalist, you can either gather your facts by observation or you can reconstruct them by talking to witnesses or consulting documents of events that happened. In fact, famous narrative journalists, like John McPhee and Mark Kramer, state that extensive reporting lies at the heart of good narratives. This often involves spending time with interviewees not in set-up meetings but in their natural habitat. In science, this means you will have to visit scientists in their laboratories, during their fieldwork, at conferences, at rallies or at their homes.

This is exactly what Denis Dilba and Georg Dahm, editors-in-chief of the German digital science magazine *Substanz*, encourage their writers to do: fully immerse themselves in the topic. Dilba tells me how *Substanz*'s authors approach stories:

> Our approach is to show how science really works. We think that most of the other publications don't really do that. Obviously, this also depends on the pieces' length: Online, a 600- or 800-word science article gets hyped for at most half an hour, and then the next article will already supersede it. Online, readers' clicks count most. But most stories don't portray science as the long-running process it really is. Instead, science often gets portrayed as one scientist who suddenly solves a scientific problem using some sort of magic trick. This approach compresses complex scientific developments that perhaps took ten years or more. Those stories miss out that research often involves sweat, tears, a lot of teamwork, calling people, finding inspiration and innovation. What we try is focus on this process and at the same time highlight the people behind it. We want to know from the scientists, what is it that you actually do? What intrigues you so much about your research topic that you decided to spend the last ten years of your life working on it? These researchers often don't even know whether their output will contribute to curing a disease. Finding out what motivates them, which should be part of every journalist's armamentarium, is crucial for us.
>
> *(Dilba 2015)*

Dilba adds that *Substanz* focuses on stories with narratives and thinks those are the publication's strong suit. But a protagonist from a laboratory alone does not make a good story. That is why they try to cover complex topics exhaustively from many perspectives while conveying the science by employing enthralling characters and narratives that connect the facts and events and using a vivid style. Ideally, the readers do not consciously notice that they learn about science; rather, they pick it up as they read through a compelling narrative (Dilba 2015).

As opposed to informative journalism, narrative journalism conveys information that sticks, which is not the case with short science morsels that you can read on the web. As amusing and entertaining those are, the conveyed information does not stick. The same is true of the inverted pyramid, as former blogs editor Bora Zivkovic writes in a blog post for *Scientific American*:

> Unlike with Inverted Pyramid articles, in which the reader's focus rapidly falls off after reading the headline, the narrative sustains focus (it

may even rise as the reader progresses through the piece). . . . Readers can actually learn and retain new knowledge, not just get temporarily informed.

*(Zivkovic 2011)*

You can also apply narrative schemes such as "a scientist struggling with a puzzle", "a race against time" or "a race against another scientific institution" (Hornmoen 2006:176). But such narratives require closure and solutions, and sometimes the depicted scientific advances do not provide that. As a result, many science journalists turn to the "semi-narrative and less absorbing form" (Hornmoen 2006:176). In fact, you will often end up using narrative elements and techniques instead of writing full narrative, as not every subject lends itself to storytelling:

> It is rather common to open with a narrative scene, which is followed by a more extensive part devoted to exposition. Characteristic of this part are attempts to describe and explain current research and its findings, before the article in some cases returns to the narrative towards the end, resulting in a circular composition.
>
> *(Hornmoen 2006:174)*

Another reason science writers hesitate to write full narratives is that such stories frequently draw criticism. Some scientists complain that narratives water down science's complexity and foster the omission of important facts and context. One caveat you should keep in mind is the persuasive power of narratives. As Dahlstrom (2014) points out, readers perceive narratives in and of themselves as valid argumentation, regardless of supporting evidence: "Narratives are intrinsically persuasive. Because they describe a particular experience rather than general truths, narratives have no need to justify the accuracy of their claims; the story itself demonstrates the claim" (Dahlstrom 2014:13616). On top of that, narratives' structures lead the readers to believe the events are logical cause-and-effect sequences that leave little room for counter-arguments, as the narrative flow creates the impression the conclusion of the narrative is inevitable, while the scientific reality is much more complex (Dahlstrom 2014).

Narratives in science are different. Scientists read a lot, and they are used to criticising each other's work. In his 2016 *New Yorker* article "Same but Different", physician Siddhartha Mukherjee writes about epigenetics and twins as he attempts to show how the environment alters the genome. Mukherjee's article drew a lot of criticism from established scientists, including from the senior editor of *Current Biology* Florian Maderspacher, who published a letter to the editor in which he clarifies that Mukherjee had misrepresented gene regulation. Some also pointed out that his literary devices, such as his metaphors, were misplaced. Science writer Tabitha Powledge called Mukherjee out and found explicit words for what she thinks about literary science writing: "Writing for Story distorts and cripples explanatory prose. The fact that narrative science/medical journalism is fashionable – and at some pubs obligatory – doesn't make it right. Or informative" (Powledge 2016). Mukherjee later added that he originally had added a part on other gene regulation factors but it had fallen victim to the editing process. Editorial constraints, together with a shortage of time to exhaustively report and research your topic, are indeed some of the main problems you face as journalists. You will always run the risk of oversimplifying when you are boiling down complex scientific concepts. Most important, whether and how you can employ narratives to tell a science story depends on the story itself. If all you do is explanatory writing, however, chances are nobody wants to read about it, as Susannah Eliott, CEO of the Australian Science Media Centre, points out:

> It's all very well to say that storytelling constitutes dumbing down the science but the converse is that worthy stories without a good narrative won't be read. So if you're happy to have science relegated to the worthy but boring pile only read by science geeks then that's fine. It is difficult to make a hard and fast rule about this since it depends very much on the type of story. Clearly there are some topics that need to be handled sensitively and the storytelling component is more about the context you provide to create the narrative – it doesn't always have to be gee whiz, quirky or humorous to have an interesting narrative.
>
> *(Eliott 2016)*

## Categories of science stories

How you tell a story also depends on what type of science story your reporting lends itself to. It seems that, for the most part, science writers consider two categories: light-hearted, cheerful stories about scientific advances and in-depth, investigative stories that offer more background. With this in mind, in a 2010 interview, award-winning science journalist David Dobbs distinguishes between two forms of science stories. First, there are "wow that's cool" stories (which he later rephrased as "nifty" stories): explanatory articles about new scientific advances that evoke readers' emotions (Schultz 2010).

Dobbs calls the second investigative category of science stories "this smells funny" stories, which he later rephrased as "fishy" stories (Schultz 2010): These are critical stories that are not just based on findings in papers and scientist's claims, but they look behind the scenes, dig deeper and look into aspects other than the mere reported scientific facts:

> That kind of story is about funding, it's about sociology of science, it's about people's motives. It's about whether or not some funny business

is going on, whether studies are being tweaked for one reason or another. You know, warped by conflicts of interest.

*(Dobbs in Schultz 2010)*

Dobbs also notes that he likes writing both types of science stories: cool stories where the science is well done and intriguing and the critical stories where the science is rather problematic. He deems both types of stories a necessity in science journalism (Schultz 2010).

Fellow science writer and blogger Ed Yong confirms this point of view in a post on his blog Not Exactly Rocket Science, which is now part of *National Geographic*'s blog network. In his post, Yong adds that he prefers writing cool stories. Even if he wrote in-depth about groundbreaking medical advances, such articles would generally attract fewer readers than articles on newly discovered animal behaviour or the colours of dinosaurs feathers; readers just care more about the latter stories. That said, like Dobbs, Yong also deems both categories of science stories important (Yong 2010), and he pays no particular attention to the story's relevance when writing nifty stories: "I often tell stories on this blog with absolutely no practical relevance. Their goal is to instil a sense of wonder and curiosity about the world, which is what the best science communicators have done for me" (Yong 2010).

Bora Zivkovic also joined the discussion about story categories and extended Dobbs's and Yong's story categories. In a blog post on science storytelling, Zivkovic adds an additional category: relevant stories. He also offers advice on how you can build a basic structure for all three types of science stories. Relevant stories are a hybrid between informative and educational science journalism in that they help readers make better decisions regarding their lives, politics and finance. Each type has a different effect on your story's narrative:" In cool stories, science is a hero, and often the researchers as well. In relevant stories, heroism is muted, though may be implied. In fishy stories, the scientist (and sometimes science) comes out as a villain" (Zivkovic 2011). If you want to tell any such science story, you should divide your story's narrative into the following three components, all centred on a scientific discovery (Zivkovic 2011):

1   A description of the world before the scientific discovery
2   A description of the scientific discovery
3   A description of how the world has changed because of the scientific discovery.

This three-part division already hints at the basic story structure, which you can read about in the next section but one.

Note that your story's hero does not always have to be human; it can also be an animal or an inanimate object (Zivkovic 2011). If you want to bring inanimate objects (and other sorts of science protagonists) alive, your means of choice are literary devices such as plot or metaphors. They turn otherwise difficult and dry scientific concepts into compelling reads, even if you have to do a lot of explanation. The next section discusses such techniques and shows how you can utilise them to write narratives.

## Employing literary techniques in science stories

"We are wired to love stories and narratives," says science journalist Angela Posada-Swafford to me; she adds that this has always been one of the primary ways to pass on information. She also tells me that she passes her evenings reading literature, analysing it and highlighting rhetorical figures that she then would like to use in her future science articles, such as alliterations. Apart from her linguistic experiments with literary techniques in science writing (including an ode to a gravitational wave), Posada-Swafford says the ultimate goal is to paint colourful images in your readers' minds. She suggests you should think in scenes and create scenes that resemble close-ups and wide-angle shots, similar to a movie director. This will put the readers right into the story (Posada-Swafford 2016):

> Narrative writing is essentially a combination of fiction techniques that are very useful in telling medical and science stories. Even if you are not writing a narrative, think of yourself as a storyteller. Use narrative writing for an entire piece or only a portion of a story. Here are the basics: details, anticipation, quotes.
>
> *(Mary Knudson in Blum et al. 2006:31)*

Set a pace so your readers can read your article in one shot. Devices that help you alternate that pace are active voice and telling verbs. They convey a sense of adventure and immediacy. If that does not matter, use past tense. Write short sentence transitions and create rhythm by alternating between long and short sentences. Alliterations are another device to convey a sense of rhythm (Knudson in Blum et al. 2006)

A fast-paced, rhythmic read is also the result the four distinctive literary techniques that Tom Wolfe employs (Kallan 1979):

1 **Third-person point of view:** Tell each scene through the eyes of a character.
2 **Scene-on-scene construction:** Move from one scene to the next and create a sense of immediacy.
3 **Extensive dialogue:** Let the characters speak for themselves through dialogue. This makes them genuine and helps your audience connect to them.
4 **Recording of status-life symbols:** Pay attention to even the smallest details if they help reveal and symbolise the characters.

Note how Wolfe's first, third and fourth techniques all focus on the human aspect of a story. You can apply similar techniques in science journalism; human-centred topics, such as medicine, are particularly well-suited for them. For example, medical journalist Sonya Collins states that when you write about medicine, you can also win over the non-affected portion of your audience by introducing them to protagonists who "live the stories – the characters need to move any story along" (Collins 2015:222).

Like Wolfe, she suggests you should draw on details and write scenically. But in science, you also need to explain complicated scientific processes and boil them down without dumbing them down. Your literary tool of choice for explaining science is the metaphor. In her article, Collins draws on an example of describing a cell as a fried egg under the microscope. Scientists might be sometimes unhappy with such depictions, but these vivid depictions help your readers understand complex scientific topics; better still, such passages can leave your readers with a satisfactory feeling that they have successfully acquired new scientific knowledge. Use literary devices from fiction and "use these tools to engage lay readers in topics readers may otherwise think are too complicated to understand" (Collins 2015:222).

You can apply many literary devices to tell better science stories. The following is a (by no means exhaustive) list of literary and rhetorical devices that many fiction writers employ:

- **Flashback:** If you start your story in the middle, you can jump back in time and explain events, weave in background information or reveal more about characters. Flashbacks are separate scenes.
- **Flashforward:** Similar to a flashback, but in the opposite direction – a jump forward in time. Unlike foreshadowing, this is an explicit scene that tells the reader/viewer something that happens in the future.
- **Chekhov's gun:** Everything in your story must be there for a reason. An item might appear near the beginning of a story and then turn up again around the climax, only then making clear its purpose.
- **Foreshadowing:** A hint at what is to come without explicitly stating it. For example, the narrator could mention it explicitly: "but when Dr. Smith went into his laboratory, little did he know he would leave it on a stretcher." Or a symbol could hint at a forthcoming event. Chekhov's guns can also serve as foreshadowing tools.
- **Turning point:** Also known as a plot twist, this is a memorable point at which the story takes an unexpected (for the reader) change of direction. (See also the case study of Phil McKenna's article in Chapter 7.)
- **Story within a story:** Nested stories, told by one of your main story's character, reveal more about the character or provide more background for the outer story.
- **Motif:** A symbolic object or linguistic construct that helps you deliver your story's theme. Motifs often recur within stories. Beware of too

obviously using motifs. You can also try to loosely connect a group of distinct objects as a motif.

- **Metaphor:** One word's attributes (vehicle) are transferred to another word (tenor). The vehicle is generally more colourful and well-known. Your number one tool to explain jargon and all non-trivial issues.
- **Simile:** A direct comparison with the same use as a metaphor. You can identify similes because they use the words *like* and *as*.
- **Anaphora:** A repetition of the beginning of a sentence. An anaphora helps you emphasise statements and persuade your readers. It also adds rhythm to your text.
- **Irony:** As a rhetorical device, irony is simply stating the opposite of what you mean. As a narrative device, you can reveal facts to your readers that your characters do not know.

You should only use particular devices when there is a reason for doing so, never as an end in themselves. For example, dialogue is not always essential but depends on the narrative arc, as Angela Posada-Swafford says. On one hand, some stories are best told through the eyes of a scientist, which is when you should visit that scientist. On the other hand, especially in science writing, sometimes your protagonist is not human but instead a neutrino or a shark. In such cases, you could draw on an imaginary inner monologue or be entirely descriptive and still write a compelling story (Posada-Swafford 2016).

## The three-act structure for science storytelling

Three is a magic number in stories. The rule of three states that information delivered in threes is particularly memorable and persuasive. Dividing the world and one's thought process into triads dates back to Neo-Platonist philosopher Proclus. German philosopher Johann Gottlieb Fichte picked up the concept and coined the triad of thesis-antithesis-synthesis: The thesis is an initial thought, the antithesis contradicts the thesis and the synthesis merges both, which often leads to the rephrasing of the initial assertion.

In stories, you can find the rule of three frequently in fairy tales such as the Three Little Pigs. You can find the rule of three also in jokes. In both contexts, often two characters' actions fail to overcome an issue, and the third one finally resolves the issue. For example, all three pigs build houses to protect themselves from the wolf. Two houses collapse, and only the third builds a strong enough house to survive the wolf's attacks. Politicians use the rule of three to deliver persuasive speeches. Businesses use the rule of three to make memorable product presentations and advertisements. For example, when Steve Jobs introduced the iPhone in 2007, he introduced it as "an iPod, a phone, and an internet communicator", an introduction he repeated three times. In fact, Apple uses triads in their product presentations all the time and sometimes uses nested triads, too. In literature, the number three is used to structure masterpieces. For example, Dante structured his *Divine Comedy* into three canticas (hell, purgatory and paradise). Each canticle is again subdivided into thirty-three cantos. Screenwriting teacher Syd Field divides a screenplay into three acts as well:

- **Act 1:** Short act that introduces the story's main characters and gets the actual story started. The inciting incident is a particular turning point that changes the status quo of the protagonist's life. Length: One quarter of the story.
- **Act 2:** The protagonist faces obstacles, the tension rises. The lion's share of the story can be found in act 2. In the middle, there is a turning point, a change of fortune. Act 2 is also the longest act. Length: One half of the screenplay.
- **Act 3:** The story's main character faces the crisis, which will ultimately end in the story climax, leading to a happy or sad end. Sometimes the end contains another, final plot twist. Length: One quarter of the screenplay.

Plot points connect the acts. They are the moments where the most noticeable changes occur. The inciting incident in the first act gets the story started, a culmination (the midpoint) in the second act is often a reversal of fortune and the climax in the third act shows whether your protagonist overcomes the main problem. To be clear, this is a fiction-writing technique. As a journalist, you are not going to mould your material into three acts if the facts do not support it. But where appropriate, you can use specific elements, and sometimes you can structure your entire story using the rule of three or a three-act structure.

In her essay "What Narrative Writers Can Learn from Screenwriters", journalist-turned-screenwriter Nora Ephron explains what journalists and screenwriters can mutually learn from each other:

> I have also learned things through screenwriting that would have been good to know when I worked as a journalist. As a young journalist I thought that stories were simply *what happened*. As a screenwriter I realized that we *create* stories by imposing narrative on the events that happen around us.
>
> Structure is the key to narrative. These are the crucial questions any storyteller must answer: *Where does it begin? Where does the beginning start to end and the middle begin? Where does the middle start to end and the end begin?* In film school you learn these three questions as the classic three-act structure. This structure is practically a religion among filmmakers. Learning it is more instinctive among journalists.
>
> *(Ephron in Kramer and Call 2007)*

So, how can this tripartite approach aid journalism? Marine biologist and documentary filmmaker Randy Olson defined a template to reduce an entire story to a single sentence: As opposed to listing facts with the conjunction *and*, the ABT (and, but, therefore) template states a few facts, connects them with *and*, progresses to the problem (*but*) and finally combines the former two parts using *therefore*:

_____ and _____, but _____, therefore _____.
*(Olson 2015:16)*

Note how Olson's template resembles Fichte's thesis-antithesis-synthesis pattern. In fact, Olson structured his book (apart from the introduction) into three parts: thesis, antithesis and synthesis. He also likens the structure of scientific papers (IMRAD: introduction, methods, results and discussion) to a three-part structure that can be summed up as beginning (introduction), middle (methods and results) and end (discussion).

Olson also shows that Abraham Lincoln used the ABT template in one of his speeches, and he identifies the ABT template in a seminal research paper on DNA (Watson and Crick 1953). While the ABT structure produces a sentence, Olson also recommends a word-level template that he coined after a geneticist who used it first: The Dobzhansky template helps you find your story's unifying theme:

Nothing in _____ makes sense except in the light of _____.
*(Olson 2015:84)*

Fill in the first blank with the topic you want to cover, and the second word is your theme or message you want your story to convey. Olson also presents a third template, the paragraph template, which comes in two variations: the logline maker and the story cycle, both of which are based to varying degrees on Campbell's hero's journey and the according twelve structural steps. Its strongest emotional point is the darkest hour, when the protagonist faces a major crisis. Ask for these moments. Showing the flaws of a scientist (perhaps an accident that later led to a greater discovery) is a another technique you can use (Olson 2015).

Both aspects make your audience identify more with the protagonist. In an article for Nieman Storyboard, associate journalism professor John Capouya suggests how you can make your audience feel connected to your protagonist: "Quickly, vividly expose the main character's most compelling attributes – be they positive or negative – as early as possible" (Capouya 2014).

Screenplays usually do not start directly with the inciting incident but first show the protagonist in her ordinary world (as in the hero's journey). In narrative science writing, however, you can start directly with the inciting incident and turn it into your story's lead, as award-winning science journalist David Dobbs tells me:

> Screenwriting is very useful, and I resisted that notion for a while, because it seems so formulaic. But they have this down to a science. You shouldn't stick to it like to a paint-by-numbers book, but there are certain principles that catch the reader's attention – like the idea of an inciting event. Maybe you don't call it that, but every time you write a lead, you are creating some sort of inciting event that grabs the reader and propels the story forward.
>
> *(Dobbs 2016)*

Capouya also recommends that you use inciting incidents to write good story leads: Character traits, a change of direction and a sense of unexpectedness are proven ingredients that will hook your audience. But unlike a screenwriter, as a journalist you must not fabricate any of these plot points. Facts are sacrosanct. If you want to use plot points, you need to find them through your reporting; simply ask your sources for these life-changing events: "You can ask flat out: 'What was the moment when everything changed for you?' Odds are, they'll know" (Capouya 2014).

The takeaway of this section is: Be pragmatic about using these techniques. Do employ the techniques that support your story. Many successful science storytellers, such as David Dobbs, Ben Lillie and Randy Olson, recommend using parts of the three-act structure as a device that conveys complex science that your readers might otherwise perceive as dry and boring. So, do use the three-act structure and other narrative and techniques, but when you do, make sure you mould your facts into a story in a way that does not misrepresent them or distort the science. Above all, never tinker with the facts just to lump them into a story that does not exist otherwise.

## Identifying narratives in science writing

Some science stories entertain readers, and some stories explain things and educate them. The best stories do both. If it is true that stories carry science and make the information stick with readers, then they should certainly be valid tools to teach science to students. That is why Stephen Klassen, a physics professor at the University of Winnipeg, shows in a paper how you can analyse and eventually construct a science story. Using the following ten elements of narrative, you can analyse science stories but not construct them (Klassen 2009):

1 **Event-tokens:** Events are central, often chronologically ordered elements that support a story and represent change: "Successive events are

made more significant in the light of preceding events. Events lead to changes of state" (Klassen 2009:410).

2  **Narrator:** This can either be an observer or one of the story's characters. The narrator selects the events, their sequence and, most important, the point of the story. You can tell the story through your own eyes or comment on it.

3  **Narrative appetite:** A synonym for suspense and one of the three ingredients of a good story. This is your story's ability to raise questions. Suspense will make your readers wonder what happens next and is a key element of compelling stories.

4  **Past time:** All events you report about have already happened in a certain order, but you can expand the chronological approach by adding flashbacks, which make your story non-linear. Recounting the story by withholding key events for a while adds suspense and makes for better stories.

5  **Structure:** Check for two kinds of story structure. The first is the classic story as a series of interconnected events that follow the classical structure: "The overarching structure of the story has an opening situation, complications that produce rising action, and a resolution in the end" (Klassen 2009:411). The second is a series of mini stories that are defined by the change of the status quo and hence create a sense of story flow.

6  **Agency:** This element refers to the characters' obligation to make decisions and subsequently cope with the consequences.

7  **Purpose:** Why should you tell this story, and why would your readers care? This should be one of the first questions you should ask yourself before writing a story.

8  **Role of the reader or listener:** Write the story with your readers in mind. Ideally, they empathise with the characters and engage with the story. Can you lead your readers to formulate higher-level, critical questions (how, why)?

9  **Effect of the untold:** Be selective when choosing events. You can never recount all of them, so you must leave certain events out. This blank space forces readers to fill it with information on their own or to ask questions about the missing information.

10  **Irony:** Capsize your readers' expectations. This element is not essential but a really good storytelling device. Readers can remember surprising turns very well.

Being a science educator, Klassen focuses on how students can learn science from good stories – a characteristic he claims differentiates science stories from stories in the humanities. He adds that good science stories make a point, and students can test their understanding of a story by trying to sum up that point after reading. Additionally, he claims good science stories raise questions, which in turn arise from a contradiction between readers' expectations and what the story actually shows them. That is why situational irony works well. This gap prompts readers to come up with questions that ask why something happens or how something is possible. Consequently, he suggests students could benefit from formulating questions in response to science stories (Klassen 2009).

The questions can be factual-level questions that involve the who, what, when and where and higher-level questions that involve the how and why. With this in mind, Klassen proposes a method for analysing and critiquing science stories that is based on the history of science. His method consists of five points, with the last point containing the actual check for narrative elements:

1  Outline the historical basis before writing the story.
2  Use reliable sources for your historical research.
3  The history used must be relevant.
4  The story must be written with the readers in mind.
5  Analyse for the ten aforementioned story elements.

How can you benefit from this methodology? First, as a science writer, you are a student of the very science you are covering. If you do not understand the science yourself, you cannot explain it to your readers. Hence, try writing down your own questions after reading about new scientific concepts and issues. Observe whether your questions belong to the factual-level or higher-level class. Second, use the aforementioned ten elements to check your own and other writers' stories for their narrative impact; this is an excellent way to improve your own analytical reading skills.

## Case study: a debate over storytelling in science

In July 2013, *Nature Methods* published an article in the journal's Points of View column in which the authors, Martin Krzywinski and Alberto Cairo, argued that graphics can benefit when scientists apply storytelling elements to them:

> Familiar elements underpin most stories: introduction, question, conflict, buildup and resolution. These can also be applied to datagraphics. For example, use the idea of a story arc and make your presentation episodic – unfold it, don't dump it.
>
> *(Krzywinski and Cairo 2013b:687)*

Moreover, they invite the reader of the column to be selective about what is presented in the graphics, to be aware that they are presenting the information for the general public and for other scientists (arguing that both groups can benefit from storytelling elements), and to imagine what the headline on their study would look like in a newspaper. Furthermore, they illustrate the employment of storytelling elements like plot twists by breaking down an information graphic into five panels (Krzywinski and Cairo 2013b:687).

The column prompted Yarden Katz, a departmental fellow in systems biology at Harvard Medical School and former postdoctoral researcher at the Broad Institute, to respond to the editors in an article that was later published in *Nature Methods*. Katz argues against the presented approach because storytelling cannot sufficiently capture the complex and experimental nature of science:

> Storytelling encourages the unrealistic view that scientific projects fit a singular narrative. Biological systems are difficult to measure and control, so nearly all experiments afford multiple interpretations – but storytelling actively denies this fact of science.
>
> *(Katz 2013)*

Krzywinski and Cairo (2013a) responded again, clarifying that their suggestion to leave out "speaks to controlling the amount of information to avoid an incomprehensible image and deferring it to the text, where it can be more suitably framed" (Krzywinsik and Cairo 2013a:1046), and they reject Katz's claim that "inconvenient truths are swept away" (Katz 2013:1045).

Yarden Katz explains to me why he thinks storytelling does not do the scientific reality justice:

> What I claim is that storytelling is not rich enough to capture scientific discourse. When scientists talk about each other, they talk about arguments and evidence in favor of particular hypotheses. They talk about the potential hypotheses that are available to explain the data, they talk about the caveats, the noise; here is evidence for hypothesis one, and here is weaker evidence, but still evidence, for hypothesis two. This is a puzzle, maybe, that remains unsolved in this current work. They speak in this language, which is much more like the language of arguments, theories, models. In that framework, there is very much room for making a persuasive argument, or a well-written argument, or communicating an argument very well. There is nothing wrong with writing well. I am not attacking narrative in that sense. But language is much richer and very different from this storytelling language. Storytelling language actually is masquerading as a communication tip or advice. People like Cairo say, "we are just trying to make scientists communicate their science better". But actually, there is an ideology to it, because the kinds of things you can frame by their notion of storytelling are particular kinds of results. So, their results have a clear beginning, a very linear flow and a very clear, strong conclusion. Scientists know this, because those who are trying to advance their careers are catering to journal editors

who judge science very much in the same way as these communication studies people judge what is a good story.

*(Katz 2016)*

Katz then adds that storytelling advocates like Cairo use this seemingly innocuous communication device to claim that they are showing scientists how to better communicate their research after they have conducted it, while they also claim they are not altering the science:

> But actually, they are. It's very telling in a way that the Cairo column was actually a visualization column. They were pretending to give you visualization advice, but I think within it, if you read between the lines, there is a kind of subtext about what your science should look like, what counts as good science and what counts as a compelling story. Scientists are acutely aware of this, they try to mould their science into this form.
>
> *(Katz 2016)*

Katz also makes clear that he is not fundamentally against employing storytelling techniques (for example, in journalism), but deems it too limited a tool to convey the complexities of science in journal papers:

> Storytelling fundamentally narrows what you can say, and it encourages scientists to look for a particular form of science, which is actually an anomalous form. Normally, what happens in the lab just gets not captured in this way. That is my main objection to storytelling. It doesn't mean that you can't write well or write compellingly or communicate your results in a good way. It just means you need a richer language, and storytelling is not rich enough.
>
> *(Katz 2016)*

I asked Cairo, the Knight Chair in Visual Journalism and a professor at the University of Miami, what he thinks might have caused the stir over his first article in *Nature Methods*.

Cairo first points out that you can use narrative structures and elements, and he distinguishes those from storytelling. Storytelling comes into play when you start enhancing these linear narratives by weaving in a human factor that makes the story more emotionally appealing. Another storytelling technique to enhance narratives is the use of anecdotes that illustrate a larger point that will follow. Cairo then proceeds to comment on where he thinks the criticism his article sparked originates from:

> Many scientists are distrustful of the very word *story*, because they believe that as writers and journalists – and this includes visual journalists – we focus too much on that fun, attractive, appealing part of the story,

and that we don't pay much attention to the actual science, or that we try to create a clear-cut narrative that does not depict the uncertainty of the data that they have. There is a crucial tension between journalism and science in the sense that science is not precise. Science is never precise. Data results are always uncertain, there are always caveats, there are always exceptions and the journalistic impulse is to come up with a clear-cut narrative. This is the point, this is the takeaway. So, how do you balance out those two things? It's really difficult. But a middle point can be reached.

*(Cairo 2016)*

In fact, Cairo points out that such a balance has already been reached:

When explaining this kind of tension to scientists here, at the University of Miami, they tell me it is possible to build a clear-cut narrative, but then they include the exceptions, caveats, and show the uncertainty in the visualization and the confidence intervals. So it is possible, but how to do it? That depends from case to case, but there is a middle point to be reached. I think the problem with the article in *Nature Methods*, this postdoc [Katz] took the idea in a wrong way, he didn't really understand what it was all about. He just said, "No, but we need to present all of the information." In my opinion, he had a quite old-fashioned idea of what the scientific process really is, or scientific communication. If I remember the article well, he was like, "But as scientists, we just want to take a look at the data and explore it ourselves." That is completely untrue. When scientists read scientific papers, those papers have a very clear structure that allows you to scan them and find the main takeaways. It is very rare that scientists take the time and double-check the data. They just read the paper. So the paper is basically communication. For me, it is not that different than writing a news story, only that it goes deeper and uses a different language. But in the end, it is also a narrative.

*(Cairo 2016)*

## Case study: understanding long-form storytelling

In 2006, David Dobbs wrote a long-form feature story on a then-novel way of treating depression, deep brain stimulation (DBS), which involves brain surgery for implanting the necessary electrodes. His story features two protagonists: one is the patient, Deanna Cole-Benjamin, whose depression proved resistant to all of the traditional depression treatments, and the other is Helen Mayberg, a neurologist who asked Cole-Benjamin to participate in a groundbreaking study. What is remarkable about Dobbs's story is that it easily manages to keep the readers' interest despite its length of more than 5,000 words. If you want to make the most out of this section, read Dobbs's

(2006) piece on the *New York Times* website before heading on. Also, get a copy of Schubert's String Quartet No. 13 (Rosamunde), D 804, Op. 29 and listen to it before reading on.

Dobbs structured his article after that very musical piece, because he was studying it at the time, as he explains to me (Dobbs 2016):

> I used a Schubert quartet as a model for this story. That was just happenstance: I was studying violin at the time, and our ensemble was working on this Schubert quartet. The teacher was very big on understanding the structure. This really resonated. . . . If you know structure, then you have a purpose. You know why this sentence is in this place, in this paragraph. Why is this paragraph here, in this section? What is this section of the story doing? If you know those last questions first, then the smaller, detailed questions are easier to answer. You will understand, for example, here I need to be brisk. You don't have to, but this way, you fit it into a plan. You decide. Perhaps you just had a long section that asks a lot of the readers, it just absorbs them with a lot of technical information about neurology, and they're learning new terms. Now, don't burden them with another long passage. This is a good time for something quick, so the rhythm of your sentences should be shorter. Allegro, presto, you change the speeds of music. I found that tremendously helpful while writing that piece.

This change in rhythm becomes evident in the following excerpt of "A Depression Switch?" The first paragraph is emotional, and the second, which is five times longer, takes the reader aside and progresses from the specific example to explanatory context and background information. At the same time, this passage shows how Dobbs connects the two paragraphs by reminding the readers what is at stake (which is a brilliant storytelling device):

> We felt we'd tried everything and nothing worked. But we talked about it and decided, "Well, what have we got to lose?"
>
> What she hoped to lose, of course, was her depression. But depression, which 5 to 10 percent of Americans suffer in any given year. . . .
> *(Dobbs 2006)*

Apart from these rhythmic changes in the lengths of paragraph, Dobbs explains that his story is basically a detective story. He explains how he weaves background information into the narrative without letting it become dry and boring for the reader:

> The basic structure of the depression switch piece, and this happens a lot in science, is a two-track narrative. This is common in a lot of genres like detective fiction and crime fiction. In one chapter you have the cop and in the next chapter the criminal. If every section is 800 words long,

this is not going to work. You need to vary the length of the sections. Whenever possible, if I have to explain something, like background or context, then instead of explaining it, I would rather tell the story of how it came to be. This way, people understand more. At some point, I needed to explain Mayberg's hypothesis she was testing and how she came to it over these years of working. So, I could have just said "Mayberg believes", and then bang away at the reader with all of her ideas. But if you show how she came across them, you watch the idea grow and expand, you see its genesis, and you expand it more. You also have a narrative of someone pursuing her desire. What does she want? She wants to figure out how depression works. And here she is, sleuthing it out. It's a detective story. Most science is, and you would be crazy not to use that model, because people love detective stories.

He also notes that when you alternate between different narrative threads, you must be cautious that no one thread takes the upper hand.

You don't want to force it, but if after a long section you get a chance to write something very short, do it, but only if it is appropriate to the material. About halfway through the story, after two long sections, I realized Deanna is threatening to disappear from the story. This is a common problem in science writing: If you are following a scientist and a regular person, then the science, A part might become predominant. So, you have to get back to that B track. You can't leave it from 10 per cent way into the story to 80 per cent. This was threatening to happen. This is a real threat in science writing, because explaining the science always takes longer than explaining the story. So I realized I needed her [Cole-Benjamin] back in. I needed to remind people of what is at stake here. And I had a scene that I didn't know what to do with, which was the scene where I'm at dinner with Deanna and Gary and he was afraid that this would end only when she killed herself. That dinner scene was originally part of a longer scene. But then I realized, no, that is the whole purpose of this dinner scene – those six lines. So I reduced those as much as I could, until it was just the essence of it, and I put that in at about two thirds of the piece.

The place where Dobbs inserted that crucial scene is relevant for propelling the story, he explains. In changing the rhythm, the size of the paragraphs reduces gradually until the story reaches its climax. Finally, you need to come back to the initial construct of your narrative, and while it looks or sounds similar, make it clear it has also changed over the course of the story:

That was inspired partly by the Schubert piece. If you listen to the piece, it is sort of two different musical ideas presented. One is very melodic and ridiculously beautiful, and the other is this sudden clash of chords, which has a lot of tension. These two get developed, and then they start to affect each other, a little bit of DNA crosses over in each one. Schubert is not going with twenty-four measures of the first one and then twenty-four of the second and so on. Instead, he is alternating. Sometimes, one gets a long statement, and then the next one is short, but in general, as I looked at the music on the stand, I could see he was building tension in the piece by on average shrinking the size of the two statements, the A and the B theme, until there is a central part about 60 per cent of the way through this movement, which is a very close analogy to building a climax in a piece of narrative. There are very rapid exchanges and alterations between the two and they come to a pitch of climax – and then a fermata brings it to a halt. Then this lovely melody that the whole piece starts with comes back. It sounds almost the same as at the beginning. Because of what it has been through, it just washes over you. It's lovely. I needed that in the story.

Finally, Dobbs recalls how he tested his story idea using the three-point checklist provided in Chapter 2. He says finding the most important criterion, a scientist who can talk well, was just a fluke:

Mayberg can talk. She just talks beautifully. It pours out of her.

## Summary

Hard news stories do not lend themselves to being told using narratives, but many features do. A story needs a protagonist who pursues a goal but does not achieve it easily. At a story's climax, it is revealed whether that protagonist achieves her goal. While conflicts are generally good to keep the audience's attention, all conflicts must be resolved sooner or later. Minor conflicts can also be resolved after the climax.

Techniques involve building tension by consciously withholding information from the reader at the beginning and letting the story unfold over the course of the article, possibly saving a twist for the end. Paradoxically, one common characteristic of award-winning journalistic stories is emotion, whether explicitly told by sources (through dialogue) or implicitly evoked in the readers. At the very minimum, a story has a beginning, a middle and an end. Turning points ease the transition from one to another and usually depict incisive moments in the pursuit of a goal. As a journalist, asking specifically for such inciting events that propel the story is a technique you can use when interviewing your sources.

Picking events, persons and dialogue and ordering these elements lies at the heart of constructing narrative structures. As mentioned before, selection is one of the critically important skills in journalism, and it is all the more important with long-form stories. Critics of narrative journalism argue that narratives are in and of themselves persuasive and invite journalists to cherry-pick their facts and mould them into the narrative. Sometimes, that is not too difficult, as some scientists already present their findings using journalism-friendly structures. In that sense, some scientists and journalists have hotly debated whether storytelling techniques are an appropriate tool to depict the complexity of science and its associated uncertainty.

## Review questions

- What are the basic elements of a science story?
- What role does emotionality play in journalistic stories?
- What is the most frequent storytelling formula?
- Which narrative strategies can you employ to entice your readers?
- What are the categories of science writing, and what merits does each have?
- What literary techniques does Tom Wolfe employ to write narrative stories?
- What is the rule of three, and how do politicians and writers utilise it?
- What is a plot point, and how can you find one in your reporting?
- Which criteria does Klassen use to analyse science stories?
- Why is there tension between scientists and journalists?

## Exercises

- Take three long-form science features and identify the following elements: characters, goals, dialogue and action. Highlight them in different colours.
- Using the same stories, highlight the narrative paragraphs and the background paragraphs in different colours.
- Identify the passages that evoke emotions in you as a reader. Which emotions do they evoke, and how are they delivered (e.g., through dialogue, implication)?
- Categorise the stories using the types of science stories. Note which elements led you to your conclusion.
- Scan the text for rhetorical devices. List them and write down what purpose they serve.
- Use Olson's ABT template to reduce each story to one sentence. Repeat using the Dobzhansky template and identify each story's theme.
- Check all three stories for Klassen's ten criteria and write down which ones they fulfil and which ones they lack.
- If one of the stories is a history of science story, apply Klassen's expanded five-step methodology to assess it.
- Formulate questions after reading the three stories. Are they mostly higher-level (how, why) or factual-level (what, when, where, who) questions?

## Reading list

Blum, D., Knudson, M. and Henig, R.M. (eds.) (2006) *A Field Guide for Science Writers*. 2nd edition. New York: Oxford University Press

Capouya, J. (2014) Want to write great narrative? Study screenwriting, *Nieman Storyboard* [Online] http://niemanstoryboard.org/stories/want-to-write-great-narrative-study-screenwritin/ [date accessed 31 March 2016]

Crumpton, N. (2015) Why the science manuscript must also have literary merit, *The Guardian* [Online] Available at: www.theguardian.com/science/blog/2015/mar/11/why-the-science-manuscript-must-also-have-literary-merit [date accessed 19 November 2016]

Dobbs, D. (2011) How Led Zeppelin + Franz Schubert = Writing, *Neuron Culture* (Blog) [Online] Available at: http://daviddobbs.net/smoothpebbles/led-zeppelin-franz-schubert-writing/ [date accessed 9 September 2016]

Kramer, M. and Call, W. (2007) *Telling True Stories. A Nonfiction Writers' Guide from the Nieman Foundation at Harvard University*. New York: Plum

Olson, R. (2015) *Houston, We Have a Narrative: Why Science Needs Story*. Chicago, IL: University of Chicago Press

## Links

ABSW, UKSCJ conference video: Narrative in Science Journalism: www.youtube.com/watch?v=1KQVG7515F4

Nieman Foundation, Nieman Storyboard: http://niemanstoryboard.org/

Wellcome Trust science storytelling (five online videos): www.wellcome.ac.uk/Funding/Public-engagement/Science-Writing-Prize/WTVM054698.htm

## References

Blum, D., Knudson, M., Levy Guyer, R., Dunwoody, S., Finkbeiner, A. and Wilkes, J. (2006) Writing well about science: Techniques from teachers of science writing, In Blum, D., Knudson, M. and Henig, R.M. (eds.) *A Field Guide for Science Writers*. 2nd edition. New York: Oxford University Press, 26–33

Cairo, A. (2016) Personal Skype conversation on 11 April 2016

Capouya, J. (2014) Want to write great narrative? Study screenwriting, *Nieman Storyboard* [Online] Available at: http://niemanstoryboard.org/stories/want-to-write-great-narrative-study-screenwritin/ [date accessed 31 March 2016]

Collins, S. (2015) Elements of storytelling in medical journalism, *Medical Writing*, vol. 24, no. 4, 222–224

Dahlstrom, F. (2014) Using narratives and storytelling to communicate science with nonexpert audiences, *Proceedings of the National Academy of Sciences*, vol. 111, suppl. 4, 13,614–13,620

Dilba, D. (2015) Personal Skype conversation on 6 October 2015

Dobbs, D. (2006) A depression switch? *The New York Times Magazine* [Online] Available at: www.nytimes.com/2006/04/02/magazine/02depression.html [date accessed 16 March 2016]

Dobbs, D. (2013) David Dobbs on science writing: 'Hunt down jargon and kill it', *The Guardian* [Online] Available at: www.theguardian.com/science/2013/apr/19/science-writing-david-dobbs [date accessed 16 March 2016]

Dobbs, D. (2016) Personal Skype conversation on 6 May 2016

Eliott, S. (2016) Personal email conversation on 3 November 2016

Field, S. (2005) *Screenplazivy – The Foundations of Screenwriting*. New York: Delta Trade/Bantam Dell

*Guardian* (2013) Tim Radford on how to be a science writer, *The Guardian* [Online Video] Available at: www.theguardian.com/science/video/2013/mar/06/tim-radford-science-writer-video [date accessed 4 March 2016]

Hornmoen, H. (2006) Constructing Karl Popper. How does science journalism employ literary devices? *Nordicom Review*, vol. 27, no. 2, 169–183

Kallan, R.A. (1979) Style and the new journalism: A rhetorical analysis of Tom Wolfe, *Communication Monographs*, vol. 46, no. 1, 52–62

Katz, Y. (2013) Against storytelling of scientific results, *Nature Methods*, vol. 10, no. 11, 1045

Katz, Y. (2016) Personal Skype conversation on 24 March 2016

Klassen, S. (2009) The construction and analysis of a science story: A proposed methodology, *Science & Education*, vol. 18, no. 3, 401–423

Kramer, M. (1995) Breakable rules for literary journalists, *Nieman Storyboard* [Online] Available at: http://niemanstoryboard.org/stories/breakable-rules-for-literary-journalists/ [date accessed 7 November 2016]

Kramer, M. and Call, W. (2007) *Telling True Stories: A Nonfiction Writers' Guide From the Nieman Foundation at Harvard University*. New York: Plum

Krzywinski, M. and Cairo, A. (2013a) Reply to: "Against storytelling of scientific results", *Nature Methods*, vol. 10, no. 11, 1046

Krzywinski, M. and Cairo, A. (2013b) Points of view: Storytelling, *Nature Methods*, vol. 10, no. 8, 687

Lillie, B. (2016) Science and the art of personal storytelling, In Wilcox, C., Brookshire, B. and Goldman, J.G. (eds.) *Science Blogging: The Essential Guide*. New Haven, CT: Yale University Press, 96–103

Linnell, G. (2014) Storytelling in the digital age, In Potts, J. (ed.) *The Future of Writing*. New York: Palgrave Macmillan, 105–114

McKenna, P. (2016) Personal phone conversation on 18 February 2016

McPhee, J. (2013) Structure, *The New Yorker* [Online] Available at: www.newyorker.com/magazine/2013/01/14/structure [date accessed 8 October 2016]

Mencher, M. (2011a) Story structure, In Mencher, M. (ed.) *News Reporting and Writing*. 12th edition. New York: McGraw-Hill, 125–139

Mencher, M. (2011b) The writer's art, In Mencher, M. (ed.) *News Reporting and Writing*. 12th edition. New York: McGraw-Hill, 140–168

Olson, R. (2015) *Houston, We Have a Narrative: Why Science Needs Story*. Chicago, IL: University of Chicago Press

Posada-Swafford, A. (2016) Personal Skype conversation on 29 March 2016

Powledge, T.M. (2016) That Mukherjee piece on epigenetics in the New Yorker, *On Science (PLOS Blogs)* [Online] Available at: http://blogs.plos.org/onscience-blogs/2016/05/13/that-mukherjee-piece-on-epigenetics-in-the-new-yorker/ [date accessed 11 November 2016]

Schultz, C. (2010) Interview with David Dobbs, *Colin Schultz Blog* [Online] Available at: https://colinschultz.wordpress.com/2010/03/13/interview-with-david-dobbs/ [date accessed 17 March 2016]

Wahl-Jorgensen, K. (2013) The strategic ritual of emotionality: A case study of Pulitzer Prize-winning articles, *Journalism*, vol. 14, no. 1, 129–145

Watson, J.D. and Crick, F.H.C. (1953) Molecular structure of nucleic acids, *Nature*, vol. 171, no. 4356, 737–738

Yong, E. (2010) The value of 'this is cool' science stories, *Not Exactly Rocket Science (DISCOVER Magazine)* [Online] Available at: http://blogs.discovermaga zine.com/notrocketscience/2010/03/16/the-value-of-this-is-cool-science-stories/#. VurTMPkrKHs [date accessed 17 March 2016]

Zivkovic, B. (2011) Telling science stories . . . wait, what's a story? *A Blog Around the Clock (Scientific American)* [Online] Available at: http://blogs.scientificamerican. com/a-blog-around-the-clock/httpblogsscientificamericancoma-blog-around-the-clock20110713telling-science-stories-wait-whats-a-story/ [date accessed 17 March 2016]

# 9
## FACTS AND FIGURES

**What you will learn in this chapter:**

- Basic statistics literacy
- Common pitfalls
- Journalistic malpractice
- Fact-checking tools
- Watchdogs
- Educating science journalists in statistics
- Legal issues: libel, accuracy and plagiarism
- Case study: analysing a health article whose author misinterpreted statistics

## Introduction

Numbers are powerful tools to persuade your readers. Like science in and of itself, they have an aura of objectivity and authority. That is why practically all journalists use them to support their claims or opinions. Could you imagine a sports, politics or science story without statistics or powerful figures? Probably not. If you report about a science paper, you will have to read and correctly interpret the numbers scientists have found and only then show those facts to your readers. This is where it gets tricky: If you are a science journalist without a background in science, you will run the risk of confusing or misinterpreting the numbers presented. Also, these numbers might be wrong in the first place. The scientists could have fabricated them. That is still no reason to get scared over statistics. In order to understand, interpret and question a paper's numbers and methods, you do not have to recalculate them. Rather, you need a sense of scepticism and an understanding of what the different statistics mean.

That is why this chapter's first section will introduce you to a few essential terms and definitions that you will repeatedly run across when you read papers and write about science. That section also highlights how some journalists prefer some statistics to others in order to conceal problematic issues or convince their audience. When this happens, it is not always the journalist who is to blame. Scientists pursue their own goals, and these goals often involve raising lots of money for their research. In doing so, they sometimes formulate their findings in a way that can mislead you into believing a study is more significant than it is.

To help you avoid falling into such traps, the subsequent two sections show you which common pitfalls exist and how you can avoid them. Also, I will define some forms of journalistic malpractice such as not reading papers, providing fake balanced views and moulding facts around a hypothesis when actually the opposite would be appropriate.

Speaking of facts, the internet is full of seeming facts, manipulated images and other content that you need to verify before you can claim they are facts. In the dedicated section on fact-checking tools, you can find a few techniques to verify photographs' authors and provenance and find out if they have been plagiarised and reused in a different context. Your primary fact-checking tool, however, is a sceptical mindset that alarms you when there is something odd about seeming facts.

This same mindset also keeps you away from legal trouble. If you take rumours or arbitrary claims at face value and simply report them, you could damage people's reputations, in which case they are entitled to sue you. In the worst case, you might land behind bars. That is why you will find a dedicated section on libel that introduces the basic concepts and points out a few differences between UK and US laws.

In the section on educating science journalists in statistics, you will find advice on how to ask questions about how scientists come up with their data. Also, you will find suggestions as for which courses you can take if you want to further educate yourself in statistics (which I strongly recommend). Finally, in the last section, a biostatistician will explain how some science journalists misinterpreted a journal paper's statistics when writing articles about cancer research. The misinterpretation went as far as to imply that cancer has nothing to do with environmental factors and people's lifestyles. The damage such articles can cause is enormous, as some people might believe these claims and stop living healthy lives – just because a journalist misinterpreted a statistic.

## Basic statistics literacy

As a science journalist, you need to know how scientists operate in order to accurately interpret their methods and results before reporting on their studies. Nobody expects you to be able to reproduce those calculations, but everybody expects you to get your facts right. Hence, you need to be able to interpret scientists' methods and results and tell your audience what a study's takeaway is. If in doubt, consult with a statistician or another pundit to clarify how you should interpret a statistic. In fact, this is what I have done for this chapter: I asked science journalists and statisticians to come up with a basic statistical term set for journalists. Before I present that, the following are a few basic notions about using numbers and statistics:

- **Uncertainty:** In science, you will rarely encounter absolute truths. Hence, beware of using (or accepting) simple, universal-truth statements that involve percentages or other figures. Science is complex and often delivers partial solutions instead of easy takeaways.
- **Data quality:** Data exudes objectivity, right? No. The data may be inaccurate observational errors. The scientists may have processed and cleaned the data. They may have excluded subsets of the data for their calculations. They may have selected small or large samples. Ask them what they did and why they did it. These questions largely reflect the five Ws and one H of journalism inquiry.
- **Limitations:** Studies' results are often valid only under very specific conditions. Watch out for limitations in the paper. If the scientists pointed out none, your alarm bells should ring.
- **False authority:** Readers rarely question numbers. Journalists rarely question scientists' claims. Both convey authority, but numbers can be flawed, and so can scientists. Researchers are human, and they follow their own agendas, which often involve funding.
- **Common sense:** Have a critical mindset and put every figure scientists feed you into question. Ask yourself, why are they telling you a specific number, and why are they telling it to you now? And, most of all, is the number in front of you logical?
- **Context:** Always put numbers in a broader context. Statistics can be powerful but misleading if they lack context. It may sound impressive that 66 per cent of the mice in a novel drug trial were cured of a disease, until you discover that the third mouse died.

I asked the *BMJ* investigations editor Deborah Cohen, John Moores University journalism professor Steve Harrison, University of Cambridge senior investigator statistician Simon White; Stanford University epidemiologist/science writer Kristin Sainani, and Senckenberg Biodiversity and Climate Research Centre biostatistician Bob O'Hara which statistical terms you should be comfortable with. You can find the distilled results in the following list:

- **Percentage and percentage points:** When you report percentages, also state the absolute base value: 5 per cent of how many people? Percentage points are the difference between two percentages. If a new drug increases the number of cured patients from twenty-four to thirty, this is an increase of six percentage points. You could also express it as a ratio (30 divided by 24), which corresponds to an increase of 25 per cent. Some scientists and journalists use the latter notation to make results appear more impressive.

- **Absolute and relative risk:** Similarly, headlines often confuse absolute with relative risks. The fictitious headline "You are 50 per cent more likely to have a heart attack when you have diabetes" might actually refer to the percentage difference between the people who do not suffer from diabetes and those who do. If the baseline risk was 10 per cent, increasing it by 50 per cent would become an absolute risk of 15 per cent. But if you sell that as 50 per cent to your audience, you might mislead the diabetics among them into thinking they have an absolute chance of 50 per cent of having a heart attack.

- **Rates:** Sometimes absolute values can be misleading. If you reported the murder rates for cities A and B as 500 and 29, respectively, it appears as if there are many more murders in city A (which, in absolute terms is correct). But it gives a false impression. Divide those numbers by their respective city populations and then multiply the value by 100,000. What you get is the murder *rate*, which is much more expressive. Assume that A's population is 8.5 million and B's is 230,000. Now the respective murder rates are 5.88 for A and 12.61 for B, which turns the picture around. Note that such calculations only have validity when they are applied within a specified time frame, for example, the year 2015.

- **Correlation and causation:** If scientists observe two phenomena or events occurring at the same time, they call this *correlation*. The events are tied or linked to each other, but that does not mean that one causes the other. Correlations are expressed through decimal values that are positive (two values increase simultaneously, with 1 being a perfect positive correlation) or negative (one increases while the other decreases, with −1 being a perfect negative correlation). Confusing correlation with causation is most likely to occur when you try to simplify your text's headline or nutgraph.

- **Study designs:** Some studies are observational, where scientists record rather than control what happens with a patient. This approach is obviously subject to how accurately a patient, for example, reports what she ate or what doses of a drug she uses. Observational studies rarely show causation in their results. In contrast, in randomised controlled trials (RCTs), researchers administer drugs to a standard treatment and placebos to a control group. Double-blind RCTs, where neither the researchers nor the participants know who receives a drug or a placebo are considered the gold standard in many disciplines because they minimise selection bias.

- **P-value:** P-values tell scientists how likely their results are due to chance. Many treat P-values as the poster child for statistics. P-values equal to or below 0.05 (5 per cent) are considered statistically significant. A word of caution: The expressivity of P-values depends on the plausibility of the hypothesis (the odds it is correct) (Nuzzo 2014) and on how strong the observed effect is. You may have a P-value of 0.01, but if a drug increased the number of disease survivors from only 74 to 75 per cent, this might not be clinically significant despite being statistically significant.

- **Sample size:** Usually it is not possible or ethical to test a drug on whole populations. Instead, scientists draw samples that ideally represent the entire population so they can draw inferences. If the sample size is too small, it may be impossible to detect whether a treatment has had an effect. This might also render the P-value useless as an indicator of how significant the results are. If the sample size is very large, then it may render the P-value inexpressive as well.

- **Selection bias:** Samples affected by selection bias are non-representative. The initial assumption that, for example, a sample of 500 bagpipe players represents all Scots is simply not true, as not every Scot plays the bagpipe. Selection biases can render a study's results useless. Apply common sense to figure out whether the method used to draw the sample is unbiased.

- **Null hypothesis:** This is the negation of an initial research hypothesis. For example, if scientists' hypothesis is that a novel drug has a measurable effect on a certain population, then the null hypothesis would state there is *no* effect and hence no relationship between the two phenomena. In order to prove their initial theory, researchers would then try to reject the null hypothesis to show there is indeed an effect. Note that the null hypothesis can only be rejected if a study's findings are significant. The null hypothesis is often denoted as $H_0$.

- **Power:** Statistical power helps researchers determine how likely it is that the null hypothesis will be rejected or accepted. The higher the power, the higher the chance it can be rejected. Studies should always state their power calculations. If they do not, that is a reason to get suspicious, so specifically ask for them.

- **Statistical and clinical significance:** Statistical significance is achieved for all P-values equal to or below 0.05. Watch out for very large samples, because those are more likely to achieve statistical significance, even though the effect size might be small. If the effect size is too small or if the cost of implementing a new treatment is too high, a statistically significant drug might still be impractical to use with patients.

- **Effect size:** This value goes hand in hand with clinical significance and tells you how strongly a phenomenon is present. Effect size is usually reported as a single value. If there is no significant change in the variable you are observing (like mortality rate), the effect size tends to get smaller. Odds ratios and relative risks can serve as the effect size.

- **Standard deviation and standard error:** The standard deviation shows you how variable data within a distribution are, or the spread. Are your values concentrated around the sample mean, and by how much do they deviate from it? In contrast, the standard error is the standard deviation of a statistic (as opposed to a sample of a population).

- **Hierarchy of evidence:** The hierarchy of evidence ranks different types of evidence and study designs in biomedical research; these are often represented as a pyramid, with the lowest-ranking element at the bottom and the highest-ranking at the top. You can find ideas and opinions at the top, followed by test tube research, animal studies, case reports, observational studies (case-control and cohort studies) and RCTs and their meta-analyses. Bear in mind that you should never suggest that a finding in an animal study works equally in humans.

Remember that P-values do not provide absolute certainty that, for example, a treatment works: "A *P* value cannot indicate the importance of a finding; for instance, a drug can have a statistically significant effect on patients' blood glucose levels without having a therapeutic effect" (Baker 2016:151). The American Statistical Association (ASA) cautions against using P-values alone to judge scientific findings because they cannot determine the truth of a hypothesis and the importance of the findings. Alarmingly, the misuse of P-values can contribute to the non-reproducibility of scientific findings (Baker 2016). That is why it is important that you apply common sense to determine how plausible it is that an effect takes place at all, as Regina Nuzzo (2014) confirms: "The more implausible the hypothesis – telepathy, aliens, homeopathy – the greater the chance that an exciting finding is a false alarm, no matter what the *P* value is" (151).

## Common pitfalls

One of the biggest pitfalls in reporting about science stems from linguistic ambiguities. In statistics, several of the previous terms are clearly defined, such as *significance, rate*, and *risk*. The problem with such terms is that they also exist in everyday language but have different meanings. You should be clear about the context in which you use these terms. Be unambiguous when you do, for the sake of accuracy and clarity.

Here is an example: *Significance* means *importance* in everyday lingo. In non-statistical terms, claiming that bulldozing rainforests has a significant negative effect on the orangutan population is perfectly valid to express that deforestation is harmful to wildlife. But scientifically speaking, it is inaccurate because there is no measurable information that underpins the claim. In contrast, significance (see the previous section) can be determined by employing statistical methods. While the number of orangutans might in fact have declined, scientists would need to test a specific effect (for example, the number of bulldozers or the area destroyed by them) for significance before issuing a scientifically backed statement.

Another example of an incorrectly used term is *rate*. Percentages are sometimes wrongly declared as rates. For example, Cope (2006) illustrates an example of an article that ran in the *Washington Post*. The article was misleadingly titled "Airline Accident Rate Is Highest in 13 Years" without actually showing rates but mere absolute values:

> The story, like many others that misuse the term "rate", reported no rate at all, merely death and crash totals. A correction had to be printed pointing out that the number of accidents per 100,000 departures – the actual rate, the "so many per so many" – had been declining year after year.
>
> *(Cope 2006:23)*

Omission is another error. While you have to select and hence omit certain events and facts when you report on a study's findings, you should be cautious when you do. If your omission distorts or misrepresents the study's actual take-home message, you have committed a mistake. This pitfall is like cherry-picking statements from quotes (see Chapter 4) and ripping them out of their context, hence distorting their meaning. As for medical studies, just reporting about the results in the treatment group is not enough; you will also have to ask about the effects on the control group. If the study authors do not mention those effects, ask for them. For example, if in a story about the side effects of tranquillisers you report that 50 per cent of study participants suffered from insomnia, that would be worrisome. However, the picture would completely change if you included that 45 per cent of the patients in the control group suffered from insomnia as well. In fact, if you omitted the latter claim, readers might refrain from taking tranquillisers when in fact they might benefit from using them.

Kristin Sainani, health researcher and educator at Stanford University, tells me another example of omission-based pitfalls. She makes it clear that in the majority of such cases she encounters, the blame is on the scientists, not the journalists:

> When you have a randomised trial, the clear purpose is to compare the treatment group to the placebo group. What often ends up happening, though, is that you can have a significant improvement in the treatment group but not have a significant improvement in the placebo group. But that is comparing the group to itself. That doesn't imply that the two groups themselves are different, because you can imagine a case where the placebo group just misses statistical significance and the improvement in the treatment group just makes it, and they might actually not be very different. I see this wrong all the time, and again, it is largely because the scientists digging for something to show in their paper say "Well, there is a significant improvement in the treatment group, isn't that great?" And then it gets reported in the media that there was a significant improvement in the treatment group.
>
> *(Sainani 2016)*

Using averages is another widespread pitfall. There are different types of averages, and you should not apply them equally to all problems. The arithmetic mean, that is, the summing up of all values and dividing them by the number of values, is usually used to describe the normal distribution of values. Here is an example: Assume you have three adult mice in a lab experiment, aged 4, 5 and 6 months. Sum up the mice's ages (15 months) and divide that sum by 3. The mean is 5. Stating the mean age of the mice is 5 months is expressive. However, if you have an extreme outlier, such as an extremely old mouse, the distribution becomes skewed and the mean is no longer a good means to describe the population. For example, the mean age of three mice aged 4, 5 and 51 months is 20 months. That mean age is highly unlikely for house mice, not to mention lab mice.

You might find the median more appropriate, as it separates the lower half of a sample from the upper half. In practice, the median of a range of values is the middle value. For example, in the aforementioned example of 4-, 5- and 6-month-old mice, the median is obtained by simply taking the middle value, which is 5. If you take the extreme outlier example (the improbably old mouse), the median does not change, as the middle value of 4, 5 and 51 is still 5. Hence, the median is less influenced by outliers. Considering that measurements in science can produce measurement errors, this is an important consideration.

There are many more pitfalls you can encounter as an aspiring science writer. The best way to eliminate them is asking more questions. These might be questions about the study design, such as how big the sample was, how it was drawn and what the underlying population was like. Was it a random sample? In polls, it should be (Cope 2006).

One prominent example of a pitfall based on study-design flaws was a personal health article written by Tara Parker-Pope for the *New York Times Magazine*. Her article, "The Fat Trap" is about the difficulties of maintaining one's health after diets. Parker-Pope's article has been widely criticized by a number of scientists and bloggers, as Freeman (2013) points out in an article for *Columbia Journalism Review*. Although he describes the article as "a well-reported, well-written, highly readable and convincing piece of personal-health-science journalism", he lists criticisms that several experts confronted Parker-Pope with; for example, they said her article hinged on a small, short-term study and pointed out that larger, long-term studies disprove the effects that manifest in the one she chose (Freeman 2013). Parker-Pope's article is also a prime example of sample size and the effect it has when it is relatively small.

## Journalistic malpractice

Always uphold honesty. What you tell your readers should be true and well-researched. Accuracy, as in the ABCs of journalism, should be among your top priorities. Your readers and your editor trust you. If you lie, fabricate facts or plagiarise, at some point it will come to light and your journalism career will be over (you will see an example of that in this section). It just never pays off. You can use the following questions to avoid some of the worst mishaps. Once you are done reporting, but before you start writing a story, ask yourself:

Did you:

- Do enough reporting, and did you fully grasp the concepts?
- Cherry-pick only the facts that support your story idea?
- Challenge interviewees' claims or take them at face value?
- Verify all of your facts?
- Consult primary or only secondary sources?
- Ask independent scientists to help you interpret a study's claims?
- Interview enough sources to get a complete picture of the topic?
- Distinguish your own words clearly from quotes and attribute those quotes correctly?

If your reporting is biased, wrong and manipulative, you misinform your audience. Because they assume you are telling the truth, they may make decisions based on what you write. Readers may place a bet on a horse and lose a lot of money because you speculated that horse is in perfect shape on race day. Readers may vote for a particular candidate because you persuade them she is the logical choice. Readers may not take a perhaps life-saving drug because you claim it shows no effect. Hence, never speculate or spread rumours. That is one of the worst malpractices.

The same is true of plagiarism. A prime example for such misconduct is the case of Jonah Lehrer. In 2012, science journalism professor Charles Seife scrutinised eighteen of the online science articles Lehrer had published on his blog Frontal Cortex. What Seife found was that Lehrer had taken quotations and passages from press releases and reposted them as his own writing, without attribution. While conceding that "journalistic rules about press releases are murky" (Seife 2012), the investigator also noted that "rules about taking credit for other journalists' prose are not". He supports this statement with a number of examples of Lehrer plagiarising content of other journalists and bloggers, either by copying them verbatim or lightly editing them before re-publishing them.

There are also a few additional journalistic malpractices that specifically apply to science journalism. One such malpractice is not reading the paper you are reporting about. Time constraints sometimes cajole science journalists into reading the press release and taking everything presented at face value. During a presentation given at the UK Conference of Science Journalists in 2014, Ivan Oransky explicitly defined this approach as journalistic malpractice. The omission of facts to frame other facts in a certain way to support an agenda is another malpractice in science journalism. Ivan Oransky and Deborah Cohen point out that especially in health journalism, press releases tend to point out positive outcomes but omit studies' limitations (Cohen and Oransky 2014).

In fact, the misrepresentation of facts and subsequent distortions of the scientific message also happen when journalists and scientists favour specific statistics to accomplish a goal, such as downplaying a risk. For example, Cohen points out that abusing relative risks to artificially inflate benefits or downplay risks is a common malpractice:

> Always try to use the absolute and not the relative risk. Because what you see in headlines is "You are 50 per cent more likely to have a heart attack if you have diabetes," that doesn't mean as someone with diabetes you have got a one in two chance of having a heart attack. That's what you call relative risk. What you need to do is look at what is called the baseline risk of having a heart attack in the population. Let's say, for argument's sake, that the absolute risk is 10 per cent. Now the statement means that someone with diabetes has a 50 per cent greater chance than 10 per cent. So their risk is then 15 per cent. Obviously, that is a far less sexy headline. Researchers are very guilty of putting this in papers and relying on relative risk. If you are reporting on a paper, go back and ask the authors what the absolute risk is.
>
> *(Cohen 2016)*

Scientist and science writer Christie Wilcox tells me she cannot stand it when journalists and scientists abuse numbers to sound like authorities. About one third of her blog posts are rants about inaccurate statistics and the exaggeration of figures. One example is a blog post she wrote on the conspiracy theory that genetically modified mosquitoes from the biotech corporation Oxitec started the Zika outbreak. The theory claims that the Zika virus outbreak started in the same spot where the Oxitec GM mosquitoes were released. But Wilcox points out that the two locations actually are 400 miles apart. Obviously, if you zoom out far enough on a map, it looks like they are close, she tells me. Wilcox has a theory on why this kind of misrepresentation happens:

> I think part of the issue is that people formulate their opinion and then try to find the facts to support [it]. Instead, they should look at the evidence and then formulate their opinions and find out whether that mashes with a specific idea. It's that hunt for evidence that gets you into that dangerous territory. I can make something look like it's true if I try hard enough.
>
> *(Wilcox 2016)*

Instead, Wilcox suggests you should take the scientific approach. Assume your hypothesis is wrong and then try to find evidence to disprove it:

> Always start from the assumption that you are wrong and find out what evidence there is for that. The first thing you can do is say, okay, I'm wrong about this. In the Zika case, what I said was "400 miles, that sounds really far. Maybe mosquitoes fly that every day. Or maybe there is a lot of tetracycline in the water, and therefore they are surviving." Start from each of the points that could potentially tear your position apart and then find what evidence there is for them.
>
> *(Wilcox 2016)*

Another form of journalistic malpractice is bias and the failure to present a balanced view. It is not difficult to select studies and quotes in a way that they support your theory. After all, for almost every scientific argument, there is a published counter-argument waiting to be dug up from the myriads of journal papers. That alone can hardly be called malpractice. The way you pick your quotations, however, may be biased. For example, if you interviewed only the PI of the study and included no further opinion in the article, it would present only a limited view on the study results, as most researchers are unlikely to pluck their own studies to pieces. Hence, interviewing at least one additional, independent source is the bare minimum you should do in your reporting.

But even if you do interview two opposing sides, the view may still not be balanced. Medicine and pharmacology professor Jalees Rehman of the University of Illinois at Chicago argues that when you as a science journalist present scientific opinions, it is your duty to also reflect the reality of consensus among the community:

> If 98 or 99 per cent of scientists agree that humans contribute to global warming, it would be wrong to give equal weight to the views of the 1 per cent fringe scientists who deny climate change and pass this off as a "balanced view".
>
> *(Rehman 2013)*

## Fact-checking tools

Information spreads faster than ever due to fast internet connections, smartphones and social media. The upside is that breaking news, images, videos and other types of information spread faster than ever before, even from places that are inaccessible to journalists. Now everybody is able to produce newsworthy material for cheap and publicise it. The downside is that much of it is scrap, fake or fabricated. But as a journalist, you cannot possibly ignore the information that floats around on the internet. In the case of a breaking event, news organisations often reuse material citizens recorded on their smartphones (with their permission). Unfortunately, however, when pushed for time, some journalists do not verify the material they obtain before publishing it. That is when they involuntarily spread hoaxes and fake material.

Whenever you run across an unverified image, video, statement or allegation released online by a non-trusted source, be sceptical about its authenticity. It is possible, if not likely, that piece of information has been doctored or is a rumour. As Gerri Berendzen, visiting assistant professor at the University of Missouri, writes in an article for the Reynolds Journalism Institute, as an aspiring journalist you should at the very least ask yourself these two questions: Who said it? How would they know? Moreover, Berendzen (2014) claims that while there are useful resources for checking how truthful a piece of online information is, journalists should be specifically trained in properly applying fact-checking techniques. One such tool is the verification handbook, which is available for free (see the Links section).

Images are particularly easy to tamper with. Take a photo, upload it, tag it, assign a location to it, write an accompanying comment and share it with your friends online. This entire process takes only minutes. Spreading false information (whether deliberately or not) has never been easier. There are two types of manipulated images floating around the internet: re-emerging photographs that belong to one event but are now being attributed to another, topical event and manipulated photographs that feature cut-outs or changed messages or that put the photograph subjects in a different context altogether.

Debunking manipulated images and other multimedia content is tricky and consumes time, so employing tools to do so is the way to go. On the upside, content that is spread digitally often contains information you can verify. Plus, it leaves traces. The internet does not forget. Just by looking at an image's file properties, you can often figure out the date it was taken and sometimes even the location and photographer.

In *The Verification Handbook*, Claire Wardle, research director at the Tow Center for Digital Journalism, suggests that "journalists and humanitarian professionals should always start from a position that the content is incorrect" (Wardle 2013:26). She specifically demands that, as a journalist, you should focus on the following four points to verify user-generated content spread online:

1  **Provenance:** Can you be sure this image or video is original content, or is it simply a scraped and re-uploaded image or video?
2  **Source:** Who is the original contributor?
3  **Date:** When was the image taken or the video created?
4  **Location:** Where was the image taken or the video recorded?

As for photographs, attached metadata provides for the most part reliable information about the origins of a digitally recorded picture. The exchangeable image file (EXIF) format is the de facto standard for recording and reading technical data such as a camera's exposure settings, shutter speed, manufacturer and model. But most importantly, attached EXIF data contain the date and time a picture was taken. If the camera a photograph was taken with contains a GPS receiver, the metadata may even contain the location. Most professional image-editing software can read EXIF data, and usually the file properties shows photograph metadata. However, EXIF data does not usually contain information regarding the originator of the file unless explicitly specified in the camera settings. Beware that EXIF data is not tamperproof and can be digitally manipulated using freely available tools that can be downloaded from the internet.

Some simple tools allow you to at least check whether an image has been uploaded to the internet before, hence implying the version you found is not the original. For example, Google's reverse image search allows you to insert a URL or upload a picture and then scours the web for similar and identical pictures and presents them in the well-known image results format. TinEye provides the same service, and both are free. If no results are found, this does not guarantee the image is an original. You can also use these tools to find out whether someone has plagiarised your own images.

Unless they have been blatantly doctored, manipulated images are usually harder to spot. Most picture agencies allow minor edits, such as contrast and level adjustments and some cropping. The rule of thumb is that you must not remove essential information or alter the photograph's context. Editing persons or objects in or out is never acceptable. In documentary photography, staging photographs is frowned upon, although there are instances when this happens, such as in the case of the Italian photographer Giovanni Troilo who was stripped of his World Press Photo Award when it came to light that he had staged a photograph of a couple having sex in the back of a car.

There are also tools that indicate whether an image has been manipulated or whether it came straight off the camera. For example, Izutru allows you to upload an image which then is processed by a number of algorithms. The software rates the image quality using a three-point scale: no manipulation, certain manipulation or possible manipulation. To avoid this altogether, Reuters joined the straight-off-the-camera movement by announcing it would no longer accept RAW photographs from freelance photographers. Instead, Reuters demands that freelance photographers deliver in-camera-processed photos that cannot be altered later (Zhang 2015).

The German weekly news magazine *DER SPIEGEL* runs the world's largest fact-checking operation; it employs seventy documentation journalists (as of 2011) and has about fifty years of experience (see Figure 9.1). *DER SPIEGEL*'s fact checkers have developed a text flow that determines

**FIGURE 9.1** Documentation journalists are checking and verifying images and image captions. Photograph recorded on 5 May 2010 in the former headquarters of *DER SPIEGEL* in Hamburg.

*Source*: *DER SPIEGEL*

who checks which parts of a submitted text and what each role can and must check. "This includes marking each individual word in the documentation which helps to prevent errors being 'overlooked' and to recognise errors adjacent to each other" (Schäfer 2011:4). Schäfer adds that documentation journalists do not reproduce scientific findings but mainly try to verify journalists' and their sources' claims and interpretations:

> The most important principle in all cases, however, is to retrace a news item right back to its original source. Even a press release by a university – generally not a bad source – can distort the content of a study (quite apart from typing errors and other banal sources of errors).
>
> *(Schäfer 2011:2)*

That said, the best fact-checking tool is not computer-based; it is your own sceptical mindset that should urge you to question each bit of information scientists, lobbyists or politicians feed you. Paired with good old common sense, this tool goes a long way. Steve Harrison confirms this:

> The first thing is common sense. The basis of common sense in fact-checking is estimation. If you can, always estimate. For example, if

people say 80 million people in the UK are going to vote in the European referendum, ask yourself, does that sound right, or does it seem too high? Could 80 million people possibly go to vote? That should ring an alarm bell and prompt you to go and check that number. If you don't stand back and think, does this make sense to me just from a point of common sense, then unfortunately, that number gets incorporated into your story, and you will apply all sorts of statistical analysis to that wrong number. If what you begin with is wrong, then what you are going to end up with is a story that is wrong.

*(Harrison 2016)*

## Watchdogs

Lack of time and money often keeps us from fulfilling one of our most important duties: holding those in power to account. To a certain degree, this reflects how science journalists perceive their daily work routine. In the *Global Science Journalism Report*, Bauer et al. (2013) carried out a survey among 592 science journalists. They found that 66 per cent of the respondents find science journalism is not critical enough. When asked about the qualities that make a good science journalist, 99 per cent of the participants responded with "reporting the facts", while only 68 per cent said "numeracy/grasp of statistics" was one such quality. "Having a science degree" was only mentioned in 35 per cent of the answers (Bauer et al. 2013).

Regarding their role in society as science journalists, 43 per cent of the 592 respondents chose "to inform", while an alarmingly low percentage of less than 10 per cent deemed being watchdogs as an important role to fulfil. Considering only North Africa and the Middle East, this value shifts to 23 per cent (Bauer et al. 2013).

Dwindling resources may be an explanation for these responses, but they are certainly not the only factor that determines who can and cannot take up a role as a science journalist. Some science journalism educators, such as Toby Murcott of Glamorgan University, argue that the degree of criticism you can develop as a journalist depends also on the scientists. In an essay for *Nature*, Murcott (2009) writes that the relationship between scientist and science journalist resembles the relationship between deity and priest: Many science journalists simply take information from the scientists and pass it on to the public without creating additional knowledge. This is also where science journalists differ from political journalists. Although he admits this problem may be partially related to a lack of resources, he proposes this relationship needs to be broken up and be more transparent about the scientific process: "One appealing way to start is if scientists helped to unmask the very human process through which science is produced and reviewed, thus dismantling their church-like roles as unquestionable authorities" (Murcott 2009:1054). Unlike politicians, most scientists have an aura of objectivity. That is why so many science articles just echo scientists and public information officers' claims. Many science journalists are just not used to critically questioning their interviewees' statements the way good political journalists do. But like politicians, scientists are human beings that pursue their own goals. These goals often involve money, so scientists' agendas are often centred around funds, as Deborah Cohen tells me:

> Some science journalists treat scientists and doctors like they are a different moral species than the rest of us. It drives me insane. Science journalists become a PR machine for scientists, rather than questioning them. What bothers me as well is they assume that scientists and doctors are unbiased – they are not. So always ask them about their funding, because increasingly, universities are commercial enterprises, just like any other company. If you were to report on a press release from a big drug company like GSK or Roche, you would look questioningly at the science. But with universities, people seem to drop their scientific questioning and their scepticism. Treat everything with the same level of scepticism. You have to remember that researchers need to absolutely promote the importance of their specialism. It's the same with charities. All researchers are competing for funding.
>
> *(Cohen 2016)*

Like Cohen, meta-watchdog platforms systematically observe science watchdogs. Such websites expose flawy science journalism, point out factual errors, spot misinterpretations and remind science journalists of their responsibilities towards their audience. This is especially true of personal health reporters, as their impact on the public's health decisions cannot be neglected. Freeman (2013) addresses this responsibility in his article for the *Guardian*. He claims that although personal health writers try to follow good practices and guidelines, "they still manage to write articles that grossly mislead the public, often in ways that can lead to poor health decisions with catastrophic consequences".

But these watchdogs of science journalism also point out positive examples of well-researched, critical science journalism. They are excellent learning tools, as most of them transparently disclose which criteria they look for. One such prominent example of a science journalism watchdog website was the Knight Science Journalism (KSJ) Tracker which was unfortunately suspended in 2014. However, the KSJ fellowship's new director, Deborah Blum, reanimated the Tracker blog as part of a new digital magazine, *Undark*, which she publishes. In addition, the Tracker's more than 10,000 old posts are again online. You can find the link to previous and current Tracker posts in the Links section at the end of this chapter.

Similarly, HealthNewsReview.org assesses the quality of health-related science articles and rates them using a five-star system. The long list of reviewers includes many established researchers and respectable journalists. What makes HealthNewsReview.org special is its openness about how it scrutinises articles. The reviewers disclose all of their assessment criteria and post detailed information about why an article does or doesn't meet them. Moreover, they explain how they award the star ratings to articles.

Although very prominent, these are not the only watchdog sites. *Nieman Reports* and the *Columbia Journalism Review* contain watchdog sections on their online portals, although they do not specifically target science journalism. In Germany, *medien-doktor.de* by Technische Universität Dortmund is the equivalent of HealthNewsReview.org, and it also discloses its evaluation criteria. There are many other media watchdog websites in Australia, Japan, Hong Kong and Canada that you should consult as part of your learning process.

## Educating science journalists in statistics

If you have a science background, you are perhaps less likely to need additional training units on statistics, although that is not a given; not all scientists are well-versed in statistics, and not all of them get their statistics right. But if you do have a science background, you may have an advantage over trained journalists who write about science. The latter group comprises the majority of science writers, so several organisations have launched training programmes and online courses in statistics that are specifically aimed at these science journalists, such as the self-paced online course in science journalism provided by the World Federation of Science Journalists (WFSJ) in cooperation with SciDev.net, which includes a module on statistics for science journalists.

Such courses are needed, as dedicated statistics modules are underrepresented in many universities' journalism programmes. The Royal Statistical Society's investigations into the state of science journalism show that of 374 evaluated undergraduate journalism programmes, not one included or mentioned a dedicated core module on statistics (Kemeny 2014). However, some programmes incorporate statistics lessons into other modules. Again, Steve Harrison confirms this by drawing on his own experience in the undergraduate journalism programme at John Moores University:

> There is no formal numeracy training at all. The only exposure to it is one optional module. They [the students] could go through the entire three years without any formal numeracy training. Now, we do obviously pepper lectures, seminars and workshops with examples of good practice and how to report with numbers.
>
> *(Harrison 2016)*

Most prominently, the Royal Statistical Society has launched an initiative to educate the public and journalists in statistical literacy. Part of this endeavour is the instalment of about two dozen statistical ambassadors who receive specialised training and respond to media requests at the Royal Statistical Society. As part of their science journalism programme, the Royal Statistical Society runs training workshops at media organisations like the BBC. One

**FIGURE 9.2** RSS ambassador Simon White teaches statistics to students and journalists

*Source*: Anne Presanis

of the appointed ambassadors is statistician Simon White. White tells me he teaches students and journalists of every level that statistical literacy boils down to critical thinking about numbers of statistics (see Figure 9.2). While he is convinced that most journalists are used to asking critical questions, he claims that "the key skill that a lot of journalists lack is that ability to critically question statistics" (White 2016).

White tells me that the four key areas of statistical literacy that journalists need to develop an understanding for are:

1   Questioning the data collection
2   Questioning the definitions
3   Questioning how uncertain a number is
4   Questioning the presentation of numbers.

Regarding the collection of data, White identifies a number of questions science (and also all other) journalists should ask when confronted with statistics. These questions essentially reflect the five Ws and one H that need to be answered in every news story:

> To come up with a statistic, there must be some evidence or data. *Where* did that come from? *Who* collected the data? *Why* did they collect it? *When* was it collected? *How* was it collected? *What* has it been

used for? These are the standard five Ws and one H of journalism, but in the sense of statistical literacy.

*(White 2016)*

White also emphasises the importance of defining the variables that describe the observed or measured phenomena. At the same time, he cautions against the innate authority that numbers in texts can convey. To illustrate this point, White provides an example of a fictitious statistic:

> If someone said every man in London was bald, you would question that. But if they said, 26 per cent of men in London are bald, some would just accept that and move on. All of a sudden, by putting in the number, that number has an authority. Now, we need to train journalists to ask questions like: "How did the person who came up with the number find out?"

*(White 2016)*

Next, definitions are important because whenever complex phenomena are boiled down to simple terms, readers might interpret these terms differently. To stick with White's aforementioned example of bald men in London, as a journalist you should ask: What exactly does *bald* mean in the context of this study? How old were the men? Does bald mean completely bald, or does a horseshoe-shaped fringe of hair count as well? There should definitely be a precise scientific definition of bald in the study, rather than the common language usage (there is a scale of baldness: the Hamilton-Norwood scale).

Another important concept White teaches his students is that numbers must be relatable. If too big a number is provided in an article, it might immediately strike the reader as impressive, although it may not be. White draws on an example of the yearly NHS budget. He says readers have a hard time picturing a budget of £100 billion and cannot easily imagine such high figures, other than deeming it a humongous number. He hence recommends you break such large figures down and explain them in everyday terms. In the NHS example, White first divides the budget by the number of weeks per year. He then divides that number by the number of receivers in the population of the UK, approximated as 60 million. The result is that the NHS spends about £32 (£100,000,000,000 divided by 52 divided by 60,000,000) per person per week, which is a scale people can relate to and is not as difficult to imagine as £100 billion.

Like all of this chapter's interviewees, White cautions against taking figures at face value and confirms the aforementioned concept of uncertainty. A lot of the boiled-down numbers in the news, such as unemployment rates:

> "Are not exactly right, because we generally estimate these numbers from samples, from opinion polls or from a selection of households.

That means there is a level of uncertainty in those numbers. Also beware false accuracy. If I said the UK population was 63,181,775 you should immediately say, no, it's not! How could you possibly know down to the person? If I said 63 million (to the nearest million) you would have no problems. Even then, how sure are we about that number? People are born and die every day. When you are given a single number, it is usually the so-called point-estimate. However, there is typically uncertainty about that number, often due to natural variability and how we worked that number out. That uncertainty can be communicated as an interval, or range, in which we believe the true number lies. For example, the UK's Office for National Statistics puts the mid-2015 UK population estimate at 65,110,000 plus or minus 0.2 per cent (64,979,780–65,240,220). Why don't we know the population size exactly? It's estimated from the 2011 Census, combined with deaths, births and migration.

*(White 2016)*

According to White, uncertainty can be found in all single numbers or point estimates. That is why he thinks you should develop an awareness of this uncertainty. Also, it is your duty as a journalist to point out this uncertainty to your readers when you employ such numbers in your articles. This uncertainty often makes it impossible to draw absolute, simple conclusions from statistical statements. At the same time, there is no reason you should be intimidated by complex statistical methods:

You do not need specific or complicated mathematical skills to apply critical thinking and question figures using common sense.

*(White 2016)*

## Legal issues: libel, accuracy and plagiarism

Good science stories involve people. Perhaps you tell their story, perhaps they help you shed light on complex scientific issues or perhaps you have to sue them to get information. All of these people have lives, jobs and reputations to lose. Especially once you start doing investigative science journalism, chances are that some of these people will feel that your article, TV or radio report soils their reputation, causing them to seek legal assistance and sue you or publisher or broadcaster of your potentially harmful piece. Clearly, this is unlikely to happen when you write uncritical, gee whiz-style science articles and act as a science cheerleader.

If you report about individuals or companies and depict them in any way that might damage their reputation, they will defend themselves. Libel is punishable by law in most countries of the world, and the types and degrees of punishment vary from country to country. Defamation trials that sentence journalists to prison are not uncommon in Italy, especially when the involved parties are – surprise – government officials or politicians. In 2012, the then editor-in-chief of the Italian daily newspaper *Il Giornale* was sentenced to a 14-month jail term for running a column in the right-wing daily newspaper *Libero* in 2007. In the column, written under the pseudonym Dreyfus, the author demands a juvenile court magistrate be sentenced to death for granting a 13-year-old girl the right to abortion.

Do you recall the ABCs of journalism (see Chapter 6)? Accuracy is one of the most important tools to defend against defamation claims. The public and the government can and will hold you accountable for everything you write. So, verifying every bit of information you include in your article is the best way to protect yourself and the publication you work for against such claims. Speculation, on the other hand, is likely to get you into trouble. Getting your facts right and trying not to speculate is, by definition, easier in traditional news articles and magazine features than it is in opinionated columns and editorials.

In the UK, the English Defamation Law regulates if and when a plaintiff can sue a defender for libel. The Defamation Act 2013 amends the English Defamation Law and clarifies, to some extent, the circumstances under which you can be sued for defamation and how you can defend yourself. You can find a link to the complete amendments of the Defamation Act 2013 in the Links section at the end of this chapter.

Before proceeding with a basic overview of the English Defamation Law, I will quickly define the basic terminology of defamation and libel:

- **Libel:** Written false statements with the potential to cause harm to the subject (and/or her reputation).
- **Slander:** Usually a spoken or oral false statement about the subject.
- **Defamation:** A false statement about an individual to a third party (for example, newspaper readers or a talk's audience). Both libel and slander qualify as defamatory statements.

The claim that libel can be any written false statement about an individual or company includes online forums, emails (not those sent directly to the claimant) and any publicly readable electronic or print publications (BBC Academy no date). Before the amendments, the English Defamation Law required the defendants to prove their truths. Defamatory statements were assumed false a priori, which put the defendants in the position of proving their statements' truth. The Defamation Act 2013 extended the possible defences and added a new one: publication in the public interest. It is necessary to point out that the Defamation Act 2013 is currently only valid in England and Wales.

If you alter quotes, you intrinsically violate the ABCs' accuracy principle, although this may improve quote clarity. That said, editorial guidelines often allow for some leeway in how much quotes can and should be edited. The Associated Press guidelines, for example, are very strict about this and allow for no alteration of a quote, not even the correction of grammatical errors. In that case, an AP journalist must paraphrase the interviewee or avoid the quote altogether.

Finally, opinions are not subject to libel claims. This means you usually cannot be sued for critical statements that unambiguously express your point of view. But beware that starting a statement with "I think" or "in my view" does not justify adding specific allegations that might harm the subject's reputation. Consider this example: The statement "I think Dr. John Doe tested in an unlawful way in his efforts to develop the cure" could land you in trouble, as it could have the power to launch an inquiry into the doctor's practices. This is a rather concrete suspicion that exceeds a simple opinion statement.

The BBC Academy's guide to defamation law explains the most important aspects of the amended libel law in the UK (see the Reading List at the end of this chapter). The US defamatory law is considered to be more defendant-friendly, as it is closely tied to the First Amendment of the US Constitution, which was introduced to protect freedom of the press. In most US states, statements regarding certain diseases (such as STDs and mental illnesses), unchastity and the involvement in criminal activities are considered defamatory per se. Defamatory laws vary from state to state, so you might also want to read the Digital Media Law Project's legal guide that includes libel and slander regulations on state-by-state basis (see Links). Also, if you are a science blogger, you should read the Electronic Frontier Foundation's (EFF) legal guide for bloggers (see Links), which covers online defamation from a US perspective.

## Case study: analysing a health article whose author misinterpreted statistics

After all these theoretical deliberations, let us now have a look at these terms and concepts in real life. The following is a good example of how scientific findings can be misinterpreted due to a lack of statistical literacy. In 2015, several publications reported about a study published in *Science* that suggested the variation in the cancer rates between different tissue types was correlated to random mutations caused by stem cell divisions. These publications depicted this differently. For example, Boseley (2015) wrote and published a health article titled "Two-Thirds of Adult Cancers Largely 'Down to Bad Luck' Rather Than Genes" in the *Guardian*, while another article titled "Most Cancer Types 'Just Bad Luck'" was published on the BBC's website. Be sure to read Boseley's article before you proceed with this section (see the Reading List).

Biostatistician Bob O'Hara and evolutionary biologist GrrlScientist (alias Devorah Bennu) point out in an article for the *Guardian* that the aforementioned titles and the entire articles "are just bollocks" (O'Hara and GrrlScientist 2015). They explain that while the original *Science* article discusses the variation, it does certainly not discuss the absolute risk of developing different cancer types: "The authors, Bert Vogelstein and Cristian Tomasetti, straight up tell you that their study explains variation in cancer risk, but it does not explain absolute cancer risk" (O'Hara and GrrlScientist 2015).

In contrast, in her article, Sarah Boseley tries to explain the researchers' findings as follows:

> In two-thirds of the cancers – 22 cancer types – random mutations in genes that drive cancer could explain why the disease occurred. The other nine cancers occurred more often than the random mutation rate would predict, suggesting that inherited genes or lifestyle factors were the main cause.
>
> *(Boseley 2015)*

Moreover, her article's title ("Two-Thirds of Adult Cancers . . ."), implies that adults have an absolute risk of 66.66 per cent of developing cancer, which is not what the study suggests, O'Hara argues. O'Hara explains to me where not just Boseley but all the authors he mentioned were wrong:

> They [the study authors] had interpreted a basic statistic called R-squared which is the amount of variation explained by a model. But the journalists had misinterpreted that statistic as the amount of cancers produced by the effects of the model. That is as if you were comparing apples and pears – or should I say apples and golf balls?
>
> *(O'Hara 2016)*

O'Hara and GrrlScientist (2015) further dissect Boseley's article and point out that the study suggests a relationship between the cancer risk and the number of cell divisions in any given type of tissue. But the paper's authors mention at no point how often cancer develops due to said cell divisions. Moreover, the expression "cancer due to bad luck" implies causation, which definitely does not hold, since all the authors are suggesting is a correlation between the two. Some news publications' interpretations have also gone as far as suggesting to their readers that the environment and lifestyle do not play a role in the development of cancer, which is in stark contrast to decades of cancer research.

In their article, O'Hara and Grllscientist wonder why Boseley and the other journalists came up with the two-thirds ratio, and they point out that in the paper this ratio refers to "the proportion of variation in the log of the cancer risk that can be explained by cell divisions". They also make clear that the variation does not determine whether the essential risk of cancer is high or low. To further explain this point, O'Hara comes up with an example of the Marianas Trench: While its variation in depth might be explained by moon phases, it does not tell anything about the trench's absolute depth.

So what led the authors to misinterpret the paper's findings? Certainly a lack of scientific literacy, O'Hara tells me, but vague definitions also played a role. What does *bad luck* actually mean? Only after having a clear definition could one find out how many cancer cases can be caused by bad luck. He also suggests that the easier approach would be to find the cases not caused by bad luck, such as those caused by lifestyle factors such as smoking, which is what the authors did in the original paper to scrutinise the effect smoking has on developing lung cancer.

O'Hara also makes it clear that science journalists are not solely to blame for said mistakes, as some scientists could also benefit from communication training in order to convey their topics and hence lower the language barrier between science and journalism. Often enough, he adds, misinterpretations start in the press releases and are then dragged on by many science journalists who solely rely on them.

Finally, O'Hara (2016) has a few very clear indications on how to improve your own statistical literacy so you can avoid misinterpreting scientific studies. First, he recommends reading *Bad Science* by Ben Goldacre ("an excellent introduction to statistic") to develop your statistical thinking without necessarily needing to handle complicated numbers. As he told me, it is more about developing the right statistical mindset). His second recommendation is to spend time with scientists:

> Learning more about the scientific process would be helpful. Try and spend a few days hanging around with some scientists. Also, there is so much citizen science going on now. Getting involved with these people might be another way to find out how science is really done.
>
> *(O'Hara 2016)*

## Summary

Buttressing claims with facts and figures is essential in journalism, especially in passages in which you explain findings, hard science and background. As a science journalist, a working knowledge and a basic vocabulary of statistics are important, because you will have to read many scholarly articles describing new findings. Separating causation from correlation, relative and absolute risk, percentages and percentage points sounds perhaps trivial, but still too many science articles in the media show that their authors often confuse these terms. One of the reasons for that is that the same terms can have different meanings when used in science as opposed to daily life.

In the digital age, not every bit of information is published in journals. Information spreads rapidly via social media, which makes it easily accessible, but it is sometimes hard to verify its authenticity. Especially for videos and images, this can be a tough task. At the very minimum, you should verify its provenance, originator, date and location. If none of these can be established, discard it. Spreading unverified material is considered journalistic malpractice. In science journalism, not reading the paper you are reporting about is also malpractice; you can't simply skim off a few numbers and report about the results without knowing whether these are significant or whether the experiments were well-designed and the applied method was appropriate. Knowing these things is necessary to fulfil science journalism's role as a watchdog.

Misrepresenting findings or reporting wrong facts can also result in legal disputes. It is important to never tamper with quotes or fabricate them. Be sure to familiarise yourself with the defamations laws and any amending acts in your country.

## Review questions

- Which statistic do journalists and scientists use to downplay a risk, and how?
- Which factors determine whether a P-value is a good indicator for a study's relevance?
- What is the difference between statistical and clinical significance?
- Which approach would you prefer: adapting your facts to your idea or adapting your idea to the facts?
- Which four properties do you need to find out to verify online content?
- How can you verify a digital image's authenticity?
- What question should you always ask scientists to determine how biased the study may be?
- How do libel and slander differ?
- Which questions should you ask scientists about their papers' data?

## Exercises

- Read three science articles that report on a specific study. Check whether the articles address limitations, funding and power calculations.
- Scan the papers the articles were based on for the following elements: sample size, effect size, P-values, limitations, power calculations and funding. Be sure to also check the papers' supplementary material.
- Find three articles that infer a drug or treatment is working in humans but that mentions the drug has only been tested in rats or mice.
- Compare these claims with the authors' claims. Can you find passages where they are fostering such misinterpretations?
- Find an image on Twitter using the hashtag #breaking. Verify when, where and by whom it was taken.

- Take the same image and find out whether somebody else has used it in a different context.
- Take a press release on a new journal paper, read it and put down an initial hypothesis for writing an article on it. Choose the facts from the press release that support the hypothesis.
- Now read the journal paper and see whether your hypothesis from the previous exercise still holds. Would you choose different facts from the paper than you did from the press release?

## Reading list

BBC Academy (no date) Defamation, *BBC Academy* [Online] Available at: www.bbc.co.uk/academy/journalism/article/art20130702112133651 [date accessed 15 June 2016]

Berkhead, S. (2015) 11 tools for verification and fact-checking in 2016, *International Journalists' Network (IJNet.org)* [Online] Available at: https://ijnet.org/en/blog/11-tools-verification-and-fact-checking-2016 [date accessed 24 November 2016]

Borel, B. (2015) The problem with science journalism: We've forgotten that reality matters most, *The Guardian* [Online] Available at: www.theguardian.com/media/2015/dec/30/problem-with-science-journalism-2015-reality-kevin-folta [date accessed 5 July 2016]

Boseley, S. (2015) Two-thirds of adult cancers largely 'down to bad luck' rather than genes, *The Guardian* [Online] Available at: www.theguardian.com/society/2015/jan/02/two-thirds-adult-cancers-bad-luck [date accessed 6 July 2016]

Cope, L. (2006) Understanding and using statistics, In Blum, D., Knudson, M. and Henig, R.M. (eds.) *A Field Guide for Science Writers*. 2nd edition. New York: Oxford University Press, 18–25

Freeman, D. (2013) Survival of the wrongest, *Columbia Journalism Review* [Online] Available at: www.cjr.org/cover_story/survival_of_the_wrongest.php [date accessed 4 July 2016]

Goldacre, B. (2008) *Bad Science*. London: Fourth Estate

Harris, M. and Taylor, G. (2003) *Medical Statistics Made Easy*. London: Martin Dunitz (Taylor & Francis Group)

Johnson, J.T. (2006) (ed.) *Ver 1.0 Proceedings*. Santa Fe, NM: Institute for Analytic Journalism

Silver, N. (2012) *The Signal and the Noise – Why So Many Predictions Fail – but Some Don't*. New York: The Penguin Press

## Links

The BMJ, How to Read a Paper (article series on statistics): www.bmj.com/about-bmj/resources-readers/publications/how-read-paper

British Medical Journal, How to Calculate Risk: http://clinicalevidence.bmj.com/x/set/static/ebm/learn/665075.html

The Digital Media Law Project legal guide: www.dmlp.org/legal-guide

Electronic Frontier Foundation legal guide for bloggers: www.eff.org/de/issues/bloggers/legal/liability/defamation

Emergency Journalism Toolkit for Better Reporting list of verification tools: http://emergencyjournalism.net/useful-links-verification-tools/

European Journalism Centre, The Verification Handbook: http://verificationhandbook.com/

HealthNewsReview.org: www.healthnewsreview.org

HealthNewsReview.org journalists' toolkit: www.healthnewsreview.org/toolkit/

Izutru (online photo-manipulation spotting tool): http://izutru.com

Legislation.co.uk, Defamation Act 2013 (UK): www.legislation.gov.uk/ukpga/2013/26/contents/enacted

Massachusetts Institute of Technology, Knight Science Journalism Tracker: http://undark.org/tag/tracker/

Poynter News University, Math for Journalists: www.newsu.org/courses/math-for-journalists

Royal Statistical Society, Statistics for Journalists (online course): www.statslife.org.uk/rss-resources/statistics/story_html5.html?lms=1

SCIJOURNO, Understanding Statistics and Numbers (online course): http://scijourno.com.au/portfolio-item/understanding-statistics-and-numbers/University of Wollongong, Statistical Literacy (online course): www.uow.edu.au/student/qualities/statlit/World Federation of Science Journalists, Science Journalism (online course): www.wfsj.org/course/

## References

Baker, M. (2016) Statisticians issue warning over misuse of P values, *Nature*, vol. 531, no. 7593, 151

Bauer, M.W., Romo Ramos, Y.J., Massarani, L. and Amorim, L. (2013) *Global Science Journalism Report*. London: Science and Development Network (SciDev.net)

BBC Academy (no date) Defamation, *BBC Academy* [Online] Available at: www.bbc.co.uk/academy/journalism/article/art20130702112133651 [date accessed 15 June 2016]

Berendzen, G. (2014) Even with new fact-checking tools, journalists still need a dose of scepticism, *Reynolds Journalism Institute/Missouri School of Journalism* [Online] Available at: www.rjionline.org/stories/even-with-new-fact-checking-tools-journalists-still-need-a-dose-of-skeptici [date accessed 7 May 2016]

Cohen, D. (2016) Personal phone conversation on 25 April 2016

Cohen, D. and Oransky, I. (2014) *UKCSJ Statistics in Science Journalism, Association of British Science Writers* (via YouTube) [Online Video] Available at: www.youtube.com/watch?v=3eOxyxYSXnU [date accessed 12 April 2016]

Cope, L. (2006) Understanding and using statistics, In Blum, D., Knudson, M. and Henig, R.M. (eds.) *A Field Guide for Science Writers*. 2nd edition. New York: Oxford University Press, 18–25

Freeman, D. (2013) Survival of the wrongest, *Columbia Journalism Review* [Online] Available at: www.cjr.org/cover_story/survival_of_the_wrongest.php [date accessed 4 July 2016]

Harrison, S. (2016) Personal phone conversation on 10 June 2016

Kemeny, R. (2014) The statistical foundations of the Fourth Estate, *Significance*, vol. 11, no. 4, 34–35

Murcott, T. (2009) Science journalism: Toppling the priesthood, *Nature*, vol. 459, no. 7250, 1054–1055

Nuzzo, R. (2014) Statistical errors, *Nature*, vol. 506, no. 7487, 150–152

O'Hara, B. (2016) Personal phone conversation on 9 June 2016

O'Hara, B. and GrrlScientist (2015) Bad luck, bad journalism and cancer rates, *The Guardian* [Online] Available at: www.theguardian.com/science/grrlscientist/2015/jan/02/bad-luck-bad-journalism-and-cancer-rates [date accessed 7 May 2016]

Rehman, J. (2013) The need for critical science journalism, *The Guardian* [Online] Available at: www.theguardian.com/science/blog/2013/may/16/need-for-critical-science-journalism [date accessed 16 July 2016]

Sainani, K. (2016) Personal phone conversation on 16 March 2016

Schäfer, M. (2011) Science journalism and fact checking, *JCOM Journal of Science Communication*, vol. 10, no. 4, C02

Seife, C. (2012) Jonah Lehrer's journalistic misdeeds at Wired.com, *Slate* [Online] Available at: www.slate.com/articles/health_and_science/science/2012/08/jonah_lehrer_plagiarism_in_wired_com_an_investigation_into_plagiarism_quotes_and_factual_inaccuracies_.html [date accessed 5 July 2016]

Wardle, C. (2013) Verifying user-generated content, In Silverman, C. (ed.) *The Verification Handbook* [Online] Available at: http://verificationhandbook.com/downloads/verification.handbook.pdf [date accessed 20 May 2016]

White, S. (2016) Personal phone conversation on 5 July 2016

Wilcox (2016) Personal Skype conversation on 25 February 2016

Zhang, M. (2015) Reuters issues a worldwide ban on RAW photos, *PetaPixel.com* [Online] Available at: http://petapixel.com/2015/11/18/reuters-issues-a-worldwide-ban-on-raw-photos/ [date accessed 22 May 2016]

# 10

# INVESTIGATIVE SCIENCE JOURNALISM

**What you will learn in this chapter:**

- What is investigative science journalism?
- Finding investigative science stories
- The story-based inquiry method
- Criteria for reviewing health stories
- Methods of proving scientific misconduct
- Freedom of information requests
- Case study: analysing an article that uncovers medical fraud
- Case study: Hwanggate

## Introduction

Much of science journalism praises new scientific advances but fails to look at limitations, misconduct and larger implications. Worst of all, many articles suggest these advances are ready to use, when in reality they are not. These articles cause an ephemeral awe, drive traffic and hence haul in advertising money. But they only report the obvious facts that scientists, charities and universities want you to report. They fail to fulfil journalism's essential role of holding powers to account, as science writer Fabio Turone tells me:

> There is a tendency to consider science journalism as different from other forms of journalism. Science journalism, and health journalism in particular, is often seen as a tool to promote health campaigns. That is not the type of critical journalism that holds power to account; instead, it is often explanatory journalism that divulges information that should in fact be up to research institutions to disseminate.
>
> *(Turone 2016)*

Most important, investigative journalism differs from that PR-style approach in that it tries to unearth the larger issues behind a wrong and expose the system that facilitates and encourages misconduct.

But investigating science entails a lot of hard work and lengthy research. Also, it does not always pay well. So why would you do it? Physician and science writer Ben Goldacre tells me that investigative science articles often do not pay, and that it does make a difference whether a journalist is paid by the hour or by the word; if you get paid by the word, looking deeply inside an issue takes more (unpaid) time, but if your motivation is to produce high-quality science articles, this is the only way (Goldacre 2016).

One big factor that drives investigative journalists is a sense of moral obligation, as you will see in the first section. But there are many more characteristics that mark investigative journalism, such as the ability to unearth documents and data some people are trying to hide. In fact, court records, regulatory decisions, disciplinary decisions and warning letters are perfect sources for investigative ideas. A dedicated section on finding inspiration for investigative stories will show you where you can find such documents and other sources.

As you pile up documents, transcripts and data, it is quite easy to lose track of your actual story. That is why you should organise your raw research material, order it and eliminate the irrelevant chaff, making sure that you report a coherent story around a hypothesis. Investigative journalist Mark Lee Hunter has developed a structured approach of doing so which he calls the story-based inquiry (SBI) method to tell all sorts of journalistic stories.

Health and the environment are two of the predominant domains for investigative journalists. The watchdog platform HealthNewsReview.org has developed its own set of criteria for reviewing and rating health stories. You will find them in this chapter, and I highly recommend you test your own stories using these criteria. If in addition you read their reviews of health stories, you will quickly get a sense of what distinguishes critical, responsible health stories from shallow gee whiz articles.

In the two subsequent sections, you will first read about scientific misconduct and which tools regulatory agencies employ to detect fabrication, falsification and plagiarism. You can use most of this software yourself to test scientists' data or figures. Next, the section on Freedom of Information Acts (FOIA) points out some differences between the US and the UK. You can get much information by filing FOIA requests, but you have to do it the right way. Also, waiting times might be long, and some public authorities can turn down your requests because they violate another act. In the worst case, you might have to sue them.

This is what investigative journalist Charles Seife did with the US Food and Drug Administration (FDA); they did not disclose the records requested or they redacted them so much that he could not make use of them. You can read in the first case study how the FDA discovered scientific misconduct but failed to take appropriate action and inform the public. The second case study, which is this chapter's final section, shows an example of a science whistle-blower that led to the resignation of a dubious stem cell researcher in South Korea. It is disconcerting that the whistle-blower faced more backlash and criticism than the culprit.

## What is investigative science journalism?

If you want to investigate science, you will not only look at what scientists feed you but also find out what they omit and knowingly (or accidentally) conceal. Once again, selection is key: Some of these hidden issues are worth pursuing and investigating, while others are not. Alan Rusbridger, the *Guardian*'s former editor-in-chief, once said you must distinguish between those stories that are in the public interest and those that are not (De Burgh 2008). Studies that involve clinical trials, health studies and environmental pollution fall into the range of publicly relevant information, because they often affect a large portion of the population and involve notable amounts of tax money. As an investigative journalist, you must dig up scientists' hidden ties to the industry. After all, how much is a study on smoke-induced lung cancer worth if it is financed by the tobacco industry?

In that sense, being an investigative science journalist greatly resembles detective work. Antonio Regalado, now a biomedicine editor at the *Technology Review*, confirms this and affirms that you should take nothing for granted in science:

> To be a science "detective" requires a more critical view of things. I tend to assume, for instance, that researchers aren't telling me the whole story. I always wonder about hidden motives. And as far as the scientific data goes, I believe that's fair game for tough questions, too.
> *(Regalado 2006:119)*

If you want to be able to critically question scientists' claims and find out what they are trying to hide, you need to acquire in-depth knowledge of the practices in their discipline. In fact, you need to become an expert in that discipline, which general reporters are often not. Investigative journalist Mark Lee Hunter tells me that specialist knowledge makes you more flexible:

> If you have specialized knowledge, you can also do general stuff. If you just have general knowledge, you can't do specialized stuff.
> *(Hunter 2016)*

Therefore, fully immerse yourself in the topic. If you have a degree in the broader field you are covering, it may be helpful, but it is not an absolute requirement:

> Whether or not you do an advanced degree, you have to do serious study, not just something where you are going to read one book and then think you are going to be able to do a good job.
>
> *(Hunter 2016)*

This expertise allows you to notice whenever something seems odd in scientists' papers and publications. Experienced investigative journalists often say they had a hunch that caused them to start an investigation. That seems like a vague statement, but it essentially boils down to experience and expertise. The more you know a field, the better you can spot irregularities or oddities in scientists' statements. This can become a source for story ideas on its own. So can tip-offs from insiders and whistle-blowers that are more likely to occur after you have established yourself as a competent journalist in a given scientific area. Both are great sources for story ideas that are often not available to generalist journalists.

Developing that expertise takes a lot of time and effort. Investigative journalism is hard work. For example, you have to do much more reporting compared to a gee whiz science story that praises a new discovery; investigative research means you have to go beyond a journal paper and consult related studies and all sorts of documents the stakeholders do not want you to see. Sometimes you will have to contend with government agencies to receive the documents you need. This ability to come up with facts other than those the scientists want you to see distinguishes an investigative science journalist from an uncritical one. In an article for the Science and Development Network, retired science journalist K.S. Jayaraman (2013) confirms this point of view: "Most science stories are second-hand, based on findings made by scientists. Investigative pieces, in contrast, rely on the reporter's own initiative to ferret out news that other people conceal." Investigative science journalists also talk to many more people than their conventional counterparts. The more sources you consult, the better you understand an issue, which will eventually improve your articles. In fact, "one academic study found that Pulitzer Prize-winning feature stories were, on average, based on interviews with 53 people" (Sumner and Miller 2013:9).

Investigative interviews tend to become tense at some point, because you will ask unpleasant questions. Contest every bit of information interviewees try to feed you. Ask them how they know that information, ask them about their industry ties and ask them what data they excluded and why. That is why you must start with your preliminary reporting long before you conduct the first interview.

Extensive reporting is one of investigative journalism's hallmarks. For example, science journalist Deborah Blum describes in an article for *Nieman Reports* how she investigated nuclear weapons laboratories. In it, she emphasises the importance of time (her investigations took more than 6 months), and she also stresses that she needed to have her conclusions "checked and double-checked" (Blum 2002). In the article, she also states that she spent many hours not only deciphering documents but also making sure her terminology was bulletproof once she started putting the story on paper. An elevated level of accuracy is definitely another trait of investigative journalism.

While you can exclude money as a driving factor, moral purpose is in fact often behind investigative journalists' diligence. As journalists, we develop that sense when our moral standards are violated, and the response may be shock. This may cause some journalists to become investigative journalists (De Burgh 2008). This ethical component also plays a role in the second case study of this chapter, where a scientist breached the ethical standards for obtaining human eggs for stem cell research and fabricated his "scientific" results. Ten years after first exposing the disgraced researcher, two *Nature* authors followed up on the case. They found that he now heads a striving cloning institute in South Korea. The moral obligation to follow up on issues of misconduct and find out if and how an objectionable situation has changed over time is another defining characteristic of investigative journalism.

You might feel that such moral obligation drives you to tell such stories, but investigative work like requesting documents people are trying to hide, filing lawsuits, interviewing reluctant sources and finally writing complex stories takes a lot of time and costs even more money. If you are just starting out, editors might not commission such stories. But don't let that discourage you from approaching investigative stories on your own:

> I think it's a waste of time for a new, unproven journalist to try and get somebody to assign them a big story. You just do the story. I spent months writing proposals that nobody approved, and then I just started doing the stories that excited me, and suddenly they were getting published. Is there a pattern? If you think the story is good, you do the story and then you get it published somewhere. And if you can't get it published, it leads to something else, but just keep doing it. Many of them don't pay, but there are so many opportunities to publish. The main thing to keep in mind is that you should be doing the stuff you think is important.
>
> *(Hunter 2016)*

## Finding investigative science stories

People are undoubtedly one of the best sources for science stories. When it comes to uncovering scientific misconduct and fraud, whistle-blowers are indispensable. These insiders can provide you with first-hand accounts of what goes wrong on scientists' lab benches. They can also often give you documents or images that prove their allegations.

Of course there is a catch. Whistle-blowers are the hardest source to get, and they usually find you, not vice versa. Becoming a whistle-blower could ruin a researcher's career, depending on which country she lives in and which laws apply (Gewin 2012). The probability is low that a researcher will approach you and denounce a colleague's scientific fraud, hence putting her own career at risk. What is required is a relationship based on trust between the whistle-blower and the journalist. The following factors increase the odds a researcher will entrust you with misconduct should she encounter it in her own laboratory:

- **You work at a high-profile publication:** For example, Edward Snowden's NSA revelations were first published in the *Washington Post* and the *Guardian*. Laura Poitras, one of two journalists Snowden initially approached, notes in an interview with *Salon* that Snowden initially was suspicious of the mainstream media (Carmon 2013). Publishing revelations in reputable newspapers has the highest impact, and sources know that.
- **You have covered scientific fraud before:** If so, whistle-blowers can assume you know how to protect them and how to work with sensitive material. Experience counts.
- **You cultivate a lot of science sources:** This means you get to know the researchers, regularly follow up with them and slowly build more know-how in their scientific discipline. Can you build a relationship on eye level and demonstrate that you are genuinely interested in their issues? If so, chances are they might confide foul play to you should they ever encounter it.

Scientists love to criticise their colleagues' work, and they often do so on their personal blogs, because they can immediately publish their reactions to new papers and point out flaws, perhaps demanding the retraction of those papers. You can find the same type of comments and reactions in, say, *Nature*'s comment section and *Science*'s letters section. But personal science blogs do not get redacted and can approach scientific issues much faster than any print medium. Some scientists even write under a pseudonym, like the author of *DISCOVER* magazine's Neuroskeptic blog. Neuroscientist and blogger Neuroskeptic is known for critically commenting on neuroscience and for raising critical questions. Such blogs can be wonderful sources for finding stories that are based on scientific misconduct.

Online watchdog publications like Retraction Watch specialise in uncovering and exposing scientific misconduct. Its authors, medical reporters Ivan Oransky and Adam Marcus, regularly write about studies that are being investigated or have just been retracted. By their own account, they mostly cover fraud and misconduct in the life sciences. Oransky also runs another platform, Embargo Watch, which examines the relationship between the media and scientific embargoes and how such embargoes influence the news. This niche in and of itself can be a valid source for pointing out the sometimes peculiar practices journals employ.

Databases and documents are generally excellent sources for investigative articles. So many reports and papers get published every day that many stories worth investigating get overlooked. The first class of relevant documents are those published by regulatory agencies. For example, you can find reports on scientific misconduct, drug recalls and food safety issues in both human and veterinary medicine on the website of the US Food and Drug Administration (FDA), although, as you will read a bit later, these can be heavily redacted. In Europe, the European Medicines Agency (EMA) fulfils similar functions and also publishes documents and warning letters. On a more local level, medical boards' enforcement databases are another great source for investigative story ideas. Many medical boards in the US, UK and Australia openly publish the original allegations, fines, revocations of doctors' licenses and other disciplinary actions. You can search and filter most of these online databases. If medical doctor misconduct interests you, you might also want to examine the platforms QuackWatch and the Bad Doctor Database. Box 10.1 contains a list of US and European databases and websites that provide many legal documents for you to consult. Most of them are freely accessible.

---

**BOX 10.1 SOURCES FOR LEGAL DOCUMENTS IN THE US AND EUROPE**

Patexia: www.patexia.com
US Patent and Trademark Office, patent litigation resources: www.uspto.gov/patents-maintaining-patent/patent-litigation/resources
PACER: https://www.pacer.gov
EU InfoCuria database: http://curia.europa.eu/juris/recherche.jsf?cid=191901
EU National case law database: www.juradmin.eu/index.php/en/dec-nat-en
EU member state database: https://e-justice.europa.eu/content_member_state_case_law-13-it-en.do?member=1
Patent litigation in Europe: www.epo.org/learning-events/materials/litigation.html
EPO case law and appeals: www.epo.org/law-practice/case-law-appeals/recent.html#201611
Patent litigation in the US: http://us.practicallaw.com/6–623–0657?q=&qp=&qo=&qe=

The US National Institutes of Health (NIH) runs the online database ClinicalTrials.gov, which registers clinical trial results; it currently contains more than 230,000 records which you can search and filter. Since the registered trials involve human participants, and given that clinical trials substantially influence health policies and the manufacturing of drugs that affect a large portion of the population, clinical trials are highly relevant for investigations. Not all scientists register their trials. Ben Goldacre tells me that clinical trial information being withheld is still the biggest problem worth focusing on in investigative health journalism. The enormous coverage in the media of such misconduct supports his claim. As a result, he has launched the AllTrials campaign, a joint initiative between Goldacre, the *BMJ* and the Cochrane Collaboration (and other institutions) which demands that all trials worldwide (even past ones) be registered and their results be reported. Goldacre says that looking into cases of missing information is an absolutely valid starting point for journalists. Health journalism has a crucial responsibility as for giving advice that people will often follow. But as a doctor, he has to have the complete information to make informed decisions about whether to prescribe a new drug (Goldacre 2016).

Following the money has always been a cornerstone of investigative journalism. In that sense, pharmaceutical, biotechnological and environmental companies' spendings are definitely worth looking at. In fact, corporations and public administrations are increasingly obliged to publish spending reports either due to legal settlements or because of transparency and anti-corruption laws. There are companies that collect this data, refine it and offer it as pre-packaged datasets that journalists can buy. In one prominent example, ProPublica has published a series of articles, Dollars for Docs, that expose how much pharmaceutical companies spent for doctors to promote their products, hold speeches and conduct research for them, which casts doubts on these doctors' objectivity. ProPublica is transparent about the methods it employs and about where the data originates from.

Some data comes from public lawsuit databases. You can use them to find out in which legal arguments and pending lawsuits large, science-related corporations are involved in. For example, patients could file lawsuits when they experience severe side effects from a drug, as in the case *Andrew McCarrell vs Hoffman-La Roche Inc.* In 1995, McCarrell took the anti-acne drug Accutane and later developed inflammatory bowel disease. The Atlantic County Superior Court awarded McCarrell $2.5 million in compensatory charges. The drug giant appealed, but the court increased the compensatory charges tenfold. As an investigative journalist, you could look at a single case and find out how the system behind it works. Were the tests flawed? Should the FDA never have approved the drug?

To locate US court records, you can use online databases like Public Access to Court Electronic Records (PACER), and individual district, national and superior courts publish their records on their websites as searchable and filterable databases. PACER contains an extensive list of these courts and their electronic records. The online database InfoCuria allows you to search cases that belong to the Court of Justice of the European Union, General Court and Civil Service Tribunal. But you can also search on a national level. Pharmaceutical cases are interesting because they often end in settlements, which means the underlying, inherent issues are not resolved.

Patent litigations are also worth looking at if you want to find investigative story ideas. Science plays a big role in patent litigations. Biotechnology and pharmaceutical companies have the highest median damages awards, according to a report published by PricewaterhouseCoopers. Five of the ten largest initial adjudicated damages awards between 1996 and 2015 involved biotechnology and pharmaceutical companies (Barry et al. 2016). Again, much information on such cases is published online. For US patent litigations, the US Patent and Trademark Office (USPTO) publishes an exhaustive list of databases you can consult to find cases, such as Patexia.com. For the EU, you can consult the European Patent Office's (EPO) website on case law and appeals, which includes a searchable database.

You can also find inspiration in the work others have produced to get a feeling for which topics (and companies) lend themselves to being investigated. For example, the following list of investigative reporters' associations (some focus on the environment) and platforms provides a lot of examples that you can access (some require that you become a member). In addition, you will find resources like presentations and tip sheets that contain advice from accomplished investigative reporters regarding the techniques they employ for planning, reporting and writing their investigative stories:

- Center for Investigative Reporting (CIR)
- Investigative Reporters and Editors (IRE)
- Reveal News (CIR run)
- California Watch (CIR run)
- Oxpeckers Center for Investigative Environmental Journalism.

One of the most important techniques is employing a critical mind-set, as journalism professor Deborah Nelson confirms. In some of her tip sheets for the IRE, she details how she helps students develop such a sceptic mind-set. She first lets them find and produce daily quick turnaround stories, she tells me. Then she sends them out again but this time tasks them with asking for examples and statistics and asking the interviewees how they know specific facts:

> Sometimes, students have a tendency to want to believe people in power and take them at face value. But when they do that additional reporting, when they discover that what they were first told is not

necessarily true, that is really eye opening. It introduces that notion of scepticism. It doesn't mean that people are lying to them necessarily for evil purposes. It just might be that the person they talked to doesn't know the whole picture.

*(Nelson 2016)*

## The story-based inquiry method

Once you have found your story idea, you will have to research it, organise your raw material and periodically check whether your facts still support your initial idea. Finally, you will write the story. In this section you will learn a specific process that covers the entire process of researching and writing an investigative story: the story-based inquiry (SBI) method defined by Mark Lee Hunter (2011), who was also a founding member of the Global Investigative Journalism Network. Why is this important? Investigative stories demand more research than shallower stories. The amount of raw material you gather during your research can easily overwhelm you. This is where the SBI method comes into play: It helps you not only to organise this material but also not lose sight of what your story is about.

Although the SBI method is not specifically targeted at science stories, its process at times does resemble the scientific method. First, Hunter (2011) affirms that in contrast to conventional journalism, investigative journalism is not reactive or passive but rather requires you to collect all the necessary evidence; this confirms the previously stated points highlighting the differences between these approaches. Although the focus of the SBI manual is not on finding story ideas, he names three sources he deems valid for finding investigative story ideas. This is what you should look for (Hunter 2011):

1   **The media:** After reading a story, do you still find that something is suspicious or unanswered and demands further questioning? If so, there could be an investigative story behind it.
2   **Changes in your environment:** Be a good observer of your surroundings. Whenever something that is familiar to you changes, ask yourself why it has changed.
3   **People's complaints:** Listen to what people have to say whenever they gather. Is their situation really immutable?

Also, do not only look at negative stories that involve wrongdoing but also at positive stories that highlight how well something has been done. When you select a story, make sure you are passionate about it or you will not endure the hard work that investigative journalism entails. Your motivation should not be fuelled by revenge but rather by the desire to lessen "suffering, cruelty and stupidity" (Hunter 2011:12).

Apart from the right motivation, you should make sure your story idea fulfils a few basic criteria that help you determine whether you should invest time and money to do the story:

> How many people are affected? (We call this "the size of the beast".)
> How powerfully are they affected? (Quality matters as much as quantity here. If just one person dies, or his or her life is ruined, the story is important.)
> If they are affected positively, can the cause be replicated elsewhere?
> Or, are these people victims?
> Could their suffering be avoided?
> Can we show how?
> Are there wrongdoers who must be punished? Or at least, denounced?
> Is it important in any event to tell what happened, so it will or won't happen again?
>
> *(Hunter 2011:12)*

Hunter's manual proposes an eight-step process that starts with discovering your subject and then moves on to defining a hypothesis. In fact, the SBI is hypothesis-based, and over the course of the investigative process, you will either prove or refute it. If you disprove it, you may have to formulate a new hypothesis or change your initial hypothesis. Starting from your hypothesis, you will derive questions that you can verify. The SBI manual's author explains of how you formulate and work with a hypothesis: "You create a statement of what you think reality may be, based on the best information in your possession, and then you seek further information that can prove or disprove your statement. This is the process of verification" (Hunter 2011:18).

A well-formulated hypothesis should consist of no more than three sentences: The current problem (the present), what caused it (the past) and what can be done about it (the future). The aforementioned questions should arise as you dissect your hypothesis, analyse the single terms and attempt to precisely define them. He is quick to add that such precise definitions are one of the four key elements of a good hypothesis (Hunter 2011). Investigative journalist and journalism professor Deborah Nelson uses a similar technique that takes a hypothesis, breaks it down into its essential components and then tests them:

> I actually use Mark Lee Hunter's book in my class. I love his book, and I have a compatible technique that I use and share with him. I did a whole environmental series on land exchanges, and it just started out with thinking: What is the biggest land exchange in the Northwest? One thing I try to do is come up with a theory, and I break it down then into what facts need to be true in order to prove it. I try to nail it down to just a handful of facts that need to be true. That is not all I

need to know to write the whole story. But it is what I need to know in order to determine whether there is a story and whether I am on the right track. The nice thing about boiling it down to three facts that I have to prove true or false is that then I pick which one is the easiest to prove or disprove. If I disprove it, I know I don't have a story. These are the essential facts I need to prove if my theory is right. You always have to try to prove and disprove a fact.

*(Nelson 2016)*

Here is a lightly adapted version of Hunter's (2011) complete SBI process. In his manual, he dedicates one chapter to each of these steps:

1    Discover a subject.
2    Create a verifiable hypothesis.
3    Consult open source data to verify it.
4    Consult human sources to verify it.
5    Organise the collected evidence as you go.
6    Put the data in narrative sequence and compose the story.
7    Do quality control.
8    Publish, promote and defend the story.

After you have formulated the hypothesis, the remaining process steps largely proceed in chronological order as you continually deal with gathering and verifying your facts. Open doors, that is, openly accessible data, are the most valuable (and overlooked) sources for finding information that some officials may be reluctant to talk about. When you interview human sources, ask targeted and precise questions that show you have some knowledge about the area you are investigating. Such confirmatory questions tend to yield better answers. Also, you should have at least four sources that can confirm your initial speculation in order to proceed with your investigations. Moreover, organising your evidence in a master file will not only help you keep track of what you have researched so far and possibly show connections between information items, but it will also serve you as a planning tool that helps you assess how much time and money you will need for your investigation. Additionally, the master file is a valuable tool to order the events, eliminate low-priority facts and finally write the story once you have concluded your research. According to Hunter, there are essentially two types of stories: chronology-based and space-based stories, where the type defines the order in which you have to connect and write down the events.

This section provides only a brief summary of the method, so read the manual to get the complete picture of the SBI method and how you can apply it to your future stories. The manual is only 89 pages, is written in an easily digestible and concise way and is available for free download (see the Links section).

## Criteria for reviewing health stories

The following sections cover methods and best practices for investigative journalists. This section first introduces the factors that health media watchdogs use to assess the scientific quality of health articles. This will help you to distinguish high- from low-quality health articles as you read them, and the criteria make for a handy checklist that you can use before you hand an article to your editor or publish it.

The health media watchdog platform HealthNewsReview.org is a de facto authority. The following are their criteria that a health article must meet. You can find a link to the entire list in the Links section at the end of this chapter:

1 **Does the story adequately discuss the costs of the intervention?** Costs should be quantified, not just approximated. When this is not possible, cite the costs of the alternatives; 70 per cent of the stories fail to report these costs.

2 **Does the story adequately quantify the benefits of the treatment/test/ product/procedure?** Again, the reviewers of HNR demand quantification, stating that many stories contain only relative data or non-representative accounts of patients.

3 **Does the story adequately explain/quantify the harms of the intervention?** Side effects, be they major or minor, should be not only mentioned but quantified. Relying too heavily on patients' accounts or scientists' comments in this sense is considered bad practice.

4 **Does the story seem to grasp the quality of the evidence?** Not pointing out the limitations of the evidence at hand or not pointing out that the findings cannot be extrapolated (for example, implying that findings in animals will have the same effects on humans) is bad practice.

5 **Does the story commit disease-mongering?** Using this criterion, HNR reviewers explicitly look for overstatements and exaggerations of conditions and the misrepresentation of normal conditions, such as baldness or timidity, as medical conditions.

6 **Does the story use independent sources and identify conflicts of interests?** The HNR reviewers split this criterion into two parts: First, at least one independent researcher must comment on the findings. Second, conflicts of interest must be addressed.

7 **Does the story compare the new approach with existing alternatives?** Omitting comparable, established and/or alternative procedures is considered bad practice. New treatments should be put in context, and not applying them at all should also be considered.

8 **Does the story establish the availability of the treatment/test/product/ procedure?** Is there promotion of a new drug in an article, and does the article imply a drug will be officially approved by the FDA when there

is no evidence supporting such suggestions? An article should point out the availability of a drug, whether it is still in trial phase or already available in pharmacies.

9  **Does the story establish the true novelty of the approach?** Is the article overstating a drug/treatment's novelty, perhaps as a sales strategy? Talking with independent experts and sourcing external information could clarify this, the HNR reviewers suggest.

10  **Does the story appear to rely solely or largely on a news release?** The HNR reviewers explicitly state that taking verbatim passages from press releases (not stating you have done so makes this malpractice even worse) is bad practice. Employing independent sources is a good sign of quality in this regard.

Other journal papers also assess the status of health-related media reports in terms of quality. For example, Hanson et al. (2016) examined 1,024 local and national UK newspaper articles containing the keywords "rheumatoid arthritis" or "research". They found that 91 of 100 articles about medical research focused on positive reporting about medical research, so they identified a pattern of generally positive reporting. Hanson et al. (2016) broke this pattern of positive medical reporting down into three components: "All the positive stories included the narrative: An **innovation** offers **hope** in the context of **burden**. Few of the articles had a patient voice and even fewer included patients' experience of research involvement" (Hanson et al. 2016:8). If the papers mentioned medical innovation, the authors often expressed that through "words such as 'breakthrough', 'revolutionary', 'pioneering', 'new approach' and 'world's first' " (4). Burden, however, was expressed as follows: "Dramatic figures were employed to show the cost on a societal level, for example '700 000 sufferers' " (4).

If you are interested in in-depth scholarly analyses of the way newspapers report about medical research, be sure to read the landmark paper written by Robinson et al. (2013) which analysed the quality of UK newspapers' health-related articles by drawing on statistical as well as cross-sectional analyses to assess their quality. They also assessed the quality of the source material and found that its quality was substantially lower for the most prolific newspaper, *The Daily Mail*, compared to the *Guardian*; the latter published the fewest health-related articles, but they were based on grade A studies (Robinson et al. 2013).

## Methods of proving scientific misconduct

Some cases of scientific misconduct can quickly be discovered using software. For example, software like Turnitin or iThenticate can detect plagiarised work by comparing an article against an existing body of work (Gewin 2012). Some universities also use this to ensure their students' essays are original and not plagiarised, although letting students proactively submit their writings to Turnitin's online service has been criticised.

Similarly, for examining and exposing plagiarising journalists such as Jonah Lehrer, browser plugins exist that allow you to verify the originality of any given article while you are reading it. These tools operate in a simpler way than Turnitin and iThenticate by comparing an article to an existing body of press releases and announcements and highlighting the matching passages. One such example is the browser plugin Churnalism, which is available in the US.

Finally, a combination of watchdogs and citizen investigative science journalism websites like the famous anti-plagiarism platforms GuttenPlag and VroniPlag in Germany were used to uncover a substantial amount of allegedly plagiarised passages in the dissertations of several high-ranking German politicians, like former Minister of Defence Karl-Theodor zu Guttenberg and former Minister of Education and Research (do note the irony) Annette Schavan. These allegations prompted their alma maters to launch their own investigations. Consequently, both zu Guttenberg and Schavan stepped down from their posts. Such platforms have to a certain degree democratised the detection and examination of plagiarism in dissertations, and said platforms currently have a number of ongoing investigations into politicians' dissertations. That said, plagiarism has to be separated from the aforementioned practices of fabricating data and results or falsifying them.

---

## BOX 10.2   WHAT IS SCIENTIFIC MISCONDUCT?

Before researchers formally file a misconduct complaint, they need to know how their university defines research misconduct. Equally, as a science journalist, you should know what counts as misconduct and what does not. Here are two definitions. The first is an intuitive and short but less formal definition by freelance science journalist Virginia Gewin:

> Misconduct is not simply bad behaviour; it is the falsification, fabrication or plagiarism of results. Honest errors, differences in the interpretation of results, authorship disputes, sexual harassment or threatening language are issues of concern, but are not misconduct. At the core of misconduct is intent.
>
> (Gewin 2012:138)

The second definition originates from the Wellcome Trust. It serves as a basis for some universities' guidelines on research misconduct and defines in more detail which actions are considered misconduct:

> The fabrication, falsification, plagiarism or deception in proposing, carrying out or reporting results of research or deliberate, dangerous or

negligent deviations from accepted practices in carrying out research. It includes failure to follow established protocols if this failure results in unreasonable risk or harm to humans, other vertebrates or the environment and facilitating of misconduct in research by collusion in, or concealment of, such actions by others. It also includes intentional, unauthorised use, disclosure or removal of, or damage to, research-related property of another, including apparatus, materials, writings, data, hardware or software or any other substances or devices used in or produced by the conduct of research.

It does not include honest error or honest differences in the design, execution, interpretation or judgement in evaluating research methods or results or misconduct unrelated to the research process. Similarly it does not include poor research unless this encompasses the intention to deceive.

(Wellcome Trust 2005)

Incidentally, ghostwriting, that is "the unacknowledged authoring of scientific papers by industry" (Bosch 2011:472), and guestwriting, a practice that "includes authors who have made little contribution to the work", should be regulated by the US Office of Research Integrity (ORI) and its counterparts in the UK and Europe. Specifically, Bosch (2011) demands that said institutions also classify these practices as forms of scientific misconduct and not simply as plagiarism.

Doctoring images counts as misconduct, and it is quite widespread in scientific publishing. That is why the ORI has developed and utilises several fraud-detection plugins for the image editing software Photoshop. These plugins find out whether an image has been tampered with before being published. For example, the ORI's "forensic droplets" allow for the detection of erased or brightened areas of an image. Also, the droplets plugins detect differences by comparing images. A modified, customisable option is to use the ORI's "forensic actions" and "advanced forensic actions", which are Photoshop actions and allow for toggling single tests. All of these tools are available for free, so you can test them on your own computer, provided you have a working copy of Photoshop. You can download the droplets and actions from the ORI website (see the Links section at the end of this chapter). Be sure to also check out the website's sample images that show how the ORI has employed the plugins to expose manipulated images.

Apart from scrutinising images using software, several scientists, such as Pitt and Hill (2013), have proposed statistical methods for checking potentially fabricated numbers, for example, by checking patterns in the data and comparing them with patterns that would normally emerge from empirical data. In microbiology, as a counter-measure to fabricating numbers in colony counting, they suggest that automatically analysing and counting colonies could deter scientific fraudsters. They also suggest that journal editors require scientists to archive and make the raw data publicly available (Pitt and Hill 2013). As a journalist, it is not always easy to perform such checks to expose scientific fraud. One way to overcome this is to team up with statisticians and experts in the field on a case-by-case basis.

Additionally, there are regulatory government institutions, like the ORI and the FDA in the US or the European Network of Research Integrity Offices (ENRIO), that do part of that work for you – namely launch investigations into alleged misconduct and then report their findings and publish them. As the first case study later in this chapter shows, these findings are not always passed on to the public. While you can obtain some of these documents via FOIA requests (see the next section), others are made publicly available. For example, the ORI regularly publishes summaries of cases where it found research misconduct, but only those with currently active administrative actions. For closed cases, you would need to file a FOIA request. When the FDA discovers research misconduct at a research institution or laboratory, it issues a warning letter, also known as Form FDA 483, to the wrongdoers. Although the FDA publishes some of these warning letters publicly on its website, some are heavily redacted (see Figure 10.1), as investigative journalist Charles Seife points out in the case study later in this chapter.

## Freedom of information requests

Freedom of Information Act (FOIA) requests allow every citizen to gain insight into documents produced by and in possession of federal agencies and public authorities. By issuing well-crafted query letters, you can obtain any information needed, provided your request does not interfere with other acts that are in effect to protect a state's secrets. If there is no such exemption, the public record keepers are obliged to tell you whether they keep records containing the information you requested, the type of records they have and how long they will need to send you those records. They are also obliged to send you the requested documents and records within a specified time period. Also, public authorities have to publish certain documents in advance, which you then can download for free.

For documents you specifically request, an authority can charge a fee that covers part of the cost it takes them to process your request. Most FOIA acts require authorities to tell you how much it will cost to unearth the requested documents, so you can decide whether they should proceed.

So far, this sounds really good. You request records, and then you get them. But public authorities also have the right to turn down requests based on exemptions that vary from country to country. For example, according to

DEPARTMENT OF HEALTH & HUMAN SERVICES         Public Health Service

Food and Drug Administration
Silver Spring, MD 20993

AUG 1 5 2012

---

**NOTICE OF OPPORTUNITY FOR HEARING (NOOH)**

<u>CERTIFIED MAIL</u>
<u>RETURN RECEIPT REQUESTED</u>

Elmore Alexander, D.O.
(b) (6)          (Home Address)

Dear Dr. Alexander:

The Center for Drug Evaluation and Research (the Center) of the U.S. Food and Drug Administration (FDA) has information indicating that you repeatedly or deliberately violated federal regulations in your capacity as an investigator in clinical trials with an investigational drug. The Center also has information indicating that you repeatedly or deliberately submitted false information to FDA or to the sponsor in required reports. These violations provide the basis for withdrawal of your eligibility as a clinical investigator to receive investigational new drugs.

The Center's findings are based on information obtained during an FDA inspection, discussed below, of the following clinical studies of the investigational drug (b) (4) , performed for (b) (4)                       . for which you were the investigator of record:

1. Protocol (b) (4)          : "(b) (4) ”

2. Protocol (b) (4)          : "(b) (4) ”; and

3. Protocol (b) (4)          : "(b) (4) ”

**FIGURE 10.1**   A warning letter to physician Elmore Alexander issued by the FDA as a reaction to Alexander submitting false information. The document was published but is heavily redacted.

*Source*: US Food and Drug Administration

the UK Freedom of Information Act 2000, which became effective in 2005, authorities can refuse your request if it is vexatious, if you have requested the same type of information before or if giving you the records would violate the Data Protection Act. Also, according to Government Digital Service's website Gov.uk, a public body can also deny you access to the information if the cost of processing your request exceeds £450 or £600.

In case your request is turned down, you can challenge the denying agency's decision by contacting the Information Commissioner's Office (ICO, a link to it is provided on Gov.uk). Scotland has its own Scottish Information Commissioner because it has its own Freedom of Information (Scotland) Act 2002, which, like the UK FOIA, became effective in 2005. The Scottish FOI act is also known as FOISA and covers authorities that are under the legislation of Holyrood, not Westminster. In some aspects, the FOISA differs from the UK FOIA. For example, the FOISA defines that, if a public authority does not hold the information you requested, it must formally notify you, while the UK FOIA does not define a specific procedure for handling that case at all. In this chapter's Links section, you will find a link to a table that shows the differences between the two acts.

How you have to write and submit a FOIA request differs from authority to authority; some allow you to send a request via email or web forms, while others demand you send a letter or fax. Practically all authorities publish FOIA request guidelines on their websites. If you search the authority's name and FOIA (e.g. EPA FOIA), the first search result is usually that authority's FOIA page. The rule of thumb is that you should formulate your request as precisely as possible. Every time you have to re-formulate your request and wait for a response, you lose time.

While you wait for a reply, you should check FOIA hub websites that often contain databases of previous queries and responses, like Gov.uk or www.What DoTheyKnow.com, which additionally features a list of the public authorities you can send FOIA requests to. For previous FOIA requests in the US, search the FOIA online database, which contains requests to major US public authorities, like the Environmental Protection Agency (EPA) and the US Customs and Border Protection. The database contains the original requests and the requestors' names and the responses, including the documents. Another important FOIA request database is run by the Electronic Frontier Foundation (EFF).

The original 1966 US FOIA became effective in 1967 under Lyndon B. Johnson, and it has been amended several times since. It is applicable to federal agencies, and state and local governments of all 50 member states have their own FOIA regulations that modulate how you can access public records on state and local levels. Also in the US, a response time of twenty working days is allowed. If an agency fails to respond within this time frame, you can file a lawsuit at a US district court for up to 6 years after your request remained unanswered. As for the federal FOIA, the following nine exemptions allow authorities to withhold the requested records (Cornell University Law School no date):

1 Classified documents
2 Personnel-related rules and internal practices of an authority, if not relevant to the public
3 Another statute prohibits disclosing the records
4 Trade secrets or financial/commercial records that originate from a person and are either privileged or confidential

5  Memoranda passed between the agency or agencies (inter-agency or intra-agency) "which would not be available by law to a party other than an agency in litigation with the agency"

6  Records that are protected by personal privacy, such as medical or personnel-related documents

7  Files that have been produced for law enforcement purposes under the condition that providing access to them could adversely affect a person in six different ways (see the U.S. Code 552 for more information on these types)

8  Documents with relation to (for example, examination) reports that belong to financial regulatory agencies, such as the Federal Financial Institutions Examination Council

9  Oil well data, including maps and any according geological or geophysical information.

Although everything seems well-regulated, it is not uncommon for authorities to unjustifiably turn down requests. In the UK, unless they deliberately destroy the documents in order not to disclose them, withholding information constitutes no criminal act and hence has no legal consequences, at least not from the ICO. As a last resort, you can file a lawsuit, but that takes a lot of time and money.

## Case study: analysing an article that uncovers medical fraud

In 2015, investigative journalist Charles Seife published an article in the journal *JAMA Internal Medicine* that uncovers how the US FDA not only knew about scientific misconduct but failed to publicise this information on multiple levels (Seife 2015a). In a 2015 article for *Slate* which appeared nearly simultaneously, Seife writes: "The FDA has repeatedly hidden evidence of scientific fraud not just from the public, but also from its most trusted scientific advisers, even as they were deciding whether or not a new drug should be allowed on the market" (2015b).

He and his students found FDA documents that show the FDA's own investigations into cases of scientific misconduct. Whenever new drugs enter the formal application process, the agency will send inspectors to their laboratories to ensure the underlying research is sound, and it documents its findings: "When there are problems, the FDA generates a lot of paperwork – what are called form 483s, Establishment Inspection Reports, and in the worst cases, what are known as Warning Letters" (Seife 2015b). He adds that he had no difficulties finding the documents, since they were openly accessible.

Over the course of their investigations, Seife and his students looked at about 600 cases but were only able to find the names of the affected pharmaceutical companies and laboratories in about 100 cases. The reason for that is that the FDA blackened those parts of the documents that would expose the wrongdoers. Seife tells me that he used FOIA requests to obtain some of the redacted passages and that he will also file a lawsuit to get the FDA to disclose what is still missing:

> I am suing the FDA right now to try to get evidence they withheld. As I mention in the piece, I was only able to decipher a small fraction of these warning letters. So I am now suing the FDA to get the rest. They do respond to FOIA requests, although sometimes you have to sue them to get to respond, but also they censor the results. In fact, they do have large redactions. I think they are redacting illegally, and that is what the courts have to decide.
>
> *(Seife 2016)*

Seife explains that in their early stages, such redactions were not sophisticated and could simply be overcome by copying and pasting the blackened passages into another application that would then reveal the characters underneath. Nowadays, such redactions are destructive, so this method no longer works. He also emphasises that, as a journalist, you should never break the law to get to information. That said, sometimes you can get creative about finding out what lies underneath:

> Even if they redact properly, sometimes, if you're smart, you can crack a redaction by counting spaces or think how long it is. Or in context, looking where something is hyphenated or figuring out where the syllable break is. You can, on occasion, if you suspect something, get pretty strong confirmation that it is what you think it is.
>
> *(Seife 2016)*

Seife and his students went a step further and found seventy-eight publications that resulted from clinical trials in which the FDA had found substantial problems such as scientific misconduct and fraud. Only three of these publications pointed out the issues, whereas "the other publications were not retracted, corrected, or highlighted in any way" (Seife 2015b).

In his article, Seife draws on the RECORD 4 study, a clinical trial that involved the testing of Rivaroxaban, a blood anticoagulant, in thousands of patients. An FDA inspection revealed that at half of the sixteen audited research sites, scientific misconduct, fraud and falsification could be observed. Although the FDA classed the study as unreliable, its results made it into prominent journals such as *The Lancet*. Seife's point is: If the FDA does not pass on its knowledge of misconduct, the public and the medical community are affected, meaning physicians could prescribe drugs that are based on flawed scientific studies.

In addition, the investigators found substantial evidence that the FDA was hiding this from an external scientific committee by withholding information and downplaying the facts when they were forced to disclose compromising information (Seife 2015b). He is also quick to add that there are patterns that can be recognised. That is why he deems pattern recognition a vital skill for every investigative journalist (Seife 2016).

The FDA referred to the fourth of the nine US FOIA exemptions in order to not disclose the requested documents because it "would compromise 'confidential commercial information' that would hurt drug companies if revealed" (Seife 2015b). Seife is convinced this justification is not legitimate, as no confidential information would fall into competitors' hands; rather, handing it out would simply expose their misconduct.

What Seife tries to teach his students in the investigative reporting class he teaches at New York University are not only the tools, like correctly filing FOIA requests, but also the right mindset, as he further explains:

> On one hand, they have to be able to look at documents, they have to learn how to use FOIA, they need to be able to manipulate data, but more important is getting into a certain state of mind – the state of mind of perpetual scepticism, even of arguments that you believe. Constantly seek out external validation to verify everything that you want to say. This can be documents or data. . . . It is a similar mindset to the mindset of a good scientist: You have a question, then you look at your armamentarium of techniques and say, "I think I can get at this – and I know how. And I have the confidence and the ability to try to lever out the truth when no one else can see it and it is being obscured."
>
> *(Seife 2016)*

At the end of the course he teaches, Seife expects his students to be able to ask critical questions and have the mindset to look around for supporting evidence, excavate it and analyse it, just like with their findings on the FDA, although their investigations are nowhere near finished, as he emphasises.

He also tells me that proposing investigative articles to editors is difficult, especially if you are a fledgling science writer or a freelancer. What makes it worse is that the amount of time and research that goes into in-depth investigations is not proportional to the often modest pay. But he highly recommends that you at least occasionally do investigative, deep articles because you can benefit from them even if you are not part of one of the big media companies' investigative journalism groups:

> One of the things you learn with investigative techniques is how to work at cross-purposes to your sources. Without that ability, you are extremely vulnerable. Even if you do not do investigative work in your day-to-day journalism, it is really crucial to be able to tear apart documents, understand when people are trying to deceive or manipulate you, and to get a story which other people do not want you to get.
>
> *(Seife 2016)*

## Case study: Hwanggate

The following is probably one of the most prominent cases of scientific misconduct that has ever been uncovered. It shows the rise and fall of Woo Suk Hwang, a South Korean stem cell researcher (then with Seoul National University) and veterinary who, in 2004, claimed to have cloned a human embryo and derived stem cells from it. For his findings, which he published in two journal papers, Hwang was greatly heralded, as they could have paved the way for new treatments for Alzheimer's disease. Little did the celebrated scientist know then that he was soon to become the protagonist of one of the biggest cases of scientific fraud in history. First, concerns were raised on the origins of the donor eggs. There were 242 eggs used in the experiments that came from 16 donors. Some of these donors were allegedly part of Hwang's research team, and several independent scientists suspected they were coerced to donate them (Cyranoski 2004). Second, it was later revealed that Hwang had fabricated his results. A commission of scientists found that Hwang had never derived stem cells from human eggs, prompting him to apologise publicly in January 2006.

As a result of his misconduct, Seoul National University expelled Hwang. He was also sentenced to a 2-year suspended prison sentence, but he did not serve time. His funds were cancelled, and he was forbidden to carry out further stem cell research. Both *Science* papers regarding his research were retracted. And yet, Hwang is still active in research.

How did the media discover the scientific misconduct in the first place? A whistle-blower uncovered the misconduct and exposed Hwang's lies. A member of his former research team, Young-Joon Ryu, was the author of the first draft of Hwang's highly acclaimed 2004 article in *Science*. In an interview with *Nature* in 2014, Ryu explains he initially abstained from informing the authorities because he did not have enough evidence to support his claims (Cyranoski 2014). In the article, he explains what motivated him to bring his suspicions forward: He had heard the stem cell researcher was planning "a clinical trial for a 10-year-old with a spinal-cord injury, whom Hwang had promised to make walk again" (Cyranoski 2014:593). Since he feared for the boy's health, he reached out to the South Korean television network MBC via email, prompting them to launch an investigation into Hwang's practices. As a result, one TV report aired in November 2005 that covered the ethical misconduct regarding the provision of the human eggs. But MBC had to defer its second report, an investigation into the fabricated results, after facing backlash and receiving threats, including possible cuts in funding from its sponsors (Cyranoski 2014).

Nevertheless, the first report prompted Seoul National University to probe Hwang's results. The investigations confirmed Hwang's misconduct (although he was never convicted of fraud) and led to the termination of his contract with Seoul National University (Cyranoski 2014).

At the time, Hwang faced relatively little criticism, probably due the fact that he was a science star in South Korea. Ironically, it was Ryu who had to go into hiding for several months after his identity was revealed shortly after the MBC report had aired. Ryu had to resign his post at the Korea Cancer Hospital where he had worked from April 2004 until his revelations came to light. Over an extended period of time, Hwang supporters threatened him and held him accountable for South Korea falling behind in stem cell research in comparison with the rest of the world. Consequently, Ryu was without paid employment until 2007 (Cyranoski 2004).

This is what one would expect for Hwang, a persona non grata in the scientific community. Instead, he remains active in research. Hwang even leads a cloning institute, the Sooam Biotech Research Foundation in South Korea (Normile 2014). Since Hwang is still barred from working with human eggs and any associated stem cell research, he now works in dog cloning. At Sooam, he manages a research team of forty staffers and has an annual budget of $4 million. His institute regularly publishes research papers and offers its services to private citizens as well as the South Korean police force. He charges about $100,000 for every cloned dog (Normile 2014). While the institute's efforts for now concentrate on the cloning and preserving of endangered animals, Hwang would like to pick up his work with human embryonic material at some point. In fact, Sooam has already requested the permission to do so, but until now, the South Korean health ministry has denied these requests (Normile 2014).

This case shows a number of phenomena associated with high-profile scientific fraud. First, by facing public humiliation and political persecution, whistle-blowers are not exactly encouraged to reveal truths. Having whistle-blowers available as sources for uncovering scientific misconduct is invaluable, as they have inside knowledge of how the research was conducted and consequently know where a paper's flaws are. This falls into line with the statements of Bob O'Hara, who told me that the whole truth and knowledge are not found in scientific papers; rather, the researchers hold a considerable amount of associated information that does not, for various reasons, make it into the paper.

Second, the forces at play in science include money, coercion, fear of prosecution and many other factors that will keep insiders from exposing misconduct. For example, Ryu's wife was a member of Hwang's team back in 2004. Although the cited literature doesn't mention this, it could be all too imaginable and understandable had this played a role in why Ryu did not come forward earlier. In fact, when he did step up, the negative emotions of the public focused on the whistle-blower, accusing him of "seriously injuring the nation" as the "entire project was stolen by other nations" (Cyranoski 2014:594).

If nothing else, this case study shows that science is a business with many stakeholders who have vital interests at stake. Indeed, it is a business with strict hierarchies, such as the relationship between lead and junior researchers and also between doctoral students and their supervisors. This can encourage some of the lower-ranking members to withhold the truth, which fortunately did not take place in the Hwang case.

## Summary

Much of the current science writing is promotional journalism – short and shallow morsels that are cheerleading advances and discoveries in science. While such articles attract a large audience and hence do have their merit, there is another category of science stories that is investigative. As a journalist, you have various tools for finding stories that people are usually reluctant to talk about. In many countries, you can file FOIA requests to obtain information regarding public entities. There are also many internet databases containing previous FOIA requests, so you can avoid the long wait. One of the best sources, however, are whistle-blowers, because they usually have a thorough inside knowledge of misconduct.

In science, a lack of data transparency, overly enthusiastic statements such as "revolutionary findings", misleading statistics and lies can hint at scientific misconduct. Many results are not reproducible, and lots of peer-reviewed papers are being retracted nowadays. Pictures in publications can be manipulated, but there are forensic software tools you can use to verify the authenticity of pictures and find out whether they have been manipulated. If you encounter cases of scientific misconduct, either by yourself or because someone blows the whistle, they make excellent examples that are worth investigating.

The SBI method is a clearly defined process that helps you formulate an initial hypothesis and then gather the evidence to support (or reject) it over the course of your research, from the early stages of pre-research until publishing and advertising of your article. Apart from that, scientists and journalists also investigate the media. Platforms like HealthNewsReview. org continuously put health-related articles to the test and have established sets of criteria that help them assess the quality of the articles. This role is particularly important with health advice articles because people make decisions regarding their own health based on such articles.

## Review questions

- Which characteristics distinguish investigative from conventional journalism?
- Which factors increase your chances that a scientific insider will approach you?
- What kinds of documents can lead to investigative science stories, and where can you find them?

- What is the central element of the story-based inquiry method?
- How can the SBI method help you structure your story?
- What role do conflicts of interest play in the assessment of health stories?
- What is a warning letter?
- Why do public authorities redact documents?
- Under which circumstances can a public authority turn down a FOIA request?

## Exercises

- Use the databases mentioned in this chapter to find a case of scientific misconduct that interests you.
- Conduct secondary research and formulate a hypothesis that takes the underlying issue into account.
- Find documents containing disciplinary actions (past and present) taken against the perpetrator(s).
- File one or more FOIA requests to a relevant public authority to find out more about the underlying issue (beware that this can entail a fee).
- Contact researchers to comment on the case and provide you with concrete examples and statistics
- Identify three facts you need to prove or disprove to confirm or deny your hypothesis.
- Find three health stories and subject them to HealthNewsReview.org's criteria.

## Reading list

BBC Academy (no date) *Defamation*, BBC Academy [Online] Available at: www.bbc.co.uk/academy/journalism/article/art20130702112133651 [date accessed 15 June 2016]

Hunter, M.L. (2011) *Story-Based Inquiry: A Manual for Investigative Journalists*. Paris: UNESCO [Online] Available at: http://unesdoc.unesco.org/images/0019/001930/193078e.pdf [date accessed 22 May 2016]

Hunter, M.L. (ed.) (2012) *The Global Investigative Journalism Casebook*. Paris: UNESCO [Online] Available at: http://unesdoc.unesco.org/images/0021/002176/217636e.pdf [date accessed 14 September 2016]

Lonsdale, S. (2013) Environmental journalism, In Turner, B. and Orange, R. (eds.) *Specialist Journalism*. London: Routledge, 59–68

MacFadyen, G. (2013) The practices of investigative journalism, In De Burgh, H. (ed.) *Investigative Journalism*. 2nd edition. London: Routledge, 138–156 (section: Digging)

Mencher, M. (2011) Digging for information, In Mencher, M. (2011) *News Reporting and Writing*, 12th edition. New York: McGraw-Hill, 229–244

Schapiro, M. (2012) Conning the climate/afterword, In Hunter, M.L. (ed.) *The Global Investigative Journalism Casebook*. Paris: UNESCO [Online] Available at: http://unesdoc.unesco.org/images/0021/002176/217636e.pdf [date accessed 14 September 2016], 80–92

## Links

Association of Health Care Journalists, Center for Excellence in Health Care Journalism: http://healthjournalism.org/
Electronic Frontier Foundation, FOIA requests: www.eff.org/issues/transparency/foia-requests‾
FOIA online: https://foiaonline.regulations.gov/foia/action/public/home
Global Investigative Journalism Network: http://gijn.org
HealthNewsReview.org review criteria: www.healthnewsreview.org/about-us/review-criteria/
Information Commissioner's Office: https://ico.org.uk
Legislation.co.uk, Defamation Act 2013 (UK): www.legislation.gov.uk/ukpga/2013/26/contents/enacted
Legislation.co.uk, Freedom of Information Act 2000: www.legislation.gov.uk/ukpga/2000/36/contents
Legislation.co.uk, Freedom of Information (Amendment) (Scotland) Act 2013: www.legislation.gov.uk/asp/2013/2/introduction
National Whistleblower Center: www.whistleblowers.org
Office of Research Integrity: https://ori.hhs.gov/
Office of Research Integrity case summaries: http://ori.hhs.gov/case_summary
ProPublica, Dollars for Docs: www.propublica.org/series/dollars-for-docs
Scottish Information Commissioner, comparative table (FOIA 2000 and FOISA 2002): www.itspublicknowledge.info/Law/FOISA-EIRsLinks/FOISA_FOIAComparative.aspx
Society of Environmental Journalists: www.sej.org
UNESCO, Story-Based Inquiry (a manual for investigative journalists by Mark Lee Hunter): http://unesdoc.unesco.org/images/0019/001930/193078e.pdf
University of Massachusetts Amherst Libraries, locating retracted publications in databases: http://guides.library.umass.edu/content.php?pid=463078&sid=3862890
The White House, Freedom of Information Act: www.foia.gov

## References

Barry, C., Arad, R., Ansell, L., Cartier, M. and Lee, H. (2016) 2016 Patent litigation study – Are we at an inflection point? *PricewaterhouseCoopers (pwc.com)* [Online] Available at: www.pwc.com/us/en/forensic-services/publications/assets/2016-pwc-patent-litfigation-study.pdf [date accessed 28 November 2016]
Blum, D. (2002) Investigating science, *Nieman Reports* [Online] Available at: http://niemanreports.org/articles/investigating-science/ [date accessed 5 May 2016]
Bosch, X. (2011) Treat ghostwriting as misconduct, *Nature*, vol. 469, no. 7331, 472
Burgh, de H. (2008) *Investigative Journalism*. 2nd edition. London: Routledge
Carmon, I. (2013) How we broke the NSA story [Interview with Laura Poitras], *Salon* [Online] Available at: www.salon.com/2013/06/10/qa_with_laura_poitras_the_woman_behind_the_nsa_scoops/ [date accessed 12 July 2016]
Cornell University Law School (undated) U.S. Code § 552 – Public information; agency rules, opinions, orders, records, and proceedings, *Legal Information Institute* [Online] Available at: www.law.cornell.edu/uscode/text/5/552#a_4_F [date accessed 22 July 2016]
Cyranoski, D. (2004) Korea's stem-cell stars dogged by suspicion of ethical breach, *Nature*, vol. 429, no. 6987, 3

Cyranoski, D. (2014) Whistle-blower breaks his silence, *Nature*, vol. 505, no. 7485, 593–594

Gewin, V. (2012) Research: Uncovering misconduct, *Nature*, vol. 485, no. 7396, 137–139

Goldacre, B. (2016) Personal phone conversation on 25 July 2016

Hanson, H., O'Brien, N., Whybrow, P., Isaacs, J.D. and Rapley, T. (2016) Drug breakthrough offers hope to arthritis sufferers: Qualitative analysis of medical research in UK newspapers, *Health Expectations* [Online] Available at: http://onlinelibrary.wiley.com/doi/10.1111/hex.12460/full [date accessed 19 July 2016]

Hunter, M.L. (2011) *Story-Based Inquiry: A Manual for Investigative Journalists*. Paris: UNESCO [Online] Available at: http://unesdoc.unesco.org/images/0019/001930/193078e.pdf [date accessed 22 May 2016]

Hunter, M.L. (2016) Personal Skype conversation on 13 July 2016

Jayaraman, K.S. (2013) How to be an investigative journalist, *SciDev.net* [Online] Available at: www.scidev.net/global/communication/practical-guide/how-to-be-an-investigative-science-journalist-1.html [date accessed 10 July 2016]

Nelson, D. (2016) Personal Skype conversation on 26 September 2016

Normile, D. (2014) The second act, *Nature*, vol. 343, no. 6168, 244–247

O'Hara, B. (2016) Phone interview on 9 June 2016

Pitt, J.H. and Hill, H.Z. (2013) Statistical Detection of Potentially Fabricated Numerical Data: A Case Study, *arXiv (Cornell University Library)* [Online] Available at: https://arxiv.org/pdf/1311.5517.pdf [date accessed 13 September 2016]

Regalado, A. (2006) Investigative reporting, In Blum, D., Knudson, M. and Henig, R.M. (eds.) *A Field Guide for Science Writers*. 2nd edition. New York: Oxford University Press, 118–125

Robinson, A., Coutinho, A., Bryden, A., and McKee, M. (2013) Analysis of health stories in daily newspapers in the UK, *Public Health*, vol. 127, no.1, 39–45

Seife, C. (2015a) Research misconduct identified by the US food and drug administration, *JAMA Internal Medicine*, vol. 175, no. 4, 567–577

Seife, C. (2015b) Are your medications safe? *Slate* [Online] Available at: www.slate.com/articles/health_and_science/science/2015/02/fda_inspections_fraud_fabrication_and_scientific_misconduct_are_hidden_from.html [date accessed 16 July 2016]

Seife, C. (2016) Personal phone call on 14 July 2016

Sumner, D.E. and Miller, H.G. (2013) *Feature and Magazine Writing: Action, Angle and Anecdotes*. Chichester: John Wiley & Sons

Turone, F. (2016) Personal Skype conversation on 10 June 2016

Wellcome Trust (2005) Statement on the handling of allegations of research misconduct, *The Wellcome Trust* [Online] Available at: https://wellcome.ac.uk/funding/managing-grant/statement-handling-allegations-research-misconduct [date accessed 28 November 2016]

# 11

# SCIENCE JOURNALISM IN THE DIGITAL AGE

**What you will learn in this chapter:**

- Attention spans in the digital age
- Influence of mobile devices on journalistic consumption and production
- Understanding the digital audience
- Producing multimedia content
- Essential web skills
- Visualising science
- Strategies for digital magazines
- Case study: the digital-only science magazine *Undark*
- Case study: analysing a successful digital science story

## Introduction

Thanks to the digital revolution, you produce more output, you produce it faster, you spread it faster and you get feedback faster – and it also appears faster on your readers' screens. In the digital world, tools like cameras, memory and software have become cheap. Also, they are easy to learn, thanks to e-learning platforms, massive open online courses, webinars and video tutorials. While journalism's established rules, such as accuracy, brevity and clarity, should always hold, the sheer amount of journalistic output produced every day makes it impossible to properly fact-check all of it. The types of articles and multimedia materials your readers consume online are often very short and to the point. If they like something you write, they will reward you with the online world's true currency: likes and shares.

More precisely, online, *traffic* counts. The more people click on and recommend your articles, the more advertising money you will make. If you run an online publication, you have a myriad of tools that tell you what topics and formats your readers like, where they come from and how old they are. These tools even tell you how long they read your articles before they get bored and close the browser tab. A lot of research hints at that our attention spans are continuously decreasing and currently are only about 8 seconds long before we get distracted. As you will read in the first section, not everybody shares that opinion, and one study's authors even show that online readers engage more with long-form than with short-form articles.

Most of these readers use mobile devices to consume news, and most traffic comes from the social media, although a 50:50 ratio between organic search and social media would be desirable, as one online editor told me in an interview. These mobile devices also influence how you produce news for your audience; in fact, there seems to be a mutual relationship between mobile news consumption and production, as you can read in the subsequent section. In the next section, a few online editors explain how they categorise their audience and how they approach and interact with it. All of them emphasise how important these steps are if you want a digital publication to succeed.

The content you produce based on that knowledge is equally important. Apart from producing indexable, findable articles that are mostly text based, you have to produce compelling multimedia material. Video is one of the cornerstones of online journalism, so a dedicated section on multimedia production will show you which basic shots you have to get when you record scientists at work and how you can connect them. Luckily, you do not need to buy professional-grade equipment to get started but can use your smartphone to produce broadcast-quality material, including live coverage of unfolding events.

As an online journalist, you must acquire a few web skills. You do not need to be able to apply all of them, but you certainly must understand how the web works. That is why you will find a section on the languages the web is made of, the most popular frameworks for data visualisation and advanced search techniques, as well as a few tips for securely browsing the web. I will also briefly touch upon the basic data journalism process before discussing data visualisation.

One of the traditional and most effective tools you can use for visualising appropriately processed data are infographics. They help you interpret and boil down your data to a core message and substantiate it with powerful visualisation techniques such as charts. I will briefly address a few of these techniques and see how infographics online differ from their counterparts in print.

Another crucial component of online journalism that has changed with the transition from print to online outlets is how you can make a profit. You need to have a solid plan (actually, a number of plans) that outlines which types of articles you run, who pays for them (some may be sponsored) and whether you want to use subscriptions in conjunction with paywalls or apps to let your readers pay for the contributions you publish online.

The first case study shows how an award-winning science journalist and professor launched her own foundation-funded magazine and how she approached some of these planning steps. Her advice: Be smart about using the social media, find your own niche and be passionate about what you write. The passion she talks about flows into the article I look at in this chapter's second case study. The award-winning multimedia reportage in "Medicamentalia" points out the differences between developing countries and the first world in accessing drugs. In doing so, the authors of the article extensively used the interactive data visualisation techniques I address earlier in the chapter.

## Attention spans in the digital age

It seems that the production and consumption of online journalism mutually influence each other: Recurring claims that our attention spans are declining have prompted online journalists to produce more bite-sized articles. The prevalence of these short morsels, in turn, could have contributed to further reducing our attention spans. In 2015, Microsoft Canada's consumer insights team released an online report that states the average attention span decreased from 12 seconds in 2000 to 8 seconds in 2013 (Gausby 2015), although the report is not a peer-reviewed study. You can read the report's findings in Box 11.1. But thriving long-form platforms like Matter, the Atavist, Byliner and Narrative.ly seem to disprove the theory that online readers are easily distracted and cannot focus on an article over an extended period of time.

---

### BOX 11.1 THREE TYPES OF ATTENTION SPAN

As mentioned, Microsoft Canada found that online readers' attention spans have declined. However, digital readers have become more efficient at absorbing and memorising information. A word of caution: This is not a peer-reviewed study.

Focusing on a Canadian audience, the report's authors subdivide human attention span into three distinct categories and propose ways that marketing professionals can address each type of attention span, as cited from Gausby (2015:13):

1   **Sustained:** Readers' ability to maintain prolonged focus during repetitive activity. Depends on digital lifestyle. Tip: Communicate on a personal level and convey clear values.

2  **Selective:** Readers' ability to avoid distraction and maintain responses in the face of competing stimuli. Not significantly influenced by age, gender and digital lifestyle. Tip: Exclude unnecessary information, make sure your message is clear and exceed your audience's expectations.

3  **Alternating:** Readers' ability to shift attention between tasks that demand different cognitive skills. Multi-screen environments improve readers' attention and facilitate the emotional encoding of memories. Tip: Interact with the audience, place calls to action and continue your communication across different screens.

The authors also cite Microsoft data scientist Danah Boyd saying that shifts in stimuli rewire our brains. Again, be aware that the tips the report proposes are intended for marketing specialists, not journalists. That said, you may find some of the proposed techniques useful and efficient for conveying science to your audience.

---

For example, a Pew Research Center report shows that US readers interact more with long- than with short-form online journalism. The study's authors analysed data provided by the online analytics service Parse.ly: A total of 71 million unique visitors accessed 74,840 articles on their mobile phones, which resulted in 117 million complete interactions such as scrolling, tapping or swiping on their screens (Mitchell et al. 2016). The study's authors found that US readers spend approximately twice as much time interacting with long-form articles (128 seconds for stories equal to or greater than 1,000 words) than with short-form articles (60 seconds for stories up to 1,000 words). These values fluctuate only minimally across the entire day (Mitchell et al. 2016). Their other findings are:

- **Engagement time increases with the word count:** For articles spanning 5,000 words or more, the engagement time was about 270 seconds, whereas it was only 43 seconds for articles spanning 101 to 250 words.
- **Readers coming from Twitter engage longer with the articles than those coming from Facebook:** For long-form articles, readers from Twitter engage for 133 seconds versus 107 seconds for Facebook; for short-form articles, the times are 58 seconds versus 51 seconds (respectively).
- **Most users are not returning visitors:** This is true of more than 95 per cent of the analysed mobile audience, differing only by one percentage point between long- and short-form articles.
- **The number of interactions is almost equal between long- and short-form articles:** Only 24 per cent of the analysed articles are long-form texts (1,000 words and longer by the authors' definition), and there is a median of about 1,500 interactions per article, independent of length.

- **Mobile users coming from an internal link spend the most time reading articles:** For long-form articles, readers spend 148 seconds versus 59 seconds on short-form articles. In contrast, mobile users coming in from a link shared on social media spend the lowest amount of time reading short-form (111 seconds) and long-form articles (52 seconds).
- **Most readers engage within the first week of publication:** With short-form articles, 82 per cent of interactions happen on the first 2 days, as do 74 per cent of long-form article interactions. The peak is by far the first day.
- **Crime is the most successful long-form topic (5,000 words or more):** The authors analysed a random sample (size: 17 per cent of the Parse.ly-provided data) to show this. In this context, "successful" means the amount of time readers engaged with the articles. In contrast, long-form science and technology articles spanning of the same length had the lowest engagement time.

Most readers come from Facebook (9 million for long-form articles, 32 million for short-form articles) than from Twitter (2 million for long-form articles, 5 million for short-form articles). Your takeaways from the study: Facebook is a driving factor in attracting an audience, but Twitter users tend to engage longer with your articles.

I addressed online readers' attention spans in Chapter 7, drawing on Robert Weatherhead's (2014) article on the *Guardian*'s website in which he stated that decreasing attention spans demand a different way of writing and structuring online articles. Weatherhead, a group operations director at Amplifi UK, commented on the aforementioned Pew study; he points out to me that the study's findings actually address who is consuming mobile news:

> My initial reaction on reading the study was that the major change is that more long form content consumers are now using the mobile as their method of choice, rather than it being shift in how people consume content. These people would previously have been consuming through the paper version. So rather than a shift in *how* people are consuming content it is a shift in *who* is consuming the content based on the sites studied.
>
> *(Weatherhead 2016b)*

Weatherhead further explained to me that there are a few limitations that the report's authors did not address, which is why he would take parts of the findings with a pinch of salt:

> The more interesting question would have been: How many people made it to the end of the piece? Did they read 5,000 words? I would imagine most people didn't do that on a mobile. You could probably

read 1,000 words in the time they propose, but probably not 5,000 words. Their findings are certainly indicative of a general shift in that more people are using mobile devices and more people are getting comfortable with them as their reading device of choice. But we don't know whether it actually means that people are going to consume long-form articles on them more often.

*(Weatherhead 2016a)*

Indeed, considering that adult readers, even trained readers (with the exception of speed readers), read between 300 and 600 words per minute, 270 seconds or 4.5 minutes seems to be an insufficient amount of time to read 5,000 words, which, considering the aforementioned assumptions, would take between 8 and 16 minutes. That is why Weatherhead comes to the following conclusion:

> There certainly wasn't anything in the study that would say to me: "Mobile is the device of choice for long-form reading." I would not go to that extreme at all. I would rather say there is a global change in penetration of smartphones and mobile devices, that means you will naturally get more people reading long-form content on them. The situation that every publisher is in is you have got to produce content that works for whatever device users are going to consume it on. Because you cannot accurately predict this.
>
> *(Weatherhead 2016a)*

## Influence of mobile devices on journalistic consumption and production

So how exactly did mobile devices cause a journalism revolution? First, it is quite obvious that mobile devices such as tablets are widely used for news consumption. In fact, they have already surpassed desktop PCs and laptops, at least with regard to news consumption. With the release of Apple's iPhone in 2007, and even more with the release of Apple's iPad in 2010, the mobile news revolution began. Today's market is saturated with smartphones and tablets of all sorts and sizes.

In the 2014 Mobile Media News Consumption Survey, Roger Fidler found that the Apple iPad continues to be the predominant media tablet for consuming news in US households. Moreover, the presence of children in a household increases the likelihood of media tablet presence (Fidler 2014). By 2013, 55 per cent of US news consumers were mobile device users, surpassing traditional news consumers for the first time (Fidler 2013). There is evidence that suggests that social media have also contributed to the shift towards mobile news consumption. For example, Mitchell and Guskin (2013) state that 85 per cent of US Twitter news consumers use mobile devices for reading news, and 64 per cent of US Facebook news consumers use mobile devices. Furthermore, they found that Twitter news consumers are younger and more mobile when compared to other news consumers. They also claim that "mobile devices are a key point of access for these Twitter news consumers" (Mitchell and Guskin 2013).

There are many more reasons why users shift towards consuming mobile news, some of which have been identified by Schrøder (2015) as the seven dimensions that facilitate mobile news consumption. More specifically, he defined the term "worthwhileness" and argued that "in order to become adopted into an individual's media repertoire, a news medium must be experienced by this individual as subjectively worthwhile" (Schrøder 2015:4). He contends that the attractiveness of smart devices also contributes to the adoption of mobile devices for the consumption of news. There are other dimensions that influence the readers' choices, such as the price and the participatory potential (Schrøder 2015).

In addition, in order for this shift towards mobile media to happen, fundamental technological, infrastructural and economical changes needed to pave the way for consumers to consume news anywhere and anytime. These changes include broadband internet access, telecommunication companies' cheap mobile flat-rate offerings and the market entry of key technology companies such as Google and Apple. Moreover, changes were not only required on an infrastructural level but also on an editorial level. Also, the development of dedicated news apps for various mobile platforms entails significant costs to news publishers (Westlund 2013).

Mobile devices have also shaped journalism in the way journalistic content is produced. For example, they can aid journalists as digital reporting tools. In 2007, Nokia and Reuters released special smartphone-based mobile toolkits targeted at journalists. Journalists equipped with mobile handsets have a tendency to respond faster to breaking events. They can also leverage the proximity to the community they are reporting from (Cameron 2009). Some BBC mobile reporters (like Nick Garnett, whose kit you can see in Chapter 4) use iOS- and Android-based smartphones together with the BBC's proprietary app PNg that allows them to shoot, edit and upload mobile videos directly to the BBC's servers. The app is only available for the BBC staff, but there are apps you can buy that have similar functionalities, like FiLMiC Pro.

If you produce stories for mobile devices, you will also have to acknowledge mobile devices' physical limitations and either leverage or overcome them. The display sizes of current smartphones are between 3.5 and 5 inches. Tablet display sizes vary from 7 to around 10 inches. Kim et al. (2011) conducted a survey at the University of South Korea and investigated the effect of mobile device screen size on perceived usefulness and newsworthiness. The perceived usefulness among the study's participants was highest for devices with 3.5 and 9.7 inches as opposed to a screen size of 5.7 inches (the standard size of phablets). The survey participants responded that they were more like to perceive video as newsworthy and enjoyable as opposed to text.

Not all mobile platforms are equally adopted. For example, smartwatch limitations are too restrictive. Robert Weatherhead says that smartwatches are not an apt consumption device; there is simply not enough space to display longer articles, only short news items that then point to a smartphone or tablet where you can read the entire text. He hence deems them a directional rather than a proper consumption device. Weatherhead thinks that over the next years, however, people may increasingly use smart, internet-connected televisions to consume news.

## Understanding the digital audience

I addressed the need of knowing your audience for blogging in Chapter 7. This section provides more information on how digital publications know their audiences. Ed Yong is an award-winning British science writer who started blogging many years ago, worked as a freelance science journalist, became part of *National Geographic*'s science blogging network, Phenomena, and is now a staff writer at *The Atlantic*. He tells me to what extent he thinks it is possible to know your online audience:

> I think you can work out where your audience comes from, what operating systems they run and which browsers they are using, but actually knowing who they *are* is much harder. I used to run a yearly thread on my blog where I asked people to tell me more about themselves. So that was one way of getting their stories. Now, every place has its own set of readers. I think *The Atlantic*'s readers are very intellectual, although they are not necessarily people who have science backgrounds. We have long had a technology channel and a health channel, but we only started a specific science channel last September. Those three channels together actually make up quite a lot of our traffic, even though *The Atlantic* is more specifically known for politics. Regardless of what audience you want to target: If you have good stories and you can tell them well, you will be able to find an audience. . . . You can think about reaching a broad audience or a narrow audience, in terms of whether you want to communicate to a general lay reader or to scientists. In that sense, it is critical. But beyond that, it pretty much doesn't matter.
>
> *(Yong 2016)*

Social media are a great way for print and online publications to engage with and discover more about their audience. Alexander McNamara, online editor at *BBC Focus* magazine, explains that he uses the social media for that purpose:

> Knowing the user? That is one place where social media can really help, because you can talk directly to the people who are looking at your website. You can say "Here is a feature I published yesterday about the top gadgets of the month", and people will come back and say "This is really cool", and you can talk to them directly about it. Our users love black holes and anything with space.
>
> *(McNamara 2016)*

McNamara subdivides his audience into two categories, according to how they access the magazine's website, sciencefocus.com: The first category arrives via search engines, and the second comes directly from the social media. McNamara tells me that most publications strive for a fifty-fifty balance between organic search as a traffic source and social media-driven traffic. The staff at *BBC Focus* magazine analyses data gained from Google Analytics and similar analytics services, which allows them to understand how many users access their website, which articles they read most, how long they read the articles and where they originate from. As such, Google Analytics is predominantly a quantitative tool. In contrast, engaging with the audience through the social media, hence addressing the second group of readers, is a qualitative tool to better understand the audience.

He also emphasises that the findability of your online articles is largely subject to search engines and social media algorithms. Should they decide to, say, stop displaying articles with clickbait titles, many articles would vanish from readers' search results and Facebook timelines. But he tells me that on sciencefocus.com, at least, a clickbait exclusion would not be a problem: "One of the things we always try to do is high quality content which speaks for itself without being clickbaity" (McNamara 2016).

Other online publications' traffic is more social media heavy. For example, VICE Media is known for being one of the most successful online media companies in terms of page impressions and market value. VICE.com is also known for using a lot of imagery and for producing compelling investigative videos, among other things. According to the online analytics service Alexa, VICE.com is currently ranked among the top 100 websites in the US, with somewhere between 60 and 100 million page views per month. Many of the readers are mobile users. Its audience is predominantly male and mostly college-educated, and it regularly accesses the site from work and home. Only about 10 per cent of VICE.com's traffic originates from searches, and people usually visit Facebook and Google immediately before opening VICE.com. Some of this information is publicised on Alexa's website, and you can find a link to it in this chapter's Links section.

According to the statistics on Alexa, VICE's science and technology section, *Motherboard*, is the second-most visited digital outlet that VICE users navigate to directly after accessing the main website. Kate Lunau, the Canada editor of *Motherboard*, expands on the digital magazine's investments in its audience:

> The fact that we are the Canada bureau means that to us it is really important to focus on and grow the audience in Canada and to tell a lot of really good Canadian science and technology stories. I think a lot about that, and on new tools and technologies that help us reach people in new ways, but without relying on social media all the time. Social media is very important, but you can't rely on it for everything. You need to get the readers seeking you on their own, too, and to become important to them as well. I am thinking a lot about how to build a readership that is curious what we are doing every day, and that wants to come check out the content, that is really important to us.
>
> *(Lunau 2016)*

## Producing multimedia content

Producing compelling stories has never been easier than today. Broadband connections, cheap memory and smartphones' capabilities to shoot and record broadcast-quality video and audio have democratised the journalistic production process. This easy access to technology does not replace solid journalistic core skills, but it substantially compresses the time from recording to broadcasting a report.

When you cover breaking news, you can easily broadcast events as they unfold. All you need is a smartphone, Facebook and a fast enough internet connection. To increase the broadcast quality, you should attach a proper microphone to your smartphone, but the built-in microphone will produce acceptable results. BBC mobile reporter Nick Garnett, who covered the aftermath of the 2015 terrorist attacks in Paris with his mobile kit, uses a windscreen to reduce wind noise. Make sure you film in landscape mode (unless what you want to cover demands you use portrait mode), and use a tripod to get some steady shots. Once the live transmission is over, Facebook makes it available as a normal video that your readers can replay. Broadcasting live on Facebook is something many major media companies like the *New York Times* do now. It seems Facebook has signed deals with some of them, so they produce and stream a range of videos exclusively via Facebook in exchange for a notable sum (Spayd 2016).

*New York Times* public editor Liz Spayd says too many of the publication's live video efforts "don't live up to the journalistic quality one typically associates with the *New York Times*" (Spayd 2016), but producing (not necessarily live) video for the web has become one of online publications' cornerstones. In science journalism, short explainer videos that often have a wow factor tell micro-stories of conservation efforts, newly discovered planets and quirky scientific discoveries. In essence, these videos are anywhere between 30 seconds and a few minutes long and encapsulate one specific phenomenon. Overlaid text explains the most important takeaways in short, succinct sentences. *National Geographic, Nature, Motherboard* and many other publications produce such videos and disseminate them via the social media. Pavlik (2000) confirmed the democratisation of video production in the digital world more than 15 years ago:

> In the analog world, the rules imposed by the broadcasting unions greatly constrained the production of television news. Each individual function, such as changing a tape or making an edit, was performed by a union member under strict rules. None of these rules apply in the digital age. In the digital newsroom any journalist can perform any editorial or production operation on the video. Thus, any reporter can produce video, editing in the field and/or on deadline.
>
> *(Pavlik 2000:231)*

During a workshop at Reporter Forum in 2016, Tom Littlewood, editor-in-chief of VICE Germany, emphasised how important producing video for their online platforms is:

> We had the magazine, we launched also websites . . . and then we started doing video, and that, for me, was kind of a tipping point for VICE – because . . . if you want to be direct in your storytelling, there is no better medium than that.
>
> *(Littlewood 2016)*

While VICE often employs traditional professional camera equipment and entire crews, smartphones have evolved enough to allow you to get started and shoot an entire, broadcast-quality video contribution by yourself, edit it on the phone and then submit it to your editor. Constantly evolving smartphone cameras with higher resolutions, high frame rates and increasing low-light capabilities are only one factor. Mobile applications like FiLMiC Pro (for iOS and Android) allow you to control your camera's capabilities better and shoot using settings that the standard camera app doesn't allow you to use. You can edit your footage directly on your phone using commercial apps or the integrated iMovie app on iOS. This immensely speeds up the entire production process as you can plan, direct, shoot, edit and publish a video contribution all by yourself and using a single device.

One of the more problematic hardware aspects is audio: The integrated microphones are not always suitable for recording audio. While they are able to cancel noise to some degree, the audio quality is dismal when recording at a distance, which is usually the case when you place your smartphone on a tripod or otherwise stabilise it. Solutions exist, from 3.5-mm jack microphones (Android) to microphones that connect to the lightning port (Apple). If you want to use professional-grade audio recording equipment, there are XLR adapters for Android and Apple devices available. But if you decide to shoot using only the integrated microphone, make sure you are not covering it with your fingers; otherwise the recorded audio will sound muffled. If you interview people using your smartphone, be sure they do not get too close to the microphone or you will hear clipping and popping.

Apart from hardware and software, the most important components are your subject, the story and how you tell that story on video. The rules of video storytelling have not substantially changed with the arrival of digital equipment. As for short videos that tell quick science news stories, Michael Rosenblum's established five-shot sequence (Frechette 2012) is the gold standard, because it answers most of the five Ws and one H in just one sequence. It consists of taking shots using the following angles. The following list is based on Andrew Lih's presentation of visual storytelling techniques, which you can find in the Reading List at the end of the chapter:

1  **Close-up of the hands:** This shows the character at work. Journalistic question: What?
2  **Close-up of the face:** Another close-up, this time of the character's face while she is performing the action of the first shot. Journalistic question: Who?
3  **Medium shot:** This shot is wider than the other ones and shows the character in context. Journalistic questions: Where and when?
4  **Over-the-shoulder shot:** Observing the character doing the action by glancing over her shoulder. Journalistic question: How?
5  **Creative shot:** The final shot is free in that you should choose unusual camera angles to depict the character and/or context. Journalistic question: What else?

You have probably noticed that there is one question missing: Why? You can answer that question using voice-over and letting your characters explain themselves while they are performing the action that you are recording. This basic technique is certainly not apt for all science stories, but it can greatly help you depict scientists at work, such as an archaeologist at a digging site.

In order to connect your shots, you should also familiarise yourself with film transitions or cuts such as match cuts, jump cuts (please avoid those), action cuts, cross cuts, cutaways, L cuts and J cuts. The latter two are transitions that employ audio to seamlessly transport your readers from one shot to the next: The audio starts either a little bit before or after the scene changes. This technique ensures that a scene change appears seamless to your viewers. You certainly can perform all these steps on your smartphone, but as memory is often limited on those devices (and editing takes up additional memory), be sure you plan your shots ahead and either create a shot list or a storyboard for that purpose.

A final remark: One important thing to notice is that many, many people have a natural inclination toward shooting in portrait mode. Please don't. Always shoot in landscape mode unless you can *only* capture your subject in portrait mode.

## Essential web skills

Starting with the simplest digital tools, such as emails, internet voice calls and video conferencing software, the digital world provides you with an abundance of enabling technologies that ease the job significantly. Get acquainted with them as you need them, and learn all about their capabilities and limitations. For example, if you are an investigative journalist and work with a whistle-blower, you should know whether WhatsApp's encryption is strong enough to hide your conversations from government agencies and know how you can encrypt your emails to protect your sources. Also, you should read where your communication service providers are located and whether they need to disclose any information to authorities upon request. Some major publications like *Forbes* offer secure online submission systems where sources can anonymously drop tips.

Apart from these communication technologies, you will also need to know how the web and social media work. The following terms should be part of your basic web technology vocabulary, as practically the whole web runs on the following three languages:

- **HTML (hypertext markup language):** This language defines a web page's structure and part of its appearance. HTML's syntax is based on tags that must be opened and closed (<html>Hello</html>). Tags can be nested and are interpreted by browsers to give the web page its look; they are never directly displayed (i.e. <html> will never be shown). Essentially, HTML tells a browser what to display.
- **CSS (cascading style sheets):** CSS language files are loaded along with HTML documents and determine the look and formatting of a HTML document. This can include the colours, fonts and layout of a webpage. The CSS syntax is fundamentally different from HTML. CSS tells a browser how to display HTML content.
- **JavaScript:** JavaScript is a programming language that enables interactive content that readers/users can adapt and change. It is fair to say that JavaScript breathes life into otherwise static web pages. JavaScript's syntax is again different from HTML's and CSS's syntaxes.

It is not important for you to program in these languages, although if you can, that is an advantage. You can find many ready-to-use frameworks based on JavaScript that you can use as a journalist. The following examples allow you to visualise data without knowing how to program. Just feed your data into the web forms they provide and configure them. Once your visualisation looks the way you want it to, you can embed them on a blog or on a website. They are cross-platform plugins that will display correctly on most devices:

- **Timeline.js:** Tell chronological stories as timelines. Readers can either navigate sequentially from event to event or pick an event from the timeline. Each event is presented as either an image or video together with text, links and the date. Developed by Knight Lab.
- **StoryMap.js:** Create slide show-like interactive maps and tell location-based stories. Your readers can navigate from location to location or pick one from a larger map. Developed by Knight Lab.
- **Juxtapose.js:** Create before-and-after sliders of two overlapping images that your readers can compare by dragging the slider to the left or right. Developed by Knight Lab.
- **Chart.js:** Create interactive, animated charts and choose from eight different chart types, like bar and pie charts or scatter plots.
- **D3.js:** Process document-based data (like spreadsheets) and create interactive visualisations. D3 (data driven document) contains a large number of chart types. The downside: It requires considerable knowledge of how JavaScript works.

Since most of these frameworks use documents as data sources, you will need to know how to use spreadsheet software like Microsoft Excel or Google Docs (you can use the latter from within a browser). Use spreadsheet software to clean, transform and organise your data before you visualise it. This ties in perfectly with the standard data journalism process: Gather, analyse, visualise and mash up data (Bradshaw and Rohumaa 2011). Software packages like the freely available OpenRefine are specifically tailored to the clean-up and transformation of data. You can also find many tutorials. Paired with a basic notion of statistics, such software becomes a powerful tool to find stories in the data you have gathered through, say, FOIA requests.

How you can gather the data also depends on how well you can operate search engines. First, Google offers an advanced search page that lets you specify whether your search should include all search terms, none of the terms or the terms with the exact wording you specified. You can also filter your results by language, region and by when the page was last updated. You can also explicitly use some of the following search operators in Google's main search field to narrow down your search results:

- **Quotation marks:** Put two or more terms between quotation marks and Google will search for these words in that exact order. For example, "Hwang's dismissal" will search for that exact phrase.

- **Exclude:** Prefix a term with a hyphen to instruct Google to not return results containing that term. For example, *building – house* will exclude all search results containing the word house.
- **Filetype:** Use the filetype: operator to return only documents using that format. For example, "gene editing" filetype:pdf returns only PDF documents containing the phrase *gene editing*.
- **Site:** Use the site: operator to search only on a specified website. For example, environment site:scientificamerican.com only returns results from *Scientific American*'s website.
- **Link:** Use the link: operator to get a list of websites that link to the one you specified, although that list is not complete.

If you are searching for sensitive material, employ anonymity networks like Tor. You can download a pre-packaged browser that lets you connect to the network, hindering data collectors from tracking you down. Using the network, you can also search the deep web, which is a great source for ideas. The downside of using Tor is that your searches will slow down. There is a great course on using Google on the web learning platform Learno.net that the European Journalism Centre (EJC) launched not long ago: Google Search for Journalists contains many tips and is taught by one of Google's media outreach managers. You can also find useful courses on online verification and data journalism. They are all available for free.

## Visualising science

Science lends itself particularly well to being presented with visuals. It is the point where art and science can intersect to convey complex issues. In an online video interview for a science journalism training module, University of Queensland lecturer Joan Leach states that explaining science by visualising it is nothing new; in fact, it dates back as far as to the sketches of Leonardo da Vinci or Charles Darwin (SciJourno no date).

But the way we visualise science has significantly changed as publications have moved from paper to bits and bytes. For example, most print media use infographics to depict science, often using charts and numbers that substantiate a story idea or further explain a scientific concept. Infographics summarise the data, interpret it and deliver a message. How they do this depends on their type. For example, cutaway illustrations and exploded details give your readers insights on how complex technology works (see the website technicalillustrators.org for a number of examples). To show proportions in context, you can create groups and highlight the members that have different properties. In the simplest case, you can use a photograph and just label it, says professor Karl Gude in a Coursera video lesson (see the Links section).

Traditionally, graphic artists created infographics from scratch, using design tools like Inkscape or Adobe Illustrator. Learning such tools requires a certain amount of time, so you can also find simpler but still powerful web-based tools like Infogram and Piktochart. They offer many templates (some free, some paid), so you do not have to design all infographics from scratch. Also, the online tools can directly access your Google Drive, Dropbox or other online folders and take spreadsheets and make visuals from them using the included templates. In print, infographics are static and hence limited; your readers can look at them but not interact and change them. Online, however, they can be interactive and change when your readers want to see more details.

Interactive infographics are designed but then also programmed, so behind the most complex visualisations are entire teams of designers, programmers, statisticians and obviously also journalists. You will encounter an example of a (technological) dissection of such an article in the final case study of this chapter. For complex projects involving lots of data sources, the entire process usually requires a whole team of experts working on crunching the numbers and visualising them interactively, but many of these tools are available for free, so you can immediately get started and experiment with them.

Many interactive visualisations on the web are maps and charts implemented using the aforementioned frameworks. They allow users to apply filters, zoom in and out and drill down into the details on selected subsets of the visualised data. This way, they can tailor the visualisation to their own interests, which in turn makes those infographics more appealing.

Should you decide to immerse yourself into programming interactive web experiences, I would suggest you read Scott Murray's book *Interactive Data Visualization for the Web*. You will find a link to Murray's website, which has free D3 tutorials, in the Links section. If, instead, you aim for infographics and storytelling and the interpretation of data and its visualisation, I suggest you read Alberto Cairo's 2012 book *The Functional Art* and its successor, *The Truthful Art*. The aforementioned infographics course that Karl Gude teaches is also worth watching. You can find links to all of these books in the Reading List at the end of this chapter.

As compelling and interactive as today's online visuals can be, they should always tell or at least support a good underlying story and not be treated as an end in themselves. *BBC Focus* magazine's online editor Alexander McNamara states that having visualisations and imagery is crucial especially for attracting a mobile audience, but he urges you to not solely focus on visuals:

> Eventually it comes down to a balance between social and search: Search doesn't work without text. If you were to create a website with just images, it would be harder to index. Sure, Google has got algorithms that are looking for that kind of content, but ultimately, when you search for something, you type in a word, not a picture. Websites

need to have text. But at the same time, visual storytelling is important. Most traffic is mobile now and not from desktop computers. Mobile is a lot more visual. You have smaller text to see, so pictures are a much better way to tell the stories on a smaller screen. It's the same with videos: People will watch videos on Facebook or on YouTube, and this is a new way of telling the story. So this depends on what kind of balance you want.

*(McNamara 2016)*

Infographics, charts and other visualisations also increasingly make it into online videos. *Motherboard* Canada editor Kate Lunau tells me the future will certainly bring more exciting technologies and tools for visualising and explaining science, but they are just that – tools that help to tell a good story, whereas a good story will always go a long way:

> Video is definitely huge. That said, in the digital environment, there are so many tools and tactics at our fingertips, whatever it is the journalist is doing, it's important not to get too distracted and also to keep telling a good story. I think that a good story will always trump the medium you are telling it in. Even talking about VR and AR, those are all going to be wonderful tools, but I think ultimately it's about telling a story that people want to hear and giving them compelling characters and voices. For that reason, I think print is just as powerful as any of the other technologies. I embrace and welcome all the new tools that we have at our fingertips, but in working with journalists, I would just encourage them to always put the story first, no matter what method they are using.
>
> *(Lunau 2016)*

## Strategies for digital magazines

At the beginning of the digital revolution in journalism, the established print publications merely re-published their print content on their websites but did not tailor it to the web. Nowadays, many large publishing houses have launched native online publications that embrace and leverage the use of technology to produce compelling online content that considers users' attention spans. For example, in 2012, Atlantic Media launched the online news outlet Quartz (qz.com) that focuses on technology and science. By its own account, Quartz has 16 million unique monthly visitors, 60 per cent of which are mobile users. Others followed, with one of the more recent additions being *Undark*, a digital-only science magazine that explores the relationship between science and society and whose editors' mission is to explicitly avoid gee whiz journalism. In an interview with *Undark*'s publisher, Deborah Blum, I discussed the strategy behind the magazine and how she brought the publication into life. The case study in the next section is dedicated to that discussion.

Launching a digital magazine may by tempting for many, because it obviously avoids the immense investments (and part of the workflow) of printing and distributing a magazine. In theory, the core journalistic values (including news values, accuracy, brevity and clarity) have largely remained untouched, but the editorial process has changed dramatically: Digital outlets produce and publish a much higher volume of articles, so they are more susceptible to errors. Due to that high volume, fact-checking online articles is only possible in a limited way.

Online, everything happens nearly in real time: Publish an article, let the readers react to it, make corrections, react to the reactions, repeat. As ephemeral the entire process seems, digital publications need strategies for assessing and measuring the audience and its reactions. In Chapter 7, I briefly touched upon tools like Hootsuite and Google Analytics that help you measure and analyse your audience. Chartbeat's approach (see Figure 11.1) shows you how well your articles do online in real time. But before you decide which tools you use (including CMS, plugins, analytics), you need to have a strategy on whom your magazine targets and also what, how and how often you want to publish.

That strategy needs to include a business plan that answers this question: How is your digital magazine going to make money? Shiny print magazines and newspapers are sold at newsstands, but digital science outlets are not. The following are just a few strategies digital publishers employ in order to make money online:

- **Advertisements:** This is the traditional but perfectly valid way of making money, as the outcry against ad-blockers shows, despite the ongoing laments that advertisement profitability is declining.

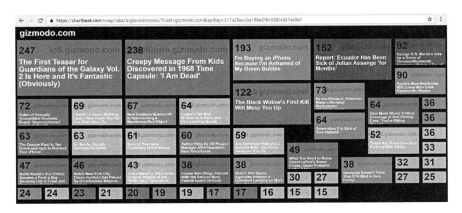

**FIGURE 11.1**  The Chartbeat Big Board Mosaic shows the popularity of Gizmodo's articles in real time. Each tile represents an article and shows the number of current readers.

*Source*: Data and visualisation by Chartbeat, www.chartbeat.com

- **Paywalls:** Users pay for reading online articles, which obviously works best with exclusive content or when the users know the quality of the journalistic research is particularly high. For example, the *New York Times* offers online users ten free articles per month. To read more than that, you have to subscribe. In Q1 2016 alone, the newspaper received 67,000 new digital subscribers, while the company expected a total number of subscribers of more than 1.5 million by the end of 2016 (Ember 2016). *BBC Focus* magazine's online editor Alexander McNamara says most publications have thought about putting up paywalls, but it is not suitable for every publication, as this depends on the brand and the business model.
- **Sponsored content:** Also known as *native advertising*. Quartz, for example, publishes articles that different companies sponsor, and so does VICE. Most of the digital magazines that do this insist that their guidelines forbid any interferences from the sponsor with their editorial values or programming.
- **Subscriptions and pay-per-view:** Articles hidden behind paywalls can often be unlocked by either subscribing or buying a single issue. If you extrapolate the costs, the latter method is usually substantially more expensive than paying for a subscription.
- **Apps:** Many publications, especially digital magazines, are released as native, often multimedia-enriched apps that contain image galleries, videos and sometimes interactive stories. Some publishers release free apps that allow you to browse and buy single issues, while others sell every issue as a new app you have to download. The downside of the latter approach is the high cost of developing apps for every issue, which is the main reason why this approach is mostly limited to well-established publishing houses.

Every digital outlet will also have to know when and how it intends to approach its audience, which channels it uses for that purpose, how it wants to grow that audience in the short and long run and how much it can extend its overall reach, all of which will form that magazine's digital strategy.

Online magazines' publishing schedules differ from print publications, as you publish much more often on the web. So you need to plan for the best times to publish (that entails reading statistics of when your readers are most responsive to freshly published articles), which portion of the population you target, which topics you run, who your audience is, what your specialisation (if any) is and what your magazine's style and tone are (think of style guidelines). Also, from a content perspective, you need to define the types of articles you run, which formats and media you want to utilise (e.g. will your publication be video-heavy, like VICE?), the rubrics that make up your magazine and how often you plan to publish contributions in each of the rubrics. One aspect you do not need to consider is a flatplan that defines which page an article will be printed on. Although it always sounds like there are no space restrictions, you should have a clear definition of each text type's minimum and maximum length.

You will also need to plan for what platform you want to publish on (as of recently, you can create digital publications for free on Medium.com); how many staff writers you need; how much budget you want to allocate for freelancers; whether you will hire a graphic artist or outsource that job; how much budget you want to allocate for illustrations, photographs and multimedia content; and how you want to make your own living.

As you can see, there is a lot of planning to do and a lot of decisions to be made before you can even think about getting your hands on technology or reporting the first article. The problem with launching digital publications is that they are so easy to set up, technologically speaking. Many advice columns focus on the technical aspects of setting up your own publication in a matter of minutes, but they mainly fail to address the planning steps. In the next section, Deborah Blum explains how she addressed these questions when she launched her new, native digital science magazine, *Undark*.

## Case study: the digital-only science magazine *Undark*

In late March 2016, award-winning science journalist and educator Deborah Blum launched the digital popular science magazine *Undark* of the Knight Science Journalism (KSJ) Program. I called Blum to ask her how she and editor Tom Zeller conceived the idea and eventually brought the magazine to life. *Undark* is especially remarkable in two ways: First, as Blum and Zeller managed to secure funding for the publication via the Knight foundation, *Undark* does not need to be profitable and hence has no need to run advertisements or sponsored content. Second, *Undark* found a quality niche where it can focus on investigative, in-depth reporting and on covering topics like the interactions between science and society as well as science and ethics. Blum (2016) tells me what motivated her to come up with the idea of launching *Undark* and letting the Knight Science Journalism fellows contribute to it:

> First, we have a lot of freelancers [among the Knight Science Journalism fellows], because that is the real world of journalism right now. Last year, some of them said: "This is partly hard as a freelancer, because one of the ways you thrive as a freelancer is by being visible, and so for this entire year where I am a fellow and I can't do any work, I'm invisible". The other motivation was: We are funded by a major journalism foundation, the John S. and James L. Knight Foundation, and they are moving toward the idea that every fellowship should have some kind of tangible product. They had done that at the Knight fellowships at Stanford and at the Nieman fellowships at Harvard: Part of your application is a research project. So, when we started talking about it,

we said: We have this really cool magazine, and it's multimedia, so you can do film, podcasts or write. Let that be their project. I didn't want it to overrun the fellowship year so they would spend the whole year consumed by a project. So these are small projects. Once a semester, they have to write an essay or a piece that is about 1,500 words. That is small enough that it is not going to overrun the fellowship program, but it will give them a place to produce, and they will become part of the gallery of *Undark*.

This means that, apart from the staff, some of *Undark*'s content will already be produced by the KSJ fellows, starting with the class of 2016–2017. The fact that *Undark* is a digital-only magazine with no print edition keeps the production costs at a minimum and allows the editorial team to assign more contributions to freelance writers, as Blum further tells me:

> The magazine's budget is almost entirely a freelance budget. The offices are on the Knight Science Journalism part of the program, as is the computer equipment. That allows us to consistently produce quality content. We don't care if anyone is mad at us, which you need for investigative reporting. If you look at investigative reporting in the US, you will see that some of the best of it is being done with foundation support. ProPublica, which partners with the *New York Times*, is foundation-funded. One of our fellows started an investigative non-profit in Seattle, and they are foundation funded, too. The Wisconsin Center for Investigative Journalism is entirely foundation funded. There is foundation money in the *Texas Tribune* and in *California Watch*. That has been very interesting in the US. When people go to foundations and say "What would you support in journalism?" a lot would say investigative journalism, because you can't have a democracy without watchdog media.

In the beginning, the editorial team of *Undark* consisted just of two people: Deborah Blum and former *New York Times* journalist Tom Zeller. That made it easy to define the publication's editorial mission and eased the otherwise often bureaucratic consensus-finding process, which reflects in how fast they launched the magazine:

> We started planning the magazine in July 2015, and then we started publishing in late March 2016. So we had a little over 6 months to get the magazine going, which was not very much. At that point, it was just Tom [Zeller] and me. We were it.

After the team was quickly established, as a first step, the *Undark* editors defined the publication's niche and mission statement, Blum further explains:

The area where you have this tension between science and society, they pull at each other, the ethical quandaries and the issues that are raised in the way science shapes society and society in turn shapes science – sometimes for good and sometimes for not so good – are essential to the mission of good science journalism. No one did just that. You could find really outstandingly good science investigative pieces throughout many publications, but there was no publication just showing this clear light right in that intersection. We saw that as *Undark*'s mission.

Blum is also quick to add that being on the same wavelength as Zeller in terms of ethics was extremely useful. Also, since both of them wanted *Undark* to make a difference, they were able to make quick decisions that even surprised the web design company that implemented parts of the publication's design, which, incidentally, was conceived by Tom Zeller himself, who prior to joining the *New York Times* had been a graphic designer.

While planning *Undark*, although the magazine has no need to become profitable, Blum and Zeller set up a business plan and a publishing schedule. *Undark* has five sections, and Blum says that they are trying to publish one podcast a month, one long-form science article a month, one science video or visual journalism article every other month, a few articles per week in the "variables" titled news section and several blog posts per week. She emphasises that the process of planning and producing articles is faster due to the fact that *Undark* is a relatively small digital publication:

> The best part of being a small digital publication? We are completely non-bureaucratic. There is only a handful of staffers, and we all get along. We don't have to go through layers of bureaucracy, which sometimes, at the larger publications, you do.

Blum also thinks that science journalists can start their own publications early in the process, be it a blog or their own publication, but she explains that a blog focusing on a niche would perhaps be best. Either way, according to Blum, it is important that you consider the following two issues before launching your own digital outlet:

> Write about something you care about, and be aware enough of the leading bloggers in your area so that you are not just duplicating someone who is there and super high-powered. Your particular insights are in fact going to stand out from the background noise. So you need to take a fresh approach. And second, be smart about social media. One of the wonderful things about being a blogger in the digital world is that it opens up a community for you, and that the community will actually move you forward as well.

## Case study: analysing a successful digital science story

Every year, the Global Editors Network first shortlists and then selects the winners of the Data Journalism Awards (DJA). Among the contest entries are strikingly often science stories, which underlines that science does indeed lend itself to interactive visualisation techniques. For example, the DJA 2015 winner (Data Visualisation of the Year – Large Newsroom category) was a story on how vaccines had influenced the spreading of infectious diseases like the measles. The story was published in the *Wall Street Journal* in April 2015 after it had taken several months to investigate. The authors state on the Global Editors Network website that they used Microsoft Excel to manipulate the data, and D3.js and Highchart.js to visualise the data. The main challenge was to mould the data into a format that allowed it to be used by the visualisation tools (the aforementioned clean-up and transformation steps). The charts are visualised as heat maps subdivided by US state and disease (included are measles, hepatitis A, pertussis, polio, rubella and smallpox). The authors also mentioned that formatting the data was the main challenge of this project. You can find a link to that story on vaccines in the Links section; be sure to have a look at it.

One of the DJA winners announced in June 2016 is the online article titled "Medicamentalia – Third World Treatments – First World Prices?" published by the non-profit organisation Fundación Civio. The investigative article addresses the accessibility of fourteen medications in sixty-one different countries and uses powerful visualisation techniques to tell the story that patients in developing countries have to work much harder to obtain treatment than patients in the first world. The article's authors are open about the process and the technology they used to create their outstanding contribution, detailing their choices and methodology in a community forum of the Global Editors Network:

> As for the technology used, the *Civio* authors (led by *Civio* editor Eva Belmonte) state on the *Global Editors Network* website that one of the main challenges they faced was to get the data. It was readily available as a web database, but due to the complex navigation, they had to scrape the data from web pages using the programming language Ruby and the XML/HTML library Nogokiri. Using Microsoft Excel and PostgreSQL, they then analysed the data in order to detect outliers and trends. In addition, they filed FOIA requests and scoured the web in order to add developed countries' data to their dataset.
>
> *(paraphrased from Belmonte 2016)*

As for the Medicamentalia website where they visualise their findings (see Figure 11.2), the article authors state that they used WordPress as a CMS. Moreover, they developed a custom WordPress theme based on the

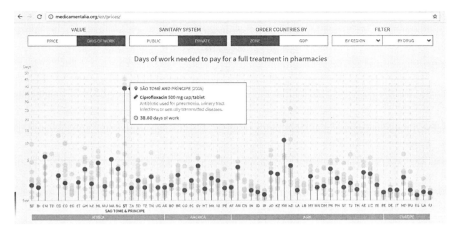

**FIGURE 11.2**   The Medicamentalia team used an interactive, filterable visualisation to show how accessible medication is in different countries

*Source*: Eva Belmonte et al./Fundación Ciudadana Civio/medicamentalia.org

freely available Sage theme. Also, they emphasise that they rendered all visual elements as web-responsive elements so the article's website adapts to users' browser width, regardless of the device they use. Moreover, the authors developed the website in two languages (Spanish and English) in order to make it more accessible to the people affected by their revelations. Furthermore, Belmonte (2016) states how the Medicamentalia team employed interactive visualisation techniques like D3:

> The [D3.js-based] visualization is a core part of the project, and allows readers to explore the full dataset, comparing countries using different filters and criteria. But we are aware of the importance of leveraging data visualization as a storytelling tool: that's why we initially guide readers through the chart.
>
> *(Belmonte 2016)*

Moreover, the images showcased in the other sections on Medicamentalia are not static but in fact little animations that start playing as mini slideshows when the user scrolls further down the page. According to the authors, a professional illustrator created these images by using the scalable vector graphics (SVG) format (Belmonte 2016). It is also noteworthy that the authors put the entire project under a Creative Commons license, hence making it partially reusable by other publications, blogs and individuals.

Most importantly, Civio has released the underlying data publicly, which is a de facto standard for serious investigations nowadays, although many publications charge fees for downloading their data. Medicamentalia allows you to filter the results by type of sanitary system, comparative value of the medication (no absolute values are given because of the lack of comparable absolute prices in the data, as the authors explain) and by region and drug.

## Summary

The digital revolution has not only changed science journalism but the entire process of consuming and producing news. Ever-shrinking screen sizes and the constant flood of news flowing onto every device 24/7 have had their effect on readers' attention spans. If you want to succeed, you need to use social media not only to better understand the audience but also to spread the content and make it stand out.

Professional-grade equipment is no longer mandatory for journalists to produce their own podcasts or web videos, as many mobile devices like smartphones cover the functionality well. What is needed, though, is an understanding of how to craft and structure such content. In addition, the web has enabled journalists to work with a variety of interactive visualisation technologies that render the users' experiences interactive. Interactive, script-based visualisations of complex datasets that allow the users to explore and further drill down into findings are particularly useful in online science journalism. Understanding and using these tools require a thorough understanding of how the web works and at least a basic knowledge of the web's languages and tools. Such knowledge is valuable for every journalist, whether she is directly developing data visualisations or a member of a team that includes developers who produce them.

On a business level, the digital revolution has turned the world of advertising upside down. Traditional, subscription-based models do not work for all digital publications; hence, successful online media companies are experimenting with blends of native advertising, traditional advertising, in-app purchases and many other models to become profitable. While online journalism has become highly competitive, and while nobody has found the magic bullet to make profit online, establishing new digital-only publications is extremely economic and practicable, provided the underlying business plan is sound.

## Review questions

- What are the three types of attention span and how can you cater to them?
- Which factors (dimensions) decide whether somebody adopts mobile devices for consuming news?
- What are the two categories of audience in terms of traffic origin?
- Which tools can you use to monitor your audience's demographics and behaviour?

- How can you improve the quality of your audio recordings?
- What shots do you have to take for a five-shot sequence, and how can you connect them?
- What should you do with your data before visualising it?
- Which advanced search operators for narrowing down search engine results do you know?

## Exercises

- Read three long-form online science articles. For each article, take a note every time you stop reading because of a distraction. Also, record the time it takes you to finish the article. What is your median reading time?
- Choose three more long-form science articles that are the same length. Read the first on a laptop or desktop computer, the second on a tablet and the third on a smartphone. Again, write down how long it takes you to read each article and how many times you stop reading. What is your median reading time per article and device?
- Analyse an online science magazine over the course of one day and write down how many advertisements and PR articles, how many independent articles and how many sponsored articles they run. How much is independent journalism?
- Ask one or more scientists at your local university if you can look over their shoulder and record them on a typical working day. Use the five-shot technique to capture them conducting research.
- Google these scientists' areas of expertise and specifically find PDFs of their research articles. Further narrow down your results by considering only your own country.
- Using your smartphone's standard audio recording app, interview one of your classmates multiple times. Experiment with the built-in microphone and the headphone microphone. Also, try different distances and locations (indoors, outdoors, the campus and a pub). Which recording sounds best?

## Reading list

Bradshaw, P. and Rohumaa, L. (2011) Podcasts and audio slideshows, In Bradshaw, P. and Rohumaa, L. (eds.) *The Online Journalism Handbook*. Harlow: Pearson Education Limited, 92–103

Bradshaw, P. and Rohumaa, L. (2011) Video, In Bradshaw, P. and Rohumaa, L. (eds.) *The Online Journalism Handbook*. Harlow: Pearson Education Limited, 104–118

Cairo, A. (2012) *The Functional Art – An Introduction to Information Graphics and Visualization*. Berkeley, CA: New Riders

Cairo, A. (2016) *The Truthful Art: Data, Charts and Maps for Communication*. Berkeley, CA: New Riders

Lancaster, K. (2012) *Video Journalism for the Web: A Practical Introduction to Multimedia Storytelling*. London: Routledge

Lih, A. (2011) Teaching visual storytelling: The five-shot method and beyond, *Slideshare* [Online Presentation] Available at: http://de.slideshare.net/fuzheado/teaching-visual-storytelling-the-five-shot-method-and-beyond [date accessed 15 September]

Murray, S. (2013) *Interactive Data Visualization for the Web*. Sebastopol: O'Reilly

Schulson, M. (2016) How journalists can hold scientists accountable, *Pacific Standard* [Online] Available at: https://psmag.com/how-journalists-can-help-hold-scientists-accountable-324e375bbe26#.o7vkhagad [date accessed 10 July 2016]

Tow Knight Center (2014) *Shane Smith on Vice Media's Business Plan, Net Neutrality* (via YouTube) [Online Video] Available at: www.youtube.com/watch?v=NkzL8F37Jfo [date accessed 6 August 2016]

## Links

Alexa, VICE.com web statistics: www.alexa.com/siteinfo/vice.com

Al Jazeera, E-waste Republic (interactive web documentary): http://interactive.aljazeera.com/aje/2015/ewaste/index.html

Andy Kirk, Visualising Data (visualisation resources and tips): www.visualisingdata.com/

BBC Academy, Filming and Recording (video guides): www.bbc.co.uk/academy/journalism/skills/filming-and-recording

Coursera, Design and Make Infographics (Project-Centered Course): www.coursera.org/learn/infographic-design

European Journalism Centre (EJC), Learno.net: http://learno.net

Fundación Civio, Medicamentalia (DJA 2016 winner): http://medicamentalia.org/en/Science Journalism Training in Australia, Visualisation in Science Journalism: http://scijourno.com.au/portfolio-item/visualisation-in-science-journalism/

Scott Murray, D3 tutorials: http://alignedleft.com/tutorials/d3

The Wall Street Journal, Battling Infectious Diseases in the 20th Century: The Impact of Vaccines (DJA 2015 winner): http://graphics.wsj.com/infectious-diseases-and-vaccines/

## References

Belmonte, E. (2016) Medicamentalia.org – A journalistic investigation into access to medicines around the world, *Global Editors Network* [Online] Available at: http://community.globaleditorsnetwork.org/content/medicamentaliaorg-journalistic-investigation-access-medicines-around-world-1 [date accessed 18 August 2016]

Blum, D. (2016) Personal phone conversation on 26 August 2016

Bradshaw, P. and Rohumaa, L. (2011) *The Online Journalism Handbook*. Harlow: Pearson Education Limited

Cameron, D. (2009) Mobile journalism: A snapshot of current research and practice, *Artigo Consultado A*, vol. 19, no. 04, 2011

Ember, S. (2016) New York Times Co. reports loss as digital subscriptions grow, *The New York Times* [Online] Available at: www.nytimes.com/2016/05/04/business/media/new-york-times-co-q1-earnings.html [date accessed 6 August 2016]

Fidler, R. (2013) 2013 Mobile media news consumption survey, Report 1, *RJI Mobile Media Research Project* [Online] Available at: www.rjionline.org/research/rji-dpa-mobile-media-project/2013-q1-research-report-1 [date accessed 29 April 2014]

Fidler, R. (2014) Mobile media news consumption survey, Report 1, *RJI Mobile Media Research Project* [Online] Available at: www.rjionline.org/research/rji-dpa-mobile-media-project/2014-q1-research-report-1 [date accessed 29 April 2014].

Frechette, C. (2012) How journalists can improve video stories with shot sequences, *Poynter* [Online] Available at: www.poynter.org/2012/how-journalists-can-improve-video-stories-with-shot-sequences/183861/ [date accessed 15 September 2016]

Gausby, A. (2015) Attention spans, consumer insights, *Microsoft Canada* [Online] Available at: https://advertising.microsoft.com/en/WWDocs/User/display/cl/researchreport/31966/en/microsoft-attention-spans-research-report.pdf [date accessed 30 November 2016]

Kim, K.J., Sundar, S.S. and Park, E. (2011) The effects of screen-size and communication modality on psychology of mobile device users, *In Proceedings of the 2011 Annual Conference Extended Abstracts on Human Factors in Computing Systems – CHI EA '11*. New York: ACM Press, 1207–1212 [Online] Available at: http://portal.acm.org/citation.cfm?doid=1979742.1979749 [date accessed 17 August 2016]

Littlewood, T. (2016) Wie VICE arbeitet, *Reporter Forum (Workshop 2016, Part 1)* [Online Audio] Available at: http://reporter-forum.de/fileadmin/mp3/Audios_Workshop_16/RF_2A_1.mp3 [date accessed 15 September 2016]

Lunau, K. (2016) Personal Skype conversation on 18 August 2016

McNamara (2016) Personal phone conversation on 19 August 2016

Mitchell, A. and Guskin, E. (2013) Twitter news consumers: Young, mobile and educated, *Pew Research Center* [Online] Available at: www.journalism.org/2013/11/04/twitter-news-consumers-young-mobile-and-educated/ [date accessed 17 August 2016]

Mitchell, A., Stocking, G. and Matsa, K.E. (2016) Long-form reading shows signs of life in our mobile news world, *Pew Research Center* [Online] Available at: www.journalism.org/2016/05/05/long-form-reading-shows-signs-of-life-in-our-mobile-news-world/ [date accessed 10 August 2016]

Pavlik, J. (2000) The impact of technology on journalism, *Journalism Studies*, vol. 1, no. 2, 229–237

Schrøder, K.C. (2015) News media old and new: Fluctuating audiences, news repertoires and locations of consumption, *Journalism Studies*, vol. 16, no. 1, 60–78

SciJourno (no date) Module 6 – Visualisation in science journalism, *Scijourno.com. au* [Online] Available at: http://scijourno.com.au/portfolio-item/visualisation-in-science-journalism/ [date accessed 18 August 2016]

Spayd, L. (2016) Facebook live: Too much, too soon, *The New York Times* [Online] Available at: www.nytimes.com/2016/08/21/public-editor/facebook-live-too-much-too-soon.html [date accessed 30 November 2016]

Weatherhead, R. (2014) Say it quick, say it well – The attention span of a modern internet consumer, *The Guardian* [Online] Available at: www.theguardian.com/media-network/media-network-blog/2012/mar/19/attention-span-internet-con sumer [date accessed 20 August 2016]

Weatherhead, R. (2016a) Skype conversation on 19 August 2016

Weatherhead, R. (2016b) Email conversation on 16 August 2016

Westlund, O. (2013) Mobile news, *Digital Journalism*, vol. 1, no. 1, 6–26

Yong, E. (2016) Personal Skype conversation on 18 August 2016

# 12

# BUILDING A CAREER IN SCIENCE JOURNALISM

**What you will learn in this chapter:**

*   Routes into science journalism
*   Science writing programmes
*   Specialist or generalist?
*   Fellowships and awards
*   Essential (soft) skills
*   Science journalism and the broadcast media
*   Case study: work experience placement at *BBC Focus* magazine
*   Case study: Carl Zimmer's science writing career
*   Case study: Erika Check Hayden's science writing career

## Introduction

Science journalism is a business, just like science. Especially at the beginning, you will have to deal with a lot of competition and rejections. But do not worry: You can take a number of steps to improve your chances to survive in this wonderful business of ours. That said, there is no guaranteed path into science journalism, which is also an advantage. Whether you have a background in science or you come from the humanities does not matter as much as you might think. Of course, it depends on whether you want to cover very specific fields and critically question them or if you would like to cover a wide range of topics. Some exceptional writers even manage to pursue academic and journalistic careers at the same time.

After showing you different types of possible routes into science journalism in the first section, I take a more detailed look at one of these routes in the subsequent section: science writing programmes. You can find some remarkable programmes in the US, the UK and Australia that I will briefly address. Apart from teaching you the hard skills, most of these programmes draw on experienced lecturers and guest speakers. Also, they require you to complete internships, which help you to not only gather early experiences but also to work with real editors and hence start building your own portfolio while you are still studying.

It is quite possible that your preferred topic or research area will emerge from such experiences. A specialisation can help you build your own brand and establish yourself as the go-to person in a specific area. The upside of this approach is that you will develop a certain level of expertise in that area, which allows you to critically question science. On the downside, being a general science journalist, you could cover more topics that interest you. It really depends on what you are passionate about.

Once you have built a solid body of work, you can consider applying for an award or fellowship. Both are great ways to set yourself apart from the competition, and editors might use these accolades to assess whether to commission one of your story ideas or whether to hire you. Additionally, fellowships allow you to immerse yourself in a project you would like to pursue for a set amount of time, which can be an invaluable opportunity if you are a mid-career journalist.

Apart from all the credentials that you earned at university or by winning awards, you will have to develop and cultivate some essential soft skills such as self-discipline, perseverance, resilience and accuracy. These skills (or traits) help you avoid frustration and better deal with rejection. Oftentimes, how easy you are to work with will determine whether you will develop long-term relationships with your editors, so this is a factor that can influence your success.

The final three sections of this chapter are case studies. One is about my work placement at a science magazine in Bristol in 2015; the other two look at highly acclaimed science writers Carl Zimmer and Erika Check Hayden. They were kind enough to share their own experiences and explain how they established their careers in different ways. By the time you finish this chapter, you probably will have gained some useful input and ideas about how you can build and eventually advance your own career in science journalism.

## Routes into science journalism

One of the academic routes into science journalism is studying for a degree in science journalism. But science journalism is a specialised genre, so you will not find as many programmes as you would if you were looking for a degree in general journalism. New science journalism programmes are occasionally launched in Europe, the UK and the US, but others disappear after a few years, like the former MA programme in science journalism at City, University of London.

Science journalism programmes equip you with the necessary skills to report on science and get published, and they also cover the business aspects of being a science journalist. In theory, you could pick up many of these hard skills through self-learning and lots of practice. These degree courses, however, are often taught by accomplished science journalists who share their experiences and provide first-hand accounts of how they reported their stories. Many seasoned journalism teachers quickly identify and nurture talents when they come across them. Also, your classmates will be tomorrow's reporters, editors, editors-in-chief and publishers. Contacts pay off in every line of business, and science journalism is no different; they can make a difference when you pitch a freelance story or when you apply for a job at a publication.

A science journalism degree is no guarantee you will actually land a job at a publication, but it certainly provides a solid foundation that you need to combine with a portfolio of science articles you have produced. Most universities with science journalism programmes acknowledge the importance of building that list of references and help you get an internship at a publication as part of your degree course's curriculum. This is an excellent first way of establishing a relationship with editors. If you approach them again after graduating, they will already know what kind of quality they can expect from you.

The opposite route is the scientist-turned-science writer. Some students study for a science degree but later discover they would rather write about science than further pursue their academic careers. Perhaps one of the most notable examples is Randy Olson (see Chapter 8), who was a tenured professor of marine biology before he moved to Hollywood, attended film school and became a filmmaker. Other scientists wear two or more hats, like Ben Goldacre, who is not only a famous science writer but remains a practising physician and academic. Similarly, Christie Wilcox (see the interview in Chapter 7) works both as a researcher at the University of Hawaii and as a science blogger for *DISCOVER* magazine. She just published a popular science book on venoms and co-edited a book on science blogging, which in a way reflects both of her roles. As you can see, being a scientist or a science writer is not mutually exclusive. You might think that becoming a scientist first and then starting to write about science might be beneficial. Charles Seife, who holds two master's degrees (journalism and mathematics) does not necessarily think this, as he tells me:

> I think a science degree is optional, but I think it does help sometimes, although it also has its negatives. We tend to have about two thirds of our students who have done a science degree, often master's or even PhDs, and then we have a number who are coming from journalism or from literature. They have different mindsets. Especially scientists, when they come from a quantitative background, have a leg up in

certain ways; but at the same time, they are also embedded in the field that they are going to cover – which presents its own problems. Sometimes they have to take a step back and be critical of things they took for granted before.

*(Seife 2016)*

Award-winning science journalist Ed Yong confirms this notion. Yong tells me the science-first route can be advantageous in certain situations, but it is not always helpful or even necessary:

> It might actually even hurt you, because it might make it harder to put yourself in the perspective of someone who doesn't have all that knowledge and scientific training. And I certainly think that there is no reason why someone who has an arts background can't be an exceptional science writer in quite a short space of time. It has happened to Carl [Zimmer] and lots of other people. It's just because they are good, because they pay attention, they work hard, and they care a lot about what they do.
>
> *(Yong 2016)*

In contrast, Ellen Ruppel Shell, co-director of the graduate program in science journalism at Boston University thinks having experience in science or pursuing a science degree can be advantageous when you have to cover complex issues, as she explains to me:

> Our students generally have at least one degree in science. If they don't have a degree in science, they have a demonstrated understanding of science, they have taken a number of university courses in science or worked in a laboratory, or they have done some work in a scientific environment.
>
> *(Ruppel Shell 2016)*

Of course, obtaining a degree in science or science journalism is not the only way of breaking into science journalism. Some science writers are self-taught through studying brilliant science writing, and others intern at media companies. Publications in Germany and Switzerland offer traineeships that can last from 1 to 2 years, with a median duration of 18 months. The advantage of internships and especially traineeships is that you are tightly integrated in newsrooms. It goes without saying that you can combine these routes, if you can afford to.

Directly breaking into freelance journalism is another option that you could consider after graduating or even while studying. A good pitch can lead to your first assignment sooner than you think. The direct freelancing route is also how science writer Alan Dove broke into science journalism.

As he explains in an essay, he "spent a few months working as an editorial intern for *Nature Biotechnology* and then declared myself a freelance science journalist" (Dove 2015:8669). But he emphasises that he could only make a living because his living standards were not very high at the time he started his business. He further affirms that it is almost impossible to predict your income as a freelance science writer, because you heavily depend on external factors. When one of his clients decided to not hire freelance writers anymore, suddenly $10,000 of his income broke away. "This is a business for people with the privilege of a robust familial safety net or a well-employed spouse" (Dove 2015:8669).

## Science writing programmes

Pursuing and completing a degree in science writing is by no means an infallible way of starting a career as a science journalist, but it does teach the fundamentals of good science writing and provide a good sense of topics to propose, which can help jumpstart your career. In an article for *Science*, Robin Arnette (2005) addresses three different science writing programmes in the US. After interviewing the directors of all three programmes, she concludes that "having a science writing degree confers an advantage when applying for certain writing jobs" (Arnette 2005). For her article, Arnette also interviewed some of the programmes' graduates. They unanimously confirmed that obtaining a degree proved an advantage in their later careers. Also, Arnette (2005) cites former *Science* editor Colin Norman, who claims that *Science* hired many journalists who could show a considerable number of clips; he also states that earning a degree in science journalism is an advantage, but not in a strict sense (Arnette 2005).

One of the degree courses Arnette (2005) mentions is the MS in science journalism at Boston University's College of Communication. The three-semester programme is co-run by Douglas Starr and Ellen Ruppel Shell. The syllabus includes modules on online journalism (including contributing to a web magazine), science news writing, science in society, reporting on controversies, a data journalism boot camp and a practical course on video journalism in science writing. Students dedicate the third semester to a practical internship. Only about ten applicants get selected each year.

Similarly, students of the MIT graduate programme in science writing (three semesters) must complete a one-semester internship as part of the curriculum. A student's final thesis is either a long-form article of approximately 10,000 words or a series of articles spanning the same length (Ornes 2014). The programme includes courses and several seminars on science writing as well as a video journalism course in which students produce a documentary. In addition, all students need to spend 20 hours at one of the MIT laboratories and then report on these laboratories, which can lead to a publication in MIT's renowned science and technology magazine *Technology Review*.

Another graduate science journalism programme is the Science, Health and Environmental Reporting Program (SHERP) at New York University. SHERP includes courses on writing and reporting as well as topic selection, ethics, investigative science journalism and medical and environmental reporting. The SHERP lecturers are accomplished journalists like Dan Fagin (the programme's director), Charles Seife, David Corcoran and Ivan Oransky. Throughout the academic year, the lecturers are joined by several guest speakers who are scientists, filmmakers, reporters and editors. Also, the SHERP students must complete two compulsive internships before they are awarded the master's degree.

In the UK, the MA in science and environmental journalism at the University of Lincoln provides a 1-year track. Its curriculum includes courses on science writing, ethics, law and broadcast science journalism. The curriculum also contains a dedicated module that allows students to specialise in a specific science discipline. A compulsory 2-week internship is also part of this curriculum.

In Australia, the Australian National University (ANU) offers bachelor's, master's and PhD programmes in science communication. The curriculum of the master's degree includes courses on communicating science with the public, ethics, science in the media, science in popular fiction and strategies in science communication. An internship and a final project are also part of the curriculum. There are several other Australian universities that offer science journalism degrees (see the Links section).

If you want to study science journalism in Europe, you can refer to the list of recommended programmes published European Commission (EC) in 2010. It contains detailed information on the programmes' syllabi; unfortunately it is outdated, so links and addresses and even the programmes' names might have changed. You can find the European Guide to Science Journalism Training in the Links section.

The list is by no means complete, but you can find more science journalism programmes in Box 12.1. Even if you do not plan to pursue one of the

---

**BOX 12.1   SCIENCE JOURNALISM PROGRAMMES**

Australian National University, undergraduate and graduate programmes in science communication

> Degrees: Master of science communication (bachelor's and PhD degrees are also available)
> Programme director: Will Grant (will.grant@anu.edu.au)
> Duration: 2 years
> Website: http://programsandcourses.anu.edu.au/program/MSCOM

Boston University, graduate programme in science journalism

> Degree: Master of science
> Programme directors: Douglas Starr (dstarr@bu.edu), Ellen Ruppel Shell
> (eshell@bu.edu)
> Duration: 1 year
> Website: www.bu.edu/com/academics/degree-programs/ms-in-science-
> journalism/

Massachusetts Institute of Technology, graduate programme in science writing

> Degree: Master of arts
> Programme director: Marcia Bartusiak (bar2siak@mit.edu)
> Duration: 1 year
> Website: http://sciwrite.mit.edu/

New York University, Science Health and Environmental Reporting Program (SHERP)

> Degree: Master of arts
> Programme director: Dan Fagin (dan.fagin@nyu.edu)
> Duration: 16 months
> Website: http://journalism.nyu.edu/graduate/programs/science-health-
> and-environmental-reporting/

The University of North Carolina and Chapel Hill, graduate programme in science and medical journalism

> Degree: Master of arts
> Programme director: Thomas Linden (linden@unc.edu)
> Duration: 2 years
> Website: http://mj.unc.edu/medicaljournalism

University of California Santa Cruz, science communication program

> Degree: Certificate
> Programme director: Erika Check Hayden (scicom@ucsc.edu)
> Duration: 1 year
> Website: http://scicom.ucsc.edu/

University of Lincoln, graduate programme in science and environmental journalism

> Degree: Master of arts
> Programme director: Gary Stevens (gstevens@lincoln.ac.uk)
> Duration: 1 year
> Website: www.lincoln.ac.uk/home/course/jouscema/

programmes, have a look at their syllabi and also at the literature lists of the single modules whenever possible. They provide excellent indications as to which skills you should acquire and hone in order to succeed as a science journalist. What unites most of the US and UK science journalism programmes is that they contain internships and courses on video journalism, so consider them in your career at some point.

## Specialist or generalist?

In Chapter 7, I addressed the question of whether a science blog should focus on a niche or a broad topic. Both approaches work for blogs, and although many of this book's interviewees have stated that writing on a niche topic can be an advantage in the beginning, the question becomes more difficult when we expand its context to an entire career in science writing. What kind of science journalist would you like to be, a specialist or a generalist? Should you gain expertise in one particular branch of science, such as life science, and perhaps narrow it further down to zoology? Or should you cover physics, neuroscience, medicine and environment alike?

There is no intuitive answer, but consider the following reflections: If you decided to specialise in zoology, there are still many sub-branches you can focus on, such as ornithology. If you cover many of those sub-branches, you might still be a generalist within your chosen field – a generalised specialist, if you will. A specialisation helps you brand yourself as a go-to person in a specific field. For example, science journalist Mark Schapiro built his 30-year career on being an investigative environmental journalist. He has covered many topics, but he is particularly well-known for covering and investigating carbon footprints and the effects of fossil fuels.

On the downside, specialising on one specific science branch may mean that you are limiting yourself to only that branch. As a consequence, you could miss out on other relevant, newsworthy topics that you could have covered. Which path you take depends also on what types of stories you are writing. Are you writing in-depth features that cover a scientist's endeavours and focus on her methodology? Are your articles investigative in nature, and do you point out research misconduct? Do you want to review other science articles, like HealthNewsReview.org? If so, you might need to acquire very specific knowledge in your chosen field. In contrast, if you want to cover a broad range of topics and write a high volume of shorter stories that do not need the same methodological depth, being a generalist can be more of an advantage. Trained scientist Ed Yong weighs in on this discussion:

> There are both upsides and downsides to being a generalist or a specialist. I have a specialism in microbiology, as I have been covering microbiology for a while, which allows me to cover those stories better

than other people because I can see the big picture, so I can see what is sound and what is not. It helps: I have respect from people in the field. If you were a specialist in infectious diseases or genetic engineering, this would have been a very good year for you, because big stories on CRISPR and the Zika virus came out. A lot of these choices make us very employable, and the people want to hear what we say. That can make a huge difference. But then again, I think you would never want to limit yourself to one particular branch. There are only so many microbiology stories that a paper or a magazine or any sort of client will take. It pays certainly to become very knowledgeable in a few topics but also to keep a certain degree of breadth.

*(Yong 2016)*

Yong's point of view that a specialism is not a strict requirement to produce excellent science articles is also supported in part by a study conducted by journalism professors McIlwaine and Nguyen (2005). They conclude that:

Journalists who are likely to treat science as another important aspect of society may be of much greater value than specialists to audiences seeking to take part in the debate about the great scientific and technological questions facing them now and in the future.

*(McIlwaine and Nguyen 2005)*

They also refute the theory that equipping general journalists with specialist science knowledge is the solution to produce better science journalists who know how to approach complex scientific topics. In fact, that theory has four inherent flaws (McIlwaine and Nguyen 2005):

1    In Australia, there is almost no demand for specialist science journalists, as generally only large media organisations can afford to hire specialist science journalists.
2    Specialist science journalists who are part of a publication's staff could be less suited to convey science to lay audiences, as they need to maintain relationships with the scientists, and hence they depend on what information these scientists feed them.
3    Specialist science journalists tend to avoid the political, social and economic aspects and implications, hence telling only one side of their stories.
4    Specialist science journalists abandon the news media after some time. Drawing on an unofficial figure, the authors say that only one-tenth of journalists trained in covering environmental issues remain in the news media. "This may be for a number of reasons, but among them must be the fact that, although scientists can learn journalism, they do not necessarily become competent journalists."

Apparently not even all large media organisations in Australia have the luxury of hiring specialist science journalists. Science reporter John Ross covers the science beat at *The Australian* and is also a general reporter who has not undergone any formal training in science journalism (Ross 2015). In light of these four shortcomings, McIlwaine and Nguyen argue that one solution could be to train general journalists in science, although they fully acknowledge that there is no simple solution:

> This paper does not attempt to argue that a little learning is all graduates need to make them competent science writers overnight. But it does suggest that if all journalism students were given a foundation of science writing – a one-semester course or perhaps even less – that articulated with other basic aspects of journalism, including the democratic imperatives of journalism, they would have a sound platform from which to approach science stories.
>
> *(McIlwaine and Nguyen 2005)*

## Fellowships and awards

You have probably noticed that many of the cited science journalists in this book carry the attribute *award-winning*. High-profile publications tend to hire high-profile science bloggers. For example, in 2013, *National Geographic* called together four well-known science writers, Virginia Hughes, Brian Switek, Ed Yong and Carl Zimmer, to form a new science blogging network, Phenomena (which is now part of *National Geographic*'s news section). Today, seven science journalists contribute to the Phenomena network. Most of them have won at least one award or obtained a fellowship. These credentials help publications select their contributors in the following two ways: First, awards and completed fellowships serve as a quality label. Second, award winners gain more exposure and are hence more likely to have already built a loyal readership, which is invaluable for fledgling science blogging networks who want to quickly increase page impressions.

Science journalism fellowship durations can range anywhere from 1 week to several months and are typically aimed at mid-career science journalists. This implies that, should you obtain a fellowship, you would need to take time out of work, which you need to arrange with your employer or school in advance. Like any form of science journalism education, most of the currently available fellowships provide fertile ground for connecting with like-minded professionals and broadening your journalistic horizons.

For example, the Knight Science Journalism (KSJ) Program at MIT selects around ten fellows, usually mid-career science journalists, each year and encourages them to follow innovative journalistic projects (which they need to outline as part of the application process) over the course of their 9-month residence at the MIT campus in Cambridge, Massachusetts. The class of

FIGURE 12.1   The KSJ Fellowship 2016–2017 from left to right: Mark Wolverton, Meera Subramanian, Iván Carrillo Perez, Maura O'Connor, David Corcoran (KSJ Associate Director), Deborah Blum (KSJ Director), Thomas R. Zeller Jr. (*Undark* Editor-in-Chief), Chloé Hecketsweiler, Fabio Turone, Rosalia Omungo, Robert McClure, Bianca Vazquez Toness, Lauren Whaley, Bettina Urcuioli (KSJ Program Administrator)

Source: The Knight Science Journalism Fellowship Program at MIT

2016–2017 (see Figure 12.1) is producing material for the aforementioned digital science magazine *Undark* (see Chapter 11). The programme's director, Deborah Blum, is a multi-award-winning science journalist herself. The KSJ fellowship's application process requires you to be a full-time journalist with at least three years of experience. The medium you work in is not important, and neither is your country of residence. Also, freelancers may apply as well as staff journalists. Applicants need to provide a number of supporting documents, too: a current résumé, five clips, three recommendation letters and a motivation letter that states why you want to apply for the KSJ fellowship. These requirements make it clear that this fellowship does not entertain fledgling science journalists. Successful applicants enjoy workshops and classes, time to work on their *Undark* project and a scholarship of about $70,000. Completing such an acclaimed fellowship can undoubtedly boost your career.

Other science journalism fellowships equip you with a better understanding of how scientists work within very specific science domains. Some of them accept applications from beginning science journalists. If you already have some published clips that tie in with the fellowship's theme, give it a try.

It is primarily research institutions that offer such fellowships, so they usually take place at those scientific institutions. For example, the Woods

**FIGURE 12.2** Ocean Science Journalism Fellows learn about the ecology of Wood Neck Beach in Falmouth during a 2015 field trip with WHOI biologist Annette Govindarajan (far left) and Woods Hole Sea Grant educator Kate Madin (left)

*Source*: Erin Koenig/Woods Hole Oceanographic Institution

Hole Oceanographic Institution (WHOI), located in the eponymous town in the US, each year chooses between half a dozen and a dozen science journalists as fellows for its annual Ocean Science Journalism Fellowship (Figure 12.2). If you get accepted, the WHOI scientists will hold lectures for you and take you on laboratory tours and field trips. The institution also reserves time for you to conduct interviews with the scientists. The WHOI fellowships last 1 week, and past fellows included freelance science journalists and staff journalists at high-profile publications including the *Los Angeles Times* and *National Geographic*.

The WHOI is also the venue for another science journalism fellowship. Every year, the Marine Biological Laboratory (MBL) at the University of Chicago invites science journalists to immerse themselves in scientific work as part of its Logan Science Journalism Program. If they accept your application, you can choose between a biomedical hands-on introductory course (aimed at science and health journalists) and an environmental hands-on introductory course (aimed at environment journalists), both held at the WHOI. Part of the 2016 environmental hands-on introductory course was a field trip to

Alaska. The fellowship duration is 1 or 2 weeks, and the MBL will cover most of the costs. You will have to prepare the usual documentation to apply, which includes recommendation letters, sample clips and a personal statement. The MBL will also assess your scientific experience and proficiency in English.

Such fellowships, especially those that provide insight into the scientists' field work, are invaluable tools to increase your own scientific literacy as a science journalist and to gain more exposure. The list of such fellowships is quite long; you can find a few more in the Links section at the end of this chapter. That said, there is another, second type of career-boosting tool that can help you become a famed science writer overnight: awards.

The quality label "award-winning" will ramp up your market value, help you gain exposure and hence draw editors' attention to your writing. As a science writer, you can submit your entries not only to specialised science journalism awards but also to world-renowned general journalism awards such as the Pulitzer Prize. In either case, you should carefully read the eligibility criteria (e.g. the contributions you submit cannot be older than 1 or 2 years for most contests) and also look at the previous award recipients' articles. Look for patterns and recurring elements to figure out what the award jury is looking for.

In 2007, Ed Yong won the *Daily Telegraph* Science Writer Award. In a 2011 article for the *Guardian*, Yong wrote about how winning it had changed his life:

> The real prize was that I had proof that I could write about science. I pitched with more confidence.
>
> *(Yong 2011)*

He also adds that the year following the award he accepted every assignment offered to him, and he tried to seize the moment and make the most out of the status he had earned then. At the same time, he strongly recommends aspiring science writers participate in competitions (Yong 2011).

By the time Yong wrote the article for the *Guardian*, the award competition no longer existed, so he recommended submitting entries to the Wellcome Trust Science Writing Award, which today is also defunct. This shows how ephemeral such awards can be: Some exist for only a couple of years, but others may be there for decades. The following is a (by no means exhaustive) list of some current and established science writing awards that you might want to consider applying for as you progress in your career. Most of them are subdivided into different categories, and all of them have clearly stated rules on their websites. You can find links to some of these websites in this chapter's Links section. Most of those listed here are annual and open to international applicants. The following list is ordered alphabetically (not in order of importance):

- AAAS Science Journalism Awards
- ABSW Science Writers Awards for Britain and Ireland

- AIP Science Communication Awards
- CASW Evert Clark/Seth Payne Award for Young Science Journalists
- NASW Science in Society Awards
- SEJ Awards for Reporting on the Environment
- TRS Royal Society Science Books Prize.

There exist many more similar awards. As soon as you have built a presentable body of work that fits into these awards' categories, you should start competing. Once submitted, participation requires little effort and commitment (apart from attending the final ceremony should you be selected as one of the winners). Be sure to also check out local fellowships and awards.

Bear in mind that you will face significant competition if you plan on entering such contests. Just as with pitching, chances are your articles will not win a contest the first time you participate. This is completely normal. What separates the professional from the aspiring journalist is that the professional has learnt to deal with rejections and to persevere. In fact, perseverance is one of the essential soft skills you need to strive for as a science journalist.

## Essential soft skills

If you are a fledgling science journalist, the difficulty of getting your first job or assignment right at the beginning of your career seems to resemble a logarithmic graph. You start out somewhere below zero, and the slope seems incredibly steep initially. But as you progress, the slope flattens and eventually becomes almost a horizontal line. Quite possibly, you will have to write your first articles for free and gradually assemble a list of references. Once you have a portfolio of published articles, you can gradually start to approach other, paying publications. Quality should always be your main focus, as editors read your clips before they consider commissioning an article. The less known you are, the more you are under scrutiny.

That is why you must be able to handle rejections and be resilient. When you are starting out, chances are you will face some form of rejection, no matter whether you are trying to find a staff job or an internship, trying to land your first freelance assignment or proposing a science book. Emma Marris notes in *The Science Writers' Handbook* that even seasoned science writers are confronted with rejections when submitting book proposals. In case that happens, you can always bring your research to life using a different format, for example, a series of articles (Marris 2013).

You must be able to deal with loneliness. Sure, you will talk with lots of people, including interviewees, editors and colleagues, but the actual act of selecting scenes and typing words on your computer and moulding these components into a coherent text is lonely work whether you sit in an office or alone at home, claims science writer Stephen Ornes. He also says that the typical sign that the loneliness is about to get the upper hand is when he starts informally chatting with interviewees. If that happens, he recommends changing your environment, pursuing a hobby and generally taking your mind off things by following social activities (Ornes 2013).

Self-confidence is one of the key characteristics of every journalist, as Mark Lee Hunter tells me. Know your value and do not sell yourself short. Internships and work experience placements are often unpaid in journalism. This may be fine while you are learning the tools of the trade, but you need to go out there and sell your work as soon as possible. Sometimes, this can also mean you have to turn down an assignment if there is no pay, but that also depends on who commissions an article. Would I turn down an unpaid assignment from the *New Yorker*? Certainly not. It would be a perfect springboard for getting similarly prestigious assignments in the future. That said, never think your work is not worth the money. If it is publishable, you should receive money for it, even if it is not much. Writing for online publications already pays less than writing for print publications. Also, if you sell yourself short all the time just to get exposure, then unfortunately you are making the situation worse not only for yourself but for other aspiring journalists, as Bethany Brookshire claims: "Every time someone is willing to come in and do the same work for free, or for less, that's one less chance for professionals to make a living. . . . The less editors feel they have to pay, the less they will offer" (Brookshire 2016:235). This may seem like the immutable generation of infinite internships and un(der)paid jobs, but publishers do earn money with journalists' contributions, so they should pay for it. Ed Yong (2016) confirms this point and points out that it is not the writers who are to blame:

> This has always been a problem. Even some paid positions force young writers to produce a high volume of not very good work that isn't going to do very much for them in the long run. This is the fault of publishers. I would never have a go at someone for taking an unpaid internship, because who am I to tell someone that the choice they have made for their career is the wrong one? They make their own decisions. But it's horrifying that publishers are still doing this. I think that people should be paid well. They should be compensated for the work and the art they produce. It's ridiculous to offer people positions or opportunities where they are just working for exposure without earning money. There is a strong line for me between having a go at organisations that take advantage of writers in that way and having a go at writers who take up those opportunities. I would always do the former and never the latter.
>
> *(Yong 2016)*

As for payment, here is a word of caution for all aspiring freelance journalists: Some newspapers and magazines will pay you on delivery, others will pay you on publication and others you will have to chase for weeks, months and even years in order to get paid. Persistence (and sometimes insistence) goes a long way in getting what you want. Professional writing is a business, just like every other line of business. Journalism is not your hobby, it is your job – and jobs pay.

At all times, be reliable and punctual. An assignment not completed on time is quite likely your last assignment from the editor who commissioned it. This is just as bad as showing up late for an interview. Beware that your sources will occasionally show up late, which leads us to the next attitude you should adopt in case you want to successfully break into science journalism: patience. This does not mean you should accept getting paid a month later. Nor does it mean you should accept that somebody does not show up for an interview at all. Rather, it means that you should show some goodwill, remain calm and be in control of every situation. In doing so, be persistent, be determined, do not lose your temper at any time and always remain confident. This is especially true as not all editors see reliability and punctuality as mutually valid principles. Some take months to edit submitted articles and more months to finally pay you, and sometimes they completely forget about your arrangements. Others are perfectly punctual and precise; that is a trait you should adopt, too.

A sense of precision and critical thinking is invaluable when it comes to science writing. Ideally, this should find expression in the way you produce and deliver your articles and in the way you run your one-person business. Even if you do not own a publication, you are still responsible for managing your image. At all times, you represent your own personal brand. Demand precision from your interviewees when they are trying to fob you off with hazy facts and especially when they are trying to dodge your questions. Demand precision from the editors whom you are working with. Did they promise to get back to you within 3 days? If they did not, follow up with them on your pitch. Especially demand precision from yourself. You can only explain what you understand yourself. A lack of precision is what waters down a science article. This is true of the conciseness of the words you choose, and of the sheer facts that you incorporate. Finally, be precise about business aspects such as payments and taxes.

## Science journalism and the broadcast media

Although this book dedicates chapters to exploring and producing different journalistic formats, it is undoubtedly the content that dictates the format, not the other way around. In other words, you may be an expert feature writer, but not every story fits into a print feature. Some stories are better told online, others on the radio and still others on television. Some stories are even better live-streamed as they unfold – it entirely depends not only on the topic but on the actual story. Before the turn of the century, media companies focused on one product: It was either print or radio or television, with television being the most profitable sector. The arrival of the internet, however, changed traditional broadcast media's dominance of that formerly straightforward media production process:

> The old media model was to reach the widest possible audience by publishing the most generally appealing content. The new media model is exactly the opposite; highly specialized content allows publishers and advertisers to reach small, widely scattered audiences.
>
> *(Dove 2015:8668)*

The fact that newspapers started producing video and television stations started producing online news (Dove 2015) may have turned the traditional role distribution of the media landscape upside down. But the platform-agnostic approach has its advantages. For example, you can break into broadcast journalism easier even if you lack prior broadcasting experience. Public broadcasters like the BBC offer writing jobs that require you to write online news to accompany their television programmes. They also offer internships and traineeships for specific television programmes, like the science show *Trust Me I'm a Doctor*, which is currently presented by Michael Mosley and Chris van Tulleken. If you could secure such a traineeship, then you would have a direct route into science broadcast journalism.

*Trust Me I'm a Doctor* is only one of many successful health advice television shows. Medical doctors and nurses are often the presenters of such shows, as their credentials lend the shows authority. Sometimes, this authority is false. For example, nutritionist Gillian McKeith, the presenter of the show *You Are What You Eat* (Channel 4, 2004–2007), faced backlash after it came to light in 2005 that her doctorate originates from a non-accredited college in the US. Also, she was a member of a nutritionist organisation that merely sells memberships without checking applicants' qualifications (Goldacre 2007). The Channel 4 show eventually stopped airing in 2007.

You can, however, find many science television programmes that are reputable. Among the well-known and high-quality shows are *NOVA* (PBS), *Nature* (PBS), *Wonders of the Universe* (BBC), *Cosmos: A Spacetime Odyssey* (FOX/National Geographic Channel) and *Scientific American Frontiers* (PBS). Of course you can also find science television shows that have little to no ambition to be scientifically sound but rather draw on sensationalism, such as *Bodyshock* and *Embarrassing Bodies* (both Channel 4). Before you apply for a traineeship for any show, you should definitely watch it and also read its reviews so you can make an informed decision.

Apart from internships at television stations, producing your own science documentaries can be another great way to break into television journalism and establish yourself, although production costs can be high and difficult to cover if you cannot get external funding or a commission from a television channel or network. Producing short documentaries can be a valid way to handle the production costs, get sufficient exposure and perhaps even win a short-film award that could further establish you in the field. Special interest groups also provide funding opportunities from time to time; for example, the National Institute of Standards and Technology that offers a $500,000 grant for producing a science documentary about the redefinition of the kilogram (see the Links section). Short film festivals such as the Sheffield Doc/Fest provide aspiring documentary film directors with the opportunity to pitch their ideas and potentially win a prize to help produce them. Science journalism degree courses do not always provide specific training for producing documentary films, but the University of North Carolina at Chapel Hill's master's programme in science journalism (Box 12.1) is one of the few whose curriculum includes according courses.

Radio is also an excellent medium for conveying complex facts, and it powerfully shows that visuals are not always needed to deliver these facts to your audience. As Clark (2014) notes in an article for *Columbia Journalism Review*, radio may be particularly well-suited to report on science. She states that the broadcasting company New York Public Radio created a new health division that produces the weekly podcast *Only Human*. Clark adds that this development is in stark contrast to the declining science desks in the print media and mainly possible due to funding from philanthropic associations (Clark 2014). You can find a link to *Only Human* in the Links section at the end of this chapter. *Only Human* also provides the transcripts of every episode. If you are interested in learning how to write for radio, listening to such shows and reading the according transcripts is a must.

Unfortunately, this book cannot sufficiently show you how to write for radio or even for television, but you will find a number of recommended books in the Reading List. As usual, consuming and analysing and then practicing goes a long way, regardless of the medium. Also, Marie Kinsey, chair of the Broadcast Journalism Council Training (cited in White 2011) notes that it is easier to change the type of media once you have gained a foothold in one. For example, if you already are an established print journalist, you can more easily switch to presenting television shows than if you had no journalistic experience. So be flexible and willing to change the medium whenever you think it is opportune: "Nobody can afford to pigeonhole themselves as a print, online, radio or TV journalist" (Jonathan Baker, head of BBC College of Journalism, cited in White 2011). Baker also confirms that it is not uncommon for broadcast journalists to start out as print journalists (White 2011).

No matter whether you plan to become a science presenter on television or a radio host, you can always apply the previous chapters' techniques for finding ideas, pitching stories, reporting those stories and eventually producing them almost independently from the medium you operate in. A good story is always a good story.

## Case study: work experience placement at *BBC Focus* magazine

The central paradox of today's working world is that in order to gather work experience you have to already have experience. This circular dependency makes it nearly impossible to initially apply for a good position. Thankfully, many activities count as prior work experience. For example, if your university or journalism school runs a student newspaper, the experience gathered there counts. If you worked as a freelance journalist before, during or after you attended university or journalism school, that will count, too.

The latter was the case for me. I worked as a freelance science journalist for various science magazines and newspapers in Germany, Switzerland, South Africa and the US both in print and online. At this point, I will add that my goal was to try out writing as many text types as possible, from short news to columns to features. If you have not guessed it already from the previous chapters, my favourite type of article is the magazine feature. The reason for that is probably that my first attempts in science writing consisted mainly of analysing and recognising structural patterns in science magazine features (like the German *P.M. Magazin*). Then I tried to apply these patterns myself and started using different techniques and tools to write the scenes of my features, like index cards. After a while, I bought a book that further cemented this knowledge. Later, I got in contact with the author of that book and attended one of his workshops on journalistic writing in the sciences. In fact, Winfried Göpfert and I are sporadically in contact to this day. He is also one of the interviewees featured in this book.

What followed were pitches, rejections, revised pitches, more rejections. Eventually, the first commissions came in. My freelance work allowed me to progress from one publication to another, writing short news, columns, magazine features and online articles. This is not the only way it works, but it is one possible path to not only building work relationships with many different editors and scientists but also continuously getting published. You can start out with smaller publications, as getting published there is easier, and this shows future editors that you are capable of producing quality articles. Also, it allows you to assemble a presentable portfolio, so you can slowly improve the credential section of your pitch (see Chapter 3). Your reputation will increase with the reputation of the media companies you work with. Have you, at some point in your career, published a piece in a high-profile publication? Congratulations; this will increase the likelihood of getting future pitches accepted anywhere, provided the quality of your work stays at that level.

I started out writing for German and English IT magazines (both in print and online); I wrote mostly technology-related articles that were highly unsuitable for the general public because they addressed specialist computer scientists, which worked fine at the time. As time progressed, I started covering more general topics, such as IT management, and I published these pieces in another category of magazines. Next, I made the leap from writing specialist technology articles to writing about science-technology interactions for general newspapers, and from there the step to writing science articles for science magazines and other newspapers was relatively easy, compared with the rocky road at the beginning. It was only then that I started studying journalism at Edinburgh Napier University.

My journalism programme leader at Edinburgh Napier University, Rachel Younger, encouraged me to complete a work experience placement, so I started rummaging the internet for such opportunities. What caught my eye was a 2-week placement at *BBC Focus* magazine, which, refreshingly, had openly accessible information on how to contact the editorial team with enquiries. Work placement experiences are traditionally shorter than internships (the latter can last anywhere from 1 or 2 months up to a full year). Work experience placements at *BBC Focus* magazine typically last 2 work weeks.

After sending an email to then editor-in-chief Graham Southorn, the process was fairly straightforward. I had to fill out and submit an application form indicating why and when I wanted to start the work experience and include a few samples of my previously published science articles. A couple of emails later, we had found an agreement, and I was due to start my placement at the beginning of 2015.

Prior to that experience, I always had the fear that internships and such placements may easily result in brewing coffee and operating the photocopier. Wrong. From the first day of my arrival, I was fully integrated into the team, and everybody was really helpful and, most importantly, prepared. Thanks to my colleagues at *BBC Focus* magazine, I could write articles that were either published in the print edition of the magazine or on the magazine's website Sciencefocus.com. The editors took turns instructing me to contribute to different sections of the magazine and they explained to me how they usually work and what they expected from me. They gave me (admittedly soft) deadlines and were always available for questions or constructive criticism. In addition, I participated in stand-up meetings where the whole team discussed the upcoming magazine's cover and the selection of the features and news, and I was also handed a current flatplan of the magazine several times a week. Hence, I gained insight into the production process but also into how an editorial team plays together. James Lloyd, then editorial assistant, took a lot of time to explain to me the various digital formats that *BBC Focus* magazine is published in and also provided great advice and constructive criticism that helped me make the most of my time at the magazine.

The 2 weeks went by all too quickly, but the impressions and the experience and insights I gathered during that time are invaluable. In fact, I am thinking of applying for a longer internship at another science publication.

*BBC Focus* magazine is still offering work experience placements, but you can also find internship positions at many newspapers and magazines. Some have specific requirements, such as being a final year (science) journalism student by the time you apply or by the time the internship would start.

## Case study: Carl Zimmer's science writing career

Every career in science journalism is individual, so there is no exact recipe that will turn you into a successful science journalist. But why not look at how one very successful science journalist broke into the business? Not many would disagree that Carl Zimmer is one of the most prolific US science writers, no matter how you measure success. Over the course of his career, he has won half a dozen awards, including three AAAS Kavli Science Journalism Awards and a number of fellowships. He writes for *National Geographic*, the *New York Times* and STAT News (which belongs to the *Boston Globe*). He also teaches a science writing seminar at Yale University, and he has written a dozen science books. In short, chances are you have already read some of Zimmer's work. Zimmer (2016) tells me how he started out, although he cautions that the media landscape has changed very much in the meantime:

> It's hard for me to talk about my own early experience in a way that is relevant to people in 2016. I was getting into journalism at a time when it was a very different kind of business. Around 1990, there were a lot of print magazines and newspapers around that were all doing very well; it was a very profitable kind of business, supported by lots of advertising and circulation. There were a lot of jobs, and you don't see that much now. Copyediting is unfortunately something that has fallen by the wayside a bit. I had to take a copyediting test to get this job, so I'm not saying it fell into my lap. That was a kind of opportunity that people today might not have. This was not a plan to become a science journalist. I had been out of college for a couple of years, and I had done various things at various kinds of jobs. Also, I was writing a lot of fiction at the time. I just thought, I should probably get a job in the publishing business. So I just sent letters to lots of different magazines but didn't hear from most of them. But *DISCOVER* [magazine] had an opening, they just got in touch and said, if you want to take the test, you are competing for the job.

Zimmer kept that position for around 10 years before becoming a freelance science writer. He has an English rather than a science degree, which he says helped him understand what a good story looks like early in the process:

> I am very glad for all of the experience I had in college as an English major, reading fiction and non-fiction as well. I learnt a lot from fiction

about how to write well and how to structure, how to have a distinctive voice to your narrative. Writing fiction as well was good. Writing a good story in science is not simply about arranging little pieces of information on a page. I always encourage people who are just starting out in science writing to look to fiction and literary non-fiction as models to learn from.

He also confirms that awards are useful in helping you get noticed. Especially freelancers, Zimmer notes, should try to distinguish themselves from the others and stand out. What is also remarkable about Zimmer's career is the broad range of topics he has covered and the broad range of formats he produces (columns, features, blog posts, videos and podcasts). When asked whether he would recommend that aspiring science writers do the same and whether he planned this strategy to become successful, he tells me:

> No. I feel very lucky with how things worked out, but I did not have a really coherent plan. I started in science writing working at a magazine, where we worked on different kinds of stories. You started out with short pieces, just a few hundred words long, then you would get to write page-long pieces, and after a while you could write features. There were columns as well. So for each one of them, we learnt what worked and what didn't work. For a 400-word piece, you can't get into a lot of history. You have to tell a very coherent story in a very short period of time. If you write a column, it is going to be longer and you are expected to have more of your personal voice in there. I learnt about how to write different styles there, at *DISCOVER*, but I was also feeling I was leaving a lot of things out in the stories I was writing. I really wanted to write books as well, so eventually I branched out into books. Since then, I have tried to do something new every year. I think it would be boring if I didn't. Journalism itself has been evolving so that there are new formats that didn't even exist when I was starting out.

In that sense, Zimmer mentions that he started blogging when blogging was still in its infancy. Like every other early blogger, he had no experience, but he paid attention to two crucial success factors of science writing that he would also like to share with you:

> New science writers should learn both the art and the craft of science writing. The art of science writing means looking at fantastic writers of the past and figuring out what makes them so good. The craft is all the logistics you have to understand to produce something: What kind of tape recorder is going to work best? How do you negotiate a contract? Good science writing and a successful science writing career depend on those two elements.

## Case study: Erika Check Hayden's science writing career

The following example shows that no two paths into science journalism are identical. Indeed, the career of Erika Check Hayden, the director of the science communication (SciCom) program at the University of California, Santa Cruz (UCSC), is in many ways remarkable. Check Hayden won multiple awards from the Association of Health Care Journalists for her coverage of the Ebola crisis in Sierra Leone. She has also won fellowships, among which is a fellowship from the Pulitzer Center of Crisis Reporting that supported her travel to Sierra Leone. Over the course of her career, Check Hayden has worked as a journalist for *Newsweek* and *Nature*, and she works as a senior science reporter for *Nature*'s news section to the present day. Since 2010, she has been one of the SciCom programme's instructors.

Erika Check Hayden (2016) tells me that she discovered her interest in science early in her childhood. Both of her parents had PhDs, and her father was a science writer:

> I never questioned whether one could make a living as a writer, and I never questioned what journalists do all day or how they work, because I had that example of my father. That being said, I didn't set out to become a science writer. But I always knew I was very interested in science.

While pursuing a degree in biology at Stanford University, she started writing for the *Stanford Daily*. This was when she realised that combining science and journalism was a career path she wanted to pursue. She remembers her first experiences at the newspaper, how she worked with editors on deadline, how she went out and talked to people and how she reported stories and recalls those experiences as very energizing.

The first story she did for the *Stanford Daily* was about a protest against the adoption of a sit-lie ordinance in Palo Alto. Check Hayden was assigned to cover the protests and immediately liked it:

> It was just so exhilarating being out there in the middle of the action, in the middle of the passionate debate on both sides. I love talking to people who have really strong opinions on either side. The whole experience was so energizing. If you want to cover science, I think it's a really good experience to also cover other things first. Being a generalist reporter of any stripe is so helpful.

She adds that getting out and talking to people who are not scientists but who are passionate about other issues is a great experience that will benefit you over your entire career. Check Hayden recommends going out on a street corner and talking to people who are passing by:

> If you live in a town that has a small newspaper, even a community newspaper, that is the best place to start, because they often don't

have science expertise on staff. They are interested to have people who are knowledgeable and interested in this, people that go out and start reporting those stories.

She adds that college newspaper editors are often eager to work with reporters who want to cover topics that their newspaper has not covered yet. That is why she soon started pitching science stories.

After graduating, Check Hayden got an internship at the general-interest, weekly magazine *Newsweek* in New York. She tells me that covering the 9/11 terrorist attacks was a defining moment for her. When she arrived at the magazine's headquarters in Midtown that morning, most of the senior-level staff was not there, because the authorities had shut down the traffic. She received her marching orders to go down to the scene and start reporting. The police had not yet cordoned off the area, so she could get close to the site of ground zero, where she noticed that "everything was covered with grimy ash." Check Hayden took the initiative and decided what aspect of the attacks she would turn into her story:

> Eventually, that became a major story: What were the potential health effects of this ash? I remember thinking at the time: This is unusual, I have never seen anything like this before. So I wondered what it is, what it's made of and what the potential consequences were. So I went back and reported some stories on the potential health effects of the ash. That experience of having to take the initiative and figure out for myself what the story was, that was a really formative experience, and it helped me realize your editors can give you guidance, your sources can give you guidance, but as the reporter, you are the one who really knows the most about a given situation. It's up to you to determine where the story goes based on the information that you are gathering.

Later that year, Check Hayden left *Newsweek* and moved to Washington, DC, where she started working as a science reporter for *Nature*. She recalls the recruiting process as "pretty intense": editors Peter Aldhous and Colin Macilwain interviewed her, and both are critical thinkers, she tells me. Specifically, Check Hayden says of Macilwain:

> He was just the epitome of the sceptical reporter. One thing that I just loved about working for him was that he really enshrined bringing that approach of a sceptical reporter into science. . . . He encouraged us all to take that approach. I think it was really excellent experience and training, not because science is somehow underhanded and we need to disbelieve the things that are reported, but science is a human enterprise, just like anything else, so it needs to be treated that way.

She adds that Aldhous was equally influential and that:

> The influence of having been supported early on in my career to really look at science as a human endeavour and to ask tough questions, that is never going to go away. That will be a part of the way I do journalism forever.

In 2006, she moved to San Francisco, still working for *Nature*. When she was covering the Ebola crisis in Sierra Leone, she decided to break into full-time lecturing and teaching. What motivated her was the difference between what her sources told her on the ground and what the mainstream media reported. She tells me that a lot of our impact can come from touching on the issues that society is most concerned about. As she realized she cannot do that alone, she decided to help train fledgling science journalists. Finally, in 2016, after long conversations with Rob Irion, then director of the UCSC's SciCom programme, and after a rigorous recruiting process, she was eventually selected as the programme's third director.

## Summary

Finding a job as a humanities graduate is often difficult. Science journalism is no exception. Many major publications have either reduced or completely eliminated their science desks, which makes it difficult to find staff writer positions. At the same time, the number of PR professionals is rising, and the quality of press releases is getting better and better. This makes it all the more important to stand out in order to get commissions, internships and perhaps find a staff position.

It is important to know that there is no one route that leads to becoming an established science journalist, apart from producing constantly high-quality articles. A thorough knowledge of how scientists work is necessary if you want to scrutinise and critically question their methodologies, results and claims. That is why some argue that getting a science degree first is helpful. Some science journalists remain practising scientists while regularly writing science articles. Others argue that being a journalist first helps you focus on the storytelling aspects and on keeping the journalistic rigour with regard to fact-checking, researching stories and interviewing.

Dedicated science writing programs try to tackle this duality and provide both scientific and journalistic knowledge. Despite their often high costs, they can pay off professionally because they are valid credentials. Other such credentials are prestigious fellowships and awards.

If you have the necessary journalistic skills and combine them with traits like perseverance, resilience and patience, a career in science journalism is certainly possible. If you add a thorough understanding of the scientific field you want to cover and if you are a critical, analytical thinker, you can excel as a science journalist.

The most important takeaway from this chapter is: You design your own career. After answering the review questions, close this book and start working on your career. If you work hard enough on it, you will make it.

## Review questions

- Why is a background in science not an absolute necessity if you want to become a science journalist?
- What elements do successful science writing programmes have in common?
- How can a specialisation in a specific science discipline benefit you, and in which way can it be disadvantageous?
- What documents do you need to prepare to apply for most fellowships and awards?
- How can fellowships and awards benefit you?
- Can you name three essential soft skills that help you strive in journalism?
- What are the advantages and disadvantages of unpaid commissions?
- Can you name two problems that undermine science television shows' objectivity?
- How can a job at a local or college newspaper help you become a better science journalist?

## Reading list

Boucherie, S. (2014) Six ways to succeed in the changing world of science journalism, *Elsevier Connect* [Online] Available at: www.elsevier.com/connect/six-ways-to-succeed-in-the-changing-world-of-science-journalism [date accessed 17 August 2016]

Kern, J. (2012) *Sound Reporting: The NPR Guide to Audio Journalism and Production*. Chicago, IL: University of Chicago Press

Stewart, P. and Alexander, R. (2016) *Broadcast Journalism – Techniques of Radio and Television News*. 7th edition. London: Routledge

Wenger, D. and Potter, D. (2015) (eds.) *Advancing the Story: Broadcast Journalism in a Multimedia World*. 3rd edition. Thousand Oaks, CA: CQ Press

White, A. (2011) Our experts said: Routes into broadcast journalism, *The Guardian* [Online] Available at: www.theguardian.com/careers/broadcast-journalism [date accessed 20 July 2016]

Zimmer, C. (2013) A note to beginning science writers, *The Loom (National Geographic)* [Online] Available at: http://phenomena.nationalgeographic.com/2013/06/24/a-note-to-beginning-science-writers/ [date accessed 8 August 2016]

## Links

American Association for the Advancement of Science (AAAS) Science Journalism Awards: http://sjawards.aaas.org/

American Institute of Physics (AIP) Science Communication Awards: www.aip.org/aip/awards/science-communication

Association of British Science Writers (ABSW) Science Writers Awards for Britain and Ireland: www.absw.org.uk/absw-awards/awards.html

Council for the Advancement of Science Writing (CASW) Evert Clark/Seth Payne
Award for Young Science Journalists: http://casw.org/evert-clark-award
European Commission, European Guide to Science Journalism Training: https://
ec.europa.eu/research/conferences/2007/bcn2007/guide_to_science_journalism_
_en.pdf
Massachusetts Institute of Technology (MIT) Knight Science Journalism Fellowship:
http://ksj.mit.edu/
National Association of Science Writers (NASW) Science in Society Journalism
Awards: www.nasw.org/awards
National Institute of Standards and Technology (NIST), Funding Opportunity to
Produce Science Documentary: www.nist.gov/public_affairs/funding_science_
documentary.cfm
The Royal Society Insight Investment Science Book Prize: https://royalsociety.org/
grants-schemes-awards/book-prizes/science-books-prize/
Society of Environmental Journalists (SEJ) Awards for Reporting on the Environ-
ment: www.sej.org/initiatives/awards-fellowships/sej-annual-awards-reporting-
environmentWNYC *Only Human* (podcast): www.wnyc.org/shows/onlyhuman
Woods Hole Oceanographic Institution, Ocean Science Journalism Fellowship: www.
whoi.edu/osj/

## References

Arnette, R. (2005) Science journalism degrees – Do they make a difference? *Science*
[Online] Available at: www.sciencemag.org/careers/2005/05/science-journalism-
degrees-do-they-make-difference [date accessed 16 August 2016]
Brookshire, B. (2016) Who's paying? Science blogging and money, In Wilcox, C.,
Brookshire, B. and Goldman, J.G. (eds.) *Science Blogging: The Essential Guide*.
New Haven, CT: Yale University Press, 233–242
Check Hayden, E. (2016) Personal phone conversation on 20 September 2016
Clark, A. (2014) Will radio save science journalism? *Columbia Journalism Review*
[Online] Available at: www.cjr.org/the_observatory/wnyc_health_unit_radiolab.
php [date accessed 10 August 2016]
Dove, A. (2015) Careers in virology: Science writing and journalism, *Journal of
Virology*, vol. 89, no. 17, 8668–8670
Goldacre, B. (2007) What's wrong with Gillian McKeith, *The Guardian* [Online]
Available at: www.theguardian.com/media/2007/feb/12/advertising.food [date
accessed 2 December 2016]
Hunter, M.L. (2016) Personal Skype conversation on 13 July 2016
McIlwaine, S. and Nguyen, A. (2005) Are journalism students equipped to write
about science? *Australian Studies in Journalism*, no. 14, 41–60 [Online] Avail-
able at: http://espace.library.uq.edu.au/view/uq:8064/science_journali.pdf [date
accessed 19 August 2016]
Marris, E. (2013) Going long: How to sell a book, In Hayden, T. and Nijhuis, M.
(eds.) *The Science Writers' Handbook*. Boston, MA: Da Capo Press, 99–115
Ornes, S. (2013) The loneliness of the science writer, In Hayden, T. and Nijhuis, M.
(eds.) *The Science Writers' Handbook*. Boston, MA: Da Capo Press, 137–141
Ornes, S. (2014) Spotlight on the MIT program in science writing, *Pitchpublish-
prosper.com* [Online] Available at: http://pitchpublishprosper.com/spotlight-mit-
program-science-writing/ [date accessed 16 August 2016]

Ross, J. (2015) Personal phone conversation on 9 October 2015

Ruppel Shell, E. (2016) Personal phone conversation on 25 August 2016

Seife, C. (2016) Personal phone conversation on 14 July 2016

White, A. (2011) Our experts said: Routes into broadcast journalism, *The Guardian* [Online] Available at: www.theguardian.com/careers/broadcast-journalism [date accessed 20 July 2016]

Yong, E. (2011) You've got seven days left to prove you're a science writer, *The Guardian* [Online] Available at: www.theguardian.com/science/2011/may/13/wellcome-trust-science-writing-prize [date accessed 13 August 2016]

Yong, E. (2016) Personal Skype call on 18 August 2016

Zimmer, C. (2016) Personal phone conversation on 25 August 2016

# APPENDIX

## An interview with a famous scientist

SCIENCE AND CULTURE

## The theoretical physicist behind *Interstellar*

What Kip Thorne loved about the new science-fiction movie and what made him cringe

*By* **Daniel Clery**

*Interstellar*, which opened last week, boasts not just a compelling storyline and dazzling special effects but also an impeccable scientific pedigree. The man who inspired the film and kept a close eye on its scientific fidelity is Kip Thorne, 74, a renowned theoretical physicist at the California Institute of Technology in Pasadena and one of the world's leading experts on the astrophysical predictions of general relativity.

In 2006, Thorne and Lynda Obst, a long-time friend and film producer, wrote an eight-page treatment for a film that sprang from the astrophysics of black holes, wormholes, and time dilation. Steven Spielberg was soon on board to direct. Six years later, however, Spielberg had to drop out and was replaced by Christopher Nolan, director of the three *Dark Knight* movies and *Inception*. His brother Jonathan Nolan, who wrote films including *The Dark Knight Rises*, worked on the screenplay, which is set in a not-too-distant future, when crop blights have driven humanity to the brink of starvation. A secret, crash attempt to find another planet that humans could colonize is under way.

Thorne writes about his experiences working with Hollywood and the scientific concepts addressed in the film in a book, *The Science of Interstellar*, published on 7 November. He spoke with *Science* last week. This interview has been edited for clarity and brevity.

**Q: How much of your original treatment remains in the final film?**
**A:** It's not recognizable as the same movie except for the scientific vision and the venue, what I like to call the warped side of the universe-black holes, wormholes, higher dimensions, and so forth.

The story is essentially completely changed, except in the broadest brush sense that we had explorers leaving the Earth, traveling out to a wormhole in the outer parts of the solar system and through the wormhole, and visiting planets. The thing that was preserved was the vision – the thing that was most important to Lynda and me – the vision of a movie in which real science, ranging from truth to speculation, is embedded deep into the movie's fabric from the outset.

Also preserved were the guidelines we laid down. First, that nothing would violate established physical laws. Second, that all the wild speculations, and there certainly are some here, would spring from science and not from the fertile mind of a screenwriter. I'm very pleased with how it came out.

**Q: Is there anywhere the moviemakers strayed outside your guidelines?**
**A:** Not seriously. The one place where I am the least comfortable is on [a] planet where they have these ice clouds. These structures go beyond what I think the material strength of ice would be able to support. Every time I watch the movie, that's the one place where I cringe. I don't think I've ever told anybody that. But I'd say if that's the most egregious violation of physical law, they've done very, very well.

**Q: In your book, you say that Christopher Nolan introduced science elements of his own to the script. What did he bring?**
**A:** The one that has the biggest impact and that I really like, is the tesseract [the 4D analog of a cube]. When he told me in our first meeting that he was thinking of using a tesseract, he didn't go into any detail. But I was very pleased because when I was 13 years old I read a book, *One Two Three . . . Infinity* by George Gamow, in which George drew a picture of a tesseract. It looks like two cubes, one inside another, and I spent hours staring at that, trying to come to grips with it. I found it so fascinating that it was one of the more significant influences on me to become a theoretical physicist.

So when [Nolan] told me he wanted to use a tesseract, I immediately saw and discussed with him how this was an ideal way to take his hero and carry him into the fifth dimension, and rapidly travel from one region of our universe to another, because distances in the [fifth dimension] will be much less than they are in our brane [our 4D slice of reality].

Q: Where did the idea of blights plaguing Earth come from?

A: This was due to [Jonathan Nolan]. When he introduced the idea, he and I and Lynda decided we really needed to find what was known about blight and other kinds of biological catastrophes. We set up a "blight dinner" with biologists who were experts and we discussed this at length, trying to identify what things could go wrong with the biology of the Earth.

Q: You worked with the visual effects team at the company Double Negative in London, providing them with equations, which they then worked into their code. What was it like seeing those equations turned into the visual representation of a black hole?

A: It was wonderful to see the resolution they got. I knew roughly what they were going to come up with, but it was just awe-inspiring to get back film clips [from Double Negative] and see this fabulous resolution and fabulous dynamics they were able to achieve.

Q: You've said that you learned something new from their simulations?

A: We learned [that] when you have a fast-spinning black hole, without any accretion disk, and let it just lens the distant sky – a star field – we saw a fantastically beautiful structure that is sort of like a fingerprint, but much more complex. It was completely unexpected with huge amounts of internal structure in it, regions where the star field appears to be quiescent and other regions where the stars seem to be whirling around in little vortices. To me it's a lovely kind of discovery in the sense that it is really very beautiful and it arises from a collaboration between a scientist and a group of computer artists. We are submitting a paper about this and about the particular method that Double Negative uses to the journal *Classical and Quantum Gravity*.

# INDEX